Gertie

Also by Faye Green

The Boy on the Wall   2012
Dicey   2013

Gertie

FAYE GREEN

authorHOUSE®

AuthorHouse™ LLC
1663 Liberty Drive
Bloomington, IN 47403
www.authorhouse.com
Phone: 1-800-839-8640

Gertie is a work of fiction. Names, characters, places and incidents are the
product of the author's imagination or are used fictitiously. Any resemblance
to actual events, locales or persons, living or dead, is coincidental.

Published by AuthorHouse 06/16/2014

ISBN: 978-1-4969-1929-8 (sc)
ISBN: 978-1-4969-1928-1 (hc)
ISBN: 978-1-4969-1927-4 (e)

Library of Congress Control Number: 2014910589

Dedication

My Grandmother, Alison Gertrude Watts Beall

In the USO, VA hospitals and American Legion,
she poured a million cups of coffee,
made thousands of sandwiches and cakes
for the men and women who served in the
United States Army, Navy, Air Force, Marines, and Coast Guard.

Acknowledgements

Every book is a journey. This journey has been almost as long as the story itself. It was tucked in my desk drawer for a long time but the life in it demanded I come back to it. I doubt that I will ever have as much attachment to a manuscript as I do to Gertie.

The story and characters_are fictional but the locations are real and dear to me. I love my hometown, Laurel, Maryland. My fond memories travel easily up and down Montgomery Street, over Prince George Street, across to Main Street and back to Tenth and Eleventh Streets—west end—where I was born. When I was growing up both of my grandmothers and a great grandmother plus countless aunts, uncles and cousins lived in the neighborhood. There is no Fergus Hill on a map of Laurel, Maryland, but there is a lovely hill on the west boundary of the town.

Hilltop Manor was inspired by Locust Hill, the loveliest home in Howard County. It was part of my teenage years and will always be part of my reverie.

One of the reasons I created this story was to use Bear Creek as a setting. It was a real and wonderful place. Now a major highway crosses the site and the family home we knew as Bear Creek only exists in the memory of succeeding generations of cousins. The big old house by the water and my grandmother's family is indelible on my heart for the warmest, grandest family heritage a girl could have. Bear Creek was as welcoming and nurturing as I depicted in this book.

I want to thank my amazing family for their support. Thanks for being excited about my books and new career. We are enjoying the fun and surprise of it together.

My heartfelt thanks go to Penny Reuss, who would not let this manuscript stay in my drawer. She actually claps her hand in joy knowing <u>Gertie</u> is finally published.

Connie Rinehold, my editor and, as it turns out, my teacher. Thank you for your guidance, nudging, cajoling and patience—wrapped in encouragement and seasoned with generous dashes of praise.

Sunny Pritchard, thank you for offering to proof read. You have done an amazing job for me on a very long manuscript. Thanks for being diligent and for cheerleading as you got into the story.

Claudette Latsko, thank you for your assistance in the final read through using your fine tooth comb to get my manuscript as clean as possible.

Kudos to my readers. My heart is warmed when you read my books and ask for the next. It is gratifying to know you are waiting for my efforts.

Finally, I want to acknowledge my appreciation to the men and women who served in the past and continue to serve today in the United States Army, Navy, Marines, Air Force and Coast Guard. I agree with <u>Gertie</u>, we should never forget those who made the ultimate sacrifice— and every day—we need to honor those who have served, and thank those who are serving today.

Chapter 1 1909

Edward walked through the west end of town eating a small box of soda crackers and wishing it was cake. It was easy to remember the taste of his mother's cake and that memory made the crackers even less appealing. When he came to the corner of Tenth Street, he looked but could not see three blocks down to the house where he was born. He cursed the crackers and threw them on the ground in the puddle made by the softly falling rain. His parents were probably sitting in the kitchen drinking coffee. He had not seen them in almost two years. He looked up Tenth Street, refused to deal with the memories residing there, and walked on. At the corner of Eleventh Street the town ended abruptly. It was a soda cracker type of town—exactly one square mile in the center of the state of Maryland, notably halfway between Baltimore, Maryland and Washington, DC—twenty miles north and south, respectively. The town ended at Fergus Hill. The hill was named, but the road was not; everyone knew Fergus Hill and the big house that sat atop it.

The big house was impressive. Three stories of clapboard beauty wrapped in wide porches and iced with gingerbread trim. In the topmost gable facing east, numbers were carved—big enough to read—1899. That was the year Mayor Fergus built it and now, 10 years later it was still the most compelling building in the town. The mayor, his wife, and three children could look out and see the whole town spreading in every direction save one—west. The west end was marked by this house and it seemed to stop any growth past this site. The town was growing and Mayor Fergus took great pride in it, and credit for it, too.

Edward was not going to the mansion. He was headed to the caretaker's house sitting fifty yards farther. It sat on the same hill, but faced the opposite way, down the hill to Walker Branch, a small stream that meandered across the west limit of the town into the Patuxent River that ran the north boundary of the town. A pastoral scene for the caretaker's lively family, who did not care to look over the town as the mayor did.

William and Patricia MacGregor and their six children had lived here ever since Mayor Fergus built his imposing mansion and made the guest cottage a dwelling place for his caretaker. In contrast to the big imposing house, this one, and its rambunctious family, was warm, lively and inviting. It was a story and a half brick home with dormers along the west roof and a porch looking down to the stream. William had lengthened the porch the full breadth of the house as soon as he moved in. Patricia had saved her egg money to get several rocking chairs to make it perfect.

"I don't know how old you have to be to think like that?" thought Gretta MacGregor, with an exclamation point etched on her brow. She softly slammed the door to the back stairs in the caretaker's house. The teenager had mastered the slamming of the door just soft enough to keep from getting in trouble but hard enough to satisfy her attitude. "Imagine Mama thinking there was anything beautiful about a rainy day in June," she said aloud. She paused by the hall mirror to check the dramatic look on her face. The day was ruined and the mood falling over the young girl was as dark as the western sky. "If I can't go to Emily's the day is wasted." She continued to talk to herself. It was a habit she had developed and was hardly aware of. From the time she learned to talk, she had told herself the most important thoughts that crossed her mind. No one seemed to notice anymore and they had even stopped teasing her about it. In this busy family it was easy to talk aloud and maybe someone standing nearby would respond with understanding or a barb. It did not matter to Gretta.

She was a pretty girl, well past her sixteenth birthday, anxious for her seventeenth, eighteenth and so on. Her name was Gretta Mae MacGregor but her family and now her wider circle of friends called her Gertie. She wanted to be called Mae, but no matter how she had tried to get Mama and Papa to use the favored name, she could not. By the time it had become important to the little girl, it was too late. She was Gertie to everyone. Now her self-confidence and high self-esteem, made the question of what she was called—not such a big thing. Unlike many of her teenage friends, Gertie spent no time mooning over her name or her looks, and she spent no time wishing to change them. She saw her beloved Papa in her own face. Her features were rounded and large but the size of her eyes made them harmonious. The eyes were bright, brown and large. They were almost as dark as her bountiful chestnut hair. She liked the one dimple in the left cheek but always acted annoyed if anyone teased her about it. Mama gave her the lovely olive tone skin which was not a favored style of the day, but which Gertie loved. She did not want to be pristine white-skinned and did not fear the sun. Her figure was hourglass, but she was very modest and made only one concession to fashion and that was to wear a good fitting cummerbund around her tiny waist. The finest features were her high cheekbones, the way her beautiful face lit with good humor, and her wavy dark hair that perfectly set off her eyes.

All week Gertie and Emily had made plans to meet on Saturday at Emily's home on Tenth Street. There was no way to console each other in the disappointment that each knew the other shared. Some families had telephones, but not these two families. Children did not use the telephone anyway. So here on the Hill, just beyond the city limits and two blocks away on Tenth Street, two west end girls moped about the tragedy of a rainy day in June. Gertie knew she probably had less than five minutes to continue this self-pity. Mama would not allow it.

Four minutes later she heard the voice she loved so dearly. "Girls! Girls!" It resonated up the back stairs in spite of the closed door down at the landing. Lydia got there first and was dispatched to find Gretta. Lydia was Gertie's older sister by two years. She came to live by a nickname instead of the beautiful sound of her christened name. Lydia was called Liddy. Gertie had given that nickname to her in her effort to speak her sister's name along with her first words.

Liddy met Gertie coming down the stairs. "Mama wants us. What is this all about?"

"She knows I'm upset because I can't go to Emily's in the rain. So she has thought of something to fill the day and cheer me up. Sometimes I just wish she would—"

"Gertie! Liddy!" The call came once more. Only little Patsy and baby Shirley, asleep in the crib, were in the kitchen when they reached it, but the door was open and a feeling of excitement was in the air. Patsy pointed to the open door. Rushing to the back porch they saw Mama giving orders to a young man standing at the gate in the rain. Gertie took a second to notice the handsome young stranger before she yielded to the urgency erupting around her. Once Mama saw the girls the orders started flying in their direction. "Gertie take Papa's raincoat and run to the big house to get help. There has been an accident on the bridge. Liddy run to the closet, get blankets. Hurry!"

Something was terribly wrong. The sisters reacted differently to the situation. Liddy immediately began to do as she was told. Gertie on the other hand, began with a quick brainstorm that had her assessing the facts another way. One-step into the kitchen and she commanded Liddy. "*You* go to the big house for help. I'll get the blankets." Liddy took the change in command and grabbed the raincoat. Gertie went for the blankets. She also got towels from the shelf and in one swift motion grabbed the large scissors, which hung from a cord in the pantry. When she reached the yard, Papa who had materialized from nowhere, and the young man from the gate, were racing down the hill toward the creek under the bridge. She caught up with them as they arrived at the scene.

Sixteen years could not prepare her for what she saw. The images of tragedy and danger flashed in her mind like lightning bolts. She began to see the problems in a checkerboard fashion. There was a steam tractor, which she had seen many times crossing the bridge—hanging from the bridge—held there by God-only-knows-what. A man was lying motionless on the ground fifty feet below the tractor. Another man was trying to raise himself up from the edge of the creek away from the suspended tractor. Three big problems. She thrust the blankets to her mother, who was hurrying toward the man, who turned out to be a boy, over by the creek. He had been thrown a good distance and was crying for help. The second problem was the man lying motionless under the dangling tractor, which could fall from the bridge at any moment. The third problem put fear in her heart. Papa was rushing to danger under the suspended machine. Her mind was screaming, *Papa, don't go under that tractor!* She knew he was not thinking about danger as he rushed to the side of the injured man.

The young stranger rushed in with Papa. He thought about the danger because right after he announced the man was breathing, he said, "We've got to get him out of here. Now!" They tried to move him but a small sapling had threaded the straps of his overalls as he fell from the bridge. In an instant Gertie was there, handing scissors to her father—scissors that only Providence could have prompted her to grab as she ran from the house. One snip and he was free.

The two men lifted the victim to the blanket that Gertie spread away from the threat of the suspended tractor when a thundering crash shook the earth. The shudder of the ground went up her spine and caused her heart to jump and her breathing to stop. It was a sound and a feeling that she would never forget. Instinctively she reached down to the earth with both hands as if to hold on and stop the shaking. At sixteen she learned that the universe could vibrate and sometimes the only thing to do was hold on. She was stooped over that way when her father wrapped his arms around her. She thanked God that Papa did not have to die today.

The tractor looked like a pile of discards from the blacksmith shop as one last cloud of steam belched from its belly.

She was tucking the blanket around the man and had just allowed herself to look into his face when Papa said, "He's dead." The commotion of arriving help was heard coming over the hill from town. She did one more thing before the adrenalin let her down, she handed the firemen some towels and pointed to her mother and the young survivor over by the creek. The rain seemed unrelenting when a sudden crack of lightning marked the departure of the storm. The wind died down as she turned to go back up the hill.

Gertie did not remember walking back to the house. Liddy was there waiting to tell her that she needed to take off her wet clothes and that hot water was ready in the tub.

Liddy had questions but right now she only got nods for answers. "Was anyone killed? Was anyone hurt? Anyone we know?"

Yes. Yes. No. The answers were all given with the nodding of her head.

"Thanks for sending me for help, Gertie. You know I'm not good at thinking and doing things so fast. I'm always better at boiling water and making food. By the way, there is some fresh coffee. Want some?"

Gertie nodded *yes*, one more time. Liddy helped her and as the blouse slipped over her head she noticed for the first time that it was still daylight. She sat in the bath and drank the dark sweet coffee that was a staple in this home. Looking at the clock, she saw that only a little over an hour had passed. It seemed a long time ago that visiting Emily and the rain were the most consuming thoughts. Gertie had grown up in a very short time.

There was a lot of commotion and people downstairs. No one seemed to notice that she was not there. Just as well. How do you go back to normal when you have seen the fleeting moments of someone's life?

Mama came up the stairs. Gertie knew her footsteps. She spoke her daughter's name and tears immediately sprang from Gertie's heart, through her eyes to her cheeks. The white handkerchief that Mama carried, but never used, the one with the embroidered flowers on it, was raised for this occasion to dry her tears.

"I'm glad you sent Liddy to the big house." Until that moment, Gertie had forgotten that she had disobeyed Mama's directions.

"I …" she started to explain but Mama touched her lips with the hankie.

Mother and daughter sat for a while and then the directions, which Gertie expected, came. "Come down and eat, you will hear what happened without having to ask any questions. Then, when you have it straight in your mind and you know how you feel about all that happened today, we will talk."

"Yes, Mama."

Her brother, Dan came in from work, full of questions, and Gertie learned the details of the terrible accident as Papa told him. "The rain had something to do with the accident on the steep incline approaching the bridge from the west. The bridge is in real bad shape and it is closed until it's decided if it can be repaired." Papa paused to drink his coffee. "The huge steam tractor fell almost immediately after the dead man was pulled from under the bridge." Papa paused again. This time he needed to gather his emotions. "The young boy has serious injuries, but is expected to recover. They were father and son." Papa paused and turned his gaze to his own sons. "The boy told me they were taking the tractor to Hauptman's garage for some repairs since it was too wet to be in the fields. I know their farm, just over the county line, but I never met them. I will go to offer condolences and any help I can. Patricia, please make some food for me to take tomorrow." Papa turned to Gertie. "Right there with blankets, and towels, and scissors. Whatever made you think to bring scissors, girl?"

"I don't know. Papa," she shrugged.

"Those scissors saved the day." No one wanted to think how it would have turned out if she had not grabbed them.

Dan walked over, messed her hair and said, "Way to go, Sis." She smiled at him this time instead of fussing about his dirty hands in her clean hair.

"The young man who came to help—what was his name?" Mama said quietly.

Only Liddy saw the look of surprise on Gertie's face. Until that moment she had forgotten the young man at the gate.

Liddy said, "He walked Gertie up the hill but she came into the house without even speaking to him."

"He did?" Gertie asked.

"He walked you up the hill, back to the house." Liddy repeated. The handsome young man that Gertie had assessed so quickly when she reached the porch eons ago, came back to mind. The curly brown hair and sharp handsome face. She had forgotten, until now. *Who was he? Where is he now? Did he come in the house?* She thought all these questions, but said nothing.

Chapter 2

Papa was still telling Dan the story when Sam arrived home. When Sam enters, the kitchen whirls in a different direction. He's everyone's big brother, but was most important to Gertie. She loved him and found in him a kindred spirit that seemed to understand a part of her that no one else did. He knew the world on the hill was too small for her, just as it was too small for him. He understood how you could love this family with all your being and still long for something more. "Wow, I heard what happened on the bridge. I missed all the excitement but I got a firsthand report."

"Who gave you your firsthand report, Sam?" Mama asked with a twinkle in her eye that shows when she talks to her oldest son.

"Edward Neal told me all about it. Said it was right dangerous under that suspended tractor. Said that was a strange way to meet my family. I told him he has to come back and meet everyone proper. He was too wet and muddy to come in today."

"So that is who that young man was! Part of the Neal family here in west end?"

Emily's brother? Gertie's interest was piqued.

"Yes, sir."

"Sam, I'd like to know more about that friend of yours but it can wait until you have at least eaten. How were things at the store today? I figure you weren't too busy with the rain keeping people home." Papa took charge of the conversation.

"Right about it keeping people home, but I work hard every day. Mr. Tasker makes sure you earn your pay."

"And well he should," said Papa looking up at Sam for the first time since his eldest entered the room.

"Tomorrow after church, Mr. Tasker wants me to come in. The second Sunday this month. The rain got to some of his storage area and we have some moving to do. You know I don't love that store, I'm not married to it. There are other jobs besides Tasker's Store."

"But you will go," ordered Papa in a soft tone. Even little Patsy shook her head as she saw the frown that masked Sam's handsome face. Everyone in the room took interest in Sam's demeanor except Papa.

"Sam, have some more potato salad and fresh coffee," interceded his mother.

Papa put his cup down and wiped his moustache clean. "Edward Neal," he changed the subject back to the man who helped him at the bridge. "He is a part of Clay Neal's family on Tenth or is it Eleventh Street?"

"Tenth, Papa." Gertie stood and sighed heavily. Her mind was racing with the knowledge that Emily's brother was the man who went under the bridge with Papa today.

"Gertie, you should rest for a while," her mother said.

"No. I don't want to rest. Come on Liddy let's get these dishes done for Mama. She's tired, too. Then you and I can sit in the parlor and look at the fashion plates Mrs. Fergus sent over, if that's alright, Papa?"

This was kitchen-oriented family and this huge kitchen had room for many simultaneous activities. Papa's big overstuffed chair had a corner by the window. The two bottom steps before the door to the stairs were Patsy's and her dolls. But summer evenings were perfect in the parlor. The parlor was cool if it had been shuttered all day. The two older sisters would be rewarded with that space tonight.

Papa took his last sip of coffee and smiled at the girls. One more cigar, a final check of the stable animals and his day was finished. Sunday was a day of rest, almost. Before church he had to feed the horses and get them ready to take the family from the big house to the Episcopal Church down on Sixth Street. Mama and the children, less Sam, walked to the Old Stone Methodist Church on Seventh Street. William MacGregor did not go to church with his wife and children, and Sam came of age to announce that he was not going either. That didn't make Mama or Papa very happy. Papa wanted his family to do *public praying* even though he was a very *private prayer* himself.

Gertie could hardly wait to get the kitchen back together as Mama wanted it. As she rushed Liddy toward the parlor, Mama called Patsy back to stay with her. So much had happened today. So many important topics to discuss that couldn't wait until bedtime. Liddy was most ied by Sam's statement, preparing the folks for the fact that he was not staying at Tasker's Store long. "Do you think Mama and Papa think so, too?" asked Liddy. "Mr. Hardy has offered him a job at the garage but it's just because Fannie Hardy is gaa-gaa over Sam. That job has strings attached."

"No. Sam told me he would starve first."

Sam was handsome and a bit taller than Dan who was the MacGregor standard, 5' 7". He had the best mix of the parent's features plus a winning personality. Sam looked a lot like Gertie, but his features were stretched over a larger face and frame. He knew every family in town that had a daughter five years younger or older than his nineteen years. His job at Tasker's Store allowed him some money to buy a few nice *sportin'* clothes. He was a favorite in the many circles he frequented, from family, to ball teams, to girls of all ages.

"You know, we can almost see Tasker's Store from here, but Sam is never home right after quitting time. Boys are so lucky. They can go places and come home just in time for dinner. I heard him tell Dan that he had been to Savage. Now how did he get way over there? Do you think he walked the seven miles? I'll bet that by the time Sam's twenty he will have been to Baltimore. Can you imagine?" Liddy rambled on. "Did you know that Sam was friends with Emily's brother? Did you know Emily had a brother named Edward?"

Gertie shook her head. "I was surprised to learn who he was. Emily told me she has two brothers that don't live at home, so I figured they were much older and married. He could be married. The Neals are in church every week, but none of us had ever seen Edward Neal." Gertie paused in her wondering. "I'll ask Emily about him, that's for sure."

"I wonder where Sam met him…and, where does he live?" Liddy asked questions that Gertie had pondered. The girls enjoyed the intrigue and speculation until a tap on the door told them it was time to go up to bed.

Gertie lay down with thoughts so mixed in her head that she tossed it from side to side on the pillow as if that would help. She decidedly kept her mind from dwelling on the most tragic and terrible scenes of the day. She was much too level-headed to romanticize the death with her *almost* meeting Edward Neal. Her life experience had already taught her about death although she had never looked at it before. She was ready to talk to Mama.

Her very last thought before drifting off was her disobedience today. It was her first time to disobey her mother since she was a tiny girl. She did not chastise herself. In fact, she was strengthened by her conviction that, at that moment, she knew better than her mother what to do. She did not know it, but right there on the back porch, she had come into her adulthood. As was her habit, she said aloud, "Papa was proud."

"What did you say?" Liddy asked from the next bed.

"Goodnight, Liddy.

❧

Gertie was sleeping fitfully when she heard a tapping on the door. "Who's awake?" Sam asked as he opened the door.

"Me," she replied. In he came and, as tired as his little sister was, she was happy that he did. He had often waited for the house to be quiet to share his life with the family member he related to best. Sam and Gertie had a strong bond. They struggled together for independence and shared a strong will. Sam sat on his chair and started his story. Gertie thought about calling to Liddy but decided to let it go. If she doesn't wake up to Sam's talking, she can be told everything tomorrow.

"I don't work at Tasker's Store anymore." He could not see her smile in the dark. Now she wished she had awakened her sister. "I haven't worked there all week."

"Wow!" The questions were flying in Gertie's head. *What about tomorrow when he has to give Papa $2. 00 from his wages*, she thought, but didn't say a thing. He came in to tell his story and she was going to listen.

"Mr. Tasker thinks I have already told Papa. I knew he was busy with the new stalls in the barn and wouldn't be seeing anyone. Mama doesn't go to the store until Monday, so tomorrow I have to tell. I've made up my mind what I want to do and Papa is going to go through the roof but I was dying in that store. I was almost fired about a month ago. I thought I'd better do something before I was fired."

"How did you almost get fired?"

"Ruthie Stallings came in and caused it. We just got to talking and before I knew what had happened Emma Farley came in and saw me kiss her. Well, ole lady Farley began squawking about not being waited on. Anybody else and I could have gotten to Mr. Tasker and explained.

She is so hard of hearing, and she was loud enough to be heard down to Main Street. Mr. Tasker came and reamed me out good. I got Ruthie out the door fast but the old lady stayed to enjoy that part."

"Sam!" Gertie could not contain her laughter.

"The next day Tasker asks me to help late and I figure I had better to make up for Ruthie. He took me to town, down to the racetrack where he keeps his thoroughbred horses. I helped him tend to them because his stable boy was sick. Then he had some business at the track office and he told me I could look around for about 30 minutes. Thirty minutes— that is all the time it took..." Sam paused as if he was thinking over something very important.

"Thirty minutes for what?"

"That's how long it took for me to know I had found my place. Not in some store, waiting on deaf old ladies, and watching for pretty young girls to stop in. I left the racetrack with one thing on my mind—how soon could I get back to the horses and all the trainers and groomers working on the glorious animals getting ready for racing tomorrow? I saw the jockey's quarters and the silks hanging ready—that's the outfit a jockey wears in a race. Each horse owner has his own color. I'm going to be there and learn by the color which stable a racer comes from. I saw the trophies and pictures from the winner's circle. That's where they take the winner after a race. You should see the track, a beautiful circle of clay surrounded by a perfect circle of hedge and grass and the huge grandstand like a colonial mansion." He was becoming more and more animated. "And then, a horse came around the track pounding, breathing hard and the jockey leaning in so tight he looked like part of the horse. A timer, standing close to me clicked his watch and yelled 'yahoo'. It was everything!" he sighed. "I left the track with one thing on my mind—*how soon could I get back?*"

"Whew," was all she could say. Her mind was already elevating Sam from favorite brother to hero. He was going, going, *doing*. Something! Action! Life!

"Are you ready for the best part?" he asked, coming over and sitting on the side of her bed. "I started telling Mr. Tasker on the way home. The words just flowed. The horses, the jockeys, the stables, the track, the people. My boss isn't that easy to talk to but I could have told the devil how I felt at that minute. I was so full of the sights and sounds of the Laurel Racetrack. You know what he said? Of course you don't. He said,

'Whoa boy,' and told me I reminded him of his self when he was a boy and fell in love with the excitement of the track. There just wasn't any use trying to keep me in the store. He can always get a new clerk, but somebody who could look after his interest at the track—that is harder to find. He said I had never stolen from him and that my shortcoming was my good looks. Ha! Bringing in girls who aren't spending money. I think he was teasing when he said that. Anyway, I don't work at the store anymore but I still work for Mr. Tasker…at the track. Only problem is, he thinks Papa gave me permission."

"What do you think Papa will do?" She was certain she knew what Papa would do. "Have you thought of talking to Mama first and get her on your side?"

"Yes, I thought about that." Sam paused, locked his fingers together, and stretched his locked arms above his head and as far back as they would go as if to squeeze some hidden energy into his being. He dropped his arms and continued. "It is different this time. You see, Gertie, I'm going to do this no matter what Papa says. You know and I know Papa doesn't know much about the racetrack but he thinks it's bad. He turned down that good job over there before coming here because the horses he would tend were racers." Sam's high mood had made a big swing but only for a moment. "He just doesn't know. I've been to the track the last four days and I know it isn't bad. It is wonderful and exciting and—," Sam hardly breathed before going on, "—anyway, if Mama can't be on my side with this, I don't want to hurt her, too. So I have to go straight to Papa. Right out."

Words of encouragement began to pour from his little sister. "You are right, Sam. Stand on that. Papa knows a lot and he knows your time is now. Oh, he doesn't know it's coming tomorrow but it was just a matter of time until you stood. Papa knows.

"Do you really think so, Gertie? Do you think I can convince him this is a good job for me?"

"Don't even try. The biggest mistake you can make is trying to convince Papa that the track is a good place. You'll never do that. Just tell him you are responsible for yourself and he should accept your decision. That's all. This is a time when too many words could work against you. I've practiced and practiced in my mind for the time when I can do just what you are doing."

"You want to work at the track, too?" he laughed.

"No, Silly. I mean tell Papa I'm ready to make my own decisions and take care of myself. Problem is, I'm a girl and not even seventeen yet. You are so lucky, Sam."

"We'll see how lucky I am," he replied soberly. "Now, to sleep. Had enough for one night?"

"I thought I had had enough for one night the first time I went to bed hours ago."

"Yeah, what a day. Heard you were rather heroic. Got the word from Edward. That is another story. Until tomorrow." He touched her hair and left the room.

From across the dark room a voice said, "I heard what Sam said."

"I'm glad. It would be a lot to tell you in the morning, wouldn't it?"

"It scares me—Sam striking out on his own. Does it you?" Liddy asked.

"Not me," said Gertie. "Not me."

Sunday dawned a new world, all washed and cleaned. Looking out the window, the torn bridge was a reminder to Gertie of the old world. Her first thought was of Edward Neal. She doubted he was married if he was a friend of Sam's. And, how she could meet him again? Would it be Emily or Sam who could assist her? Her mind was made up. It would just take some planning. She would find a way. So much had changed for Gertie. She had changed. The family, not even Liddy, knew about the sense of excited anticipation she felt or her knowledge that nothing would ever be the same for her again. Sam was going to begin his life and Gertie was ready to begin hers.

There was a note on the table from Sam saying that he had gone on to work and would surprise Mr. Tasker when he got in from church. This made Papa smile and raised his confidence in his son. Second best thing to seeing Sam go to church with Mama was his obedience to his father and going to work as Mr. Tasker expected. Papa failed to see the biblical view on this.

Mama did not smile as she read the note. On the way home from church Mama thought to stop by Tasker's Store and see Sam, but Gertie and Liddy prevailed upon her not to. They suggested that they would bring Sam a lunch after they ate. Mama thought that made good sense.

The walk from the Old Stone Church on Ninth Street was difficult after yesterday's hard rain. At times it was best to walk in the road and in some places better to walk on the neighborhood lawns. Mother had insisted that boots be the footwear of the morning. Papa could have hitched the carriage for them but he saw, as the Fergus family headed down the hill, that it was difficult going and it was better by far that the family walk.

Sam was in the kitchen with Papa when Dan, Liddy, Gertie, Little Patsy, and Mama, carrying Shirley, walked in. Steaming cups of coffee sat on the table for them.

"Sam, I am surprised to see you home," Mama said.

"Sit down, Patty," said Papa. He did not often call her by his pet name. Usually it was when he disagreed with her or when he needed her attention. Dan was trying to decide just how serious were the things Papa was about to say to Mama. Sam's face showed nothing. He didn't know what Papa was going to say, either.

"Do I get to take off my hat, Papa, or must I get right into this without a fine cup of coffee like you are enjoying?" This tickled Gertie and she loved her mother even more at this very delicate minute.

Mama removed her hat, put her Bible right where it belonged, and turned to get the cup of coffee that would give her hands something to do while she found out what Sam was up to now.

"Yes, Papa…." She smiled.

It was not a discussion. Papa simply told her that Sam was working at the Laurel Race Track for Mr. Tasker and that he didn't approve. Sam would not be turning his wages over to him any longer, but would pay Mama room and board if he decided to stay in the house. "As of today." He concluded.

Mama hardly batted an eye. "Very well." She stood to end the meeting. "Come girls, we need to get dinner on the table. If the meal is good enough, Sam may not want to burn all his bridges."

Chapter 3

The MacGregors were an open family, always sharing, but no one was prepared for Liddy's announcement.

Liddy was pretty, like Mama, but shy. She never made announcements. While everyone was getting ready for the big mid-summer celebration, Liddy was working on her own agenda.

The summer was growing more humid each day. The grass on the hill toward the creek was the only green lawn left on the whole of Fergus Hill. The house felt cooler when you first entered but shortly the slight relief from outside temperatures was gone. Papa had opened all the windows and pulled the heavy shutters closed on the south and west side. That let the breeze in, if there was one, and kept the devil rays of the sun at bay. The big house was even hotter because it stood so tall and alone on the hilltop. The smaller house had the lovely Norway maples and tall cedars to shade it.

Liddy had been working in the big house for almost two years—whenever Mrs. Fergus needed her. This summer three young grandchildren and their father, Lon Fergus (who lost his wife when little three years old Marcie was born) returned to live in the mansion. The extended family could always use the willing and capable hands of Liddy. Mama missed her when she went to the big house for she was the only one of her children who was happy and comfortable at home—content to be busy with whatever it took to keep the house in order. Even now while steadily employed at the big house, she kept her duties at home. She had never had a beau and quietly grew into womanhood without looking beyond her own family for happiness. Even her tasks at the big house were an extension of opportunity to make people happy in the confines of *home*.

Late one evening a while back, Papa had asked Mama to come back to the table after dinner was cleared away. The children had dissolved into their own activities and he had something on his mind. Papa continually twirled the end of his moustache and she knew it meant something was in the wind. Mama sat quietly and waited in her usual manner. He took a moment to admire his wife in her flowered house dress and the mismatched apron.

"Liddy," he began, "just doesn't seem to have any interest off this hill." He was about to tell his wife of his concern for the oldest daughter's future and the choice she was making to keep her attentions and activities here on Fergus Hill. "She can't be planning to stay at home all her life." As Mama sat down with him, he again noted that Mama was just an older version of Liddy, slightly more beautiful. Both had soft brown curls and perfect, delicate features atop a slight figure that gave no hint of changing through the years. "Liddy should be getting married and yet she is not going out with the other children and meeting the young men of the town. Has she ever spoken of an interest in marriage or of some boy?" he asked.

She shook her head from side to side.

"Shouldn't you talk to her, Patricia?" It was serious when he used her given name. "Make sure she is doing what she really wants to do. Maybe there is a job on Main Street where she can meet people or I could ask Mayor Fergus if there is a position in the town office for her. We could insist she go out more with Gertie and Sam, or make her come down from her room when the young people are here." Papa continued to ramble on with every idea he had had since the thought crossed his mind that Liddy would soon be nineteen with no prospects. "Could we afford to send her to the Academy to finish her education? At least we are lucky the Academy is here in town and room and board would not be needed."

Mama thought he had not even taken a breath but she did not interrupt him.

"Would it be a good idea to send her to Susie's for...?"

"William!" Now she interrupted him, using his given name, too. "Liddy is not going anywhere. She is definitely not going to tend to Aunt Susie. It is the 20th century and we do not send young spinsters to care for old spinsters anymore...especially not Liddy. What are you running on about? Liddy is Liddy and she will do what she wants if I have any say in it. We didn't raise her to wait for us to tell her what her options are. Now, if you are serious about her education, I will discuss that with her. It is the one good idea you put on this table tonight. Go to Susie's, I never...." Mama was finished raging.

Patricia reached over and touched his arm and noted how strong it was. She softened her tone and continued. "Papa, I know you want Liddy to be happy and I do, too. All the guidance you have given her through the years will take care of her future. You know that. You are a good father. I will talk to her, though. I think you forgot your cigar tonight," She changed the mood. "Why not get one and let's go to the side porch, I see the breeze stirring from that direction." She had done it again—held things together and taken charge. She was a wise woman who gave her husband the power, still knowing that he depended on her strength and force.

Papa's sigh was not one of frustration. He put his arm around her as they sat on the porch.

Gertie had not meant to ease drop but she was sitting right outside the open window shelling peas just as Mama had told her to do. She started to leave until she heard it was about Liddy and not some intimate subject between her parents. *Maybe I shouldn't.* She said to herself but she had not even started to pick up the pot of peas when the subject of Liddy's future made her stay. She was most impressed at the way Mama handled Papa. She resolved to be just like her mother if ever she should have a husband. *I'll be firm and think things over the way Mama does,* she thought. Just before shelling the last pea and dwelling on the scene, Gertie reached another truth. *Papa not only loves Mama, he respects her,* she thought. "I want that." was what she said out loud—as was her habit.

The next day Mama watched for the chance to sit and talk to Liddy. When she came in from the big house right after lunch, she looked tired. "Come, have some lemonade and sit for a while with me." Liddy wiped the stubborn curl away from her brow and sat lifting her dress to cause a refreshing breeze to sweep under her petticoat.

None of the children passed the chance to sit with their ever busy Mama. It seemed that lately these two had not had the usual time together so Mama made a point to find the time today. She had promised Papa. Liddy told of the unusual activities at the big house preparing for the4thof July. It has been so hot. The baking was finished and she would not have to go over before the sun brought the heat of the day making baking impossible.

18

"It will be a lovely4[th]. It's nice that our families join for the picnic. Sam's getting crabs?"

"Of course, we can't celebrate the 4th without crabs."

It was obvious to Mama that Liddy was worn out from the work and not by dissatisfaction with her work. She went right into the plans to help Mama with the fried chicken. It did not matter how hot it was while getting ready for the picnic, heat was a part of the occasion.

Liddy told Mama all about her day as she enjoyed a glass of lemonade. Mama got her a second glass and began the subject that was on her mind.

"Liddy, Papa has said that we could let you go to Academy if you still want to. In two years you could have that teaching certificate that you used to talk about. That is if you still want that."

The girl went silent.

"This is a good sign," thought Mama.

«My goodness. I'm surprised. I haven't thought about that for such a long time, I've been so busy. The Academy. Me? I always wanted to go—but not board. I wouldn't like living there." She reached up to brush the curl away but her hair was not out of place; her hand was moving air in a nervous way.

"No need to board, you would just have to make the extra effort to rise early and be there on time each day. A mile walk."

"It is so hot," she said sweeping her dress up to catch a breeze again, "I can hardly think. When do I have to decide?"

"You would have to take your entrance exams by August fifteenth for the fall session which begins on September 5th. You have time to think it over." Liddy fell silent, thinking again, bringing more sweat to her brow.

"We are sorry that we could not send you to Academy when you finished high school but now that Sam, Dan and you have been earning your own way, Papa feels we can and he believes you deserve it. You have worked so hard for the Fergus' and here at home. He was afraid you felt we depended on you, and although we do, you can do as you wish and this family will go right on."

"I know, Mama," she nodded somewhat embarrassed by her mother's compliments. She took a deep breath and said, "I'm going up to change. Does Gertie know about this?"

"No. I wanted to talk to you first."

"Good, I want to tell her myself. It's a lot to think about." She was up the back stairs, two at a time, mindless of the oppressive heat.

Liddy did not give her parents an answer the next day. In fact, she seemed somewhat distracted when she came home from work and went right upstairs. There was no lift in her step and Mama began to believe she would decide not to go. The truth was that not even Gertie knew how Liddy was leaning in the decision.

"I'd go to Academy. I'd go in a heartbeat." was Gertie's opinion.

❧

The Fourth of July dawned bright, sunny and hot. The sun came up a fiery red ball in a blue sky that had just a white cloud or two floating by to make it perfectly patriotic. The picnic preparations were part of the fun. The chicken was fried before sun-up. Extra ice had been secured and the chest was packed with lemonade and the best potato salad in Maryland. Sam left early for the Racetrack to tend to the horses and to meet his friend from Annapolis who promised a bushel of blue claw crabs—fresh and live from the Chesapeake Bay. Dan was quietly making everything easier for everyone. First he tended to the horses so Papa could feel he was on holiday. Then he moved the tables and chairs under the shade trees and watched to make sure the women did not have to lift or tote anything. He set up the badminton net and horse shoe pegs. Lon Fergus was his assistant. Dan and Lon began to wait on the ladies in both houses, to be at their beck and call for all errands. Lastly the two workers built a fire and brought the large iron pot to cook the crabs. Papa showed up to give his advice. "Build the fire far enough away so we can't feel the heat, but close enough so we can smell 'em cookin'." The water was set to boiling and the steam was rising when Sam's *wha-hoo* call announced he had returned with the basket of treasure from the bay. His friend had given him a secret blend of spices in a small brown paper sack. Dan stuck his head in the sack to smell and came up gasping for breath from the spicy aroma. He pronounced it *wonderful.* The live crabs and spices were spilled into the pot and covered. The small amount of water and vinegar in the bottom produced steam that melted the spice and poured the flavor into the white delicate meat of the favored crustaceans.

At exactly noon, family members from the little and big house spilled out to the picnic area as if intoxicated from the aroma of the crab pot. Friends began to come up the hill and the lawn filled with celebrants in white dresses and shirts. It was the only color to wear on such a sultry day. The sun rose unrelentingly. The rays broke through the large maple leaves like quiet fireworks. Laughter was infectious.

This would be a special holiday. The tables under the trees were spread with the most wonderful, traditional treats. All of the cakes and pies were baked by the ladies. Liddy—apple, Mrs. Fergus—cherry, done in those wee hours in the Fergus kitchen. Liddy also made her famous yeast rolls. Gertie and Mama made the cakes—one chocolate, (struggling to hold up in the heat) and one coconut. Dan cracked the coconut and Gertie shredded it to make her specialty. The white and wonderful cake waited in the ice chest with the salads so it would be refreshingly delicious on this hot day. Everything was covered by a white cloth to keep insects from enjoying the first bites. The smallest children could not resist lifting the cloth to see the wonders and maybe lick a finger full of chocolate frosting.

Nearby a table was designated for crab eating. It was spread with butcher paper that Sam had bought from Tasker's store. Little cups of vinegar and red spiced pepper were spaced around. There were wooden mallets piled in a basket. Each one had been carved at one time or another by the men in the family. Some were the smooth skillful work of Papa. Some were the rough work of a beginner. Sam had one with his name carved in the head. The Fergus basket had lovely ash wood hammers bought in Baltimore. Mayor Fergus even had one forged of steel and engraved with a fancy "F". From the youngest to the oldest, the art of picking crab meat was refined. Only the tiniest Fergus's grandchild, and the youngest MacGregor, had to be helped with the task. Gathering at this table was a Maryland summer ritual, especially on the 4th of July. It was polite to select the largest crab which was in front of you but not to reach in front of anyone else to get a big one. Eat the crab with your fingers after using the wooden knockers to break the shell. Everyone was expected to raise the crab by the red claw and declare it a *good one* before beginning the process. Then you could begin the banging and eating. First open the crab and discard the inedible and devil's finger lungs. The youngsters had to have their crab inspected and declared clean and ready to eat. Now the job is to pull every bit of meat from every crevice. It would be very bad if your sibling or parent could point out a morsel missed. The finest lump of crab meat came from behind the large flapper and each picker had a special way of handling this *filet* of crabmeat—some went right for it first, others saved it for the last bite. No matter, the spice from cooking, coated the hands and got into the mouth with the meat. Pleasure was written on every face. The families gathered on Fergus hill today knew exactly what to do. The best crab feasts are those where you eat some crabs, socialize a while, enjoy the fried chicken, salads and desserts, and come back to eat some more crabs. This was that kind of feast.

Eventually everyone had to sit down and do nothing. The badminton games and horse shoes had worn out many players. There were boastful winners and quieted losers. The food and games and heat mandated a quiet time. Lon Fergus strummed a guitar as his small children crawled over his knees. Dan napped against the tree. Mama, Papa, Mayor and Mrs. Fergus were sitting in lawn chairs reminiscing about past holidays such as this. Gertie and Liddy had some secret that they were teasing each other about. Sam rose to his feet.

"I think I will wander down to Tenth Street to see if Edward is there. He is probably bored with his family by now, too. They are probably *ground hogs* like all of you!" With this, Dan threw the volley ball into Sam's gut as Liddy sprang to her feet and went over to where the guitar player was sitting and said, "Wait, Sam. Don't leave. I have an announcement." Sam feigned a swoon and fell dead to the ground. Liddy standing in the center, calling attention to herself was more than he could believe and he couldn't resist having his joke on her. "Go ahead, Sister, speak," he said from his dead position.

Papa and Mama looked at each other and smiled at their lovely daughter. They were most pleased that she had enough poise to tell everyone gathered what her plan was. Gertie froze with her mouth dropped open. "What's this?" she wondered aloud. Gertie was as astounded as Sam when Liddy took center stage.

"Lon and I are getting married..." He took her hand and stood with her as she continued, "...next Sunday. You are all invited." Liddy's eyes were on her parents, looking for a smile of approval, which she got first from Papa and then Mama who were the only ones present who knew about the marriage plan. Then she turned to Lon as he put his arm around her, the only outward sign of affection that would be shown here. The look on Gertie's face was hidden behind her hands, but Liddy didn't think to glance in her direction.

Soon everyone gathered around the couple giving hugs and congratulations, except Gertie. Later as the family quietly settled down to visiting after a day of feasting and games, and until the sun went down and the fireworks were set off, there was nothing for Gertie to do but think about Liddy's announcement. Marrying Lon was the most stupid thing she could imagine. She even said, "Stupid," so she could hear the word and convince herself that it was the right word for the occasion. She continued to muse with deep furors across her brow. Lon was twelve years older than Liddy—with three children. Most of all he was just old—so, so *old*. He was an old widow-man over thirty.

The problem was that Gertie had never looked at Lon as a suitor and never imagined him as someone anyone she knew would want to marry. Sitting here this afternoon, she tried to look at him with new eyes and assign some of the criteria that she was developing for prospective suitors and she couldn't. He didn't fit anything. No adventure, no excitement, no mystery, no fun. And not handsome either. He even lacked authority by letting Liddy make the announcement. Gertie was not finding anything on the positive side and yet *her sister* was going to marry Lon Fergus next Sunday.

The week passed quickly with arrangements made for a small church ceremony and reception at the Fergus Mansion. Liddy and the children were all dressed in white. Gertie, maid of honor, wore her soft blue dress. Mayor Fergus was best man for his son and that made up the wedding party. Gertie had to admit that Lon looked fine, tall and distinguished in his dark suit. He stood close to Liddy and smiled warmly at her, just as he did to the children.

Liddy looked wonderful in the new dress she bought for herself, declining to use Mama's wedding dress, knowing that she would look too much like her mother. And that was true. She looked her own, happy person in the dotted white organza and carrying the yellow roses from the arbor. Gertie hardly remembered the food and guests who gathered on the mansion porch to avoid the heat. By three o'clock Liddy and Lon were off to Baltimore for their honeymoon.

She did remember her last words to Liddy. "I'll miss you…and you thought you would never get to Baltimore."

Lon owned a house in Elkridge, about ten miles from Laurel and ten miles from Baltimore. That was the worst part. Liddy was moving away. Lon and those children were taking Liddy away. Ten miles, might as well be a hundred. Liddy was choosing to leave us and go away with plain, old, balding Lon.

Sixteen year old Gertie was left to sit in the bedroom she had shared with Liddy, to sort out the reasons why this unbelievable thing had happened. For the first time she thought about marriage as a part of her own future. *One more year of school. What about me? Could I go off with a man and leave this family?* "What about me?" she asked her friend in the mirror. Marriage? The Academy? If Papa could send Liddy, he could send me. Teacher? Nurse? Spinster?" she asked her reflection.

"No teaching. No nursing. No spinster." she announced. The desolate girl crawled into bed but could not sleep, tossing and turning until the sheet was a mass of rocky mountains that would not let sleep come to the girl. She got out of bed and ran to Mama's room, stopping short. Only an emergency could cause her to knock on that door at night. If only Liddy were here. By the time she got back to her room the tears were dripping off her chin. Taking hold of the pillow to bury her face, she let herself go into body quaking sobs. She wanted to shout No, no, no! She tried not to think of Liddy but she couldn't. How do you try not to think of something? Maybe Liddy wishes she were back here this very moment. The thought that maybe Liddy was unhappy pleased and tormented Gertie and caused her heaving chest to ache. Trying to sleep but unable to get her mind to leave the troublesome thoughts, she tossed and turned. Things have always been such fun here. Liddy changed that. She did. *How could she do that?* Anger began to move into Gertie's being. She seemed to get overly warm under the sheet she was clinging to. "I don't care how hard it is for her. I hope she doesn't like Lon after all," she thought. Drifting toward sleep, she muttered, "Serves her right."

Gertie's anger brought her wide awake. She was hot. She seemed to be sweating and chilled at the same time, as shivers consumed her body, her dinner came up. "Mama" she called just as she got to the night pot by the bed.

She was still heaving when Mama put her hand on her forehead and held her so she wouldn't fall. "Gertie, you have a fever. Why didn't you call me sooner?" Mama took care of Gertie and soon after romancing the pot, the exhausted girl slept. She awoke to the soft morning light and a cool breeze coming in the window. A summer rain was falling breaking the heat wave. She just lay there thankful that the night was over. When she moved to get up the room swayed and she found it much better to stay put. A terrible thirst that made her call out to her mother who came in the room with a pitcher, a glass and a soft wash cloth. After pouring the glass for Gertie, she wet the cloth and placed it on her forehead.

"The fever is gone," she announced.

Gertie raised her eyes to Mama, and the tears started again. They held each other and cried softly together.

"Gertie, you made yourself sick last night. Let that be a lesson to you. If you had called me, we could have shared our tears and it would have gone easier on you. Our emotions can help us face challenges. They can also make us sick or cause us to make grave mistakes. Don't deny your emotions, Gertie, but don't allow them to cripple you either. You may have thought Liddy's marriage made a dead end street…."

"I did, I did." Mama was so right. "Last night I was on a dead end street. I didn't know what to feel or which way to go."

"Liddy's marriage is not your dead end street. In fact, Gertie, there are no *dead-end streets* in life given to us by others. The only real dead-ends are those we make for ourselves. This marriage is a wonderful opportunity for Liddy and Lon and for us too. A family is an ever changing thing. Sam, Dan and now Liddy have made their way and you will too—someday, not too soon, I hope. You'll see."

She continued, looking straight into Gertie's brown eyes circled with red. "Now you must think about what you let your emotions do to you last night. Emotions are good; anguish is not. Things are always better in the morning and with a little time to mellow your feelings they are always more reasonable. Women are stronger because they learn early on how to use the energy of emotion. When you took Liddy's decision as a personal blow you became defensive and angry. Self-pity is foolish and if you let anger be the controlling emotion, you lose because you can't make a good decision when angry. You lose if the battle is with yourself. Remember what I am telling you."

"Yes, Mama." Gertie took a deep sob ending breath. "I miss her so much."

"She deserves her happiness and you, my love, will get over your loneliness and will be glad no one knows about this, especially Liddy."

"I already feel that way. Can we keep this as our secret? I don't want Liddy to know…or Sam either."

"You stay right here until lunch is ready. You get soup, nothing else. After lunch you will be fine."

Being the obedient daughter, she did what her mother said and thought long and hard on what happened last night. The memory of the agony was strong. She felt the fear and anger again and knew it was foolish. *Things do look better today. If I can make my body sick, I can make it well and happy.* "I chose that." she proclaimed aloud as she promised herself to never forget the lesson learned although she had no idea how important that lesson would be to her own future happiness. She went downstairs to hug every member of the MacGregor clan who happened to be available. But, she really only wanted to hug Liddy.

❦

Three days later, sitting on the porch in the late afternoon playing jacks with Patsy, she was feeling her old self and mentally planning some activities for her friends. Patsy was excited about moving into Liddy's bed and sharing Gertie's room. She shared her little sister's excitement. It had been lonely in that room the last few nights. At that moment Liddy was coming across the lawn from the big house.

"Mama! Liddy's here." Gertie called as she raced to meet her. Amid hugs Liddy, who looked just the same to Gertie, settled into the porch swing. In fact Gertie was looking her big sister over very carefully to see what outward changes could follow marriage and she could not find any except the animation as Liddy started talking.

"Lon and I are here to talk with Mother Fergus about the children. We have decided that we need time to set up the household. Lon did not realize how badly things had deteriorated over the past year and a half when the house was empty. We saw all that should be done to make a new family home there in Elkridge. We have come to ask Mother Fergus to keep the children until we get it done. So the children won't feel left out we will be coming here to see them twice a week until the work is finished. He's in town now, gathering some materials and hiring workers. It may take a month or more." Liddy's animation was a delight to her mother and sister. "So I'll be seeing you on Tuesday when Lon will drop me off on his way to work, pick me up after work. We will bring the children back on Sunday. Won't that be nice? It is going to be such fun and when we finish you all will come to see our home."

"Gertie, would you like to help Mrs. Fergus with the children for the next month?"

She had not expected to have the opportunity to earn money so soon. The idea appealed to her and she said "Yes," while looking at Mama for approval.

Gertie and Mama could not remember seeing Liddy so excited about plans before, not even when she made her announcement at the picnic. They were both thinking the same thing and started laughing. Soon all four women were dissolved into giggles, just like old times.

Gertie was thinking, *I'm so glad Liddy is not unhappy.*

Chapter 4   1910

Gertie was not the prettiest girl but she knew how to dress and how to make the most of a tiny waist and full bosom with the fashionable Gibson style. She favored the wide sash and liked to tie a bow at the back which forced her to sit up straight. That knot pressing into her back pushed her breasts out and kept her shoulders straight. Gertie noticed that many girls did not look as good sitting down and she had figured out why. She did not have a pale white complexion because she would not hide under a hat. Hats were to be worn until the first possible chance to remove them. She had thick, chestnut curls that were hard to contain in buns or braids. Whenever possible Gertie took an outside chore and had already begun to enjoy gardening with her mother. It seemed that when the other girls wore black or blue, she came in white and vice versa.

Gertie grew up knowing Liddy was prettier. She did not look like her mother; she looked like Papa. However, she knew other things catch the eye of the opposite sex. She was not a shrinking violet. She had always come forward to meet men on equal ground, always honest and too often, outspoken. Gertie became a student of human Nature, studying Mama and Papa and the dynamics of her family. It was apparent to her that Papa's sternness and Mama's tenderness cemented the family together. Her big problem was with the traditional roles for women. She watched Mama manipulate Papa instead of just standing her ground when she was right. Gertie was not sure she could do that or that she would want to.

At the dinner table one evening, soon after the bridge accident, Papa announced, "Sam, I want to meet Edward Neal. See if you can arrange to bring him home for dinner. How about it Mama, can we set another plate one day for a fellow hero?"

"We sure can. It might be a little tight here with three heroes at the table." That caused Papa to let out a belly laugh while Gertie lowered her chin to her chest and smiled.

"I'll ask him if I see him tomorrow. He works in DC and doesn't come to Laurel every day."

❧

"We are having a guest for dinner tonight," Mama announced at breakfast Wednesday morning. "Sam is bringing Edward Neal home."

"Today? He is coming today. Why didn't anyone tell me? I will be at the big house for dinner tonight." The disappointment in her voice was written on her face.

Over at the big house, Gertie found it hard to concentrate on the children, their meals and baths that evening. At eight, her duties were finished and she took her sweater and started across the lawn on the well-worn path between the two houses.

"Sis, over here," Sam called from the porch.

Her heart tripped in time with the quick stumble of her feet as she turned to his call. She slowed at the steps and forcibly slowed her breathing.

"Gertie, this is Edward. Edward, Gertie," Sam said with raised brows.

"I have wanted to meet the girl with the scissors," Edward said, taking her hand, squeezing it gently, and then releasing it as convention dictated. "Whatever made you bring scissors that day? You may have saved my life."

"I was just grabbing blankets and towels and they were hanging there," she replied, disappointed at the break in contact. A lovely thrill had rippled up her arm. "I grabbed them. A lucky happenstance, I guess."

"I don't even want to think what would have happened if you hadn't." He stepped past her toward the steps. "Well, I hate to leave good company, but I've a train to catch. Thanks for the invite, Sam. Pleased to meet you, Gertie."

"Come again anytime." Gertie said, because she meant it and she wanted to see him again.

Edward started down over the hill and Sam took Gertie into a head lock. "*Come again, anytime*," he mocked in a sing-song voice. "Even I can figure that out."

"Sam, you think you're so smart. I'm just being polite."

"Polite, my foot. That's the first time you have ever acted like you wanted a boy to come again. I know your take *'em or leave 'em* attitude. What's with Edward?"

"What are you making a big thing about?"

"I don't know...*who is* making a big thing about it? Not me." he laughed and took off running into the house with her flying behind him.

That night she was full of dreams of Edward. He had turned her head and she couldn't decide why. He was handsome, but she knew other handsome boys. He seemed more a man—working in DC—riding back and forth on a train. His clothes and manner were sophisticated. Gertie didn't really understand chemistry; she had never felt this way before. "I wonder if I will ever get to Washington?" she said aloud, though Patsy was asleep.

Sam came in and took his chair, pulling up close to her bed. "Is Patsy asleep? I want to talk to you."

"Yes. You won't bother her. What's up? Things going OK? You aren't here to spend the night much anymore."

"Things are fine with me. I just have more and more responsibility at the track and it is easier to stay there. I have a bunk, but I do miss Mama's cooking." He patted his stomach, and leaned forward. "I know how determined you can be when you want something. Do you have a crush on Edward Neal?"

"Sam, I hardly know him, but ..."

"Here's my take on Edward. He is nice enough but a little mixed up. His family is a good one, and because of some disagreement with his father, he walked away from them. When he has a chance to blast his father he does it with a vengeance. He is a lot of fun and loves a good time and I do too, but I would have to know Edward a lot better before I would want him with my sister. I think you should give yourself every chance to get to know him before you fall for him...seriously I mean."

"I get it! Thanks, Sam."

❦

Gertie looked forward to Edward's next visit and she was not disappointed. He found time, after the first meeting, to climb Fergus Hill. She did not become the giddy teenager for this sophisticated suitor. She spent some quiet evenings analyzing how she felt about him and how she wanted him to see her. She decided to be herself. When Edward asked her a question, she answered it as directly as she could and he liked that in the girl he had decided to pursue.

Their courtship was fun and easy. Edward would come to town on the train and show up on Fergus Hill. Sometimes he would see his sister Emily and sometimes Sam would be there. In the last year he had walked up Tenth Street to see his mother twice; he never saw his father.

The few hours each Sunday were highlights for the couple. Gertie let Edward know the time together was important to her. Her hair and dress were fresh and becoming each afternoon, no matter the temperature. She had his favorite cake or treat to take with him for the trip back to the city—believing the adage—*the way to a man's heart is through his stomach.*

Edward admired Gertie's appearance and enjoyed her vivacious, generous ways. Moreover, he was physically attracted. Edward understood chemistry. Gertie became a prize and Edward was experienced enough to devise a plan to win her. He learned, in his city social circle, how to make sure a girl knew he was looking at her. He waited for her to notice and looked down at the moment he was sure she knew she had his attention. He brushed her hand without taking it and whispered in her ear whenever he could. Edward never had to compete with other men because his technique with a woman was never obvious to other men.

Edward quickly ascertained that Gertie's family was important to her and that he had to court them as well. His upbringing included manners and so he spent time with Mama and Papa when he came to see Gertie. At times, he acted reluctant to leave the family circle and go off with Gertie for a walk or sit on the porch swing. Mama noted this and thought he must be missing his family just two blocks down the hill. He took to having a cigar with Papa after dinner and the two talked about the railroad. Edward did make one mistake in his courtship of Gertie—a common mistake made by men. He thought Gertie was a lot like his mother but someday he would learn that she was not like his mother at all. And so, Gertie and Edward fell into a very casual courtship that included family activities. The only times they had alone were walks around the Fergus estate. He held her hand on the walks but never reached for it unless they were alone.

On one occasion when she asked about his family and leaving home, he was quick with his reply. "I just don't live there anymore. Nothing more to tell." His tone of voice closed the subject.

Edward was a lot of fun and everyone enjoyed his good humor. To Gertie he was thoughtful and romantic. His gifts were small—flowers picked when he saw his mother or picture cards of the monuments in Washington. He remembered her favorite things like ice cream and dancing. And took her to the town's bandstand where they could share both.

Emily was delighted to have her brother around more often; she thought they were a perfect match. Gertie's other friends were jealous.

School was fine and her activities filled the week while she waited for Sunday. Her good grades and work on the Student Council brought her attention from the Academy. They offered her a scholarship for next year.

"Exactly what does the scholarship mean, Gertie?" Papa asked.

"They will pay for my first year but my grades have to compete with other students to get it the following years. If I am not in the top five percent, I will have to pay for the next year."

"Can you do that?"

"I don't know Papa. If not, I can always stop after one year."

"I think it is a great opportunity and you should go. There is no reason not to," offered Mama.

But, Gertie was falling in love with Edward. She kept meaning to tell him about the scholarship but never quite found the right time.

He came every weekend while the weather was nice and the mile walk from the train station was easy. With fall, he came less often and she never knew when it would be. Gertie tried to understand the days were shorter and cooler but her desire to see him took her to her wits end before he came again. As they walked across the yard, hand in hand she would forget the hours she had felt so tormented since last Sunday when he did not come. Gertie melted at the touch of his hand. Their courtship had been going on for months, and yet, he continued to wait until the last minute before kissing her.

After his kiss and departure to catch the 6:45, she began to wait the wait for nest Sunday with strange burning on her lips—a feeling that only another kiss could put out the fire. Gertie had her unfulfilled passion and his single kiss—which she held on to.

One warm April evening, the world stood still with his words. "We can have it all; you and me. I want to show you the city. You'll love living there."

His off handed remark struck her dumb. She could not say a word. *Was that a proposal?* She thought over and over again. It was a dream and she wanted it. She wanted it all. Gertie wanted to see new worlds; to live in a city; to be with Edward. And, he wanted to give it to her. She felt he would not want her to go to Academy but she never really asked him. Maybe there was time to go to Academy and be with Edward, too.

❦

The next week, everything changed. Mayor Fergus was gravely ill. Liddy and Lon Fergus were called home from Elkridge. Mama, Gertie and Liddy worked around the clock to keep the Fergus family fed while the vigil was held. The whole town was shocked at the great loss of the Mayor and benefactor of this small town. The new school which he built was just dedicated and he was gone.

Two weeks after the MacGregor family assisted the Fergus family with the funeral, they gathered in the warm kitchen. Gertie noticed the rain beating the windows when Papa stood and rapped his cup with a spoon. In his usual factual way said, "We will be moving. I have just taken a job in Sparrows Point. We will go in the summer after we help Mrs. Fergus through this hard time. She is not going to live in the big house; she is giving up her stable of horses and will not need a caretaker."

Mama knew where Sparrows Point was, as did Dan and Sam, but to everyone else he might just as well have said Timbuktu. It was Gertie who finally said, "Papa, where's Sparrows Point and why do we have to move?"

Papa did not realize that his announcement about moving would change everything for Gertie. She would not move away from Edward.

Chapter 5

They were married in the parlor. Rev. Harrison came up Fergus Hill from the Methodist Episcopal Church. Gertie wore a white organdy dress that came to her ankles. It was the fashion length for this year. When Mama wore it, it touched the floor but Mama was shorter than Gertie. Mama removed the puff sleeves and added a band and a pearl button to fasten it fittingly to the arm just above the elbow. The shirred cummerbund accented Gertie's figure which was fashionably hidden in the generous bosom of the dress. Mama had carefully washed and sunned the dress until it sparkled white. Papa bought her a pair of white dress shoes. Liddy let her wear the gold watch Lon had given her for their first anniversary. To have something blue, Gertie tied a small blue ribbon to her camisole.

Edward was breathtakingly handsome. He was a man of distinction, with a fine job in Washington, DC and he was in love with this splendid girl. It seemed to radiate from him. His demeanor was optimism. Everyone listened as he spoke of his future as if it were reality instead of a dream—especially his bride. Edward liked to see admiration in the eyes of the people around him but most of all he liked to see it in Gertie's eyes. He knew he was almost more beautiful than the bride and he liked that about Gertie, too.

They stood, Gertie and Edward with Emily, sister of the groom as Maid of Honor and Sam, brother of the bride, as Best Man. The parlor only held Rev. Harrison, the bridal party and Mama and Papa. There were MacGregor children of all ages on the porch, peeking in the open doors and windows. The family and friends of the happy couple filled the home and spilled on to the lawn. The kitchen and the porches were full of food and drink served in a more formal manner than this family usually presented—but just as hospitably.

Liddy enjoyed seeing everyone enjoying her baked ham and candied sweet potato casserole. Her rolls and fresh churned butter were delicious. Lon provided fresh fruits which he had sent from Baltimore. The most spectacular wedding cake of six layers awaited Gertie and Edward to slice the first piece and feed the multitude. The lovely couple delighted in each other and in the company of their loved ones—minus Mr. and Mrs. Clay Neal. That bothered Gertie but Edward seemed oblivious to their absence.

After everyone had eaten, the men went for a game of horse shoes and the ladies stretched out on blankets on the lawn. Everyone complimented Gertie on her dress and her new husband. Edward stayed close by with Papa and a few men who enjoyed talk more than lawn games. Sam led the conversations, talking about the horses and the track. Papa had long since stopped objecting to Sam talking about his world where the best horses won the hard races and poor ones lost because of the lack of good jockeys.

"I'd ride, if I were small enough," Dan offered.

Papa looked sternly at Dan. "I'll not have two of my son's at the abominable racetrack. Eat up, Dan. Have another piece of cake."

Sam never let a good tease go. "Papa you will be over in Sparrows Point. How will you be able to count your children at the track?" With that the conversation turned to the impending family move.

"Can't you stay in Laurel? I will be in Washington, Sam will be here, Liddy is in Elkridge and everyone else will be in Sparrows Point," Gertie lamented.

She rose from her place and walked over toward Papa. "I know. I know…you have a home and a job." She paused and took a deep breath and went to stand beside her father. "When are you leaving and how are you going to move the whole family across Baltimore?"

As she passed Sam, he reached out, tripped her and caught her in one sweeping move. Raising her above his head, he spun her around, laughing and shouting. "Hush, you old married lady. You only need to worry where Edward is!" The only blush of the day crossed her cheeks and she swatted him and squirmed to the ground.

Papa smiled and answered, "We will be moved by August and it will take most of the summer to get the job done. I have to go where I can provide a home for this family that cannot be taken from under us due to unforeseen circumstances. I've found that at Bear Creek. There will be room for everyone and for those children who only come to visit. You, Liddy, Sam… and Dan. He is staying here in Laurel and will be working in Washington just like Edward."

Dan had decided not to move with the family. This was news to everyone except Mama. She let her children go from the nest without fussing. Although she did ask Gertie, just to make sure, if she was getting married to keep from moving. Gertie assured her she loved Edward. It was in the wee hours that Mama wept at their going and comforted herself with the young ones that will still be with her at Bear Creek, Sparrows Point, Baltimore.

As distressing as this news was and talk about the family being split by a move, it still did not dampen the spirit of the wedding party and celebrants because Papa and Mama would not allow it. Their quiet confidence in the family ties was not contrived. This family would always manage to be together and the values they held dear would not be diminished by the miles. Because Papa knew it and Mama knew it: everyone there knew it.

Even Edward was learning—this family formed a whole, which was so foreign from his. As Papa stopped talking a buggy pulled into the drive and out stepped Elizabeth Amsterdam.

Edward said, "Gram," and ran to meet her.

Gertie and her parents came across the lawn to greet the late arriving, but very important, guest. The meeting was polite and gracious. It was not until she was seated and had a glass of lemonade and a piece of wedding cake that she spoke. "I want to express my best wishes to the lovely bride and congratulations to my grandson on their wedding day. Edward you are to be congratulated for picking a young lady from one of the finest families. Of course, I am sure that was not the criteria for your selection. I can see that a lovely face and manner were more important to you." The quiet laughter broke the ice and the visit evolved into a most enjoyable time. The afternoon breeze softened the temperature and the increasing shadows made the lawn very comfortable. The whole wedding celebration glowed.

Gertie relaxed and paid attention to Edward's grandmother. She saw and admired her manner of speech. It was as if every sentence was a proclamation and did not require response. She saw Elizabeth Amsterdam as a very confident woman who had no problem coming here unescorted, and saw no need to explain why her daughter or son-in-law had not come also. She was happy with her grandson and happy about this occasion. Her enjoyment of the company and the food was obvious although this was the first time she was a guest at the MacGregor home. She made a mental note of names that were familiar from church rolls or mill workers her husband had overseen.

Elizabeth Amsterdam knew when the visit was over and when it was time to go. She said her good-byes; rose and placed her arm through Edward's, took Gertie's hand and allowed herself to be walked back to the carriage She placed in Gertie's hand a wedding gift and left. The bride and groom stood staring at the cameo surrounded in diamonds. Gertie read her note

> *Dearest Gretta,*
> *It is important that you know you always have something*
> *in reserve. Keep it safe; it is yours. Knowing it is there is*
> *its real value.*
>
> *Always,*
> *Elizabeth Amsterdam.*

The wonderful afternoon turned to evening. The bride and groom were preparing to go to the big house to spend their wedding night in one of the bedrooms in the manor. Mrs. Fergus was still visiting her sister since her widowhood. Lon Fergus was a generous man. It was he who proposed this as the refuge for Mr. and Mrs. Edward C. Neal for this night in May. Since his marriage to Liddy he was ever mindful of her family and tried to do them a kind deed whenever Papa would allow it. He and Liddy had enjoyed opening the room with the best view and preparing it for the bride and groom.

Gertie and Edward were delighted that they would have this special place for tonight. Tomorrow they would leave for Washington and Edward's little hotel room. They had just announced that they were retreating from Sam's teasing remarks when Emily Neal stepped forward and handed Edward the envelope that her mother had bid her bring to the wedding. It had *Edward* written in his mother's fine hand. Emily had waited to the last minute fearful that whatever it contained could spoil the day for her handsome brother and her best friend. The envelope did not spoil the day because Edward placed it in his pocket unopened and continued painstakingly long good-byes to the MacGregor family who seemed to be having trouble watching Gertie leave for the big house on this evening.

Mama took extra care helping Gertie change from the twice used wedding dress. They talked of Patsy and Shirley and wondered if it would be used again in years to come. Liddy bustled around the room putting things away, placing the jewelry Gertie wore and the beautiful cameo in Mama's dresser box, and laying the undergarments aside for hand washing later. Mama had thought very seriously about the words she would say to Gertie before she left with Edward. It was difficult to send such a capable daughter off without confidence in her choice as a husband. Mama had watched Gertie make choice after choice, small and large, important and insignificant, throughout her life. Always they had built confidence in the girl. It was with unusual apprehension that Mama spoke to Gertie today.

"Everyone has a right to happiness, Gertie. Your father and I want you to be happy, as we have been happy. We learned early that the best way to assure the happiness of our family was to be happy in ourselves. It is the only way it works. I have stitched a sampler for your wedding gift." With that said, she presented Gertie with the labor of her love. Tears sprang to Gertie's eyes as she read:

Your happiness comes from within.
It is not a gift from God
But a gift to God.

It was done in beautiful script and embellished with hearts, flowers and the tree of life.

Gertie hugged her mother until the tears were over. Then she dried her eyes and smiled brightly. She was so happy.

Papa held her to his ample chest and simply said, "Always remember who you are," as he squeezed her. Then he held her from him and with a twinkle in his eye challenged her to their annual horseshoe match on the Labor Day in their new home on Bear Creek. This was so warm and reassuring to the young girl who had no fear of forging ahead in marriage because she had family and knew what that meant.

Gertie and Edward went to the big house to begin their life together. The wedding bed was large, ample for two. Neither Gertie nor Edward had ever been in such a large bed. Liddy had place fresh linens and flowers in the room for them. Every comfort was there for the newlyweds. Each could imagine that this large manor home was theirs. On a wedding night nothing is just-for-one-night.

The room was beautiful. White linens seemed to sparkle on the bed. The pillows were edged in soft lace that would not scratch. A hint of lavender and roses wafted in the air. The flowers in the wallpaper softened the walls. Gertie noticed it all and held to each image, especially the softly moving organdy curtains. She would recreate this room some day in a home of her own.

Edward waited very patiently as Gertie prepared for bed. He was a man of experience and was determined not to frighten his bride. Since he was fifteen and was led to bed by Ann Moore in her very own home, while her children slept in the next room, Edward was disillusioned by sex. After that experience, he concluded that it was a mechanic act that gave momentary satisfaction. Later he found pleasure in a girl his own age who aroused feelings of affections to align with sexual pleasure. His conclusion was that this was definitely a better arrangement. Edward's subsequent experiences with women were of the non-affectionate nature while he looked for a wife that could be the perfect combination of affection and sexual enjoyment. Edward had two definitions of sex. One had absolutely nothing to do with the other. He was alive with anticipation of love with this wonderful girl that he had married. Edward was confident that he could love Gertie and satisfy himself.

Gertie was shy but her usual straightforward nature kept her from being a giggly, flighty bride. She came right to Edward, for him to put his arm around her as he had done on so many other occasions. She leaned on him for the kiss that was familiar to her and felt the tingle through her body that was also familiar to her. She looked right into Edward's eyes, again taken by his good looks, and asked, "Tell me right now, Edward, what we will be on the wedding bed... and then give me a chance to understand and appreciate what is happening."

Never in all of Edward's experience had a partner spoke to him like this. As he began to vocalize the acts of sex for Gertie as she asked, he became incredibly aroused such as never before. Edward had not expected his wedding night to be so spectacular. He thought he had experienced sex to the optimum but this bride of his was not a passive thing; she was alive and wanting to know and to do. Edward led Gertie through her wedding night as if he were the giver of all knowledge and gifts. She took all his knowledge and gifts and made them hers—to give back to him.

The next morning they were as one. They talked and dreamed and hoped and schemed. They were both hungry but Gertie was reluctant to face her rousing family across the lawn from this fine bridal suite. She knew without a doubt that Sam would be ready to tease and not even Mama could stop him from smiling with his eyes at the new bride.

When Gertie opened the door to their chamber a tray of fruit, ham and wedding cake and coffee was sitting on the floor. Sometime in the early morning someone had brought food. The coffee was cold but sweet. The bride and groom went back into the room to eat and to stay for hours more.

It was near noon when Edward dressed and folded his good suit to put it into his bag. That is when the rustle of the paper reminded him of the letter from his mother. He pulled it out and Gertie gasped. "We forgot to open your mothers wedding letter. How terrible, Edward."

He opened it and read aloud. "After your wedding guests have left tonight we would like for you to come to see us. It is important that your family extend their wishes to you and Gertie today. Your Father and I are expecting you. Love, Mother."

"Oh, Edward, this is terrible. We have no excuse for not reading that yesterday and going the short distance to see them. I feel awful."

Edward was not so contrite. "Don't let it bother you, Gertie".

Gertie urged him to go the very short distance to the Neal home on Tenth Street. He was not inclined. He knew that his father would be angry. It was only Gertie's insistence and her reminder that his mother deserved a response to the letter that he consented to go. Edward was still in a mood that this letter had even come and a little put out at Gertie for taking a side in this.

Gertie took more than just a *side*. She began dressing for a visit to her in-law's house. She combed her hair thinking about meeting Mr. and Mrs. Neal as Mrs. Neal herself. She straightened a very becoming yellow dress, musing about the impression that she could make on

Mary Amsterdam Neal—all the while portraying to Edward that it was settled. They were going this afternoon.

Edward thought it was still a matter of discussion but he was wrong. Gertie laid out his fresh shirt and completed packing his bag. They would leave from Tenth Street for the railroad station after the visit. She even put Sam on alert, he would drive them in time to catch the 4:30 congressional southbound. Edward was certainly taken aback by her organization and direction but he was amused also. *This is going to be interesting,* he thought as he watched his wife. Edward liked things to be interesting.

They walked to Tenth Street. He opened the gate and led his bride to the door, wondering if he should knock or walk in. Before he could decide, it opened and Mary Neal invited them in. She gave Gertie a hug and reminded her of the many times she had visited Emily. Then she turned to Edward and embraced him as if it had been only yesterday since she saw him. All the days and weeks and months of hurt were gone with one look into his blue eyes and handsome face. She took in a big breath but dared not issue a sigh. Edward hugged her and nearly shouted, "Mom you are as pretty as ever, the best cook in the world, and I love you." Mom Neal was again ready to give her first born the world—but it was not hers to give. The conversation was light and full of the events of yesterday. Never was there a mention of why the Neal's had not come to the wedding, nor was anything said about the failure of Edward and Gertie to respond to the invitation for a visit last night.

Edward told his mother about their new apartment in Washington and about his promotion with the railroad. Gertie told about her family's move to Sparrows Point to a place called Bear Creek.

Finally, as conversation slacked, Mary said, "I will go tell Clay that you are here."

Clay Neal knew that they were here. He saw them come up the walk from Montgomery Street. He was sitting on the back porch and heard the exuberance of Edward's greeting of his mother. And, he saw Gertie's pretty yellow dress. Mary's countenance had changed when she returned with her husband. Gertie was frightened and when she touched Edward's arm, it stiffened. He pulled back, ever so slightly, and hurt her feelings.

Clay walked in, waited for his wife to take her chair, and began. "I have something to say to both of you. There was an invitation to come here yesterday. Gertie, I didn't know if Edward would want to come but I expected you to see to it. I'm disappointed." He raised his hand to halt Gertie's response. "You," he addressed Edward as if he could not say his name, "cannot take Gertie to live in Washington, DC. I have the utmost respect for the MacGregor family. William gave me help when I needed it. I am honor bound to prevent you from taking her to the city. The home at 405 Eleventh Street has been secured for your residence at the rate you would pay to live in the city." With this Clay slid a door key across the table and rose to leave the room and its startled occupants. He hesitated and turned to his son. Pointing his finger he said, "Visit your mother once a week," and left.

There was no invitation to eat although Mary would have loved fixing a meal for the couple. She did not mention it. She offered coffee or lemonade but Edward and Gertie declined. In truth, none of them could swallow a thing, Mary least of all. She had no idea what Clay planned to tell the children when they were summoned. She had waited in dread all last evening when they did not come. She feared that her husband would spoil their wedding day but providence kept them away. Her first easy breath came when they rose to leave and she had not even begun to digest the surprise her husband had presented to them all.

Gertie and Edward needed to go back to Fergus Hill and talk over this strange turn of events. A home instead of a hotel apartment. A gift from an unexpected source.

Edward walked without talking. He clutched Gertie's hand so tightly, cutting off circulation, that it tingled. His strides caused her to struggle to keep up. It was almost as if he was pulling a rag doll—almost dragging her.

"Edward, I can't keep up," she cried as she pulled her hand away. He moved on ahead of her and took a seat on the MacGregor porch step to wait for her.

"Edward…" His hand went in the air to interrupt and stop her. Gertie kneeled before him so she could look him in the eye. It was hard to ignore someone so close, but he did. She was near tears when he finally spoke to her.

"I've seen the house at 405 Eleventh Street but for the life of me, I can't even remember what it looks like," he paused and twisted the key in his fingers. "I'm sure it will be fine for us." He made the decision alone. "We can go to my apartment for the next few days just as we planned and enjoy my two days off. Then move into the house on Wednesday. No need for you to take much to Washington." Suddenly he was warm and tender to his bride. "Let's go have our honeymoon, Gertie"

She was disappointed. She really wanted to live in the big city; instead she would be living right here in the west end of town. But the excitement of her newly-wed state carried her from that disappointment into her husband's arms, saying, "Yes, Edward." It didn't matter that he never asked what she *thought* about this turn of events.

Chapter 6

The house on Eleventh Street was nice but small, yet, more than Gertie ever expected. It was one of the narrow but deep, two story homes of small mill towns at the turn of the century. There was a living room, a dining room behind that, and a kitchen behind that. On the back of the house was a closed-in porch with the newest in toilets—installed. The toilet had a storage tank for water and a pull cord for flushing. There was no trap with water to keep fumes out so it was installed on the porch out of the house. The porch was hot in summer and very cold in winter, but the convenience of having a toilet in the house was wonderful. The steps to the second floor rose from the dining room. At the landing a left turn went into the front bedroom; a right turn led to the back bedroom, and an unfinished storage room. Gertie and Edward were very fortunate to have this house. She began nesting and trying to deal with the impending move of her family. At least she would have her brothers and friends near.

"I'm glad we will be close to your parents. It will be perfect," she declared.

"I doubt that," was Edward's off-handed reply.

Gertie was optimistic that roses would grow, the sun would shine, and life would be colorful, fragrant, and wonderful. The small white house would sit in the center of green grass and her happy world. She would show Edward the world as she saw it. "Papa and Mama will soon be moved. Your family will be my family, now."

Edward was tired of her foolishness. "Come here, wife. Look at me—I'm your family." He stopped her talking and thinking with a kiss.

Edward liked the house and the status it brought, but it meant he had to commute to work. The train ride was free, but every morning and evening he had a one mile walk to the train station. In bad weather he would have to stay in the city away from his bride. The gift from his father was accepted; Edward was a *taker*. He wondered why his father had provided this house, and finally concluded that it was given to him because he deserved it. Once a week, when the rent was due, he visited his mother.

Gertie washed dishes, made beds and revisited her dream of going to the Academy. *Married women don't go to school*, she wondered. "Why not?" She proclaimed aloud. Her happiness with Edward and the fun of keeping her own house would bring new dreams. But, the old dream came in mid-day and often late at night.

"We will live on Eleventh Street and I will take you on the train—to Washington for holidays," he promised, as he drew her to his lap. "We have it all."

Gertie believed and wondered.

Life in the house on Eleventh Street fell into a pattern of lovely summer days and a couple in love. Gertie became the housewife. She cooked her mother's best recipes, planted flowers by the front walk and a climbing rose on the railing. Their home became a warm and pleasant place for gathering just as the caretaker's house was on the not too distant hill. The little house began to look as she had dreamed it, idyllic—lacking only the white picket fence.

Edward was getting to know Gertie and used all of his charm to get his way with her. He allowed her to dote on him. She quickly assumed polishing his shoes and bringing him his coffee. He complimented her on all her meals and the special touches she made for the house.

Gertie had a strange feeling of gratitude toward Edward for allowing her to do these things for him. One quiet evening on the sofa, listening to the radio, her contentment inspired her to ask the question that had been on her mind. "Edward, what do you think about me going to Academy? I was offered a scholarship for one year."

"What? Is this a joke?"

"I'm serious. I have a scholarship to Academy starting in September."

"You want to go back to school?" Edward could not believe what she was saying. He was too disarmed to be angry.

Gertie snuggled closer, almost teasing with her body for his compliance. "I want to..." she drew closer, "...if you agree. The Academy offered it to me at graduation. I gave up thoughts of going until it turned out that we were going to live here. But, since I am here, I wonder—"

"Never!" His voice took an edge and his body stiffened against her.

"Edward?" She put her hand on his chest. "I would be in class while you—"

"No—a thousand times—no." He lifted her hand. "Your place is in the home. Isn't being a wife enough? Tell me now. Is it enough?" The tight grip on her hand eased and he kissed it. "Am I enough for you?" he asked as he turned her on the sofa so she could feel manly pressure against her thigh.

Gertie laughed to relieve the tension as she relaxed to him. "Can we talk about this tomorrow?" She kissed him.

His lips whispered, "No," as they formed the kiss that lingered on her lips and mind.

She muttered with her returning kiss, "There is still time to talk about it." In his aroused state, even her insistence was good with him.

* * *

Gertie's stubborn streak kept things interesting. Edward never thought that he would be satisfied with one woman, but his bride seemed to be ready to challenge him and lay with him every night. It was beyond his wildest dreams, from boyhood through the challenges of manhood, to find such pleasure in his wife. She was willing and loving until he was worn out. There was no doubt—Gertie was his finest possession.

Her marriage was not her only dream, but her commitment was total. Her joy was Edward, and she was losing herself in him. Her every thought was tempered by what Edward would like, or think, or do. Eleventh Street was her world. She would help Edward climb the ladder of success, raise their children and keep this house—so that he had no worries.

During long boring days, after the daily chores were done, she thought about going back to school, and tried to find the argument that would soften Edward's stance against it. "Why can't I do it just because I want to?" She asked the chicken she was preparing for the oven. The time never seemed right to bring it up to Edward that day or the next.

"How long is this honeymoon going on? Sis, you have eyes like a puppy all the time." Sam teased.

"Sam, you won't understand until you find the right girl...I mean the perfect girl. I have found the perfect man."

To which, Sam raised one eyebrow.

Eleventh Street became a center for their group of young people. Sam was always the welcome and unexpected guest. Gertie provided the home setting since their parents were breaking up the household on Fergus Hill. When Sam came it was usually with a new young lady in tow—always pretty.

"Gertie, meet Eloise." Sam exclaimed as he arrived at the porch where several young people were already gathered.

"Hi, Eloise. Sam, introduce her around while I get iced tea. Edward will be here soon and we will eat."

This same scenario was repeated each week except Sam would have a different girl.

On the longest day of the year, a picnic was planned down by the Patuxent River. Sam and his date, Emily and her beau Walter, with another couple gathered with food baskets on the porch.

Edward was late.

"Go on ahead. We will catch up. Edward must have missed his train." Gertie gave her voice a light air, which she did not feel. Her concern was hidden from all, except Sam.

"OK. Walt, grab that basket. Emily, get the blanket. I've got the drinks. We will see you down at High Rock, Gertie." Sam took the lead to get everyone moving as Gertie suggested. He was sure she would only be more anxious if they waited with her.

She waved them off and took a seat on the front step. *Something must have happened,* she worried. *Train wreck?* "No." she admonished herself. "Missed train, that's all." She spoke to her hands twisting in her lap and refused to let her mind wander to a possible tragedy. Arrival time for the 6:45 train came and went and her anxiety grew.

It was eight o'clock when Edward got out of a carriage at the end of Eleventh Street and walked to 405. Gertie breathed a sigh of relief when she saw him coming. Her heart jumped and her voice quivered in her throat. "Edward." The only tears of the day burst from her eyes but they were dried on the hem of her skirt before he reached the porch.

"Hi, Sweetie," he said and sat beside her on the step. "Anything going on tonight? No Sam? Nobody coming by?"

Gertie was amazed at his nonchalant way of ignoring the two hours that he was late. In her usual manner she went straight to the subject. "It's our picnic night. Edward, please… tell me what happened to make you late. I've been so worried." Edward said nothing. "Sam and the others have gone on ahead to the river."

"I'm here now," he said and again posed the questions about their friends. "I forgot this was the night we were going for the river picnic."

She nodded and went on in her direct manner. "Edward, why are you are just now getting home?"

Edward was finished trying to pass over this unpleasantness with Gertie. She could see the cloud pass over his eyes as he rose and stood before her. It was a look she had seen before, but never directed so piercingly at her. "Gertie, your stubborn questions are making me angry. Shut up." He tried to control his anger. "Let's go on to the river. I'm hungry." He took both of her arms and jerked her to her feet. "Now!" She felt his tight fingers go into her arms and then relax into a gentle hold. As suddenly as the cloud came, it passed. A smile radiated his face as he kissed her. "Let's go." He held her hand lovingly all the way to the river path to the high, flat rock where their friends awaited them.

Gertie said nothing while they walked. Edward talked incessantly and did not even notice that Gertie was quiet.

The picnic was spread and warm greetings came from their friends on the river's edge. Gertie and Edward blended in to make the most of a moonlit summer night. The river streamed silver over rocky rills that provided a gentle gurgling background to laughter and song that filled the summer night.

"Come, Sweetie. It's too beautiful to miss. Look at the river." Edward pulled Gertie to sit on their favored spot.

Gertie was relaxing into the spirit of the picnic when a strange feeling in her arms caused her hands to rub the places where Edward grabbed her. First she felt the tenderness. *I'm bruised.* Then her hand felt a knot on the inside of each of her upper arms.

Sam was the only one who saw a darkening of his sister's countenance. He filed his thoughts away for another day.

"What's for dessert?" Edward demanded. "Didn't you bake a cake today, wife?" Gertie remembered the chocolate cake sitting on her table waiting to be brought to this picnic.

"In the rush to catch up, I forgot it."

"Let's go back to the house and eat it." Edward gave the invitation and she smiled assent though she could not wait for the evening to end.

Sam noticed that her weak smile did not echo Edward's invitation.

At last the cake was eaten, the men sang *Good Night Ladies*, and everyone left.

Gertie cleared away the dishes and crumbs, tired and unhappy. It no longer mattered why Edward was late, but it mattered that he pushed her and her inquiries aside. She felt disrespected and belittled. And it mattered that she had two bruised and sore arms. Gertie needed to tell him how she felt, and she knew only one way to do it.

"Edward, I was worried this evening. You ignored my question—what made you late?" He said nothing. Hardly above a whisper, she gently suggested, "I deserve an answer." Gertie was unprepared for his response.

He broke out in laughter and went upstairs. She listened to him mocking her words "deserve... answer" drifting back down the stairs and into her being. She heard him throw each shoe so the sound would travel down to her, slam each drawer and bang the bedroom door. The last made her cringe. She took the afghan, wrapped in it and curled up on the sofa trying to be comfortable. Her sore arms roused her with every slight turn to either side.

In the morning, she awoke to the smell of bacon cooking. Edward was whistling a tune as he turned the bacon and began breaking eggs.

"I wouldn't think you'd like sleeping on the sofa," was his greeting as he brought breakfast to the table and crossed the room. At the edge of the sofa, he found a place in the curve of her body, and sat.

Gertie's eyes were wide with questions when he pushed her hair from her face and touched her gently and lovingly on the cheek and shoulders. Confusion reigned as she breathed in his scent and the aroma of bacon. What hunger was keeping her from telling him about her bruised arms? He spoke to her hesitancy.

"I love you, Gertie. This was just a spat, all newlyweds have them." He smiled knowingly, "You still love me?" He didn't need or wait for her answer. He kissed her repeatedly until he felt her soften against him. "After breakfast, I will take you upstairs and remind you why you don't want to sleep on the sofa." His smile worked its magic. "Come. Eat"

She ate and discovered that she was famished. Everything seemed better on a full stomach in the light of day. She hadn't eaten anything last night. The terrors of last night were far away in the light of this warm, satisfying morning. Breakfast was good and hearty. Edward filled her plate with the salty, savory tastes of eggs over easy in bacon drippings. He buttered her toast more generously than she would and insisted on jam, too. It was all good. *So good,* she thought.

Edward did not hurry through it. When he led her to the stairs she was excited and thinking only of the answer to his last question. *Yes, I still love you.*

They climbed the stairs in the house Clay Neal provided for them as a wedding present exactly a month ago. Later Edward was spent, happy and asleep.

Gertie was in the bathroom throwing up her breakfast. Along with her breakfast came the heaving of the dream of using the scholarship to the Academy. It all went swirling down the toilet.

Chapter 7   1911

When you need to talk to your mother, no one else will suffice. Gertie often went to tears when she thought of her mother. *What's with these tears?* She asked herself. The tear stained face laughed back at her in the mirror. "Who are you?" she asked the only slightly familiar reflection. Her hormones were raging, trying to reshape her body, playing havoc with her emotions and forcing her to go into her womanhood. She needed to see Mama and she needed to tell Edward—soon.

"Gertie!" He called when he came in from taking the rent to his mother. "Mom sent a note."

Gertie, I'd like to see you.
Will you come tomorrow morning?
Mom Neal

Gertie was comforted to hear from Edward's mother when she was crying for her own. The next day, as soon as the house was straight, she crossed the street, cut through the White's yard, over the alley, across the Neal's back yard to the house on Tenth Street. She walked past Clay Neal's garden full of tomatoes, green peppers and straight rows of pole beans. She passed the arbor and wooden swing swaying in an unusual July breeze.

"Hello, Mrs. Neal"

"Gertie, please call me Mom Neal. All the children and their spouses call me Mom Neal and soon grandchildren will, too. It is good to see you." Mary Neal had much to say and she went on with her prepared lines. "You need to be comfortable in my kitchen and I want you to come whenever you like or whenever I can help you."

"Thank you."

"Are you pregnant?"

"Yes." Gertie lost her breath. *How does she know, when I haven't told Edward, yet?* Now, the only person who knew important news was this distant woman, mother of her husband.

"I can tell. Women my age can tell when we meet a young pregnant woman. Sometimes we can tell before the girl herself knows. Have you told Edward yet?"

Gertie shook her head.

"I thought not because he didn't mention it last evening."

"Tell him soon before someone else guesses. But, that is not why I asked you to come and talk. This may be even a better idea now that I know about the baby. I need someone to do some hand sewing and ironing. Before I ask Mrs. Pole if she wants the job, I thought I would ask you. I have worried that you have time on your hands... and maybe you and Edward could use some extra income."

"I would like to do that, Mrs. —" she corrected herself. "Mom Neal, but I must talk to Edward first."

"I have already mentioned it to Edward and he said *yes* for you yesterday."

Gertie did not like that, but she held back telling her mother-in-law. She turned her thoughts to a few extra dollars for a layette and some clothes to fit her soon to be swelling body. Her mind rushed forward in an eight-month leap when Mary Neal's next words brought her back to the here and now.

"I want to help all I can. Your wage can pay the rent and take some pressure off Edward. If you come two days a week, I can tally for each piece repaired, washed, starched and ironed and it will equal the rent due. I will enjoy your company and get to know you."

Mary Neal rambled on but Gertie was not listening. "Excuse me, please." Gertie rose, saying, "I am suddenly very tired, I will see you Monday at ten o'clock." Actually she was exhausted by the facts gleaned from this conversation. By the time she got home her head ached as if it had been tightened in a vice. A cool cloth soothed her head but did not stop the thoughts that raced. *Edward hasn't paid the rent to his parents!* Her mind went over the words Mom Neal said. *He has agreed to put me to work to pay it without talking to me. His suit is new and he talks constantly of owning a car.* Alarming conclusions were lining up in her brain. Finally she spoke aloud. "What's he doing?" She was angry and she needed time to think, but she was so sleepy. The tiredness finally won and she drifted off. Her rest was fitful and she woke up after an hour, calling aloud, "Mama."

By dinner time, the table was set and food was ready. Since Gertie's manner was to be direct, if the time wasn't right to speak her mind, she chose to say nothing. Her issue would be saved until eating was finished and coffee served.

Edward was more cheerful that usual when he bounded onto the porch. "Gertie, look at this." he shouted. A watermelon was rolled on to the table. "Mr. Grimes picked me up, gave me a ride and this watermelon. It will be dessert." His quick kiss and fleeting glance did not pick up Gertie's mood. Edward sat at the table still talking of the day's events, rambling on and ending with the question: "So… when do you begin working for Mom Neal?"

Gertie was on her feet in an instant; her chair fell to the floor behind her as her fist landed on the table causing the dishes and silverware to rattle. Edward's slap across her face took her to her knees.

Gertie struggled to get up before Edward could strike again or reach to help her. She wasn't sure what he intended as he bent toward her. The anger in Edward eyes dared her to speak, but it did not stop her. She came to her feet, using those seconds to compose herself.

"Edward, I will go to work for your Mother on Monday." She took a breath. "But, she will pay me. It will not be part of a plan to keep your father from knowing that you aren't paying the rent. I will ask her tomorrow if she will agree to this. The wage that I earn will be used to buy a layette for the baby that I am expecting in the spring." She paused to read the look on Edward's face. It showed nothing—nothing to reassure or scare his wife. Nothing.

"That is the first time I have ever been hit," she delivered her words precisely, "…and it has to be the last time." As she spoke, Gertie backed away in case he tried to strike her again. The fallen chair tripped her and she fell again, this time striking her head and taking her to the floor.

Edward carried her upstairs without saying a word. Her eyes flickered once and did not open again. For the first time since the bridge accident, eons ago, she did not want to see his face. Edward put her in bed and pulled a quilt to her chin. She turned toward the wall to silently cry again for her mother before accepting sleep and taking refuge in it.

The house was quiet and dark when she woke up. The sun was down. *How late is it?* She wondered. The clock answered, chiming to announce nine o'clock. *Was Edward sleeping downstairs on the sofa?* The terrible events came to her suddenly, along with a headache. Reaching up, she felt the knot on the side of her head. An overwhelming thirst was pushed aside by her fear of moving. Her hand gently pressed over her abdomen. There was no pain in the stomach or pelvic area. Her self-diagnosis assured her that all was well. Physically she was fine.

Gertie was a different person now. It might not show in the mirror, but she knew she was not the same girl who rose from this bed this morning. She instinctively drew her hands around her face and traced the line of her chin and throat, looking for the familiar in the dark. She pulled her hands through her hair to remember her father's dark curls. Her fingers twisted together. They were strong and reassuring as she rubbed them gently, pausing momentarily on the gold ring. Gertie picked a single tear from her cheek and put it in her mouth to taste the saltiness of herself. It infused strength and self-worth. Her mothering instinct, unnamed, washed over her as she placed both of her hands again over her womb and slightly pressed.

"Baby William, I *can* take care of you. Nothing... no one... will harm you."

If she was careful, she could go for a drink of water. Sitting first on the side of the bed then rising slowly and carefully, she took a step and was relieved to be steady on her feet. The drink of water was refreshing, and coming to an upright position seemed to help the headache. She was alone in the house on Eleventh Street. When bedtime came, she was still alone in the house.

Edward did not come home that night.

Sam came the next morning. He was driving a car and honking the horn. Sam was the first west end boy to have his own car. Mama and Papa would be aghast to see him driving like a proud peacock through Tenth Street, Eleventh Street, and Fergus Hill in that shiny black coupe. Wives at the clotheslines were waving at his continual honking. Even Clay Neal saw him and said, "That Sam MacGregor!" in not an unkind way. Sam pulled up to 405 Eleventh Street, as Gertie stepped outside to check on the commotion.

Why she started crying, she did not know. "Sam you're here. Today!" She shouted. *On the very day that I need you so badly.* He was the answer to one of her prayers.

"Guess what. Tomorrow I am taking you to Bear Creek—my first automobile trip. How would you like to see Mama and Papa?" He followed her into the kitchen and waited for Gertie to pour him a cup of coffee. His eyes were more serious when she sat down. "Gertie, what's with the tears? I know you aren't so happy to see my car that it brought tears. What's wrong, Sis?" He mussed her hair on the side of her head opposite to the lump she was hiding, and gave a brotherly embrace, which she took into her core.

"I got up this morning wanting to see Mama so badly, and the sight of you just brought the tears and I do have some things bottled up, but we can talk on the way to Bear Creek."

"I'm not asking Edward to go with us tomorrow. He came by the track on his way to catch the train this morning. Tells me you are homesick for Mama and that it has caused you to be emotional and irrational. Well, I know you better, and I say, let Gertie tell me about herself. I don't need Edward Neal to tell me about my own sister. What's going on? Tomorrow is soon enough, if you say so. Are you alright and will Edward be upset by us going without him for overnight?"

"I will be fine until tomorrow and Edward will not object." Gertie said, perfectly composed. "What time will you be here?" She couldn't predict how Edward would react to their plan, but she was going to see Mama tomorrow—no matter what.

"I think we should get an early start. It gets light around 6:30."

"Why not come back and spend the night, Sam? We can be on the road at first light. I will pack biscuits, coffee, and lunch." *Yes, Sam, spending the night here is the best plan,* she thought, not yet ready to be alone in the house with Edward.

With a quick hug, Sam left. Gertie sat on the porch and closed her eyes. "Thank you, Sam…thank you, God." she whispered.

As soon as she finished cleaning up her kitchen, she combed her hair and headed to see Mom Neal. Sam's visit gave her courage. She set her shoulders and walked over the back path to Tenth Street. Inside the garden gate, Clay Neal was sharpening tools on the grinder.

He looked up, "Hello, Gertie." In her surprise, she turned toward him, and decided to have her first conversation with her father-in-law.

"Mr. Neal, good morning. I hope you're well today. I have good news. Tomorrow, I'm going to visit my parents at their new home."

"That is good. Give them my regards."

"Mr. Neal, starting next week, I will be working for Mom Neal on Mondays and Wednesdays, if we can work out the arrangements." She paused, renewed her courage, and gave the next words great importance. "There's a problem with the rent on the house on Eleventh Street."

Clay stopped the grinding wheel and looked at Gertie for the first time.

"Problem?"

"I have learned that we are behind. Responsibility for the rent is Edward's. The wages I earn working for Mom Neal will not be used to pay rent. Any money I earn will be used for things that are a wife's responsibility."

Clay stood up. He towered over her, but Gertie was not intimidated.

"I've come to ask Mom Neal to pay the wages to me to use for our expected baby...or I will not come to work here on Monday."

Clay walked to the path and stood before the girl, now turned woman, standing just inside the gate. He wiped his hands on his trousers and ran them through his hair. Gertie looked at him and for the first time saw the older version of her own husband.

"Go home, Gertie. It is done." he asserted. "It is agreed." As she turned to go, he held the gate for her. "Take care of yourself, girl," he said, so softly she wondered if she really heard it.

She glanced back to see the old man taking long steps toward the house. He was still holding the hoe that he'd been sharpening as he reached the door.

Her mission was accomplished. She was ready to go home and prepare dinner and wait for Edward. She enjoyed fixing the meal that would have excellent leftovers for Edward while she was gone and the lunch she would take tomorrow. Ham was the best choice and she had one to bake. The bread and butter for sandwiches were on hand and she had time to bake cookies, which traveled well.

As she worked her spirits rose. The afternoon was cool for this time of summer and she decided to make a cake to take to Mama. The meal plans were done, the picnic made, and food for Edward was ready. *I can nap,* she relished the thought. *Almost an hour before Edward and Sam come home.* The early pregnancy days begged little naps. She fell asleep quickly and soundly.

Edward came into the room and saw her asleep on the sofa. He stood for a long time before he tried to rouse her. His thoughts were mixed as he recalled the terrible events of the past evening. Edward was filled with remorse and confusion. *How did that happen? She must realize that she brought it on herself. A wife cannot bang her fist on the table at her husband.* Even as he stared down at her, his remorse lessened. "Why did you make me hit you," he said out loud, but Gertie did not hear him. "Gertie, wake up. Are you alright? Gertie, Gertie," his voice became concerned.

As he touched her cheek, she opened her eyes. And, at the waking moment, she forgot the last things that happened between them. Her arm went around him in an almost reflex action and she kissed him. Then she was awake. "Edward."

He was most anxious to hold her in this moment, but he couldn't. She stiffened, and sat up, her posture straight. "Edward, before we can go on from this I want to tell you some things that may make you angrier than you already are—"

"Don't, Gertie," he interrupted. "Don't. I am not angry. I don't want to be angry."

"Wait. Listen. I must tell you."

"I'm listening."

"I went to your home and intended to talk to your mother, but your father met me at the gate and I told him."

"Told him what?" His voice was calm.

"He agreed that the rent is your responsibility and I will receive my own wages working for your mother. I don't know why you have not paid the rent, but the payment is now between you and your father. I will go to work Monday for your mother. The money I earn is to be used for this family that we are beginning." Gertie instinctively pressed her hand to her stomach and waited, but Edward said nothing.

He just watched her intently, as if he were puzzled about something. "Family…. we are beginning?"

"Yes."

"Family? A baby?"

"Yes, Edward, a baby, in the spring."

He put his head down as if he could not bear the burden of the news. Time stood still for Gertie and Edward, both. A deep union breath was drawn.

"Are you alright?" he finally asked, giving into his old, hidden values. "Tell me you're alright, Gertie."

"I'm fine. I carry your son, Edward. I'm sure."

The only thing Edward could do was touch Gertie's stomach in an easy, searching way.

"Sam will be here soon to spend the night. He and I are going to see Mama and Papa tomorrow...and we will stay overnight. I've made dinner, packed a lunch for Sam and me, and prepared enough for you until I return." She took a breath.

"Okay. I'll wash up and maybe Sam will be here in time to eat with us, too. I'm starved."

An amazed and confused Gertie got up to put dinner on the table.

Chapter 8

They were on the road at the planned time. The car fascinated Gertie. She settled in with an air of excitement. Sam was ready for the first long trip in his new automobile. He wondered how to open the conversation with Gertie. He needn't have worried because Gertie, in her usual manner did it for him.

"A girl's brother should not be her knight in shining armor but when you showed up yesterday, I thought I saw your armor sparkle."

"That was my wickedly charming smile, Gertie." Laughter broke the ice and set the mood for the trip. There was some territory to cover, but the MacGregor children were prepared for the trip.

Gertie did not open the conversation and Sam could not wait any longer.

"I saw Edward at the track yesterday—"

"Yesterday?" Gertie interrupted. "Yesterday was a work day."

"Edward has been betting the horses almost every day with a bookie he meets at the station in the morning. Sometimes he stays to see an early race. I guess he goes to work late. He is very quick to tell me when he picked a good one, but he doesn't know the horses well enough to come out ahead. Has he told you of his wins or losses?"

"No, I didn't know he was betting on the horses, but I have just learned that the rent has not been paid on the house. I'm not sure how far in arrears we are. He and his mother worked out a wonderful arrangement where I was to do sewing and ironing for her and it would cover the rent. Of course, Clay Neal would not know about it. He'd think she was paying me from the rent Edward brought, yet no money would change hands. She said this would take the pressure off Edward."

"Damn. Excuse me Gertie, but, damn, damn!" Sam almost drove off the road and again the brother and sister were laughing. His foot seemed to press the accelerator as he spoke.

"Maybe we should not talk about Edward if we want to arrive alive," she chuckled.

"Let's stop at Liddy's for coffee. Won't that surprise her? Don't know why I didn't think of that yesterday."

Liddy could not believe her eyes. Sam, Gertie, and a new car. Coffee and buns were served for their party at 7:15 am. It had been a long time since one of these gab fests between MacGregor siblings and a coffee pot. Each had so much to share. Liddy was doing just fine taking care of Lon and his children. It was obvious that he was prosperous, but they were not ostentatious like the big house on Fergus Hill. Lon worked in Baltimore, and during the school year, the older boys attended a private boarding school in the city. Lon could bring them home for any week-end they wanted. The youngest, Marcie, was Liddy's favorite probably because she was young enough to relate to her as a mother. She was happy to have her at home with her. "I miss my family so much. It seems a great distance across the city to Bear Creek. Lon has taken me once and we are going for the Labor Day picnic."

"We will be there, too. I wish you could go with us today."

"I can't. Lon has gone to get supplies to put in a greenhouse and I could not leave without talking to him first. I'll just keep Labor Day in mind—that will get me through. Tell Mama and Papa and the girls *hello* for me, and that we will see them in September. You'll get the plans about Dan's coming marriage before I do."

"Dan? Getting married? Mabel?"

"Yes. A Christmas wedding. Isn't it wonderful? Lon saw Dan last week."

It was a happy farewell full of plans for Labor Day. The travelers pulled back on the road, not wanting to lose too much time.

"It is good to see Liddy so happy."

"I wonder if most marriages are happy. Mama and Papa always seem happy, don't they, Sam? Or wasn't I really looking?"

"Oh, they're happy."

"I've thought about it a lot. It seems to me that Edward comes from a family so different from ours. All families have problems or squabbles but the Neals never resolve anything. Since we have been married, I have found Edward expecting me to ignore any *unpleasantness* and go on with the diversion of the moment. His parents are the same way. No issue is ever talked over or settled. Issues become chisels that chip away at the individual and break apart the relationships in the family. That's happening with Edward and me right now."

"Whew! Gertie, that's pretty profound. I'm not sure I understand what you mean."

"Well, Sam, with us—you saw Edward so congenial this morning, kissing me good-bye. He really has no concerns about us. To him, everything is fine, he ignores the rent. That is *not* fine. Mrs. Neal did not even ask Edward why he didn't have the money to pay it. I was shocked about the arrangement he made with his mother for me to work off the rent with her." Gertie took a breath and shook her head. "I blew up yesterday and I didn't even know about the horse betting. This morning Edward did not have a care in the world." Gertie decided not to tell Sam that Edward hit her. "My first inkling of how the family works, and how it would affect Edward and me, was the day after the wedding. Clay Neal held *me* responsible for not inviting them and for not going to see them after the ceremony when it was Edward's decision. Mr. Neal stated it and closed the subject. Edward said nothing to clear the air."

'What does Edward say if you ask him about these things?"

"Edward says nothing. He answers no questions."

Sam drove on with his thoughts.

They passed the Baltimore city limits, and Gertie was about to see the big city for the first time. She was engrossed in the sights—so many people, so many cars. Cars out-numbered the horse carriages. When she saw the street merchant, she begged Sam to stop so she could get a melon and some blackberries. She used the dollar that Edward had put beside her place at the table this morning.

Sam drove the car like he lived life—confidently and finding ways that would get him through. He was never rude or pushy with his car and even took his hands off the wheel to wave at people who had to yield the right of way.

"Should you take your hands off the wheel, Sam," Gertie asked.

He threw his head back and laughed out loud. "By God, Gertie, next you will think women could drive this thing."

"I am sure I could learn to drive it. You did."

"That'll be the day when women are out diving motor cars."

"Just watch, someday I will be driving."

"No doubt, Sis. You'd be the one. I will watch out for you and give you plenty of room."

And so they crossed the city, around the harbor where ships moored at the pier were larger than Gertie could imagine, and down Broadway past Lexington Market. There was some bustle at the market on Saturday and she asked Sam to stop and let her watch for a while. The trolley coming down Broadway clanged past them. They turned east and passed the row homes where the streets were filled with children in all colors and sizes. Women were scrubbing the already glistening white marble steps that led to each home. A glance down Monroe Street showed the steps like stacked pieces of white nougat, cut in perfect rectangles and looking like a tasty geometric delight. Gertie would remember this introduction to the city forever. She fell in love with this big mechanical, living, thing—Baltimore City.

They stopped for lunch out near Camp Holabird. Sam said they would be at Bear Creek near one o'clock. They found a shady and grassy spot where the soldiers mowed the grass on the roadside. The blanket that Sam pulled from the back was perfect. Gertie smiled as she supposed he had done this many times before—but not for a sister.

As they ate, Sam opened the hand drawn map to Bear Creek on the ground to study Lon's directions. Gertie paid close attention as Sam assigned her the navigation duties. He handed the map to Gertie. "Keep this on your lap and be ready to tell me about each approaching turn. If we get lost, it will be your fault." He glanced at his sister to gauge her mood. He had a few more things to say to Gertie before they got back on the road.

"You know that you and Edward will have to come to common ground on these problems. We both know that all marriages aren't made in heaven and many men and women have to compromise. I am deeply sorry if you will not have the marriage that you hoped for. Maybe a lot less than you wanted. Can you still be happy for yourself? Can you live day to day with Edward? There really is no choice that I can see. As long as he does not hurt you, and as long as he supports you and the children you have… can you live with a man like Edward?"

She fidgeted with his mention of Edward hurting her, and then concentrated on hiding her discomfort. Sam always seemed to know when she was lying, even by omission. "That's a good question. I love him and I'm pregnant—"

"I'm to be an uncle. I was waiting for you to confirm what Edward told me yesterday. Wow, Gertie! A little girl or boy." He flashed a grin at her, and then sobered. "There really is no choice now. You will have to make the best of things. Can you do it knowing that I'm there for you?"

"Oh, Sam you can't always be there for me. You have a life of your own. How you have escaped wedding vows is a wonder to me. But, if you will listen and lend a shoulder... it is my life, my marriage, and I will live it." She straightened her back as she spoke.

"The only advice I can give is don't close down, don't stop talking and don't stop being yourself. Remember you are a MacGregor. Don't ever forget who you are." He spoke the same words Papa spoke on her wedding day. Sam walked over to check the car, looking under the hood. "All this talk about marriage reminds me... I've been meaning to tell you about Nora. I want to bring her to Bear Creek soon." Sam had lost his audience. Gertie fell asleep in an instant as women in their first months of pregnancy are prone to do. He gave her ten minutes, knowing that she would not like to sleep and delay their arrival at Bear Creek.

The final turn on Lon's map took them down a narrow dirt road beside a railroad track. It was a dreary area, all black and dusty. They crossed the tracks and saw a big, beautiful Victorian house set a quarter of a mile away in the midst of a sea of green lawn. Beyond the lawn, the water of Bear Creek sparkled. Gertie drew her breath at the beauty of it. In her wildest dreams, she had not pictured such an idyllic place. She had a warm feeling. *Bear Creek will be a special place for me and my little boy.* Sam and Gertie were amazed at the size of the house; not as big as Fergus Manor, but as lovely.

Sam started blowing the horn as he approached and he did not stop until Mama and his siblings ran out of every door. Sam reached Mama first and got his hug. Gertie was next. Neither Mama nor she wanted to let go. "Oh, Sam and Gertie, what a surprise! Wait until your father finds out you are here. He's on the bridge. Let's go in and call him. I'm sure he can see that someone has arrived in the yard, but he won't figure it to be you—in that car."

Papa's new job was as bridge tender for the B&O railroad bridge over Bear Creek for a spur going into Sparrows Point Steel Mill. He got a lease on the house for just one hundred dollars as long as he works for the railroad. When the tracks isolated the house, B&O intended to demolish it because access was only thru the rail yard. Then William MacGregor took the job, and made them an offer for the house, B&O had nothing to lose. They may have found a way to keep a man at this difficult to fill, isolated post. There was room for the family, and space to grow and enjoy the country and the water. In the huge kitchen, at the familiar table, Mama poured coffee and asked about Edward. News of Liddy was passed on as well as the plans for Labor Day weekend.

"Gertie lets go into the parlor where it is cool. You can relax while we talk." Gertie went to the sofa; Mama sat where her sewing basket was waiting. "We have all evening to visit, rest first." She watched her daughter fall into a peaceful sleep and contented herself to sit and watch her. Mama could not help thinking how quiet Gertie had been since arriving. Maybe the car trip wore her out or maybe it was because she was going to have a baby.

"Mama, I'm pregnant," were Gertie's first words upon waking.

"I know."

"I guessed you would. I figure the baby will come in March. I might as well tell you that the choice I have made in Edward may not be the best, but I love him and I know what I must do." Her mother didn't question or interrupt. "I am going to have a baby. Just think of it, a baby. I will have to take care of the baby and of Edward and myself. I'm not sure how I will do it, but I will." Mama waited patiently when Gertie paused to find the right words. "I am trying to understand Edward. All of his life, people have spoiled him. I guess it is not his fault that he is irresponsible with finances and obligations. Thank goodness he goes to work every day and he wants to make advancements there. It would be wonderful to believe that the coming child will help him to take life more seriously, but I don't know if it will. I am learning to expect less and less from Edward."

Patricia MacGregor was very good at keeping her feelings off her face. Her heart broke at these words, but she smiled and went over to hold her daughter. Gertie, who loved life and knew how to be exuberant, was going to live life far from fulfillment. She was proud of her daughter and the way she sorted out the problems she faced, but she didn't know how hard marriage can get—even a really good marriage. A few months into this one and her daughter, who should still be on a honeymoon, already had some serious doses of reality. "Marriage is forever, Gertie. You will not be the first or the last to find disappointment in it. I have confidence that if there is a way to work with Edward, you will find it."

"Mama, I love him and he loves me."

Oh, Dear. Patricia MacGregor knew Gertie's love was not going to make it easier. In fact, it would make a more difficult and heartbreaking path. Edward's love could destroy Gertie if he used it as an excuse for bad behavior. *Oh, Dear God…*

"Come, let's begin dinner."

"Mama, I brought a watermelon and some berries in Baltimore. Let me tell you what I thought of Baltimore—"

At the dinner table Mama announced to everyone that Gertie would have the first grandchild in this family. Patsy and Shirley ran around the table to squeeze her. It became a celebration and Gertie felt the first happiness since realizing she was with child. "It will be a boy; I know; I'm positive. His name is William after Papa and Edward."

"Fine, it's probably a girl named William." Sam joined the conversation. Patty and Shirley turned to him and tickled him until he fell off his chair. Mama broke up the pandemonium by asking for help clearing the table.

"Sam will do my part. I must get my rest, you know," dramatized Gertie as she carried her plate to the sink.

The balance of the daylight was spent exploring the sandy beach beside the river that somehow was called a creek. Papa explained that the river widened here and from up on the bridge the shape of a bear could be seen. It was alive with crabs and fish. They would have all the crabs the family wanted for summer parties. All they had to do was tie a piece of chicken on the line and pull them up to the net. Swimming was excellent and the water clear. It was rare that the pesky sea nettles ever came up this far from the bay. A small abandoned rowboat was repaired and readied for the ambitious rower. Several fishing rods lined the wall next to the back door of the shed, where Delco batteries ran the generator providing electricity. Worms hiding under an old log or the large grasshoppers flushed from the grass, were bait. Summers at Bear Creek would be fun, full of adventure and bountiful, especially now that Sam had a car. It was not a far off place.

Gertie was comforted by that.

The house was two stories and an attic. The kitchen was the largest room in the house. The great cooking stove and large table did not begin to fill it up. To one side was a fireplace and Papa's over-stuffed chair and ottoman was by the back window so he could be warmed as he watched the bridge. The coffee pot was ever ready. The aroma of coffee puffed out the open door inviting all to enter.

In the dining room, the table was used for card playing. The whole family played pinochle or Parcheesi but Mama did not allow it in the kitchen. With a family this size the kitchen table could be needed at any time. The dining room and parlor had fireplaces and long floor to ceiling windows that looked across the lawn. Mama's good furniture was in the parlor, but it was not stuffy nor shut off from the family. Everyone used the parlor, yet respected it as Mama's room. She loved to sit and sew by the tall window. Her favorite pictures hung on the walls. There was one showing the corn fields of Illinois where she was born and another one of her mother and father in a large dark oval frame.

William MacGregor was happy that they made the difficult move to Bear Creek. It turned out better than he hoped. The house was going to suit the MacGregor clan very well and he liked his work. The bridge had to be tended twenty-four hours a day, seven days a week. The only way he could do this job was to live within sight of it. The train schedule required a man to make sure the bridge was closed for six crossings a day. The bridge had to be closed for him to come down to the house. While he was in the house, he watched for tall boats so he could open the bridge for them. Papa was in his chair if he was in the house during the day. The whole family learned to watch for tall boats for Papa. Usually by the time they blew their horns, he was on his way across the trestle to the ladder and turn house.

The happy clan reluctantly called it a day and headed up the stairs to bed. Gertie crawled into the bed she slept in as a girl. She stayed awake for the expected visit from Mama.

"Are you asleep?" Mama asked as she came to the room.

"No, I waited for you. Come sit for a minute…and then you can tuck me in." Gertie reached for her hand and placed a small box in her palm. Open the box, Mama" Gertie tilted the lamp shade for more light.

"It's the cameo that Elizabeth Amsterdam gave you on your wedding day."

"Yes. I am not sure if she meant it for Edward and me or if she only meant for me to have it. She told me to take care of it and keep it in reserve. I don't want to keep it at my house so I decided to bring it back here for you to take care of again. I would never sell it and use the money for myself, you know that, but I have to think of the baby. If it is ever needed for him, I want to be sure I still have it." Gertie paused and relaxed. "Put it in a safe place, Mama. Someday when you and Papa go to Baltimore, can you get it appraised? I may need to know its value." Gertie was talking about the brooch but thinking about herself and the unborn child. Her hand rested across her stomach.

"Yes, Gertie, we can. I love you." The kiss she planted on Gertie's forehead was long and deep. "Good night."

As she put the cameo in the box she had a strange thought about her daughter. "Gertie's in a box, too." The brooch slid into the satin lining where it had been stored before.

Patricia MacGregor paused to wipe a tear and utter a prayer.

Chapter 9   1911

"I love you, Edward." Gertie greeted him with words of assurance, turned, and walked back into the house on Eleventh Street. "But, I'm not sure about us." She stood across the kitchen from him and wanted more than anything to be in his arms. Instead she took a seat at the table. "I'm not sure...," she repeated, letting that thought go. "Sometimes I wonder what you're sure about." Her desire to make everything right for her baby burned deep inside but she did not know how to bring Edward to understand her feelings.

"We're going to be alright. I'm sure about that. You love me. I love you."

"Love means more than just saying it."

"There you go. Gertie... making everything so complicated. I said I love you. What else do you want?"

Please apologize, she begged in her mind. An apology would help at this awkward moment. *Acknowledge something.* She knew, without a doubt, that if she mentioned the reason she left this house three days ago Edward would end the conversation. The wall going up between them left a lump in her throat. *Will my baby be safe?*

"Have you thought about the baby? I really am pregnant, you know."

"I know you're pregnant." His voice was arrogant.

"I'm not the only one who has to protect and take care of this child."

"You do your part; I'll do mine." He spoke with a softer, confident voice.

"And, your part is?"

"I'll provide for my family. And make sure nothing happens to either of you."

"Edward, I have got to be sure about that."

He walked over to her and put his hand in hers. She took his hand and placed it on her stomach. "He's right there, Edward."

He pressed slightly but there was nothing to feel. He had to take her word for the changes in her womb.

"Don't forget, even before he is born, his life is precious and must be cherished... by both of us." She was moving close to putting Edward on the defensive.

"I won't forget." He promised.

Oh, God... please God, she prayed.

❦

Gertie celebrated her eighteenth birthday by organizing a routine and reaching into the community as an adult. She went to the Ladies of Mercy Circle and joined the church choir. She loved the choir—its rehearsals, and every Sunday morning—its anthems. Although she had no musical training, she was a natural with a pure alto voice and good memory for notes. She learned to read music and was given occasional solos.

The Ladies of Mercy Circle helped to fill the void because Mama was so far away. The group adopted Gertie with the announcement of her pregnancy. The ladies in the Circle inquired about her progress and led her to explore her feelings. She needed that, and she needed the information they shared from their birthing experiences. Every doubt and question was easily asked of these friendly women and Gertie was at ease doing it. So, when Edward came home in the evenings and had no interest in talking about the baby, Gertie was alright with it.

Edward was always more pleasant when their friends were around, so Gertie encouraged their gatherings. When they were home alone, he was often silent and distant. She found herself constantly planning card parties just to have friends over. Everyone found him charming and Gertie did, too.

"Edward why do you talk to me when our friends are here but have nothing to say when we eat alone?" she asked, taking the direct approach one evening at dinner.

"I don't know what you are talking about."

Gertie did not want to accept his disassociation but she did, rather than spark a disagreement.

When there were disagreements, he walked out the door. The most incidental things like purchases for the house or dinner menus were not discussed. It appeared to be harmony, but it wasn't. When he was late coming home, she did not worry. He would come soon enough.

Grandmother Amsterdam was a lighthouse in Gertie's stormy seas. "Gertie, please come and visit. I would love to have you. Edward stops in sometimes on his way from work but I need to see you, too."

"I could come on Sunday after church. Would that suit?"

"Yes, my dear. I look forward to it."

Every week, if the weather was agreeable on Sundays, Gertie went for the visit. Her relationship with Edward's Grandmother was the most important connection to his family.

Edward gave into his temper on occasion, but did not strike Gertie. He raised his hand but held back. There were times when he grabbed her arm and bruised her, but he stopped short of hitting her. At other times he grabbed her defending hand and twisted. His regrets were quick.

"Sit here, Gertie. Take this pillow." Although she wanted to relish these tender moments, she knew he was atoning for the newest bruise on her arm or the finger that had been twisted in his grip. Other times he just said, "I'm out of here," and headed to the door to give himself time to forget what he had almost done to his wife. No matter the mood, he was ready to be romantic when they were in bed. Sometimes he told her he was sorry for his temper. But that was rare.

Gertie refused to walk on eggs fearing him, so she stood her ground, prepared to protect herself if she needed to, and waited for him to act as if the *unpleasantness* never even happened. She even rationalized that Edward would grow up. She was wise enough to know their problems were bubbling just below the surface, but right now only the baby mattered.

Things were changing in the house on Eleventh Street. Gertie was busy sewing for the nursery and making clothes for her changing body. She chose prints that could be used again later for William's play clothes. By winter, a nursery area was set up in their bedroom.

"Why here?" Edward asked. "Why not in there?" He pointed to the back bedroom across the hall.

"William should be right beside us at first."

He walked around the crib and noted the crowded space. "Not much room."

"You still have room on your side." Without yielding her position, she led him with compromise. "I want the crib close on my side."

"At first, right? Soon all this will go in the other room, right?" He reached into the crib. "And, what's this?" Edward asked as he picked up a blue rectangle pillow.

"It's to pad the sides from William's head when he rolls over."

"William! Beats me how you can be so sure it's a boy. If we agreed on a name, I don't remember."

"You said you would not talk about names because it could be girl. If you want to pick a girl's name go ahead. William for a boy—agreed?"

"Sure. That's my middle name, although I figure you were thinking of your father when you picked it."

Gertie was warmed by the discussion and his attention to her preparations. He could not be engaged very long on this mysterious subject—an unseen baby, floating in a womb. But, she relished the minutes and the precious connection with Edward and their child.

That same evening, a card table was set up for a gathering of friends. Tonight was important. "Let's tell everyone about the baby tonight. I'll be showing soon."

The festivities began with Edward's announcement. "We are going to have a baby."

"Congratulations."

"How wonderful."

Hugs and handshakes went around the circle. Edward enjoyed the attention the baby announcement brought from their friends. Gertie smiled her joy. Theirs would be the first child in the group.

"We need to toast Gertie, Edward, and the baby."

"Give me a minute, I'm making punch." Gertie announced as she headed to the kitchen.

Edward's voice followed her.

"Gertie says it is a boy and he'll be named William. I'm not so sure. It could be a girl, you know. She talks as if she has seen it and knows for sure." He paused for the soft laughter. "We set the crib next to our bed for the first weeks. We even have little pillows to protect his head. We'll be ready when the time comes."

"When is the baby coming?" asked Emily.

"March."

Gertie stopped what she was doing to listen to Edward and breathe deeply, which caused the baby to move inside her.

Edward called to Gertie. "Early or late March?"

"Early."

❦

The last three months moved slowly. Quiet intimate times became more and more rare. As she moved into the last phases of her pregnancy, Edward seemed uncomfortable looking at her. Gertie was consoled by the child growing and moving inside her.

Edward's family expressed interest in the coming event. Handmade gifts were made for the baby. Mom Neal stitched a quilt with ducks.

"William is Clay's middle name as well as Edward's."

"I know. And it is Papa's name, too."

"I hope it is a boy."At last the two women had something in common.

As all expectant mothers do, Gertie handled some pieces from the layette every night.

Her silhouette was stretching. She was eating right and resting often. As her body blossomed with the baby, her personality and maturity bloomed. Gertie became more beautiful—her skin and hair seemed to glow. The beautiful girl had become a beautiful woman.

Edward noticed the radiant changes in her, and told her, "I love you," as they sat beside the small Christmas tree on New Year's Eve. She yielded to his sentiment and held her belly with new promise.

"I love you, too." It was so true… and so hard. The words in the air became a renewed commitment to this family that Gertie wanted so badly. In the glow of the holiday and promise of a new year, it was easy to believe they could be a happy threesome.

❦

Sam worried about his sister and questioned her occasionally about Edward's temper. "Are you afraid of him?"

"No. I don't think he will ever hit me again."

"You never told me he hit you." Sam was obviously shaken. "Tell me. What happened?"

"No point, Sam. That was before he knew I was having a baby. He isn't going to hit me again."

In the quiet of the night she often wondered about love and the feelings that were so strong for Edward. His breathing beside her was the only sound in the night and she could not imagine living without it. Her fantasies took her back to their courtship and that first night in the big bed on Fergus Hill. She wanted her baby to be named for her father, but she hoped he looked just like Edward. As imperfect as her marriage was, it was hers and she was committed to it. These quiet thoughts usually ended with the conclusion that Edward would grow up one day and see how blessed he was to have a devoted wife and family. She was sure that her love for him and the coming baby would bring joy and bliss to the marriage. Gertie was positive that she could do what it took to make their love last. She often said to herself, *I can do it.*

Hurry. Grow up, Edward, was her final thought before drifting off to sleep on nights like this.

January and February were mild the winter of her pregnancy. There was very little snow and ice so she was able to walk to her favorite activities and to Mom Neal's.

Edward had been doing his own late night thinking.

"I want...I mean... I need a car."

"The weather isn't that bad. Soon it will be spring."

"Yeah, and then I'm walking in the rain." He was getting angry but knew he had to be careful or Gertie would walk out the door.

"We just can't afford it with the baby and—"

"Baby! Baby! That's all you can think about. What about me?" His voice was rising. "I'm the one earning a living for you and that precious baby."

"Edward, I know a car would be a help to you—" She tried to appease him.

"Help, hell! I'm working extra hours and you sit on your butt with that cameo."

She knew the demand for the cameo was coming and she knew this was going to be a difficult, almost impossible discussion. To gather her thoughts, she rose from the table to get another cup of coffee. "Let's talk about the cameo and our options," she said as she was pouring.

She brought him a cup and saw him settle slightly with her willingness to discuss the cameo.

"That cameo is more than enough to get us a car. I wouldn't have to walk to the station every morning. You could even learn to drive. Emily is driving now and so are other women."

"You know, Edward, I have been against getting a car. It's more than we can afford..." Edward shot to his feet, anger boiled, flushing his neck; he raised his hand. Gertie instinctively placed her hands across her belly to protect her baby and sat down with her cup making sure the table was between them. Her breathing was heavy but she kept her composure. She knew how to sidestep his anger, but the knowledge that he wanted to hit her stayed with her.

"Now, now, Edward, hear me out. Maybe it is expensive, but rather than use the cameo, I will give you my earnings. You'll be surprised how much I have saved in almost two years."

"Really... how much? You mean you will stop arguing against an automobile?"

"Yes. I'll go along with getting one but not if the cameo has to be sold. I have almost one hundred and fifty dollars. I saved all that your mother paid me and Mama and Papa gave me fifty as a wedding present. Do you have to take it all? What does a car cost? I need to have some for the baby and to pay the doctor."

Surprisingly he took the compromise and only one hundred dollars. Of course the money was immediate and selling the cameo would take time and be another delay in getting the car. As always when his anger was spent, he was a most pleasant companion in bed even though she was beyond the time when intercourse was allowed.

It was a quiet but unsettled time. Edward voiced his anxiety to have the baby born so we can *get back to normal.* But, the normalcy that Edward wanted would never return to the house on Eleventh Street.

Meanwhile life went on. Monday and Tuesday morning Gertie cut across the yards and alley to go to work for Mary Neal. She enjoyed the task of handling the family linens. She loved the fine cloth and intricate embroidery. This week she was ironing curtain ruffles. Mary appreciated the attention she paid her task and complimented her work. On Tuesdays they ate lunch together and Mary laid Gertie's pay on the table beside her plate. This Tuesday was different.

"Gertie, I have put some extra there for you."

"Thank you, Mom Neal."

"Today will be your last working day, but if you would like to come during your last weeks, just for coffee, that would be fine."

The two women developed a respect for each other but it was not a friendship. No hard questions could be asked that could possibly help her to understand Edward better. No intimate exchange of feelings or family history was shared.

On Wednesday, Gertie walked to Circle, and on Thursday she walked to choir rehearsal for the last time before her delivery.

*

On March 5th, Liddy entered the house on Eleventh Street like a guardian angel.

"Liddy, what a wonderful surprise."

"It gets better. I'm staying until the baby comes."

Gertie melted into smiles and tears. No better joy could come on this snowy day in early March. "I can't have Mama. I'm overjoyed to have you."

"Lon is taking Marcie to Mrs. Fergus. The boys are at school and I am yours."

"Yes, mine and William's."

"Are you still sure it's *William?*

"As sure as rain."

They settled at the table with coffee and the fresh cinnamon rolls that Liddy brought.

"How is Edward handling all this?"

"Not well at all. He just wants this birthing part to be over. And, he thinks we will go back to *normal.* He doesn't realize that everything changes with a baby."

"Typical." Liddy turned her attention to the job at hand. "These final days are all about you… and what I can do for you. The only man we will need is the doctor. Maybe we will need Edward to go get him."

"Don't need him for that either. Mrs. White, across the street has a phone and said she will call the doctor for us."

"Good. Tomorrow we will set up for delivery. I'll use Mrs. White's phone to talk to Dr. Smith. Then you and I will begin the waiting."

"I hope Edward is at work when my time comes." Gertie hated it when she said it. Later that night she thought how unnatural to want the father of her baby away when he pushes into the world.

Five days later Gertie's labor started. A warm clear liquid ran down her leg and she knew William was on his way. Liddy settled her on the bed prepared in the parlor and went to Mrs. White's. When she returned, Gertie was calling her name.

"Liddy! Liddy! The pains are coming quickly. William's as anxious as I."

The sisters worked together to prepare the setting for the new life. White sheets, clean water and soothing voices awaited him.

"Oooh, he is coming. I don't think the doctor will get here in time."

"Go ahead and push."

Gertie grimaced with pain.

"You can do it."

More pains.

"You can do what you need for your baby—"

More pains, harder—with hardly any time between.

"—and if you have to—"

"—you can do it without help." Gertie took her sister's hand and bore some of her pains as she squeezed repeatedly.

Liddy's words were prophetic for the beautiful baby boy and for Gertie's future.

Doc Smith arrived in time to cut the cord and pronounce William healthy and strong.

Before she drifted into happy sleep, Gertie talked to William. "I love you baby boy—my William." Then she turned to Liddy. "When Edward comes, wake me. I want to show William to him myself."

Edward was greeted with the news when he arrived three hours later. He walked in to the parlor to see Gertie holding the baby.

"So, were you right? Was it William all along?"

"Yes, Edward."

"How are you?"

"I'm fine. Come hold him." She carefully placed William in his father's arms.

Edward took the bundle very gingerly. He pulled the blanket down from the baby's head and chin so he could see his dark hair and full face. Then he walked away from Gertie to the window where the waning, glowing twilight lit the little face. Edward studied his tiny son for minutes.

When he turned back to Gertie, she saw tracks of tears down his face. She promised herself never to forget the first minutes Edward had with William. It was tender and important.

Liddy entered the room in time to see Gertie propped up on the pillow, Edward sitting next to her holding William—all together on the bed. William, peacefully sleeping, was the only one not crying.

If Liddy had asked Gertie and Edward why they were crying, neither would have been able to give an answer.

🐌

The return to normal that Edward expected did not come. The demands of a newborn wore heavy on him. Night feedings, crying, and rearranged schedules tested his nerves.

"What did you expect, Edward?"

"I don't know but it wasn't this. I'm going to stay in town this week and get some sleep."

"Please don't do that. William will be six-weeks old next week and I can take him to Bear Creek. You'll have uninterrupted sleep then."

"I can't wait another week. I'm gone. I'll tell Sam on my way to work."

Gertie could manage without him. He did not help with William anyway. "Please get these groceries in before you go." She handed him a list.

When Sam came she assured him she could manage this week without Edward.

"Actually, it will be easier without Edward. I can take care of my baby."

"I'll come and spend the nights here. Just put a pillow and blanket on the sofa, Sis."

The next week Edward came home and the trip to Bear Creek was postponed. A new plan was made to visit during Easter. The arrangement became a pattern. Every few weeks, Gertie tended William, Edward escaped, and Sam came so Gertie would not be alone at night. When it worked for Sam, Gertie and William went to see Mama and Papa.

Edward now had a car parked outside, when anger flared, he walked out of the house, got in the car and drove away to cool off. Gertie breathed a sigh of relief. *Getting a car was a better idea than I realized.* She didn't care where he went as long as he took his anger away.

At times Edward lost control and pushed Gertie, but he did not strike. Gertie's abuse was just as real as a blow. She knew at any time she was vulnerable. When he lifted his fist and hit the wall, her safety was measured in inches.

Edward did not like Gertie's dedication to William. Most times he ignored his jealousy unless William needed Gertie's attention at the same time he wanted it—usually in the bedroom. On those occasions when Gertie and Edward were intimate and William cried, she agonized. *Why does Edward want me to choose between him and William?*

"Let him cry."

"I've got to see what's wrong, Edward." She knew that she would not be welcomed back to her husband's arms after their son was settled again. A quick walk to his crib and diaper change and the babe was ready to sleep again. Gertie turned to see Edward in the doorway.

"Was that life or death?" He asked mocking her.

Gertie chose not to answer.

"What about me?"

"What about you?" She replied walking past him.

Edward lashed out and pushed her into the door jamb. "Please, don't," she pleaded.

He pushed her again, this time causing her to fall beside the bed.

"Edward, help me."

"Call William, maybe he will help you up." Edward gathered his clothes and shoes headed out of the bedroom. "...or Sam," he spit back at her.

Gertie stayed on the floor. She wasn't hurt; she could not find a reason or a will to rise. She suffered the exhaustion of tending a new baby while trying to keep a childish husband happy. And, she suffered an agonizing pain from his cruel words.

William kept Gertie busy and gave Edward an excuse to be away as much as possible. He was quick to let Gertie know that little William, was her responsibility—or as he said—*her problem.* She loved caring for her baby and the love that came to her from the child was beyond wonderful.

In the quiet of the night, she prayed that Edward would find joy in his son. "...and dear Lord, please make it soon."

Chapter 10   *1913*

Life settled in to for the busy mother, growing child and disconnected father. Gertie was not happy but her days were full. Edward was at times, warm and caring. That managed to give her hope that he was growing up.

His temper was always just below the surface. There were bruises from tight grips and occasional twisted hands but he did not strike her. However the walls and doors in the house on Eleventh Street showed evidence of abuse.

Little William was two. His birthday party would be a grand occasion. March 10th was warm for an early spring party. Gertie enjoyed baking his cake and preparing dinner for their guests. Edward's parents were coming but Mama and Papa could not leave the bridge unattended. The invitations went out; the door was open. The Neal's extended families and all their friends were expected.

"Edward, bring the chairs from the kitchen to the living room, and bring the high chair, too."

The ham and baked beans filled the house with delightful aromas. Side dishes would be carried in and the table would be full. Edward seemed busy and preoccupied as Gertie went about her tasks trying to have everything done by noon.

"Look, William is asleep in his play pen. All this activity has worn him out." Gertie joked.

"Worn me out, too," Edward countered as he headed for the door. "I'm going to Mom's to get more chairs."

Liddy and Lon were the first to arrive and while they listened for William asleep in the warm corner of the kitchen, Gertie went upstairs to freshen up.

Nothing prepared her for the sight in the bedroom. Every drawer was pulled out and emptied on the bed. The dresser was stripped. The mattress was cockeyed on the bed. The armoire was askew. Gertie let out a gasped breath. "What happened here?" she said as she sat down in the piled mountain of everything she and Edward owned. As she was trying to figure out the mess, she heard the sounds of arriving guests downstairs and finally William's awakening whine.

The party was a big success and William had the best time of all. Poppa Clay and Mom Neal brought a beautiful stuffed teddy bear, which William carried under his arm all day. Edward's mood was light. He enjoyed his son's birthday party. Gertie at times was distracted by the thought of the condition of the room upstairs.

As she closed the door when Sam, the last to leave, departed, Edward said, "Where's the cameo?" Before Gertie could digest his question, he repeated, "Where is the cameo?" He walked over and stood so close his breath moved her hair. "I said—where is my grandmother's cameo?" Gertie put his question together with the problem troubling her mind all day.

"It is not here, Edward.

"It's not here? It's not here? Did you lose it? Where is it for Christ's sake?" He was shouting in her face and William began crying. Gertie very slowly moved from Edward to William, taking him soothingly in her arms and talking softly to keep alarm out of her voice. "Edward, sit down and have a cup of coffee while I put William to bed."

"I don't want a cup of coffee!" Edward raised his voice and advanced toward Gertie and William.

Lowering her voice to a most pleasant whisper, Gertie said, "I can put William to bed and come talk to you or I can walk out that door and let you continue to tear this house apart looking for something that is not here." She picked up a blanket, wrapped William and walked to the door. "Well?"

Edward walked to the coffee pot without a word.

Gertie trembled as she climbed the stairs to William's room. By the time the birthday boy drifted off to sleep she was calm and ready to face Edward. With a blanket and pillow in arm, she entered the kitchen. "Be careful about raising your voice and waking William. I don't know where you are going to sleep tonight, but I am going to sleep on the sofa by the stairs so I can hear him. If you sleep in the bed upstairs, you will have to clear it off and put it back together. I'm too tired." It was a tense moment while she waited to see if the storm would continue or if it was over. Edward left the house. Gertie went to the sofa and slept like a tired puppy.

$

"Get up," Edward said, his face only inches from hers. Her startled mind did not know where she was or what was happening. In the darkness she felt Edward's breath on her and smelled whiskey, and she knew the storm would go on. Gertie decided to say nothing and Edward decided to hit her. She rolled from the sofa to the floor. His kick landed squarely on her right hip. Gertie grabbed his other leg and caused him to crash to the floor. She could hear wood splintering as Edward came down.

Pulling herself to the stairs, she crawled up to William's room, closed the door, securing it with a chair propped under the knob, and placed herself as an obstacle between the door and her child.

Oh God, can it get any worse? Please…, she pleaded silently, afraid to even make a sound. She listened for William's baby breaths and cried.

William's stirring brought Gertie awake and she saw the early morning light across his dark curls. When she tried to get up she felt the sharp pain in her hip but she was able to get to her feet. William reached for the spot on her face, which made her flinch. All she could think of was getting the diaper changed and fixing his milk and breakfast. She recalled that it was Sunday and she would miss singing in the choir today.

Gertie was shocked when she saw Edward still on the floor in the kitchen. One leg was broken off the table and it sat like some geometric figure tilted on the floor. Edward was sleeping—at least Gertie thought he was sleeping—leaning against it, just as he had fallen. His chest moved assuring her that he was breathing. Blood was caked on his face. She stepped over him, keeping William's face turned away from his father.

Gertie picked up William's milk, oatmeal and coat. "Let's go see Mrs. White, Sweetie."

When she returned, she stood at the doorway and gathered her strength for what she had to do.

"Edward, wake up." She was afraid to touch him with the washcloth and startle him. "Wake up," she urged.

He looked at her.

"Here, wash your face." She handed him the warm cloth. "You cut yourself when you fell."

He went to the sink and looked in the mirror at his not so handsome face. The sound he made was not quite human. He began talking under his breath. "You did this to me. I'll teach you—"

"Edward, I don't know why you want the cameo or why you didn't ask me. It is not here. It's in a safe place and I can't give it to you. Your Grandmother gave it to me—not to use but to keep it in reserve. Now, if you want to go to her and tell her why you want it and ask her if I should sell it or give it to you, do so. Then I will do what she tells me to."

He wasn't listening to her. "How can I go to work with my face cut and my eye black? Look what you've done."

Gertie moved to the other side of the table.

"Just look what you've done." He repeated, raising his voice. "What'll we tell our friends and family? How *will you* explain all this?" he said waving his hand across his face and pointing to broken table. He was oblivious to the bruise across her cheek.

"*I* will not explain anything. You're responsible for what happened here."

"You... you... poor excuse for a wife. Know-it-all," he accused. "You think you know what you are doing. If you don't stop crossing me, you'll be out on the street." He stepped over the broken table leg. "Who do you think you are in this town without your husband? Nobody!" He closed in on her position. "You think I don't know you put me down to your family and friends."

Gertie moved toward the door, reaching for her coat. Two steps and her wounded hip gave way and she took the arm of the sofa to keep from falling. "I'm not going to stay here while you rage." It took all her strength to stay firm against him and upright on her feet.

Edward moved quickly between her and the door. He pointed his finger in her face as she stepped back. "I know... I know you've been to the bank trying to have accounts without telling me." He pointed again.

"Edward, I saved money—money that bought your car." She tried to explain but realized he could not—would not—listen to reason in his rage.

She side-stepped and moved toward the back door. *Away! I've got to get away.*

"I know. You never did understand that a wife is to obey her husband. You are to do as I say and as I want." He turned away and turned back for emphasis. "You are nothing without me. When I ask a question, you are to answer me. Do you hear? Am I going to have to teach you a lesson?"

She continued across the kitchen. He moved to block her again.

"*You* are to keep the peace here. *You* need to learn how to get along with your husband." He banged his fist into his hand. "I've tried to be patient. But I ask you, what is your choice?" Rage burned on his brow and in his eyes.

Gertie's emotion moved from fear to strength. "Edward, I don't know what all my choices are, but I can tell you this—I choose not to be pushed, slapped, kicked, or beaten by you."

Gertie walked with great difficulty to get William and go to the Neal home on Tenth Street. Mom Neal was surprised to see her at church time. Clay left the kitchen as they came in. He took a seat on the back porch, out of sight, but in ear range.

"Are you all right?" Mom asked as she looked at her daughter-in-law's face.

"I must tell you that Edward hit me last night and it is not the first time." Gertie took a deep breath and smiled down at William, gaining strength by looking into the child's eyes. "It will be the last time, though. I will not stay with him. I cannot—I will not—risk myself and little William."

Mom Neal's head was reeling with the words she was hearing. *Oh no. This cannot be true. My Edward wouldn't do these terrible things. What does Gertie do to provoke him?*

Clay held his head and pondered the problems spilling over from Eleventh Street. *This girl is just too strong for Edward.* He walked back to his workshop.

Gertie waited for some offer of help, for William, for herself… or for Edward. None came. William's grandmother did not touch him or look at him. Gertie rose and left without another word. This clean, well-organized, highly respected home would never be a safe haven for her. Gertie was beginning to see the way things would be with the choices she would make.

Edward was drawing his conclusions, too. If he had to teach Gertie a lesson in getting along in marriage, he would—as soon as he got the brooch. There may be love lost, but satisfaction was easily found. No big thing. Edward had his women in Washington, anyway. He would work with Gertie. Break her spirit—even enjoy doing it. She was still wonderful in lovemaking and if she resisted—all the better.

Edward believed he knew what marriage really was now. At last he understood how men and women lived a lifetime together. *If only she weren't so hard headed.* Edward smiled as Gertie entered the house on Eleventh Street.

Gertie saw his smile and knew he was prepared to forget all about their fight. But, she knew the cameo would continue to be an issue. *The best thing would be to give it back to Grandmother,* she thought.

Edward fixed the table leg while Gertie put the room back together and began preparing lunch. She hobbled around holding on to the table or sink to support the hip that was hurting more and more. The leftovers from yesterday would make a fine Sunday brunch. She usually enjoyed the busy work that brought the house back to order but the pain was excruciating. The table was finally set and the family of three sat to eat.

"It would be best if you left, Edward," she said, very quietly, before the first mouthful was taken.

"Leave? I am not going anywhere. No one is. This is how it is. Our marriage will be *'til death do us part.* Shut up your nonsense and eat your meal. I will tell you when to talk and I will tell you what is best," Edward replied with a smile on his face and a lilt to his voice.

"Then I'll go."

The disarmingly soft conversation continued. "You aren't going anywhere and neither is William. Don't think I will let you take that child out of here. Don't even think it."

They were talking in tones to soothe the baby. Edward enjoyed playing a role.

Gertie did not imagine that Edward would hold her or that he would even think of William. He barely spoke to the boy. She thought this was just going to be about her and Edward. *Why is he talking about William?* Suddenly, Gertie was in a state of confusion, her knees were shaking, and her hands could not lift her cup. She was devastated by the thoughts that rushed over her. William ate and played with his food. His parents' seemingly kind chatter kept the child happy.

When Gertie rose from her chair her hip gave way and she fell to the floor. Edward watched her for what seemed like forever and finally

84

came to help her as she got to her feet. The pain in her hip brought her down again.

Edward bent to her.

"No! Give me a second. I can get up."

"Put your arms around my neck." He carried her to the sofa and pulled her dress up and her underwear down so he could see the hip. She was in such agony that she did not move. Edward laid his hand on the terrible bruise and baseball size knot on her side. He laid it very tenderly and withdrew it sharply as if the pain passed to him.

Edward bit his lip to keep from saying he was sorry. "Do you think this needs a cool rag or heat?" he finally asked.

"Cool rag."

William brought his blanket and cuddled beside his mother on the sofa. Gertie straightened her dress and accepted the cloth Edward brought to tend her hip. He went upstairs and she and her baby boy fell asleep to the sounds of Edward reassembling the bedroom.

When she heard him come down the stairs, she crawled from the nest William made with her on the sofa. She had reached an immediate plan, but could not clear her mind enough to figure the future.

"Edward, I can't climb the stairs. Please bring William's crib mattress down so I can make him a place here for the time being."

For five nights Gertie slept on the sofa downstairs with William on a pallet next to her while she healed. It was obvious that she could not walk up the stairs until that hip mended. It wasn't broken or she would not have been able to walk at all. With the help of a cane she was tending to William and getting meals on the table. She did not go to Mom Neal's to work on Monday and no inquiry came from Tenth Street as to why she was not there. Edward assumed life would go back to the usual.

Gertie set her first plan in motion. By Friday she had a bedroom set up in the front parlor. William's crib was moved down and a single iron bed was set up with fresh linens from the closet upstairs. Some of their clothes were stacked neatly in the bookcase by the front door. She decided to continue to sleep on the sofa through the week end—in case Edward went to the tavern. On Monday she would make him aware of the changes. Gertie forgot that this week was Palm Sunday. She missed choir rehearsal and was quite surprised by a visit by Mrs. Stevens, the choir director, on Thursday morning.

"We missed you at rehearsal last evening, Gertie." She began while sipping the coffee Gertie offered. "I'll leave the music. Can you practice and be ready to sing on Sunday?"

Gertie was too embarrassed to admit that she forgot what Sunday was coming up. "I am sorry, but I couldn't presume to sing without attending rehearsal. That's the rule, Mrs. Stevens. Don't break it for me. I just can't do that."

"Gertie, we really need you Sunday. Both Sarah and Ruth will be away. You know what that means to your section. I chose an anthem that we have used before. Look at it. You know this music, don't you?"

"Yes…yes, I guess I do, but—"

"No more excuses. We'll be expecting you."

"My, but William is growing so fast and starting to talk. What fun." She gathered her coat and went to the door. "See you on Sunday?"

"Yes, I'll be there." Gertie felt better when she said it.

"I must go now. I have to clean the choir loft myself since there is no one cleaning the church. I think Rev. Harrison is going to clean the sanctuary. Isn't it awful? John Blaney walked out and said he would not be back to work. No one else to do it."

Gertie hatched plan number two. Tomorrow was going to be quite a day. Early she was going to see Rev. Harrison about a job and in the evening she was going to let Edward see the new arrangement in the parlor. She would not see Mom Neal again this week.

Gertie dressed William and herself in work clothes instead of *go-to-meet-the-preacher* clothes. If he gave her the job, she would stay and clean today. She was feeling light-hearted as she packed lunches and prepared to walk down Montgomery Street to the church. New breezes were stirring, and the warmth made a promise. Gertie felt a renewal. The forsythia pushed yellow trumpets out of stiff brown branches and the bravest daffodils bobbed their heads. A sweater and light jacket would be just right for the outing. She debated taking some favorite scrub brushes but decided that was not the thing to do.

They headed down past Tasker's Store where Sam used to work and crossed over at Tenth Street. She was amazed that the hip was willing to walk and knew it was because she set mind over matter. She looked up just as Mom Neal came to the same spot.

"Good morning," she greeted. "Are you walking downtown today?"

"Yes, I'm going to the church." Mary Neal wanted to know where Gertie was going and she even wanted to invite the girl and her child to walk with her but her staunch Scottish ways would not allow it.

"I'm headed that way, too. Shall we walk together?" asked Gertie. They passed two blocks in silence, except for William's chatter over the things he saw. "I'm recovering from my injuries," Gertie said casually. "The bruises on my face are gone and it is good to be back in the choir. The long walk to town will be a good test to see if my hip is fine again." She decided to clear the air and not let their last meeting seem like a bad dream. Mary Neal must be reminded that *it* did happen.

"I'm glad to know that. I didn't realize that you hurt your hip."

"Be sure, Mom Neal, I did not *hurt* my hip. Edward kicked me and I've been laid up all week."

Mom Neal stopped. Gertie stopped. William walked on yelling, "Come on."

"Gertie…" the older Mrs. Neal was at a loss for words.

"It is important for you to know what goes on in your family. At home, I was taught that things under the table cause more trouble that a good sweep of the broom. I don't tell you these things to hurt you or Edward. They are what happened. When Edward, William, and I make choices you will understand why. Do you see?"

"I believe it is our job to keep the family life sacred. As a wife and mother, we are expected to do all we can to keep our husbands and children wrapped in that sanctity. You are expected to put others before yourself. Find your joy and happiness within the marriage you have made. If it is not in the man you married, it may be in one or more of the children you will bear. I can only help you, if you understand this. Do *you* see?"

"I cannot do that. I just can't." She shook her head in disbelief as if to shake the words out of her ears. "No… No. I don't see."

The two women stood together on the walk leading up to the church, yet they were worlds apart. The older one went in, the younger one, holding the little boy's hand walked on. Without thinking, she made two turns and found herself at the yard where Grandmother Amsterdam was picking boughs of barren lilac to take in to force into bloom.

"Gertie and William, come in. Come in. Oh, what a surprise." Her delight was apparent. "William let me see you. Can you say 'Hi, Great Grandma'?"

"Hi, Gama"

"Yes, that will do, 'Hi, Gama'. Again William."

"Hi, Gama."

It was an all-encompassing hug for Gertie. She melted in to the arms of Edward's Grandmother as a ship goes into a safe harbor from a terrible storm. Her tears were torrential. There was so much joy in the greeting that William was not upset by his mother's tears. Gertie resolved to take William to see her own parents at Bear Creek soon. The boy should have such greetings more often. Mom Neal had not even spoken to him when they met earlier. While Grandmother Amsterdam was getting tea, Gertie tried to line things up in her mind so as not to show her disappointment with her mother-in-law just minutes ago. After all she was Grandmother's daughter.

"Gertie, let William go into the yard and play. The fence will keep him safe and we can watch him from here. William, take this box of toys to the porch." She held the door for William, and then sat down across from Gertie. "Do you need to talk or just to sit and have your tea?"

"I'm not sure Grandmother. I was on a mission this morning and I started out sure and confident... but now I'm unsure and lost."

"You aren't lost. You're here and I'm so very glad to see you. How is Edward and how is your family?"

"Edward is fine and I hope Mama and Papa are, too. I haven't seen them for over a month, just letters. I trust everyone is doing well."

"Well, if they are all doing well and if Edward and William are doing very well, you are the only one not doing well by my estimation. I can tell by looking at you and all those tears—they were not tears of joy. They came from way too deep for that. You don't have to tell me anything if you don't want to. Maybe not today—maybe tomorrow."

"Something is helping; maybe it's the tea or maybe it is just being here with you. You make me feel good about being me. I'm beginning to wonder who I am and why I don't see things as others around me see them."

"Child, when you feel that way, maybe you should look and see if you are around the right people. It is very important to find kindred spirits who understand you, and when you do, spend time with them. They will help define you. Your own family is the best place to get that kind of support. It is too bad that you are located so far from them." Then she asked the question that was upper most in her mind. "Is Edward a kindred spirit?"

"No." She spoke barely above a whisper and with only the slightest hesitation. Gertie raised her sad eyes to meet Grandmother's as she refilled the teacups with a suddenly shaking hand. She set the teapot down and took time to put sugar and lemon in her tea before meeting Gertie's gaze.

"Gertie, I am going to tell you a story. A beautiful young girl fell in love with a good man and married him. He was handsome and strong and hard working. He toiled for her. He brought home his pay and provided a beautiful, well-kept home. He was faithful and passionate enough to father many children. The young girl had no time or encouragement to follow her love of the arts. No time to read or go to musicales. Art works offered by her parents were not accepted as frivolous adornments to the home. Besides they were reminders to him that he had not provided everything his wife wanted." Grandmother walked to the window to check on William and returned to her chair and the story without Gertie saying a word. "Although she was raised to follow the events of the day and to develop opinions, she could not express them so she stopped keeping up with current events. Her passion for the suffragettes was lost. She had no desire to vote. Her husband's demands were all within the walls of their home. The distance between her and her parent's home widened and soon she was embarrassed to be with her parents because she somehow felt she disappointed them. She became a different person. She accepted his demands. The light in her eyes dimmed and her compassion for her fellow man died. It was as if she could not feel for others because she stifled her own feelings." She paused to inhale the aroma of the tea and to move her spoon in the cup as if she were stirring up memories. After a deep breath to aerate her soul, Elizabeth Amsterdam went on.

"The only things the beautiful young girl could provide for her children were creature comforts. She could not solve her own problems, and she could not help with theirs. The young girl stopped sharing with her mother. They discussed only the weather. Her mother never saw her cry, not even when the children were born." Grandmother stopped and took a breath, looking off into space. She seemed so far away.

"Wasn't there anything the mother and father could do? That is the saddest thing—to think she lost herself."

"That's what made me tell you this story when you said you didn't know who you were." Grandmother took Gertie's hand.

"I wish she had come to me as you are doing and told me a long time ago that she didn't know who she was. Maybe, just maybe, I could have saved Mary Amsterdam Neal for herself and for me." Grandmother's look was warm and loving and there were no tears. She'd finished crying for her daughter long ago.

But, Gertie cried and cried and cried.

Suddenly William jumped up on the porch with an earth worm to scare his mother. "See. See." The two women laughed with the delight the child brought to them.

"Gertie, do you still have the cameo brooch?"Grandmother asked as she was leaving.

"Yes, Grandmother, it is in a safe place. In fact, only this week I considered giving it back to you."

"No, Dear. It is yours now. I will not take it back. Treat yourself as you do that brooch."

It was time to go. William was tiring of the toys.

"Bye, Love"

Gertie and William started the long walk home. William skipped, hopped and ran part of the way. Gertie struggled to keep up. Soon they arrived at the church. Rev. Harrison was sweeping the steps.

"Hello, Gertie and William. How are you this fine spring day?"

"Good, thank you, sir. And how are you?"

"How you?" echoed William

"William, let's sit here on the church steps and rest awhile before going home. There is a cookie in this lunch bag. Rev Harrison would you like a cookie?"

"I could use a rest myself," Rev. Harrison replied as he sat down with them. "I never refuse a cookie, either. I have divided the church into five sections so I can clean some each week day. You know, John quit."

"Yes, Mrs. Stevens told me. Reverend Harrison, I could clean the church." Gertie jumped right in.

Her pastor reached over and patted Gertie on the head. "That is very nice of you but we can manage for a while. No need for you to worry or feel sorry for an old man with a broom." A chuckle came into his voice.

"No, No, you don't understand. I'm not just trying to be nice, I want John Blaney's job. I'm very serious."

"Gertie, you don't want this job and I can't have you do it. How would it look—the daughter and daughter-in-law of two of our most faithful families—cleaning the church? No, it is impossible. Whatever would prompt you to ask for this job?"

She thought for a moment, preparing every word she would speak. She decided to talk only of herself, not of Edward or the problems she faced.

"I need to act with independence, Reverend. I am setting goals for myself and for William which will require that I be independent. Some women pursue higher goals for themselves and they want a good education for their children. If they are wealthy, it is fine but, if they need to work to provide these things—it is not fine. Does that mean women like me cannot work and choose what is best for themselves?" Gertie tried to look in her pastor's eyes but he kept them diverted. "What better place for me to work and save money than here at my church? I wish I were a nurse or a teacher, but I'm not and I have William to think about. He could come here with me while I work."

"Gertie take your son and go home. Your work is there. You are provided for and William will grow and find his way. I cannot hire you to clean the church. You are very zealous and I admire that. Spend that energy and intensity on your marriage and home. The fulfillment is there, believe me. A contented husband and happy family will make your life complete. If you have time on your hands we always need Sunday school teachers and communion stewards."

She stood to go, saying only "Good-bye."

"Peace my child." He was so pleased with himself in the sound advice he gave the young mother. He was so sure he had assisted her onto the right track. Rev. Harrison turned back to the church and his task with a satisfied smile on his face.

Gertie spent the time walking home thinking of the pastor's words. She wondered if she failed to express herself well or was his mind just too closed. Gertie became more resolved than ever. The great disillusion of her marriage and even greater disillusion in trusting Edward for her security and future became indelible mistakes in her mind. Mistakes she would not make again, but mistakes she has not yet been able to correct.

"But, I will!" She said aloud to herself. She was only ten minutes ahead of Edward but she had the coffee on and the home smelled like Mama's kitchen. It made Gertie so homesick.

"That coffee smells good. How about a cup?" Edward entered the kitchen from the back door. William was asleep after his long day in town. Edward did not even ask about him but went straight away upstairs to change his suit.

This was not the time she picked to tell Edward about the parlor. After a good meal—that was the time but, today was definitely the day. Edward walked out onto the porch to smoke a cigarette as Gertie worked to get dinner on the table. A cool breeze came in the partly open door. It carried the pleasant aroma of his cigarette and mixed with the coffee, she could close her eyes and almost believe that Papa was nearby. The terrible homesickness passed over her again. The table was set for the bean soup and cornbread dinner—one of their favorites. Fresh butter was on the table and a glass of milk and a cup of coffee sat at each place as was her family's tradition. Gertie remembered Papa always drank half of his milk and then poured his coffee into the glass, added two big spoons of sugar and saved it for dessert.

She was in this reverie when Edward returned from the porch. "What are you daydreaming about, Gertie?" he asked, startling Gertie to attention as he closed the door and sat at the table to eat.

It was very quiet without William to entertain during the meal.

"I was thinking about Papa." Gertie said into the silence.

"Is this the weekend you go to Bear Creek?"

"No, not until Easter—next week."

"Why is William napping so late?"

"We took a long walk this afternoon and he was worn out and late getting to his nap. In fact we only got home a few minutes before you."

"And, are you going to tell me where you went?"

"We packed a lunch and started walking down Montgomery Street. I thought we would eat at the churchyard, but we went on farther and saw your Grandmother in her yard. We ate lunch there. It was nice to let William run free in a fenced yard. I will have to watch him extra closely in our yard now. He's so adventuresome." She paused, "Then we walked home again."

"Goodness, that is about a mile to Grandmother's."

"I know but we stopped often going both ways. It is alright for the boy to be worn out with exercise on a beautiful spring day. He loved it. I believe he will want to go again tomorrow…but we won't."

In Edward's usual manner of avoiding hearing what he might not like, he did not ask anything about the visit with his Grandmother. He was sure Gertie told her about the awful scene they had after William's birthday party. *What do Gertie and Grandmother have in common?* He wondered.

As Gertie cleared the kitchen from dinner, William stirred in the parlor. "Is William in the parlor?" Edward rose to go to him. Gertie was surprised for Edward rarely went to William when he needed attention. She stood in the middle of the room while Edward opened the parlor door. He brought William to her and went out the front door without a word.

"Please," she prayed, "don't let him go to the tavern. Please, please." Her words circled the kitchen and came back to her. "Please…"

It was late when Edward came back to the house. William was in bed for the night and Gertie was prepared for bed. She was beyond tired. She was exhausted. The aroma of coffee was gone from the kitchen. Thoughts of Papa were far, far away. She knew Edward had not gone to the tavern because she saw him coming across the hill from the river. She would wait and talk to him if, in fact, his head was clear. She would accomplish something on this day.

"Is that your bed in the parlor?" were his first words to her.

"Yes."

"Was your hip well enough for you to move William's crib down those stairs?"

"No."

"Humm. Where did the single bed come from?"

"I bought it from John Dannon with money I saved. He brought it here and I asked him to go upstairs and bring William's crib down."

"All that trouble for a temporary arrangement?" he asked.

"It is a permanent arrangement for so long as I live in this house."

His jaw clenched and he went up to bed without a word.

She fell into her bed and listened to William's sweet breaths until she fell into a deep sleep. In the morning the soft spring rain beat gently on the side of the house. It was dark and when she saw the clock she realized that they had overslept. *Edward missed his commuter.*

Racing to the kitchen, she was startled to see him sitting there—just sitting there.

Chapter 11   1913

"Make some coffee Gertie. I'm not going to work today."

"Are you sick? You never stay home."

"Today I'm not going to work. We have some work to do."

"I knew we had more to discuss and I appreciate that you let me get some rest last night before we began this. I will make coffee and I ask you to please let us try to keep our manner civil as we work through this day."

"Our work is to put the parlor straight again. I cannot live in this house with a wife sleeping in another room." He was struggling to keep his voice calm.

"I cannot live with a man who beats me." She was cold as ice.

"I cannot have a wife who hides money and valuables from me. Who lets the bankers in town know that she wants accounts without my knowledge. Who lets the local merchant know that separate bedrooms are arranged in this home." He was reciting the words he had planned.

"I cannot have a husband who gambles away our assets and would hock the one important piece of jewelry I have. One who stays with other women in the city, believing it has nothing to do with our marriage." She was doing her own reciting. Neither of them denied what the other said. No argument formed. It was a speak-and- be-heard attempt at clearing the air. But, the air was not clear. It was heavy with incrimination, anger and fear.

"You know, Gertie, divorce is out of the question. The only way you can get a divorce is if I abandon you. I will not leave. Now, you can leave… abandon me and I can get a divorce. Then the courts will leave William with me."

"Don't do that Edward. Don't close all possibilities for me. You know I cannot leave William. Why do you play that card against me?

Who would tend William? Who would care for him?" Gertie was losing ground as her emotions took over. "No. No."

"You can go. My mother will take care of William. You can see him but you can't take him anywhere. I talked to her about it yesterday after dinner."

"I will not leave William with you or your mother. He needs to be with me. Can your heart be so hard against your own son? Your mother pays no more attention to William than you do. She is a stranger to him. She is worse than that. He knows she is *somebody* to him but her coldness hurts him every time he sees her." Gertie paused for effect. "We aren't going to talk about my leaving William."

"For now, you can stay in your room with William." Edward pointed at the parlor. "You will continue to keep the house and make a pleasant mealtime for us all. I'm trying to keep this civil. There are many marriages that have arrangements like this for the good of all concerned."

"Do you really want me here? Do you want to live like this for the rest of our lives?"

"Why not?" was his cold, hard answer.

She turned her attention to preparing the baby's breakfast.

"Edward, I need some time. I would like to go to visit my family. As soon as I can arrange it with Sam, we will pack and go."

"That is a good idea, Gertie. Go, but be sure to set a date for your return or I will come after William, Now—," he smirked, "—I am sure you can complete the move of your belongings to the parlor. After your long walk yesterday, I assume you can master the stairs."

"Yes." She turned to go see if William was awake. Edward reached out, took her arm as she passed his chair, and pulled her to his lap. She could feel his erection as he held her tightly to his lap. She held her breath.

Is he going to force me?

"Gertie, I'm not going to hurt you." It was almost as if he read her thoughts.

"I'm not going to insist on my husbandly rights now, before breakfast… but you feel the reminder that we are young. We are one flesh. Do you really think we can live here in separate rooms?" He took her chin and turned her head toward him. "Can you keep yourself from wanting me when you know I want you?"

She closed her eyes and held her breath

"I can resist you right now and keep out of the parlor…. can you trust yourself to keep your hunger from bringing you to me?" He took her chin. "Look at me, Gertie."

She looked at him.

"The solution is so easy. Come back to the bedroom. Give up this foolishness. Stop the agony over leaving me. Make the best of our marriage. It will be more good than bad. Don't I always make everything up to you? Lighten up, girl. You love me… you know you do."

"No, Edward I don't know that," she said without turning her gaze. Gertie pulled away from him as he grabbed her wrist and held like a vice. He squeezed and squeezed; her hand throbbed from the constriction.

"Let go!" she demanded. "Edward," she pleaded.

He twisted.

The words, "This marriage is over," came from her mouth as the snap of her bone sounded in the kitchen. Gertie managed to stay on her feet. He dropped her wrist the instant he felt the bone break. His face showed agony; hers was full of hate.

She took the tea towel and tried to make a sling but it was too short and she could not manage with one hand. A sweater hung on a hook by the door and as she struggled, he took it from her, tied the sleeves together and put it over her head to hold the wounded arm.

"Take William to Mrs. White," she ordered.

As soon as he left, Gertie walked out the back door and down the back alley to get help. She turned west to Fergus Hill and the big house. It never seemed so far away as each step brought pain up her arm and into her shoulder.

As soon as Mrs. Fergus' girl opened the door, Gertie stepped into the house where three short years ago she and Edward spent their honeymoon night. It was a good choice. Mrs. Fergus had a phone and the doctor came to tend to Gertie before Edward could figure where she went. Even as the doctor was setting the arm, she was insisting that she needed to go get William.

Dr. Smith was talking to her and trying to keep her calm while he worked. "It is a butterfly break, very nasty. How did this happen? This kind of break is usually done when the arm is caught and twisted in machinery. Most of the breaks like this happen on the farm."

"How long will it take to get it in a cast, Doctor? I must go get William."

"Mrs. Fergus, this young lady cannot go anywhere today. Can you put her to bed?"

"Of course. Maria, prepare the front room for Gertie."

"No! No! I cannot stay. Thank you very much, Mrs. Fergus, but I must go to Mrs. White's and get William."

"There, there, Gertie. You rest right here and I will send Maria to get William."

A feeling of helplessness washed over her. If only she had the strength, she would get up and out of here. She could have William in minutes. She used to run down Fergus Hill faster than her brothers and sisters. *I am trapped by my own weakness,* she thought. *Oh Edward, why?*

"Maria, quickly, take this note to Mrs. White on Eleventh Street. Bring little William Neal back with you."

Dr. Smith put a cast on her arm and prepared a powder for Gertie which she drank and fell into a fitful sleep. The doctor and Mrs. Fergus noticed her tears flowing, even in her drugged state. The sleep lasted only two hours and Gertie awoke with a start. First, her arm panged so sharply that it jerked her out of slumber with a cry. Then, she asked for William.

"William is with his father. Edward has taken the day off to care for him. You can rest at ease Gertie. If he cannot be with you right now, it is best that he be with his father. That way you can get the rest you need. You will not go home today."

For the rest of her life, Mrs. Blanch Fergus would never forget the terror she saw in Gertie's eyes as she spoke those words to her.

"Dr. Smith left another sedative for you if you need it."

Gertie shook her head. "I don't need it; I will rest now. Thank you." She closed her eyes until her hostess and Maria left the room. Alone, she began to work through the events and implications of her plight. Maybe it was the leftover drugs or the need to open her mind, but she spoke aloud in the air. "I have brought this on myself because I failed to do what was best for me and William." She pounded the pillow with her good arm and started an important conversation with herself. "I'm stupid. I made a fatal error in delaying when I knew…I knew Edward would hurt me again." She relaxed her neck muscles and enjoyed the comfort of her pillow. "Now, I can't delay. He could hurt William while I am making excuses for him. But, I can't do anything until my arm is better." She held her cast up and studied it. "Maybe twenty-four hours. Yes, I must be stronger than I am right now. Stronger. Stronger. I must think. I must think...no more sedatives." The pain in her arm was nothing compared to the pain constricting her heart and the aching in her gut. *No more—no more,* were her last thoughts.

The first light coming into the room on Fergus hill slowly enticed Gertie to wake. She was quietly remembering all the warm and wonderful times she spent in this big house with the Fergus children and her own siblings. She remembered the times she and Liddy made every bed and mopped the shiny hardwood floors. Even the aroma of breakfast floating up to her was part memory and part reality. Gertie came back to the thoughts of her broken arm and the need to be reunited with William. She came back without panic or fear. It was with a quiet determination that right would prevail. Surprisingly the arm, though it ached, did not generate the radiating pain it did before her good night's sleep. The white curtains gently filtering sunlight reassured her. The breakfast Maria brought to her looked wonderful.

Maria was delighted to see Gertie smile. "Good mornin', Miss Gertie. Great day, Miss Gertie. You are going to be so much better today... and, don't forget to be thankful it is your left arm and not your right one. There's always blessings in everything, Miss Gertie. See, you can feed yourself. Even I can be thankful for that. I never did like feedin' folks. Don't get me wrong...I'll do it if you want me to."

Gertie smiled at Maria's ramblings. She looked like a schoolgirl nestled in the big bed. Her hair always seemed to fall into place and she was one of those women who woke with hair neat and skin refreshed. Her cheeks lacked the usual glow today, but the brightness of her dark eyes lit her face. She had a mysterious way of looking young and mature at the same time.

"No, Maria, I am thankful that I can feed myself and, thankful for this breakfast."

"Excuse me; Mrs. Gertie someone is at the door and it's so early." The breakfast was wonderful and Gertie ate every bite like a puppy that finally got to the kennel bowl.

"Well, I see a broken arm does not necessarily take one's appetite."

"Sam! Oh Sam!"She cried in her brother's arms as he came to hold on to her.

"I got a note from Doc Smith this morning telling he tended you yesterday and where you were. Glad to see me?" He took a moment to assess his sister. "Are you going to be laid up in bed with this?"

"No, Sam, as a matter of fact, I was wondering where my clothes are so I can get dressed and go home. Doc and Mrs. Fergus insisted I stay here last night and it was a good idea. He gave me some medicine that knocked me out. It was like a happy land juice." She smiled.

"Maybe it was bourbon. Works for me. What happened? How did you break your arm?"

"Sam, I am so glad to see you. I'll tell you all about it when you take me home. I'll be ready in no time."

"OK. I'll wait downstairs. Take your time. Nice to see Mrs. Fergus in this house again, isn't it? I wasn't sure she would come back after the Mayor died. I love being here again, don't you?"

"I was thinking the same thing before you arrived, but I'm ready to go now. I can't thank Mrs. Fergus enough for helping me yesterday."

Mrs. Fergus tapped on the door. "I have a note for you, Gertie. Edward dropped it here last night, but you were asleep. I told him you would get it this morning. He also brought your clothing. Remember you arrived yesterday in your sleepwear and robe." Mrs. Fergus left and went to her chores.

"Open this for me Sam, please." She put her cup of coffee down and read.

> *Gertie, I will be back to work tomorrow. William is spending the night with Mom Neal and she will be looking after him while I work. I told her not to expect you to pick him up. Edward*

"OK, Sam. Wait for me downstairs. I can be dressed in ten minutes. We're going to get William."

§

Gertie's blinders were removed. She realized that Edward had held himself back from hitting her many times. He did it once; he did it twice. He almost broke her hip and now her arm was broken. This marriage was over. She would not even allow herself to believe it was for William. The marriage was over because she had too much self-esteem to allow this to happen again. Something was wrong with Edward and she could not fix it. Gertie was a MacGregor and MacGregors were not fools. She would look at Edward as he was; not as she wanted him to be. The tears flowed as she struggled into her clothes. This one time she allowed herself to cry for Edward and the dream of love that was gone.

In the same room where she started her marriage, she ended it—in her mind and in her heart. Gertie would not lose herself.

Chapter 12

At last, she was in Sam's car and headed to Tenth Street to pick up William. *Where can we go?* The question hammered in her head. There was only one place.

"Can you take us to Bear Creek?"

"Sure. When?"

"What day is it…goodness, I can't think. Wednesday, right?"

"Yes."

"I don't guess you could go today."

"I have to get back to the track. I could go tomorrow."

She said nothing as her mind tried to sort out her possibilities. She looked for options, but was still fuddled when they arrived at the Neal home. The two blocks from Fergus Hill hardly gave her time to plan what she was going to say to Edward's parents much less what she was going to do after she got William.

"I'll go in and get him," offered Sam.

"No. I have to myself but come to the porch with me."

They walked to the door. Gertie was surprised how weak and unsteady she was. Sam held her arm and supported her with his smile.

The door opened before they knocked. Mom Neal stood in the doorway. Gertie did not speak—she waited for an invitation to come in. Mom Neal hesitated and obliged.

"Come in."

Sam took her arm and led her in letting her feel his decision not to wait on the porch.

The kitchen was bright, spotless and filled with the aroma of baked sweets and coffee. Mom Neal looked at Gertie's arm with the slightest raised eyebrow as she invited them to sit at the table. The wood cook stove in the corner rendered pleasant aromas and overbearing heat. A spoon jar and a huge sugar bowl stood on the table along with several clean coffee mugs. A plate of cookies centered the table. Everything for coffee and cookies was there except the invitation to enjoy.

"Where is William?"

"He's asleep."

"Where?" Gertie asked again as she rose to seek the place where his bed might be. "I will look in on him. I have missed him so much. It was hard to sleep apart from him, even though I knew he was safe. Is he in here?" She continued walking toward the door leading to the hallway.

"Gertie, sit down." It was not a question it was a directive. "We need to talk before William wakes. Edward said you would be at Mrs. Fergus all day and I was to keep William here until he returns from work."

"I'm much better than expected. You do not have to keep him all day. I'm taking him now."

"He is to stay *here* until his father comes." Mary pronounced with emphasis.

Gertie's continence changed. Her jaw set and her heart began beating faster. Swallowing fear, she raised her head and looked into Mary Neal's eyes. It was the older woman who broke the gaze.

Sam decided to take a part. "Mrs. Neal surely you do not want to keep William from his mother today. Gertie should take care of her little boy, if she is able and you can see…" Sam went to stand beside Gertie, "… *she is able*." He made his own emphasis.

"William is to stay here. He is fine. He slept well and ate his meals. There is no need to disturb his routine." Mary addressed Sam, to avoid looking at Gertie or the arm cast. "Gertie should go back to Mrs. Fergus and stay today as her husband said. Edward will be home at 5:30. He'll pick up William and take him home." Her face and mind were set in stone. Her eyes stayed averted from Gertie.

Gertie rose from her chair. "Mom Neal, it has been over twenty-four hours since I saw William. Now, I'm going to him. Shall I go looking for him or will you tell me which room?" Gertie was out of the kitchen. She checked the parlor to the right and then went the stairs leading to bedrooms. At the top of the stairs she found the room with a crib and the little fellow sleeping.

William, my little boy! At last this eternity was over.

Gertie walked to his bed and resisted stroking his hair. She contented herself watching her beautiful child sleeping so peacefully. The chair, silently drawn to the bedside, became her observation seat. She did not think of Edward's mother or Sam waiting down in the kitchen. She did not care how long they would have to sit and wait. Strength infused her body and soul as she watched William. With each breath raising his tiny chest, Gertie's mission became clearer. It was up to her. *I must protect him.* She could not see the difficulties spread out before her but it would not matter. The strength she was gathering would be enough to meet every challenge for William.

"I will give you peace for every dreaming moment, William," she whispered.

From this day forward, she would take care of her little boy and give him every chance to overcome the hardness his father would inflict upon him.

How can I take care of William if I am battered and broken? She asked herself. To do all these things for her son, she would have to take good care of herself. She could not risk broken bones, body or worse. *I will not sacrifice my life in this marriage thinking it is best for William. Nothing—no one on Tenth and Eleventh Street can stop us—me and you, my precious child. No power on earth."* She would not wait on the power of God, although she would willingly welcome His Holy intervention. "Forgive me, Oh God for my selfishness. Help me to be the person I need to be. Please hold my little boy and me in the care of your Holy Arms," she prayed aloud.

When he roused from his nap, it seemed a dream to see her face smiling at him. He jumped. He squealed. "Momma. Momma. Momma!" He cried. "Gertie, go."

"Yes, sweetheart, we will go. I've missed you. Are you my little boy?" she asked.

"Big boy," he answered with arms stretched over head to show her how big and to beg her to lift him from the crib.

It wasn't easy but she raised him over the rail and set his feet on the floor. He wanted to be carried but she insisted he stay on his little legs as she led him down the stairs.

"Mom Neal, we are going home to get our clothes and then we are going to Bear Creek. Edward knows about the trip and agreed. Please give me some paper so I can write him a note. He wants me to tell him when we will be coming back."

"Gertie, you cannot take William now. You'll have to wait until Edward comes home tonight. That's final. Come, William."

When Mary Neal reached her arms toward William, he sensed something was wrong and scurried onto Gertie's lap and threw his arms around her neck and hid his face in her hair.

Gertie was determined that he not feel the tension building. She tickled his ribs and moved toward the door which Sam was opening for her.

At that moment, Clay Neal had his hand on the outside knob, entering the room as his wife spoke her last words.

"That boy needs to be with his mother. He cried for her all night. For God's sake, Mary, what reason do we have to hold that baby here.…. because Edward said so? No." He took two steps into the center of the room. "Aren't you making something out of nothing, wife?" He turned to Gertie. "If you are able to tend William, do it, Gertie. We will tell Edward that you have gone home."

"Thank you, Poppa Clay, but we're not going home. We're going to Bear Creek. It is something Edward and I discussed. He only wants to know when we are coming back. I would like to leave him a note but you can just tell him if you want."

Poppa Clay was stepping in to help her again and she was not going to lie to him and let him think she was going to Eleventh Street with William.

"Mary," he turned to his wife, "give her something to write on."

Gertie wrote the note.

Edward,

We are going to Bear Creek. I will be home to keep an appointment with Dr. Smith on April 7.

Gertie.

Clay followed them down the walk to the car. He touched Gertie on the shoulder and asked, "Your arm? Did you break it?"

"No, Sir. I didn't break it; Edward did. I am not going to tell you how this happened. I will only say that it will never happen again. I'm going to take care of myself and William. I'm not sure how but I will …"

Sam drove away with the happy little boy and his troubled mother. The first stop was Eleventh Street.

"The door is locked. Do you have a key?"

"No, I left without a key."

"Stand back." Sam broke the window and got into the back porch. He opened the door and let Gertie and William in. She put William in the highchair and went straight to the parlor and upstairs to gather their clothes and items needed for their trip. Sam made lunch for everyone while chatting with the little boy. He cleared the table, made coffee and poured milk for William. When Gertie came back to the kitchen Sam was entertaining his nephew with crazy faces and weird noises.

"Where do we go from here? Can't go to Bear Creek today, you know."

"Can you take us to Elkridge? We could stay with Liddy until you come for us."

"I can take you after the last race. So, I guess it is off to the races for you. Want to see the horsey, William? Giddy-up, giddy-up."

Gertie wrote Edward another note telling him exactly what they did to get in the house and what she was taking. She cleaned the kitchen and put everything back where it belonged. Sam took a piece of cardboard and taped it over the broken window. He also left money to repair the window pane and they were gone—to the races.

The Laurel Race Track is a beautiful thoroughbred track nestled in the trees off of US 1 north of Laurel. Its brick pillars and winding drive led to a grandstand patterned after Churchill Downs in Kentucky. The brick wall had a colonial look. The white clapboard clubhouse and dome sat high above the trees. The red clay track made a pretty picture with green grass surrounding it along with a bracelet of white rail fence. It was especially nice today because the prevailing wind was from the west and the stables' smells traveled away from the zealous attendees. The fifth race pounded the track when they arrived. Gertie had never been to the Laurel Race Track. She listened to the crowd and the sound of the horses running—so many people in her small town! Sam carefully led them toward the club house. He was greeted on all sides by everyone they passed.

"Do you know everyone here?"

He answered with his ever ready smile.

"Gertie, we're going to the clubhouse office. It's a quiet place where you can rest and wait for me. It is 3:15. The last race is over about five. You'll be fine. How's that arm?"

"It hurts, but not bad. I'll be fine."

"Hi, Laurie," he greeted the receptionist. "Anyone in CJ's office this afternoon?"

"Are you kidding? Of course not. You know where CJ is during the races."

"Can my sister and nephew wait for me in there? Is that OK?" He smiled. The smile was not wasted on Laurie.

"Sure."

"Gertie, William, this is Laurie Shaffer. She's a friend and she can be trusted to take good care of you. Laurie—Gertie and William."

They settled into the office. It was rich and full of mahogany and leather, but the feature of the room was the huge plate glass window looking out on the finish line of the track. Gertie was fascinated and so was William.

"Horsey!" he said over and over.

The clay oval surrounded by grass looked like a large brooch from above. The trumpet sounded bringing Gertie and William to the window to see the horses march around the track to the starting gate. The roar of the crowd excited them. Gertie and William melted into the large overstuffed sofa and watched Sam's world turning below. She did not realize how exhausted she was until she began to have trouble keeping her eyes open. She fought sleep and finally rose to ask Laurie where she could get some coffee.

Laurie assessed the situation and knew that Gertie needed to rest and William needed someone to watch over him.

"Can I take William for a walk while you rest?"

"Yes, that would be nice." Gertie set the coffee cup on the table and closed her eyes. Her mind was going over the events of the day when sleep demanded her concession. The cast made finding a good position difficult but soon she was sound asleep.

❧

A noisy commotion aroused her. She shook off sleep, wondering how long she dozed. Some instinct deep inside told her the commotion was an alarm as the hair came up on the back of her neck. She ran to the door and looked into the reception room.

"Where is William?" she screamed at the sobbing Laurie who stood alone in the reception room door. "Where is my boy?" Gertie took the girl's arm, shaking it. She tore for the door screaming "William... William!"

Laurie followed, mumbling. "A man took him...asked *me where are you going with that child*...picking him up... shoving me—"

Gertie went out the door of the clubhouse and into the grandstands. Stairs spread out like spokes on the wheel. The crowd was a squirming, squealing monster. *Where to turn? Where to go? Where to look for William?* So many people... so much noise... so hopeless.

"William! William!" she screamed to blend with the noise of the race fans. She moved on, searching— her face wild. The stairs tripped her. With both arms stretched to stop the fall, she screamed again in pain. That scream was lost to the thundering hooves crossing the finish line.

Laurie stopped following Gertie and ran to the stables. *Sam'll know what to do.*

Suddenly as Gertie turned to run up the next aisle, a man took hold of her and said "Gertie?" He looked into her terrorized eyes. "Gertie! What is wrong?" It was Doc Smith. He put his arm around her and set her in his seat. "What is it girl? Are you calling William?"

Gertie's composure was gone. Her hair was wild and her eyes wilder. She couldn't stand; she couldn't sit. Doc Smith held her in the seat with both hands on her shoulders.

Sam arrived just as Doc Smith was corralling Gertie. The two men led her back to the clubhouse and the sofa without saying a word.

"Listen, Gertie. It was Edward." Sam bent down on his knee to look in Gertie's eyes. "Edward took William. When Laurie described him, I knew...and she said William called him Daddy." He spoke the words slowly and softly so she could take them in.

Laurie and Sam filled in the events for Doc Smith and the distraught mother. As Laurie went over what happened, all three of them knew it was Edward. He didn't go to work today; he came to the track.

Gertie took strange relief in this knowledge. At least, William was not abducted by a stranger. Gertie began to exchange fears in her mind. *Oh God, now I have to deal with Edward. How can I get William back?* Her mind raced round and round like the horses on the track below.

The sudden roar of the crowd cheering the last race startled Gertie and the first tears came.

"Sam, I hope I have the strength to go back to Tenth Street again and get William from Edward or his parents."

"You do… if it is what you have to do."

Laurie kept saying, over and over. "I'm sorry…I'm sorry."

"It is not your fault, Laurie. He is safe. It was his father. We are sure."

"Gertie, do you want to stay here while I go to see if Edward left the track, went home or to his mother's?" Sam asked.

"Let me look at your arm and check you over." Doc Smith stepped to the sofa and forced Gertie to lie down. "Mmm. Swelling is way up and I suspect you are in pain. Heart racing. I want you to take this medicine but you need to be in a place you can rest for it to work. Can we take you back to Mrs. Fergus? You can't go all the way to Elkridge."

"I'm not leaving Laurel without my son. Doctor, give me the medicine. I will take it soon."

She looked to Sam. "Take me to the Amsterdam home on Prince George Street. It is close and a safe haven for me. I'm welcome there. Then go and see where Edward and William are." Then she made a sad admission, "I will not be with William again tonight," and started to cry—a soft, heart wrenching cry. Her heart was breaking for William. It was breaking a harsh twisting break.

"Alright Gertie, let's go. If at all possible, I will bring William back with me."

Gertie was right about one thing, she was welcome in the home of Edward's grandmother who did not ask questions. It was apparent that Gertie needed help. She just began providing for her needs as soon as she saw her being led in by her brother. Although she was distraught to see Gertie with a broken arm, the story could be told later. They went upstairs to the back bedroom. The comforter was pulled back from the high bed. Gertie was changed into a big nightie that went easily over the cast. The medicine and a warm glass of milk and honey helped her to relax.

"Grandmother, Sam will tell you what has brought us here this evening. I am going to give into the medicine and sleep. Please waken me when he returns." She put her face into the pillow and cried. Gertie forced her legs, her arms and spine to relax by methodical steps. The aching, broken arm lay elevated above her head across the pillow.

Three hours later Grandmother quietly opened the bedroom door and brought the freshly bathed, fed and pajama-ed, sleepy, little boy into the room and slipped him in the bed with his mother. Gertie nestled him and herself back to sleep.

Grandmother whispered, "Sam will be here tomorrow afternoon to take you to Bear Creek."

Chapter 13

The next morning the sun was high in the sky before they opened their eyes. William was playful and happy with this new bed and his bed partner. His newest words made her laugh.

"Yockey. Gertie. Horsey and yockeys."

He pointed to the cast and demanded a word for that. She taught him to say cast and she explained that her arm was broken but the doctor fixed it. William kissed it to make it better.

Gertie studied her son as he studied the cast. His eyes were brown and his curly hair was very dark. It was a mop this morning. How could a child look so much like his father and still remind her of her own father? William's thinking skills foretold his brightness and she was becoming more dedicated to his development, even as she lay there looking at him

He was gentle with Gertie's hand. He understood that it was hurt.

Nothing wanted to move in Gertie's body. Her hip was aching and her shoulder was tired from carrying the cast. Her hand was full of pins and needles because swelling under the cast cut circulation. It would have been very easy to stay in Grandmother Amsterdam's bed.

"We are going to Bear Creek today, William". The words, that were supposed to get him excited, worked magic on her as she said them. "Yes, going home to see Mama and Papa." She helped William to the floor and started to dress when she realized again that she could not do it without help. The frustration was unbearable. She hated to ask Grandmother for help but she had no choice.

Grandmother Amsterdam was good at anticipating Gertie's needs. "Sam will be here at lunch time so you do not need to hurry. Go down to the kitchen and have coffee while I tend to William. Then we will see to your clothes."

Gertie gathered the large skirt of her nightie and went down the back stairs to the warm, bright kitchen. The huge white table and chairs had tufted cushions that welcomed her sore hip and made her sigh in relief. She sat there for a minute and took in the security and warmth that this room gave her. With her good right hand, she poured a cup of coffee and started to gather bread, butter and applesauce for William's breakfast. She noticed oatmeal on the stove and prepared two bowls. This would be a fine substantial breakfast for their travel. *Always*, she thought, *I will always remember this difficult time and all that Sam and Grandmother did for us.* She found a kindred spirit in Edward's grandmother and her grateful heart seemed to swell in her chest.

Then Edward came to mind with a surprising thought. *I want to love you, Edward.* She shook her mop of uncombed hair and tried to reconcile her feelings for Edward and the terrible happening in the last couple of days. She took a deep breath and admitted to her troubled mind—*But, I don't know what love is anymore...maybe I never knew.* Aloud she said, "I do know who deserves love—William—and maybe me, some day."

Sam arrived right on time. Gertie bade Grandmother farewell with tearful eyes. She could not begin to thank her and Grandmother would not let her. "Just take care of yourself and this little one. I love you both."She handed Sam a lunch basket. "Write to me Gertie. And, come see me when you come back." She turned to Sam. "Bring my picnic basket when you have time. I'd like to see you from time to time."

They were off.

William went right to sleep, and Gertie slept for the first twenty minutes. "Shall we go by to see Liddy?"Sam asked.

"Yes!" She roused up to answer.

Liddy was glad to see them all, especially William who had grown so much since she last saw him. They spread their lunch out. Liddy added fresh baked cookies and joined in for a festive meal. The story about her broken arm was recounted. Sam heard the detail of Gertie's ordeal for the first time. She left nothing out, including the stoic attitude of Edward's mother, the matter-of-factness of Clay Neal, and the generosity of Grandmother Amsterdam.

"What are you going to do? Where are you going to go when you come back to Laurel?" Liddy brought the question that Gertie could not answer. It was easy to tell her brother and sister what she was not going to do but she had no positive plan for hers and William's future.

"We'll never live with Edward again," was the only thing she could say.

Heavy thoughts invaded and the conversation faltered. To end the visit on a better note, Sam brought up Easter.

"This Sunday is Easter."

Gertie promised William a visit from the Easter bunny. He had no idea what that meant but it sounded like fun as he imitated, "bun-ny."

"And, we will gather eggs to color—red, blue, green, yellow."

That sounded like fun, too.

"Lon and I are coming to Bear Creek Saturday afternoon. Do you have to come home today? Can you just stay through the week end?" She directed her question to Sam.

"Is Dan is going down home for Easter?" Gertie wanted to see everyone.

"Now that I recall, he did say that would be his next trip down and he is bringing his sweetie, too. I'm not coming back tonight. I'm staying for the weekend, too."

"Let's go, Sam. I'm anxious to get there." Gertie was on her feet to make a, not so successful, attempt to help clear the table. "I can hardly wait to see the whole family together." But, as she said it, her mind wondered. *Not everyone. Not Edward.*

✿

The house at Bear Creek and the water beyond sparkled like a dream to Gertie. The sun was just low enough to catch every window pane and every ripple. She thought the driveway would never end. And then she was in Mama's arms. Shirley was hugging and lifting the squirming little boy who kept saying, "Walk! Will'um walk."

"Let William walk, Shirley. He wants to show you what a big boy he is." Mama would have her time to hold him when he was ready.

"Gertie, you have a broken arm! Come on Sam, let's go in. You can get the things later."

It was all there—the warm cozy kitchen and the sweet hot coffee, the down home feeling. Dinner was cooking on the stove. Gertie thought she smelled roast chicken. Papa was on the bridge waiting for the last train before coming home for the night. Gertie looked at her mother and saw the gray increasing in the hair and the wrinkles giving more character to her face. She noted again how much Liddy looked like Mama

"Sit. Are you alright? Is it hurting now? I want to know what happened. Did the doctor say it would heal and be fine? Do you have any other injuries?" Her questions came quickly.

"Mama, I will tell you all about it, but for now I am fine. It is not hurting too much but it is swollen under the cast. I have to keep it elevated. That should go down soon."

"Sam, come here boy and hug your mother."

"Well, at last someone noticed me. Am I invisible? Next time I will put a cast on my arm up there on the road like Gertie did—so I can have all the attention and the best seat in the house." All the while he was lifting Mama off her feet with a bear hug. When he sat down, Shirley came to climb on his knee and William tried to follow onto the other.

"I'm not going to be much help while I am here, Mama. I feel bad about that—in fact you are going to have to help me dress and take care of William. I'm going to be here until April 6th. I have to see Doc Smith on the next day to have the cast removed… hopefully."

Patricia MacGregor raised her eyebrow and looked at her daughter. It was apparent that Edward was not mentioned, and now she learned it would be an extended visit. There was more than a broken arm to deal with. "You stay as long as you want."

"How about you, Sam? Is your visit extended?"

"No. I go back Sunday after the big meal you're gonna feed me. By the way, Liddy, Lon and the children are coming and so are Dan and Mable.

"Everyone will be here for Easter." She said, as if to God, in thanks.

Chapter 14

Laurel was a true small town. The streets were usually quiet except when they were buzzing with stories waiting for new ears. The week before Easter gave the west end—and the whole town—a lot to talk about. The stories spread back and forth—to churches, to stately homes along Montgomery Street, to small mill houses on the side streets, to Main Street businesses, and to bars and taverns on US 1.

Mrs. Drake lives three doors down at 409 Eleventh Street. She saw Gertie hurrying toward Fergus Hill that early morning. She noticed that the girl was in her night clothes and robe. "She isn't even dressed and I wonder where little William is…," she muttered under her breath as she washed her dishes and looked out her window toward the alley. She went straight to the phone.

Mrs. White was startled to have Edward at her door with his little boy—early but long after he should have been at work. "Of course I can look after him for a while," she said. And when Edward returned in less than an hour to get the boy and take him to his mother's for the day—that was even more puzzling. "Where's Gertie today?" she wondered but did not ask. She would not get to discuss the events with Edward, but she discussed them with all her neighbors on Eleventh Street and some of those across the alley on Tenth Street. The coffee they shared, as well as the gossip, was strong and bitter.

Maria came to work for Mrs. Fergus two years ago when she returned to live in the Manor after Mayor Fergus died. She liked her job, especially when something different and exciting happened in the big quiet house. She knew to keep her tongue about the Fergus' affairs but Gertie wasn't a Fergus. Maria grew up in the west end. She knew the Neal family and the MacGregors, too—even attended Gertie and Edward's wedding. *Edward is beating up on Gertie*, she surmised. *That's what is happening and nobody can do anything about a thing like*

115

that. 'Poor thing' became the name Maria assigned to Gertie. Maria's brother worked at Laurel Feed Company along with Edward's best friend Johnny—a good avenue for a good story with lots of suppositions.

Jerry Hobson was working the concession booth at the track the day Gertie came in with William. "Well, I'll be! I reckon that is the first child I ever saw at the racetrack. I thought Gertie had better sense than come to the races much less bring her baby. You just never can tell about those church-goers." He told his mother what he saw. Mrs. Hobson was the organist at the Methodist Church.

Ziggy Camp tended his bar just up from the track on US 1. He was distressed to see Edward come in that afternoon with his little boy. This was no place for a child. *Why didn't Edward leave the boy home with his mother?* He wondered.

Edward told a wild story about finding William wandering around at the track. Edward was very drunk; the boy looked frightened. Ziggy called Charlie's Town Cab to hire a ride to get Edward and the boy home. It was worth the price to get that scared little boy out of his tavern.

"I'll drive you home, Edward. Don't need a cab." Mike Stein offered but Edward insisted on one more beer.

"Then ya can take us to Elevenst Streest." Edward was already slurring words and staggering, but everyone in the bar knew there was no use arguing with Edward when he is this far into his cups. The most they could do was keep an eye on the little boy until Edward finished the beer. Mike ordered a coke and waited. William sat quietly on the chair Ziggy brought for him.

Mike would not take William to Eleventh Street. Sam came in and took the young boy away from the drunken father without a whimper.

Sam bent down to look William in the eye with a big grin on his face. "Hi, my man. You ready to go with Uncle Sam?" In one sweeping motion, he took William to his chest as little arms circled his neck.

"Go." William exclaimed. Two strides took him to the door and out on US 1 in the fading sunlight.

Ziggy's hand was frozen in motion drying a glass, the patrons, drinking at the bar, sat motionless. Was there going to be an altercation between these brothers-in-law? Edward shrugged, drank his remaining beer, and said, "Mike, I'm most ready."

Alice Camp was astonished at the story Ziggy brought home that night. She called her sister who was Dan MacGregor's fiancée's best friend. The story was fourth hand by the time Dan heard it.

The next day, Mrs. White just happened to be looking out the front window when Gertie, Sam and William left 405 Eleventh Street with two suitcases and a little potty chair. Each *concerned* citizen did their part to put the story together for everyone else in the town.

Doc Smith knew that Gertie didn't have an accident. It was his practiced hand that felt the broken bones and knew it had been twisted. He could see the bruising at the wrist where it had been in a vice-like grip. She wasn't the first wife he mended and sent back to—God-knows-what fate. Gertie would get over the broken arm but his concern was the future of the very likable young woman. Unlike others gossiping in the town, he would not discuss Gertie's accident or fate.

🐦

Sam returned from Bear Creek to this little town and resumed his chores at the track on Sunday afternoon. Things had to be done each day for the animals. Fortunately, Sam was well liked and his friends picked up the slack when he left so suddenly. There were several notes tacked to the door above his locker. Most of them were work related but one was from his friend, Doc Smith.

> *Sam, I'll be at the track Monday.*
> *Want to talk to you.*
>
> *Doc*

Monday morning Doc Smith found Sam. He knew his way around the track and was a regular in the stands or back in the stables just jawing with the horse people. He was always hoping to get an inside tip. Sam assumed that was what this note was about. Doc often came to Sam to see if he concurred on some of the hottest information he gleaned. Sam was wrong today.

"Sam! I've been looking for you." Doc called across the grounds.

"Hey, Doc! How you doin'?"

Doc got right to the point. He wanted to talk about Gertie. "Sam, I've seen a lot of this husband-beating-on-wife thing in my practice. It is, without a doubt, the most frustrating thing to deal with…especially if there are children, and there usually are. I don't get to see the wife until a bone is broken, or worse. That means it has been going on for a while."

"She told me he hit her once, but I thought after William was born…" Sam was overcome with guilt. "I should have seen it."

"Gertie and Edward haven't been married that long. The years stretch out ahead." Doc paused to shake his head in frustration. "In this town it is whispered about, but the wife doesn't get the help she needs. Some of the most *upstanding* men in this town beat their wives. I just put them back together and send them home for more punishment. The wealthy ones even send the wife on a vacation if bruises are visible. Gertie will live in this hell to raise William… and most likely, have more children that will keep her grounded in a marriage that is slowly killing her." The doctor went on with words fired by his passion on this issue. "I hope she didn't go home to Edward. Where is she now?"

"She's at Bear Creek with my parents."

"That's good. These characters rarely beat again immediately. Remorse comes after injury but doesn't last long enough. I'm concerned about when she comes home."

Sam sat holding his head, finally facing Gertie's fate.

"There is one thing that might help your sister. I hesitate to suggest this but knowing you—you may have already thought… " He paused to gather his purpose. "Most wife beaters are cowards. I've known Edward all his life. He's a pretty boy and not much backbone. You'll have to take him on. Let him know what will happen to him if he dares to hurt your sister again. This will work to keep him in check for a while…. and when he takes time to think. It won't be magic. I hate to say this, but he will beat her again…because, when he is in a rage, nothing you do or say will stop him." Doc shook his head. "Believe me, I know—he will hurt her again."

"I agree, Doc. I already decided I would tear Edward a lick. Driving home from Baltimore yesterday, all I thought about was when and where. I'm looking forward to it. I think I'd kill him if he wasn't William's father."

"I know, Sam, I know." Doc eased, fearing that he might enrage Sam over the boundaries. "But, be careful. Edward can mess up a lot of lives. And if you seriously hurt him or worse, you could end up in jail because of that SOB."

"I have mentioned divorce to many of these women and it is a certain fate worse than possible beatings. First the husband does not want a divorce and the wife risks losing everything. She will not have the support in the community. Everyone will say—it is terrible what he's doing to her—behind her back. She is expected to make the most of it… even try harder not to infuriate him. What a crock of shit. I get so angry when I think about the corner your sister, and the other victims, are in."

"Thanks Doc." The two men shook hands, gripping tighter than usual.

"Let me know if I can help." He was gone, shaking his head and kicking dirt clods in disgust.

⚓

Sam was waiting by the back stoop at 405 Eleventh Street on Monday evening. He stepped out of the dusky shadow to greet Edward as he started up the steps.

"I've been waiting for you, Edward. Open the door." The two men stepped into the house and Edward flicked on the kitchen light.

"Just the person, I wanted to see," was Edward's reply. It didn't dawn on him that Sam was there to hurt him. "You know I can have you arrested for kidnapping William last week. You took—"

Sam took Edward by the collar, choking his words in his throat. He was lucky to draw a breath before his head bounced back from the blow Sam landed squarely on his right cheek. Edward's hands came up to grab Sam's sleeve trying to get his grip off his throat. Sam sent the second blow into Edward's face. His head bounced back again like a balloon bobbing on a string. Edward finally raised his right fist as if to hit Sam, when the third punch caught Edward over the eyebrow. The beaten man had no force in the only punch he landed on Sam's left arm. Sam lifted Edward with a strength coming from deep within, slightly tossed him upwards and put his fist into Edward's gut as it rose to Sam's eye level. It was like throwing a ball into the air and hitting it squarely with a bat. Edward fell to the floor drawn up into a heap. He was motionless. Sam reached down to get him to his feet and Edward started half crawling, half squirming to get away from Sam. But Sam persisted and set the trembling man on a chair. Sam wanted to look in Edward's eyes.

"That is payment for what you did to Gertie. If you ever hit her again, I will kill you. You better believe me, Edward. I mean it. Don't touch my sister. Remember, I'm not a coward like you. I'll do it!" Sam opened the door. He turned and in a lower tone, with precision, annunciated each word. "I... will... *kill*... you... " Sam lifted his strong hands to make sure Edward saw the threat. "... with my bear hands."

It took less than five minutes to give Edward new perspective and Sam sweet revenge.

When Edward went to the train on Tuesday, to the racetrack on Wednesday and all the local hangouts along US 1, his battered face became new gossip in town.

Chapter 15   1914

"Sam!" Edward's voice carried through the stable as Sam filled the last oat bucket. "Sam! You here?"

"Yeah, I'm here," was Sam's less than enthusiastic reply to his brother-in-law.

Edward moved to the stall where Sam's voice led him. "Gertie's doctor's appointment is tomorrow. She's got to come home."

"I know. I'm leaving as soon as I finish feeding. Bear Creek by noon and back before dark." Sam kept his voice civil, although he hated answering to Edward.

"I want to pay for the gas to bring my family home." Edward reached into his pocket as Sam turned his back and took two steps away.

"Keep your money. I don't need or want it."

"Thanks—"

"And, I don't want any thanks from you, either. I'm going for my sister and nephew. Your money or thanks have nothing to do with it." Sam was not going to soothe Edward or mend fences. He might as well know right now, how it was with his former friend.

When Sam turned back, Edward was gone.

❧

Sam put Gertie's suitcase in the car while William struggled to carry his own. "Will'um do it."

"Sure enough, my man. Ready for another ride in my car?"

William nodded enthusiastically.

In the last minutes, family members moved out of the kitchen. Gertie and Mama hung back, allowing them a few minutes alone.

"Come, sit with me before you go," was Mama's invitation as she poured a cup of coffee.

Anticipation of her return to Eleventh Street was taking its toll on Gertie. She was pale and worn out by the problems mounting before her. *I wish Mama had a magic answer,* she thought as she offered her mother a weak smile.

Mama added cream and a generous scoop of sugar to the cup as if those extravagances could soften Gertie's life.

"Doc Smith isn't going to take that cast off for weeks. How are you going to manage? William is a handful." She smiled thinking of the delightful boy, but yielded to a frown with her next thought. "Stay… so I can help."

"I can't… I wish we could, but I told Edward we would come home today, and I must be good to my word." Gertie's face darkened "It's important that Edward know I mean what I say."

"I am afraid for you, child. This is the only safe place for you… and William."

It was difficult territory but it needed to be crossed. How could she clear the stumbling blocks and say what she needed to her daughter? "Edward is not the one to be considered now—"

"Mama…," Gertie interrupted. "Edward will take William from me if I don't stay in Laurel. He's sure he can do that if I abandon him. That's his one threat, and the only one that frightens me." Gertie replaced the coffee cup on the saucer and took her mother's hands, reaching for understanding.

"How can you—"

"Wait, Mama—" Gertie was prepared. "—I have thought this out since I came here. I am going to Eleventh Street just long enough to get a job and move out with William. But, it will have to be in Laurel." She paused before yielding her other thoughts to words. "This broken arm is an inconvenience and constant reminder of what *I must* do." She raised the cast and placed it between them on the table.

Mama lifted her cup to drink and thought carefully of her next question. "So, you will live separated from Edward?"

"Not separated." Gertie took a deep breath. "Divorced."

Patricia MacGregor's heart lost its steady beat. "Divorced?" *Oh no, not divorce. Not in this family. Not in any family. Asunder, before God. Not Gertie.* She said it again. "Divorced?" Her body and soul twisted in knowledge of what this meant. The awful word made her shiver and spill the coffee she was trying to sip.

Gertie saw physical and emotional stress enveloping her mother. She rose to embrace her and gently take up the spill with a napkin. "It will be alright, Mama. *We* will be alright." She corrected her words to include William and more determination.

Their eyes met—Gertie's were set; her gaze unwavering. "This is what I have to do." She knelt down before her mother. Recollection swept over her as she bent down and remembered the trembling earth the day the tractor fell from the bridge. Gertie touched the floor with her good hand and held it for the smallest instant before looking again into her mother's eyes.

"My marriage is over. The only sure protection William and I will have from Edward is divorce. He cannot have *any* claim on me. I can control his time with William and make sure it is quality and worthwhile time." She placed both hands on her mother's knees. "This decision is over two years coming. These years with Edward have been some of the highest highs and lowest lows imaginable. I thought I could keep Edward happy but it is not in him. He has problems that I can't fix. Problems that make him lash out."

Gertie rose to her feet. Patricia MacGregor remained seated and in that moment, Gertie saw that she was no longer her mother's little girl. She was upright, strong, and most importantly, ready to take care of herself and her son.

"William will *never* see me damaged by Edward again." She squared her shoulders. "Never." She walked to the window and looked off into space as if she stood alone in the universe. "If I have learned anything since William was born it is this: Edward will rain down violence again and again. No matter how contrite he is, it happens... over and over again." She closed her eyes and saw Edward's face. "Mama, it is not easy to leave Edward, but I do not have a choice. I never thought he would break my bones or hurt William." She turned back to look across the room where her mother had not moved a muscle. Gertie pulled the cast to her chest. "I was wrong about the bones." She lifted the cast again in defiance. "I cannot... " Her sobs took her breath away. "... risk being wrong about him hurting William."

Time and space dissolved. Reality descended. Gertie cried with total abandonment. "Oh, Mama. I wanted to tell you all this without crying."

Patricia MacGregor girded herself for what Gertie was saying. She let her own tears flow. Gertie's hands, wet from catching tears, held tight to her mother's.

"Go ahead, child. Cry all you need to."

"I want to be strong," she sobbed, "not cry like a baby."

"Here," Mama pressed the familiar fragranced hankie into Gertie's wet hand. "We will cry mother's tears together. They're not tears of weakness; they're tears of love. And they're tears for what we know we must do. Cry when you must… and dry them when you must."

Gertie was finished with crying. She regained her composure so she could leave her mother with a strong image. "Mama, I can do this. Now that I have decided that Edward can't hurt me anymore I can go on." She paused, raised her arm, and tapped the hard, rigid surface of the cast. "Never again. William will not grow up in violence. And, I will not live in it either." Conviction was on her face and in her voice.

"Divorce." Gertie dried her last tear with Mama's hankie.

"Not separation." She softened her countenance.

"Not on again off again living with Edward."

"Divorce," she said again, softly to convince her mother and herself.

She walked back to her mother's side to gather warmth and strength from her presence. "Mama, my love for Edward hurts too much. It hurts more than the breaking of this bone."

"Oh, my wonderful girl! I love you and hurt for you, too. I wish there were some way to keep you here."

"No, Mama… I must go."

"I understand. Don't forget, you are not alone, Gertie. Never. We are family. You and William won't be alone."

"We'll come as often as possible. Knowing you and Papa and the rest of the family are here, means so much. Sam will look out for us."

"Without asking, you have a home here—always."

"Mama, fetch the cameo for me. I may need to sell it." *I hope not,* she thought.

The farewell hug was long and strong.

❧

Normal family life could not resume for Gertie and Edward on Eleventh Street. She and William slept downstairs; Edward upstairs.

Fear gripped her on the first night back under the same roof with him. Gertie thought she was strong enough, but fear was a new emotion. Fear burst like a volcano when the lights went off. Fear robbed her sleep in the nights when she heard Edward's footsteps on the stairs. Fear was a stalking dragon when Edward was late from work and possibly at the tavern. Fear was a disease taking her sleep, her appetite, and her energy. Most of all, she feared for her child. And, that was a fear she could not live with.

Edward recovered from Sam's beating, and had a *fear* to live with now, too. At the most unlikely times Sam's words came back to him. *I will kill you*. Edward did not doubt it—not for one minute. It became a recurring nightmare. When he awoke from Sam invading his dreams he was angry with Gertie and wanted to tear her apart. Edward's own violence was terrorizing him. That scared him most. For the first time in his life he was concerned about his self-control. Edward felt cornered. Life in the same house became impossible in a matter of weeks.

Edward vented his rage by slamming doors or kicking chairs.

One night a tapping on the parlor door awakened Gertie.

"Gertie, can I come in?" He asked in a quiet nighttime voice. She pretended not to hear him and prayed silently.

"Gertie, I just want to talk." She listened for his hand on the door knob. The sound of it turning made her heart skip a beat.

"Gertie." In the darkness she could hear the door knob turn back as it was released. Her breath went out. Edward retraced his steps up the stairs. She listened for the squeak on the third step from the top. She drew another breath. Gertie got out of bed and touched William for reassurance and courage.

The next day it took her two hours to install a bolt on the door. Gertie had to get out of this corner, and take her baby boy to a better place.

Their life included tense courtesy and good meals, dutifully prepared, but nurturing was lost. The atmosphere included the constant worry about a storm and the possibility of a damaging lightning strike.

"How much longer are you going to go on with this, Gertie? Pretending you'll never want your husband again." He pointed at his chest and smiled the old enticing smile. "Our best times may be behind us but what about the years we have ahead?"

"*We* do not have years ahead of *us*, Edward. The sooner you realize that, the better for you, for me, and for William."

"This will be our *arrangement*." Edward answered waving his arm to include the kitchen, parlor/bedroom and stairs.

"No… no *arrangement here*." Gertie moved her own arm.

"No?" Edward put his hands in his pocket as a form of control. "Tell me, how do you plan to live apart and support yourself and William? He has a home here. Where will you go? Not Bear Creek. Don't even think it. My son will live in Laurel."

"I understand that. I will get a job and an apartment here." Gertie responded with calm and conviction, which she had to feign.

"Good luck with that, meanwhile, how about bean soup and cornbread for dinner tomorrow?" He was finished with this unpleasant talk about their problems.

Edward was wrong about one thing; Gertie's sexual desires did not bring her to him. She never came to his bed in the middle of the night as he predicted and fantasized. In fact, it was his desires that brought him to the parlor door. He discovered the bolt lock and took his anger and frustrations back upstairs.

Gertie heard Edward retreat up the staircase. She heard him kick the wall and slam the door. There would be no sleep in the parlor except the gentle slumber of the innocent one in the crib. Gertie went to William, and put her hand on his gently rising and falling chest. The warm little body gave her a measure of comfort even in her dark place.

Soon. Very soon. She promised herself and her baby boy. Her resolve glared in the black room.

❦

Edward was gradually showing interest in changing the arrangement. Gertie was as determined as ever to get the divorce. Not unlike the day Edward walked away from his family on Tenth Street seven years ago, he as easily turned the corner and looked to his renewed freedom from responsibility and answering to anyone.

Despite prejudice against it, as soon as possible Gertie filed for a divorce. It was good that Mama and Papa did not still live in Laurel and suffer the stigma among their friends. Sam, Dan, Liddy, and Lon offered support—financial, moral, and tangible. They were the only ones who did.

I'll sell the cameo to pay them back, if I have to. Aloud she repeated, "If I have to."

Two weeks later, she had news and waited on the porch to tell Edward. He smiled at her sitting there, waiting for him. The breeze caught her curls and lifted her skirt from her knees. He had a silent wish. *Is today the day Gertie comes to her senses?*

Gertie saw his smile as she drew her dress tight to her legs. His pleasant demeanor took her back to the days she waited for his smile as he climbed Fergus Hill. That was a lifetime ago and a slight tug pulled at her heart for something that was gone.

"Edward, Mrs. Pole has an apartment for rent. Two rooms and shared bath. We'll be over on Tenth Street, 403."

It was not the greeting and news he wished for, but he did not give himself away.

"Really?" He changed the subject. "What's for dinner?"

"I asked her for it." Gertie refused to be sidetracked. "Mrs. Pole's apartment will be perfect for me and William."

"And, how are you going to pay for it? You figure that out and then we'll talk about it." He went past her to the door. "Let's eat."

After a satisfying meal, he was not totally negative about the apartment. "I shouldn't give you anything. William has a perfectly good home on Eleventh Street, but," he leaned forward slightly to emphasize his terms. "I'll help with one half as long as you live at Mrs. Pole's next door to Mom and Poppa. I'll ask Mom if she will keep William while you work. Do you have a job?"

"Not yet. I'm looking."

"You have the cameo." Edward did not know its actual value, but believed Gertie would use it would support them, even give her the means to live apart without a job. It never occurred to him that she would hesitate to sell it.

❧

The date finally came for Gretta Mae MacGregor Neal and Edward William Neal to appear before Judge Marshall. With affidavits from Doctor Smith, Mrs. Fergus, and family members, Edward did not contest. He wanted the whole thing over. It was handled discreetly in the judge's chambers as requested by Elizabeth Amsterdam, sister-in-law to the judge.

"Edward," Gertie called to him as they left the judge's chambers, "William is your son. I promise I won't do anything to keep him from you...unless you hurt him. Then..." She shook her head, cutting off the sentence. "He will be close, playing on Tenth Street."

"Not that close—I'm moving from Eleventh Street."

"Well, you know where we will be." She did not ask his plans.

Gertie spent the next few weeks looking for a job. There were none for her in Laurel. The merchants, many fellow church members, would not go against the community feelings and put Gertie Neal, *divorcee,* in their stores. So she headed to Baltimore and got a sales position in the Hecht May Company cosmetics department. It made a long day, including bus commuting, but she could support William if she was careful with her money. And the cameo would remain safe—at least for now.

On the day she and William moved from Eleventh Street to Tenth Street, Clay Neal came to see her. He knocked on the door and accepted the invitation to come in, but made only two steps into the apartment. He declined the offer to sit.

"Gertie, Mary will take care of William every day as long as you live next door. It is a good arrangement and Edward can come whenever he wants to see his son. He did not make his life easy; your divorce may make yours even harder, but William is safe. You are safe, too. Have no fear. I will watch over you."

She could only stare at him in shock. She never expected Poppa Clay to be her protector.

Chapter 16   1915

Sunday was a glorious day. Spring pushed the temperature up to a balmy 58 degrees. Gertie was up before the sun today—awake early for no reason, except it was Edward's birthday and the date and the remembrance took her sleep away. *Is he happy on his birthday?* She wondered… and, surprised herself with her next thought. *I am.* "Alone for over a year and sometimes it seems forever." Each holiday, anniversary, birthday made Gertie count the weeks, months, years since her divorced life began.

The cup of coffee warmed her hands. *Maybe not happy, but contented,* she conceded. Gertie began counting her blessings. The first on the list was William and the counting went on and on.

The morning sun broke the horizon and streamed in her window. "And, I am thankful for this day,"

"Rise and shine, William. It's a beautiful day."

William was less impressed with the abundance of sunshine and the proclaimed beauty. He scooted down in the bed, unwilling to relinquish the dark warmth.

Gertie pulled on his big toe.

"As the big toe goes, so shall the boy." she shouted to her son. "If you get up right away, I'll have time to make pancakes before church. We are going to Great Grandmother's after church. What do you think of them apples?" She tugged on the toe once more.

"O-o-o K. OK, Gertie. Let go of my toe."

❧

Gertie no longer took her son to Sunday school. She felt uncomfortable and unwanted in the class with her peers. William was just as happy to spend one hour each week in the worship service instead of two hours if his mother included Sunday school. Church had been a challenge for Gertie since the divorce, but she was resolved to go every week. It was just another of those things she set her mind to—and did.

She would never forget the first choir rehearsal following the divorce decree. Mrs. Stevens told Gertie that she would not be doing the duet she was rehearsing with Burton. It was apparent, as every eye was diverted, that the choir knew of the decision and its reasons before that night's rehearsal. Mrs. Stevens' words came out in a well-rehearsed stream.

"Gertie the duet with Burton will be done by Ruth. I'm sure you understand. Take your place there and let Ruth move to the front." The words rolled off her tongue like hot bullets. She seemed to sputter as she tried to get them out before they burnt her tongue. They still had enough power to burn Gertie. The deed was done.

She turned her gaze away from Gertie, pointed to a seat in the second row of altos, and addressed the choir. "Open your music; let's begin wit the anthem. Are you ready?" She asked the organist.

"You want me to understand?" was Gertie's only comment as she gathered her purse, walked down the steps, through the chancel, and passed the gleaming cross and communion plates.

Nothing in the girl, who was raised by William and Patricia MacGregor, *could* understand. Nothing would allow her to smile and make everyone feel good about this injustice. Nothing in her eyes or stance would admit to the Christians in the choir that she was guilty of anything or that she needed to take a step to the rear. They'd known her all of her life. They'd attended Sunday school and church picnics together. And, they were the ones who could deliver this cut into her soul. A diagram was just drawn of what her life would be in this small town. If she could be treated like this in her church choir, what could she expect from everyone else in this town? These thoughts whirled about, but they didn't have time to settle in her brain.

It was a long walk to the door of the sanctuary. Gertie listened for footsteps or maybe a familiar voice to come after her. Maybe Emily or even Ruth to say, "Don't go, Gertie. It's a mistake." The only sound was her own footsteps and the firm *click* of the door latch behind her.

Gertie began the walk home, glad for the cool moist air softening her clothes around her. As if in sympathy the skies began a cold rain and each drop punctured her skin. She cried bitter tears with every step but the tears lost their distinction as they blended with rain on her face. *I am the same person I have always been,* she thought. "What have I done to deserve this?" she asked the cold rain.

She suffered pangs of self -pity and chastised herself as Mama would. "Give it up, Gertie." She told herself. The rain pounded her head as her thoughts pounded her brain. She claimed her reason again. *I couldn't live with Edward and give William a safe home.* "That is what I have done." she said aloud.

Gertie stopped at the corner and turned to look back at her church. The beautiful stained glass window glowed in the semi-darkness. The walk to the mahogany doors was inviting. The steeple with its wet shine, pointed heavenward. "Emily!" she shouted and took two steps back toward the place where her best friend was. "Emily," she whispered. "Please come get me. Aren't we friends?"

Gertie waited but the big beautiful wooden door did not open. No one came out of the church to the cold place on the sidewalk where Gertie stood pleading in the rain. She and Emily were not friends any longer. A new pain coursed her body and joined the old ones that resided there.

Instinctively, she pushed back her wet curls and tried to dry her eyes. With both hands she rubbed her face as if washing off a mask that hid who she was. *I'm Gertie—always have been—always will be. I'm just not married any more.*

Looking back at the church, Gertie wanted to ask Mrs. Stevens and each member of the choir –"Who, exactly… who are you?" Her question banged on the closed door.

Gertie's steps resumed homeward. Her mind closed down and her concentration centered on the cold rain. But, that exercise did not last long. Soon her thinking returned to her problem of being not married but, not single. *Not married, but not single.* Gertie smiled crookedly at this contradiction floating in her brain. Once more she realized how very different she was from other girls her age. They all wanted to be married, or if not, they wanted the active single life looking for a husband. *I don't want either.* "I have a vision of marriage that I hope you never know," she confessed.

The tears were gone and a new realization came. It was hard to recognize prejudice. She never practiced it in her life, but at this terrible moment, she knew that she was a victim of prejudice. She knew that it hurt very much, and the cut was deep, but bloodless.

Gertie was getting cold and there were three more blocks to go. She broke into a sprint and opened her mouth to catch the rain to soothe her dry throat. The cold wet run up Montgomery Street was bitter and long. It taxed her strength, yet it was nothing compared to her walk out of the choir loft.

"What is a divorcee?" She asked herself and realized she had never used the word before.

"Divorcee!" she shouted. The sound of her own voice made her stop running. She panted, drew a shallow breath and hissed, "Divorcee," with attitude and condemnation. It sounded just as she imagined others were saying the word.

As always when facing a problem, she began looking for a solution—a way to regain her place, her favor, her happiness in this town. She didn't know that she could do nothing to change the problem because it was not her problem—it belonged to the town and the people who lived up and down the streets where she walked. The only fear that gripped her stomach was that William would experience the same unkind rejection she experienced tonight. It left her with an uneasy feeling and a desire to hurry to their little apartment on Tenth Street to be with him and to prepare him.

Sleep wasn't easy that night; she tossed and turned. In her dreams she saw the word 'DIVORCEE', painted on mailboxes and on street signs. It was in a thousand different places, in every conceivable color. She awoke in a sweat and shaking as she dreamt that William was writing *Divorcee* all over his homework. She must have called out because the next thing she heard was his little voice.

"Gertie, wake up! You're dreamin', Momma."

❧

On the first Sunday after leaving the choir she took a seat in the front pew with William's hand firmly in hers so he would know to be on his best behavior and not say a word. Although Gertie was making a statement of new resolve in church today, she did not want to take anyone else's seat, knowing how folks like to have their regular places. No one ever sat on the front pew. Today Gertie and William took those seats. As the choir filed in from the side entrance, each one noticed Gertie and William. She sought every eye and did not turn away from any. Rev. Harrison nodded and she nodded her head in response. She sat with a warm smile on her face and embraced the new place she took in the church. Her faith gave her the courage she needed to stand up to everyone in the choir, church, and community... at least on Sunday mornings.

The choir did not sing their best; they were a bit off key. Gertie knew it was not her absence; it was something else that diminished the joy and perfection usually projected from the choir loft.

✍

The world turned and turned and 1915 did not bring any changes for the girl who had become a divorced woman. She struggled with the notion that she could prove herself again in this community. But, once the community decided that she belonged over *there*—a short distance away, far enough for everyone to feel comfortable—there was nothing she could do. She had to live in Laurel as part of her divorce agreement. For the first time, she knew it was a sentence she had to serve. Gertie had a new identity in her hometown and it was a label that everyone saw before they remembered going to school with her, walking familiar streets together, or joining voices in the choir.

"Tish-tish," was the kindest remarks uttered just out of her ear range. Pity was not any easier to bear.

No matter how proper and careful Gertie was in her demeanor, she was a divorcee. Gertie was not the only one trying to understand what that meant. Women could not decide if she was a married or a single woman. They had no definition and therefore Gertie could not fit in their circles, especially if they included husbands, fiancées or boyfriends. And, Gertie was raising a child—living proof that she was a sexually experienced woman without a husband. Was there anything more threatening than that?

Gertie was doomed to fail in the social arena; she was living an unacceptable independent life.

At school meetings attended by parent couples no one sat alongside her. Friends looked the other way as she passed them on the street or in stores. Gertie never challenged their averted eyes.

Her efforts to secure a position in a business on Main Street were the subject of gossip.

"I couldn't have *her* wait on me."

"I heard she applied at Sachmore's Clothiers."

"Mannie Sachmore won't hire her. Sadie told me."

"I'll bet she regrets what she did to Edward."

The town was forgetting the gossip that blanketed from Main Street to Fergus Hill when she wore a cast and William was rescued from Ziggy Camp's Tavern.

Gertie was forced to look for a job in Baltimore, thus entering the man's world—working, commuting, striving to advance. In that arena, men had to be very careful not to cross the lines drawn by their women. The seat next to her on the bus was always empty.

The Divorcee was a threat to the accepted norms in this community. Gertie could not waste time and energy trying to understand it or fight it—she had a child to raise.

❦

The church, full of flowers and candles, was crowded for Palm Sunday. In the tradition of Easter season, hope and halleluiahs seemed to fill the sanctuary from ceiling to the waving palms along the chancel rail. William was smartly dressed in short pants and high socks; Gertie looked lovely in her yellow dress. She hummed quietly with the organ prelude as they walked down the center aisle and took their regular place—front pew, under the lectern. Turning her head slightly to the left, she could see Grandmother in her usual pew, halfway back, on the center aisle, east side.

Grandmother smiled knowingly at the odd couple—mother and son.

The sermon of Christian benevolence was well received by the congregation as was the beautiful music attributed to Mrs. Stevens and her choir. After shaking the pastor's hand, she and William turned to find Grandmother and walk the block to her home.

William was the first to spot his father's car parked on the street in front of the house. "Look, look, Daddy is here!" He broke out running.

There he was—a tall version of the boy—handsome, smiling and dressed as sharply as ever. He could take the breath from most women.

Gertie remembered, but did not allow herself to be moved by the sight of his square handsome face, wavy hair combed straight back, or his deep blue eyes.

Edward smiled for the only family he had. He lifted his son and swung him around. "Good morning. How lucky to see you all together," he greeted Gertie and Grandmother. "Am I in time to eat?"

His happy infectious mood was contagious.

"Yes. Give us a chance to put it on the table. William, your ball is in the foyer basket." Grandmother invited father and son to play. "Gertie, let's get these men fed."

The ladies removed their hats and began setting out the food, which had been prepared earlier. A party atmosphere developed to the happy sounds of William throwing and chasing the ball. Grandmother was delighted to have William, Edward, and Gertie together, but she did not pretend they were a united family. These were her dearest ones, but her heart's desire did not change that they were separate in their lives.

Lunch was delicious and conversation stimulating, but limited to William's world. Although the threatened war in Europe was the most popular topic of conversation across the United States, it would not be at her table this Sunday.

"Daddy, how fast does the train go? Faster than your car?"

Edward answered the many questions and spun yarns. His undivided attention was William's. Today, he did not break up the visit to hurry to something else. Gertie was the one who moved to end the visit because Grandmother was tiring.

"William, put your ball away and gather your things. It's time to go."

Edward got his coat and walked over to Gertie. "William's a great kid. I'm glad I got to see you today." He touched her arm without noting the surprised look on her face. "Take care. Bye."

Gertie was mystified by this almost fond farewell.

"Give your father a hug." Because she wasn't sure what was happening, she turned attention to William. "And, Great Grandmother, too."

"Bye, Daddy. When can I ride in your car?"

"Next time, son."

Edward did not offer to take them to Tenth Street; he knew Gertie would refuse. Before the car turned the corner and went from sight,

Edward turned and waved again, looking at both Gertie and William. He did not flash his famous smile.

Edward and his shiny automobile were gone.

"We had a wonderful time. I know you're tired. Will you rest now?"

"Yes. Tired but such a happy tired." Grandmother walked Gertie to the gate.

"I'd better get going; William is getting ahead of me. I'm happy, too. William had such a good time with Edward. We'll be at Bear Creek for Easter. See you the Sunday after. We love you."

"I love you, too." After her lingering hug, she reached in her apron pocket. "Here is a letter Edward left for you. He left me one, too. I can't imagine what it is all about or why he waited to the last minute to give them to me. He could've given this to you."

Gertie followed William up the sidewalk while opening the envelope and reading.

> *Gertie,*
>
> *I've joined the army. I leave Tuesday for Ft Bragg, North Carolina and don't know when I will be home again. There are a couple of things I want you to know.*
> *I am hoping that the Army will help me. I don't know why I always seem to be hitting someone. There must be something wrong with me. I did not marry Dora although she was still willing after I hit her last month. I am thinking maybe the Army will be able to use me before I mess up really bad.*
> *William is all I have now. He is a good boy and you have done well by him. I set it up so the Army sends something for him every month. It won't be much, but it will be more regular than I have done in the past. If I go overseas, I will send all my pay. He is my beneficiary...just in case.*
> *You take care of yourself and William.*
> *Edward*
>
> *PS I never hurt William, I am glad of that.*

Gertie stopped in her tracks to reread the note.

"Freeze," she shouted to William. He froze his footsteps, joining the game to keep him from getting too far ahead on the sidewalk. Her slow, deliberate steps toward him allowed her to face her mixed emotions. Edward was going away and she didn't know how she felt about it. She couldn't conclude how she felt about him going away but she knew immediately that she did not want any harm to come to him.

"The Army," she said aloud. And then she prayed. "Dear God, Keep Edward safe. Let this be in your plan for him. Bless, protect, lead, and keep him. Amen."

"Un-freeze!" They continued toward home.

She walked along with her thoughts. *Life has not been what Edward and I expected—not at all.*

Chapter 17   1917

Before going in the army, Edward came at the most unexpected times. Now his visits were rare—only when he got a three-day pass. Weeks would pass and then suddenly his shiny Buick coup would be parked at the Neal's.

"Your father is here," Gertie announced and William came running. It was *circus time* with high excitement.

"Something for my boy." Edward flipped a shiny dime in the air and William caught it.

"Thanks. Can we go get a soda at Tasker's?"

"Next time, Son, I don't have much time." The visit passed quickly for William and then his father was gone. Try as he might he could not keep the excited feeling going for the small coin in his palm. Sometimes the dime got lost before it could be spent.

❧

Three long months passed without a visit or a letter from Edward. Gertie tried to ignore the lapse but when she saw William with his treasure box, re-reading old letters, she was angered.

Gertie looked at the calendar—March 10, 1917. *Hard to believe William is seven,* she thought as she walked into his bedroom humming *Happy Birthday.*

William was awake, lying motionless on his pillow.

"I want Daddy to come home for my birthday. That's the only thing I want, Gertie."

"You know the army tells Daddy what he can do. He'll come if he can."

"No letter, no card, no Daddy!" William was showing a temper as he pulled the pillow from his head and hurled it across the room. While her son showed his temper, Gertie contained hers on the same issue. *He could have sent a card...something.* She understood William's feelings and did not chastise him for his anger.

"Mom Neal baked you a cake and I'm sure you will have another one at Bear Creek. How many boys get two parties?" She ruffled his hair.

They walked across the yard where assorted Neal family members were waiting for him to blow the candles, eat cake, and open gifts. *Two cakes, no Daddy*, he thought as he blew the candles and wished that his father would suddenly appear.

❧

Playing in the sun had burnished William's chestnut hair with golden highlights. He was on the verge of moving from cute to handsome. His chin was definitely squared like Edward's, but his eyes and forehead were from the MacGregor clan. William was well on his way to being a tall boy, already inches taller than his classmates, even the girls. His curls were faithfully smoothed down each morning but found their own way by mid-morning. One curl fell across his forehead and he threatened to pull the tuff out. Gertie knew that if his hair was combed straight back a wave formed above his brow just like his father's. She combed it with a part. His slim young body was marred with skinned knees and elbows from his dedication to sports. William was determined to excel in everything. He played to win and didn't expect to lose—ever. Gertie was nervous watching him play because he would risk life and limb to catch a ball or beat a tag. The first time she saw him fall over a fence to catch a fly ball, she was mortified. Running the bases was even worse—sliding in the dirt was a life or death situation, too. William ran with a most excruciating look painted on his face. It was as if tensing his face muscles could help him run faster and win. Gertie did not want William know she feared him hurting himself. In rare moments when he allowed a long caress, she could feel his strength and zest for everything.

"Letter from Daddy?" William asked every day.

"Not today."

"I keep thinking you might forget to give it to me."

"Now, William, you know that would never happen."

He knew. He just hoped there was some other reason he didn't get one—other than his father did not send one.

Edward had written four letters and called his son three times in the past year. William wanted letters. The phone conversations were gone when they were over. The letters could be read again and again. William wanted letters to put in the box where he kept his special things. Each and every day, he continued to hope for a letter.

"Get some paper from my desk. You can write to Daddy again tonight."

School work was much too easy for the boy. He went at the tasks that he liked the least, accomplishing and putting them aside first. Math was a breeze and he could not find the challenge.

"Just wait, William, it won't always be so easy," Gertie cautioned.

A spelling list was copied and put away; he was ready for that exam. William was an excellent reader. He knew how to read before starting school. He and Gertie included reading every evening. His studies got easier and he continued to wait for mathematics to challenge him.

William's after school routine allowed him almost three hours before his mother came home from work. After Mom Neal's fresh cookies or hot cinnamon rolls, William wandered the neighborhood looking for his pals and maybe a ballgame. On rainy afternoons, William went to the book shelves in his grandmother's home.

"Gertie, did you ever read Huckleberry Finn?"

"Yes."

"Oh, geez, I was going to read some of it to you tonight."

"Please do. I'd love it, especially the part about Jim and the raft."

"That's the part I like, too." He read; she listened. "Will I ever see the Mississippi? Is it as big and powerful as Huck says?"

"I'm sure it is. Someday, William... maybe someday, you will see for yourself."

She ruffled his hair and joined his reverie. Gertie and William were travelers on the pages of his books.

❧

Sam arrived right on time on Saturday to pick up Gertie and William for the weekend at Bear Creek. As the years passed Sam came first with Nora, his bride, then with Sam, Jr. and Elwood. It was a happy riotous group. Gertie and William could not wait to climb in the car for the weekly excursion.

"Did you bring sandwiches, Sis?"

"Sure. I know the admission price to this automobile."

The three children began their chatter as the adults caught up with their news.

"I swa—nee, Gertie, is that you? William, is this your mother?" Gertie was sporting a new hair-do, and Sam took the first opportunity to tease her. "Is this the new you, Sis?"

"How'd you get the nerve? I've thought of letting my hair down but I'm afraid," was all Nora could say.

"I loved wearing it down when I was in school. I see women in magazines without those buns and knots. Why is it just for girls? I'm even thinking of getting a bob-cut."

The new hair-do gave Gertie a carefree air. She laughed and tossed her curls around her shoulders. Even her brother was taken by the change in his sister who had become so matronly lately.

"I like it. If you like it, Nora, go ahead—let your hair down."

"Gertie says she might get a bob-cut. Should I do that, too?"

Sam blinked a time or two. "Let's not get carried away." He changed the subject quickly. "It has been so hot. The water at Bear Creek is probably warm enough for swimming. Not always the case in late May."

Decoration Day weekend promised to be full of events and good food—as always.

Little had changed at Bear Creek through the years. Mama and Papa aged, but not much. Patsy and Shirley were growing up fast and the list of grandchildren was getting longer.

Gertie was happiest on the weekends when she saw Liddy. This Saturday afternoon, she was sitting on the end of the pier watching the children in the water when Liddy approached over the back lawn.

"I brought Marcie. Didn't think you had enough swimmers to watch."

"Oh, Liddy!" Gertie jumped to her feet to give a warm hug to her sister and moved over to make room. "I'm so glad to see you."

"How are you doing?"

"It has been a hard week. Edward's grandmother is failing. I'm going there several evenings after work. William falls asleep at the Neals. Some days, we have only the mornings together—except for Bear

Creek. I like lifeguard duty and the chance to be with the kids." She turned her attention back to the swimmers and blew her whistle. "Too far. Everybody back!" She waved her arm toward shore and waited for her directions to be obeyed. "Good."

"How long has Mrs. Amsterdam been ill?"

"All last week. She was upset and didn't want to be the reason we would miss coming here this holiday weekend. She wouldn't settle down until I said I would go. I try not to worry, but at eighty-four, she is fragile. Her body is failing but her mind and heart are as strong as ever. Such a lady and such a wonderful support for me and William. She has done so much for us. There are times when I feel she is my only friend in Laurel. She was Edward's best gift to me...other than William."

"Let me know if I can do anything."

"I will, but there is nothing. She is comfortable and cared for. Mom Neal is spending every day with her."

"You still haven't told me how you are, Gertie."

"Look at me, I'm fine. New hair-do."

"I see and I like it." She put her arm around Gertie's shoulders. "Sis, really, tell me about *you*!"

"There is nothing to tell. I work. I take care of William. I work. I take care of William."

They were interrupted by a call from the house. "Liddy, its time."

"I promised Mama I would get the chicken ready to fry. I tell you what—after things quiet down tonight, let's meet in the parlor like we used to on Fergus Hill. Girl talk."

"Good plan. I'll bring a decadent treat."

After two dinner seatings at the big table, all were fed. It took a while for the big house to settle down, but finally the children slept, a pinochle game was underway, and Gertie and Liddy stole off to the parlor, closing the door behind them.

"How are things in Elkridge?" Gertie started the conversation, taking the focus off herself.

Liddy felt a little guilty recounting her near perfect life with Lon, compared to the life she knew her sister was leading. "We are fine. Lon has his greenhouse going. He is propagating chrysanthemums and selling them to landscapers. He loves it, spending all his spare time there. The children are so grown up."

Gertie listened, but her mind wandered from her sister's words to the room. It held the exact furniture from Fergus Hill. The same curtains, reworked, hung at the windows. Mama's sewing basket was beside the south one. Liddy looked the same—hardly changed.

I've changed. I'm not the same. The impending requirement that she open up to Liddy sent a shiver down her spine. *I don't want to do this.*

"Let's talk about you." Liddy was going to insist.

Gertie said nothing. Silence and the blank look on her sister's face alarmed Liddy.

"Gertie, are you OK?"

"Yes." Gertie came back to the moment and took a piece of fudge, which delayed talking for another moment or two."William and I are fine. We really are. He loves school and does well in all subjects. Edward's mother takes good care of him. In fact, she spoils him, but he handles it well and seems to understand our unusual family and the ties to Edward's family next door. He's an amazing boy."

"Wonderful. I'm happy to know William is doing well...but, we came in here to talk about you." Liddy took the plate of candy, set it aside, and required Gertie to look into her eyes. "Sis?" Her voice was pleading and could not be denied.

"Liddy... dear Liddy. I don't talk about my life, except in terms of William. That's all I have. What can I say if you don't let me talk about William?"

"Do you have friends to confide in?"

"No." Gertie's answer was short and sure. There was no weakness and no tears.

"No? Not one?" Liddy couldn't believe her gregarious sister had no friends.

Gertie moved her head back and forth.

"Emily?" Liddy questioned.

"No, not even Emily."

"Emily's not your friend anymore? You were so close."

"I know...but not now. Emily couldn't side with me against Edward and couldn't figure how to stay my friend. In the Neal way, she distanced herself from our problems. When I divorced, she wasn't strong enough to stand apart from the town's condemnation." Gertie paused. This was the first time she tried to explain what happened—to anyone or to herself. "When I was pushed aside by the choir, Emily let me walk out of the church hurt and belittled. But, she had already stopped being my friend. I just saw it clearly that night. I was angry... but what does that get me? Emily's married and lives in Richmond."

"Gertie, I'm so sorry."

"It feels good to talk about it. Emily rarely comes to Laurel. I've learned that the Neals don't face problems and Emily is, after all, a Neal. Just like Edward in some ways—turn and go another way." Gertie paused to think. "I'm not angry any longer. No time for that."

"Who do you talk to?"

"Sam."

"But there are things you can't talk to your brother about."

"You're right. I've decided not to open the box that holds my doubts, fears, and feelings. I can't afford to." Gertie spoke in a dry monotone. "I simply can't. I'm holding everything together and it takes all my focus and energy."

Liddy sat on the arm of her sister's chair, caressing her shoulders. Gertie could not look at her. She stared straight ahead and began talking without animation. "My life is lonely. After William goes to bed the hours until I go to bed are endless. It's a solitary existence... a day by day struggle." Gertie responded to Liddy's kiss in her hair by leaning into it. "The day I realized marrying Edward was a mistake—I told Mama, 'it's my life and I'll live it.' That's what I am doing... as well as I can."

She took a deep breath. "It would be nice to believe there is something more for me out there but I've got to be honest—there's nothing. It takes all my time and energy to provide for William and me. I'm an outcast in Laurel. Divorce is not accepted in the churches and therefore—no place. No one wants to admit they even know me, much less be my friend. I'll accept that until I can make a better life for us. Meanwhile, I thank God every day that I have a good, healthy son who is wise beyond his years and a natural scholar. I am very careful not to require too much from him. He has his childhood—I make sure of that."

"Gertie—"

"Liddy," she interrupted, "don't try to say something to make it better—you can't. That's why I didn't want this conversation."

An unusual quiet settled in the parlor while each sister did some sorting.

"Out there," Gertie pointed to the parlor door, "... are all the wonderful people who would like to make things right for me. All *you*, and all *they* can do, is be the family you've always been. You have to believe, as I do, that I can do it."

Gertie hugged her sister and whispered in her ear."Believe in me, so I can, too."

She saw Liddy's eyes filling."Whoa! No tears. Crying is in the past. We are at Bear Creek; it is a laughing, loving, and living time." She pulled her mood up and put on a cheerful face.

"Look at William. He's the inspiration for whatever I need to do." Gertie smiled. "Give me another piece of fudge—chocolate may be the only answer." She rose from the chair and took Liddy's hand. "Let's go check on the card game. I'll bet Papa is beating them all. No one can bid a hand like he can. Bring the fudge, I'm tempted to eat it all, but it will be best for my waistline if we share."

Liddy followed her amazing little sister with a heavy heart.

Sam looked up as they rejoined the family. "I was wondering who stole the fudge."

🍂

Life on Tenth Street was much quieter than at Bear Creek. Mom Neal became very attached to William. She saw Edward in him and began doing for him as she had done for her first son many years before. William's favorite treats were baked and special likes were catered to. She looked forward to his arrival after school each day and missed him terribly on Saturday and Sunday when he went to Bear Creek. William was allowed to choose what he wanted to do after changing clothes and eating his snack. She never required him to do schoolwork. Her permissiveness was apparent to William and to Clay. When Clay asked the boy to do a chore, Mary quickly stepped in, sending him out to play. But, when William had the chance, he wandered to the shed to get involved with Poppa Clay in some task that would teach him about tools, gardening and repairs.

"Can I help?"

"Come here, boy. I'll teach you to sharpen on this grindstone."

It was apparent that the boy had a knack for mechanics and Clay put aside his concerns about William's homework. He felt the boy would not need much more schooling with so much natural ability.

William loved his time with his grandfather. He learned to evaluate a task, set a procedure for completion, work hard, and appreciate the finished project.

"Good job, William."

Poppa Clay's compliment was as good as catching a fly ball.

At quiet times William evaluated his unusual family. He saw around him families with mother, father, and children in a traditional setting—a mother at home, father at work, brothers, and sisters. He longed for siblings, but he had cousins galore in this two block area from Tenth to Eleventh Streets plus those that gathered at Bear Creek. Among the brothers and sisters of his parents, he had more than enough mothers and fathers who treated him as their own. There were his two sets of grandparents who, each in their own way, were a big part of William's life.

And there was Gertie. William had begun calling her *Gertie* with his first words. He seemed to love the guttural sound of saying *Gertie* and try as she might, she could not stop him from using the nickname. The family thought it was cute and this reinforced the name when he was a toddler. Only in times of fear or pain did the little boy call out to his *Momma*. On his first day of school William learned a lesson about his mother's nickname.

"Gertie will walk me home after school."

Mrs. Blake frowned and a stern storm of retribution crossed her face.

"William Neal, you will not use your mother's nickname. Come up to my desk."

"Yes, ma'am."

"Now, tell me again. Who will call for you after school?"

"My mother will walk me home after school."

"Better." She did not smile; she pointed at his desk. "Sit."

He went back to his seat and heard nothing else said that day. At school she was *Mother* at home she was *Gertie*. William was very careful to tend to this requirement.

They were a team. The apartment at 403 Tenth Street was their special place. Gertie felt lucky to get these three rooms next door to Edward's parents. It was the winning point for Edward at the divorce hearing. The judge endorsed this compromise and it seemed to save face for Edward.

The apartment was set up as nicely as she could manage. A folding screen in the bedroom partitioned her bed and chest from William's. The living room was also divided so that the boy could have his things on a long bookcase on the far side. She had a floor lamp and pillows on the braided rug for him to sit and read or spread out and play. The kitchen area was cheery and inviting. It was the place she and William went at 6:30 every evening to do homework and make dinner. The table had a small wall lamp situated to give William the best reading light while working at the table. It lit his work, his hair, and his face. Gertie got through the day to get to this. The house had a large front porch and yard, which Mrs. Pole gladly shared. Clay made a huge wooden box for William's play things and placed it on the porch.

❧

Monday through Friday, at 5:45, Gertie stepped from the bus at US 1 and Montgomery Street. She changed to her walking shoes for the one mile trek ahead. She did not have to walk in the mornings because Clay's brother-in-law gave her a ride. He was family, therefore did not generate gossip for giving the divorcee a ride.

Some evenings, the ten block hike was a refreshing pleasure—others, it was a torturous ordeal depending on the weather or the difficult work day. She knew three people who got off of her bus and drove to the west end. She also knew she would not be offered a ride.

Once Jake Murray tried awkwardly to explain why he could not offer her a ride. "Sorry Gertie, my Annie wouldn't... I mean it wouldn't look... what with you being divorced and all...."

"Forget it Jake," she said to put him out of his misery. At least he made this half-hearted apology. Listening to him stammer about the things she already knew was worse than the walk itself. Jake and the other west end men could not be seen driving through town, up Montgomery Street one end to the other, with the town's only divorced woman.

But she wished Ellie Hanson would offer her a ride on cold rainy days. Gertie had known Ellie all of her life. Sometimes, watching Ellie drive off while struggling with an umbrella or an extra neck scarf angered Gertie. She sputtered and fume at the injustice but after a couple of blocks let it go. "Shame on you, not me," she proclaimed to the passing tail lights.

When snow was blowing and sidewalks were treacherous, Sam met her but; he would not be here today.

And, today was different. Gertie got a call as she was leaving work.

"William is running a fever. I've called Dr. Bryant." Clay was not comfortable on the phone.

"How high is the fever?"

"High, very high."

"I'll get there as quickly as I can. Tell William I'm on my way." She moved quickly, but nothing would rush the bus schedule or the twenty mile trip from Baltimore. *I've got to get a ride to Tenth Street,* she concluded. She thought about the men who would get off with her and of Ellie. It was obvious; she would ask Ellie.

Should I ask while on the bus or wait until we get off? She pondered. *I'll wait.* She quickly changed her shoes, organized her belongings and gave herself over to prayer for William.

"Please God, please, please," she whispered, confident He was listening.

Gertie stepped off and walked to Ellie as soon as she was on the sidewalk."Ellie, I need a very special favor. I wouldn't ask if it wasn't an emergency. Could I ride to Tenth Street with you… this one time? My little boy—"

"No!"The word stung in its force."Don't ask." Ellie seemed to plead. Her embarrassment required some kind of excuse and things got worse."We are not the same kind of people… " She moved away.

"The air of self-righteousness is mighty heavy tonight," a deep voice interjected.

"W-what?"Gertie stammered to the stranger who had stepped into this little scene with the two women. Ellie, with tears in her eyes, turned and ran toward her car. For an instant Gertie forgot her plight and smiled.

"Oh dear, now you have done it." Gertie knew she would pay for this insult at some later date, in some unknown way. With that she started a quick step toward Montgomery Street. She could not waste another minute; she needed to get to William.

"Wait," he called, "if I've put you in a bad light with one of Laurel's upstanding citizens, you might as well let me give you a ride to Tenth Street. You say there is an emergency?"

"My son is ill and I must get home quickly." She hesitated for only a second before following the stranger to his car. "Thank you so much. My name is Gretta Neal."

"Jesse Morgan."

It was a quiet trip through town. Jesse Morgan could tell the young woman was uncomfortable and not wanting small talk from a stranger. Feeling her discomfort, he concentrated on driving. Gertie went back to her prayers for her son.

"Here, right here." She said, pointing at the Tenth Street sign. "Let me out at the corner. Thank you, I'll walk from here."

He ignored her directions and made the right turn. "Last one on the left." Gertie assembled her things, and got out of the car quickly. "Thanks, more than you know," she called back as she ran for the house—just short of being rude.

Clay met her at the door. "Dr. Bryant just arrived." Clay took her arm and led her to the stairs. "William keeps asking for you, Gertie."

Dr. Bryant was in the room at the top of the stairs. William was motionless in the bed. Mom Neal stood in attendance. Everything was heavy and dark. William's face seemed to glow red, giving an alarm signal to Gertie. *William seemed so well this morning. How can this be?*

"William, I'm here," Gertie whispered. She touched his head and felt a fever that burned into her being. Her pain for his fever punched her stomach and gripped her heart.

She turned her questioning gaze to the doctor as he finished his examination.

Dr. Bryant looked at the distraught mother, her face etched with concern for her son.

"Now, now, Gertie, William is very sick, but he is a strong boy and you must have faith that he will be alright. We aren't sure what is causing the fever, but listen very carefully and I will tell you what to do."

"Mary, go down and get a pitcher of warm water and several washcloths. Gertie, it may take all night, but I believe William can fight this off—if we help him. Pull these heavy covers down. Take off the pajama top—just a sheet to keep him from chilling. Put a small pillow under his head. I don't want him lying flat."

Doctor Bryant continued. "Wring the cloth in room temperature water and wipe him down from head to foot. When his fever heats the cloth, take the other one. Give him only water to drink. His stomach will reject anything else while this fever rages. I have a medicine to make him feel better, but right now he would not be able to keep it down. I will decide on that when I come back." He put his hand in the water to test its temperature. "Good, slightly warm." He looked back at Gertie. "Your job is to fight the fever with him. I have other stops to make this evening and I will come back here when I finish." He touched her arm for emphasis. "Gertie, if he begins to have difficulty breathing, call Mrs. Bryant. She will know where I am and I will come back immediately. Understand?"

"Yes doctor, thank you."

William tossed about, but did not say a word. He was so glad to have his mother here to make everything better. He looked at her with glassy, pleading eyes.

"I'm here, now. We will make you better, soon." She turned to the doctor. "Dr. Bryant, before you leave would you explain everything you have told me to Mary Neal? It will be so much easier if she understands I am following your orders." Gertie knew how to head off possible problems with her mother-in-law.

"I understand. I'll give her a job—feeding you. You will need your strength."

When the doctor returned William's fever was down, but not gone. He took the medicine and asked for water.

Gertie was fed and a cot set up after she protested at the suggestion that she go home to sleep. Gertie was prepared to sit up all night. The cot was a welcome solution.

Dr. Bryant was pleased with William's progress, but cautious in his manner. "William is a very sick boy. I have seen several cases of measles lately, but it may be scarlet fever. It is very likely he will break out in a rash. Keep his room dark tomorrow and continue bathing him. Only water until he asks for food. We'll keep his diet light—no milk. I'll leave a list of recommended foods with Mary. The first three days are the most serious. Soon we'll know what we are dealing with. I'm encouraged that he is doing better, not worsening. I will see you tomorrow."

William slept. Gertie thought over the events of the day, recalling how she felt when Clay called her at work and how she felt when Ellie stung her with her words. The two sets of emotions seemed to be on a scale in her mind—balancing one against another. William's survival was her whole life. Ellie's rejection was only a surface scratch. William was the heart of her being; Ellie represented the attitude of most women in this town—a sad, sad situation—nothing more.

Gertie reached some conclusions at William's bedside. The years of coping with her divorce had taught her to prioritize her emotions as well as her options. Pondering and re-pondering of her position, within and without the family, became a regular exercise. Reviewing today's events and visualizing them on a balance scale, brought her a focus she'd sought since her marriage dissolved.

Gertie's life since divorcing Edward had been a trial. The *trial* was over tonight—not guilty. She would bear no verdict or serve a sentence. Gertie was exonerated in the only place that really mattered—in her own mind.

She reached over and touched the warm, wonderful head of her child.

"Get well, William. We have a weekend at Bear Creek soon." She thought he was asleep but he nodded and gave a sweet smile, as if he had just received the best medicine.

The days passed slowly with steady improvement, although he had some setbacks and the fever daunted him for the next three days.

"Can I take him home, Dr. Bryant?"

"I'd rather you wait until the fever is gone one full day before you move him."

Gertie was disappointed; Mary wasn't. She delighted in making special broths and soups for William and having Gertie at her dinner table.

Early each morning, Gertie got up from her cot, checked William and ran home for a quick bath. On Tuesday and Wednesday, she called her employer. "I can't come to work, my son is sick." Very early on Thursday, Mrs. Pole was at her door announcing a phone call from her supervisor in Baltimore.

"Mrs. Neal, are you coming to work today?"

"I'm sorry, Mr. Proctor. I was about to call you. My son is still sick. He has scarlet fever and last night broke out in the rash. I cannot leave him."

"You have lost two days."

"I know, sir."

"Mrs. Neal, I will expect you at noon today, otherwise you are terminated."

"Please, Mr. Proctor. I cannot come to work today and... I need this job."

"Can you promise me you will be in at eight tomorrow?" It was his only concession.

Gertie took a deep breath. William still had intermittent fever. A rash covered his abdomen. She could not, she would not, make that promise.

"No," she said, hardly above a whisper knowing what that answer meant.

"We'll mail your partial pay for this week. You are terminated. Good luck, Mrs. Neal."

Gertie hung up and melted into pieces in Mrs. Pole's living room. Her landlady came to her with a hankie and gentle words. "Now, now, dear." They were nice words but did nothing for the devastated, overwrought, sleep deprived, anxiety ridden, weary woman.

"I lost my job," she sobbed.

"Shall I call Sam for you?" He was the only family member Mrs. Pole knew.

"No."

"Anyone?"

"No one," she told Mrs. Pole. "No one," she told herself.

Gertie walked up the stairs to face the girl she saw in the mirror. "Now, what?"

Chapter 18

"Gertie's changing and it isn't only the hair. She is trying to find the right time to tell you that she is going to move. So when she comes to you to talk, make some room for her." Sam had cornered Mama as soon as they arrived at Bear Creek. "A lot has happened since William was sick last month."

"Move? I hope she will move to Bear Creek. You children have always come down home when there were troubles, but not Gertie."

"Mama, she's too independent. Let her tell you of her plan. She isn't telling you to get advice, save that for me. I need it more than Gertie."

"Right, Sam. Here is my advice for you. Two children already. Slow down."

"Pow! I asked for that and Patricia MacGregor delivered it right between the eyes." He kissed his mother's hair. "Remember, Gertie has been making her own choices for a long time."

"Sam, I advised Gertie to mend fences with Edward long ago before the divorce—before he broke her arm. I worried so much about the attitude of people in Laurel if she divorced. She took a hard road and I'm afraid she has refused our help because she knew how upset I was about divorce. But you know we support her—whatever she decides. I just wish Gertie and William would come to Bear Creek."

"Gertie will not come here to live, you know that—and it isn't because of how you feel about divorce. Now, you aren't going to show her that sour face, are you, Mama?" Sam, in his usual manner, was about to lighten the conversation.

"My face isn't sour," she retorted

"Yeah, you look like lemons taste." Mama smiled and headed to the kitchen as Sam disappeared across the lawn.

It had been over a month since William's battle with scarlet fever. He was looking stronger and color was back in his cheeks. Gertie, on the other hand, did not exude strength or color when she came into the kitchen. The downward turn of her mouth came back to her face immediately after the soft smile she gave her mother.

"Mama." She crossed the room. "Give me a hug. I need one."

"Here's your coffee with two scoops of sugar." Mama said, while wrapping her arms around her daughter.

"You are treating me like a teenager. I'll take it and love every sweet drop." The smile came back and they took a seat at the table. "Where's everybody?"

"Crabbing. Do you want to go down to the water, too? I see Sam and William setting up the pot in the yard," she said, looking out the window. "They must have a good catch."

"No, I want to stay and visit with you. I'll do my part when it comes time to eat."

"You cut your hair. I like it."

"Me too, but I thought after the first snip, maybe I was making a mistake. The hair kept falling to the floor until I was afraid to look in the mirror. Soon it was ankle deep but once I started there was no turning back." She lifted her hand to puff her locks up as they followed her chin line where the natural curl turned the edges in smoothly. "I expected to look like a shorn sheep. I even worried about the shape of my head. Maybe it would be knobby and make my hair stand on end. There was a bushel of hair on the floor—all from me." She allowed a relaxed smile to engage her mother. "I love it."

"Goodness, I don't know how you were so brave to take scissors and *bob it off.*"

"Remember, I have a reputation in this family for grabbing scissors. That day seems a lifetime ago… but, I don't think Papa will let me forget."

Mama walked around Gertie's chair, touching her hair and declaring, "I like it, too."

"Sometimes after you do something that seems to take a lot of courage, you realize it isn't hard. You just have to take the first step. I'm making some other changes, too." Gertie's voice had a defiant edge to it.

"Tell me."

"I've decided to move from Tenth Street." Mama was ready, thanks to Sam, for her news. She had a warm smile in place and waited for Gertie to go on.

"I lost the job in Baltimore. They fired me for staying home with William while he was sick. The third day they called me and said come to work or be fired. They didn't even give me two weeks—just said 'don't come in'. I am looking for a new job and I want to move."

Their conversation was interrupted by a search for crab seasoning and knockers. When fresh crabs go in a pot, the whole family is part of the circus. Sam and Shirley searched the drawers for the necessary implements, while Mama emerged from the pantry with the seasoning. Gertie followed them out to the crab pot with a glance back at her mother.

"Later, Mama…"

The next day after the sandwiches were made and in the ice box for lunch, Mama made a point of staying in the kitchen as everyone scattered. Gertie cleaned up her work space and drew another cup of coffee. "Mama, want some more coffee?" The two sat together, a study in contrasts—Mama with her delicate features, thin gray streaked hair, and small hands; Gertie so much like her father with full features, wide forehead, big eyes and thick, curly, but short, hair.

"William looks good. And his appetite is good. I would worry about him if he didn't eat his share of crabs."

"No worries there."

"Yes, I think he's back one hundred percent. It was a scary time. I missed you most that first night when his fever was so high." She paused to recall that night. "All's well that ends well."

Mama did not say anything.

Gertie drew in a deep breath. "It is time for us to look to the future. I've made a decision that has been coming for a long time. I thought living on Tenth Street was in the divorce agreement, but it wasn't. It was a verbal agreement that made sense at the time, but not now. We are going to move."

"What will Edward think?"

"Edward will have to accept what I think is best for us. I don't think he will give me grief over it, though his mother will not take this news well. I don't look forward to telling her." A less than confident air passed over Gertie. "I hope it will help when I assure her that William and I will visit often. And, we want to remain close to Grandmother Amsterdam, too."

"So, you will stay in Laurel, just not on Tenth Street."

"No, out of Laurel. It depends on where I get a job and frankly, I can't get a job in Laurel." Gertie knew what her mother wanted. "We cannot come here. Please try to understand."

Patricia looked down to her useless hands resting in her lap. Gertie did not want to tell Mama all the reasons for her decision. Staying on Tenth Street would always keep her in the shadow of Edward and his family. The stigma of divorce was a part of every breath she drew in the west end neighborhood.

"I'm tired, Mama—tired of living in Laurel." She sighed deeply. Gertie wanted more, and with that knowledge came the realization that William would have more too.

Gertie did not tell her mother about the difficulties she faced every day in her hometown. She did not want to trouble Mama's heart with the rocky road she traveled. Why she had to move was as clear as the clean summer air. Where she would go was another matter.

Please trust my judgment, please believe in me. Her mother did not disappoint her.

"Gertie, you've proven yourself in every difficult place in your life— from the time of the bridge accident, through your life's choices and problems—not of your making— that you have faced. Your father and I are proud of you and William. He is a wonderful boy and a testament to you." She reached over the table and took Gertie's face in her hands. "I believe in you."

"William and I deserve more than living in shadows. I'm going to search for that place."

"Yes. You and William *do* deserve better. Please consider coming here. Live with us for a while—until you get your feet on the ground. Come for the rest of August—until school starts again. I'll fix up the two front rooms. Perfect."

"We can't. I must continue my search for a job It is enough that we have this home to come to on weekends. That means the world to William and to me. As long as Sam brings us; as long as he doesn't fill his car with so many children that there's no room for us." A smile crossed her face as she thought of Sam and his growing family. "But seriously, I must live where I can earn a living for us."

"I have been thinking about my cameo." She lightened the mood. "I cared for it. Brought it to you. Took it home again. Brought it back to you. That pin has been like your children, coming and going to Bear

Creek—to be cared for." They both smiled with the analogy. "I need to take it again. I really may have to sell it this time. Our plight now might be the reason it was given to me. Fetch it for me again, Mama."

"Of course, sweetheart." Mama rose and went to her bedroom and returned with the lovely brooch in the box that Grandmother Amsterdam had brought it in.

"Gertie, I hope you have forgiven me for being so upset by your divorce. I was honest with my feelings, but I have learned that I cannot know what is best for someone else. As difficult as your path may be, it is still better than it would have been with Edward. I think you helped him more by ending it."

"I never thought of it like that before…but you may be right. He seems to like the army. I worry about Edward. I'm afraid for him. Now that the United States has declared war, he could be sent over…" Gertie stopped herself.

"That is the role of women in wartime. We worry and believe me; I do my share for Sam and Dan. They have to register for the draft next week."

"I think about Edward… but, I'm focused on what's best for William and me."

"It is a lot to do on your own. If you need help, ask for it." Patricia MacGregor covered Gertie's hand with both of her own. "Remember, no one can hurt you if you resolve not to let them. Nothing takes the sting out of words like discounting the speaker. Be careful, Gertie. You cannot run away from your problems, a change for change's sake does not always work. Hurt among strangers has its own pain."

"Yes, Mama."

"How is Elizabeth Amsterdam?"

"Very frail, but holding her own. She does not go out much, not even to church. She loves to have visits, and we try to go a couple of times a week."

"Please remember us to her on your next visit."

❧

The job search was becoming more and more frustrating. Days were turning into weeks. Each morning, after William left for school Gertie was challenged to find something to do. She turned her attention to the cameo. It was a good day for walking.

She entered the Laurel Jewelry shop and approached the counter. "Mr. Sharpiro, would you look at this cameo and give me an appraisal?"

"I know this piece. I cleaned it for Elizabeth Amsterdam before she gave it away. Are you the lucky recipient?"

"Yes, sir. She gave it to me on my wedding day."

"Ah, yes. I remember—for a bride." He put his glass to his eye and held the brooch as if it were a delicate flower. "Lucky bride."

"It is a precious gift."

Mr. Shapiro went to his file.

"This cameo has increased in value since then. Mmm, 1910. The casing is solid eighteen-carat gold and the stones around the lovely face are diamonds. 2.75 carats." He thought a moment. "Fifteen-hundred dollars was the original appraisal."

"Oh, my. That much?" Gertie was flustered at the figure.

The jeweler held it tenderly. "It was based on the gold and stone value at the time—and that has increased. This is an Italian cameo—museum quality. That makes it harder to judge. I would have to show it to a collector to get an accurate sale value."

Gertie was amazed. It was too dear to keep and too dear to part with. She thought about Elizabeth Amsterdam. *Oh, Grandmother, so much!*

"Oh, dear," was all that Gertie could say as the jeweler laid it back into her hand.

"I know collectors in the city," he added. "Let me know if you ever want to sell it."

Gertie stepped out in the fresh air and breathed deeply. She was shaken by the figure from Mr. Shapiro. "Sweet cameo, you are going into a safe deposit box." She pushed her hand into her purse to be sure the small jewelry box had not evaporated in the few seconds since she put it there and headed to the bank.

"I'd like to speak to someone about a safe deposit box."

The receptionist pointed to a seat in the waiting area and went about her duties.

Gertie waited for ten minutes. "Please... about a safe deposit box..."

Without acknowledging Gertie, the receptionist brought out a form and began filling it out. "And… what name do you use?" the girl asked in a snide manner

"My name is Gretta Neal. What's yours?" Gertie asked, beginning to see an attitude in the bank employee.

"I'm Martha Hanson." Gertie looked into the face of Ellie Hanson's little sister, and a flash of recognition came from years ago when she and Ellie played and a small girl followed after them. It was obvious that Martha recognized Gertie and the question about her name was impertinent.

"Well. Martha, if you will hand me that form, I will fill it out completely. You need not be concerned about my name. It's legal and I intend to rent a safe deposit box with it. If you have a problem with that, call someone else in this bank to help me."

"Maybe you should go to another bank," Martha muttered hardly above a whisper.

With that, anger flashed. Gertie was on her feet walking toward the huge mahogany door with a shiny brass name plate that she did not bother to read. Anger flourished with each step. She opened the door and continued past the secretary, busy in the anteroom. Before she could open the next polished wooden door, the secretary had Gertie's elbow.

"May I help you?"

She looked back at Martha Hanson, and said, "I intend to find someone to handle my affairs." The cameo in her purse seemed to be radiating courage. She had no idea how her dark eyes flashed.

The door opened slowly and a gentleman stepped forward. "Gretta Neal, nice to see you again." He took her arm and led her into his office.

Gertie had hardly regained her composure at hearing her name, when she found herself in a fine leather chair looking at a face she recognized, but could not immediately place. *This must be one of Sam's friends. No. Sam doesn't know bank officers. He must know or be related to Edward's family—they know everyone. Maybe he belongs to the church. No.* Her mind raced.

"How is your son? I hope he has recovered from his sickness."

Yes! Jesse Morgan. He gave her a ride from the bus six weeks ago when Ellie would not. Ever since that day, Gertie wondered if she would meet Jesse Morgan again. She had even come to believe that she did not remember his face well enough to recognize it. But here it was right in front of her. His desk nameplate confirmed her recognition— Jesse R. Morgan, President.

"My son is doing very well, thank you." Gertie relaxed and let go of her anger at the thought of William. "He was quite ill, but he's a strong boy and you'd never know he was ill to see him now. Thanks again for coming to our rescue."

"You are quite welcome. I'm glad to know he has recovered well. Now, is there something I can do for you, today?"

"I need a safe-deposit box." She decided not to speak of the receptionist's rudeness. "I have completed the form. If you will outline the terms, I can pay in advance." Jesse Morgan took only a moment to have the key to a box ready for his new customer.

"Miss Logan, escort Mrs. Neal to the vault and explain the procedure for accessing her box."

"It seems I'm always in your debt, Mr. Morgan. I thank you again."

"My pleasure, Mrs. Neal."

Gertie paused a moment as she passed Martha Hanson's desk. "Good day." With a confident and genuine smile, she offered Miss Hanson unspoken forgiveness. Gretta Neal did not have to hurt Martha Hanson to gain something. As she left the bank she let her feelings of hurt and anger fly away in the cool breeze. She had won some vague victory.

It was a good day for walking so she headed south on Prince George Street to Grandmother's house. If she timed it right, she could visit and be on her way to the elementary school at dismissal. As always, Gertie was warmly greeted by Edward's grandmother. The two women found joy in each other's company through the years. Grandmother was aging so gracefully and her snow white hair was like a crown on her head.

"Grandmother, it's so good to see you in the sunroom. You're looking so much better."

"I'm feeling better. It is always wonderful to see you. How is William?"

"Good. He's doing well. I'll bring him to see you after church on Sunday, if the weather holds. It has been a rainy September."

"Then I will use one of my prayers to ask for sunshine on Sunday."

"I was downtown today to put the cameo in a safe-deposit box. I lost my job and I might have to sell it if I don't get another one soon. You told me to keep it in case I needed it. I was surprised to learn of its value. I want you to know; I'll do all I can to keep from selling it. I treasure your gift very much."

"I know you do, child, but it is only a material thing and it is yours—has been since the day I placed it in your hand. Do as you must." Love and support shown through her warm gray eyes. Gertie took time to share her story about William's illness and the possibility of moving.

"Gertie, move if you want to but don't think you can run from your problems, they have a way of following you."

That's almost what Mama said, Gertie thought while continuing to listen.

"Make your changes one at a time. If it seems events are moving you, put on the brakes and make sure you are moving events. I know you have the best motives and your priorities are in order. God will see you through; He has so far. You and William are in my prayers... as is Edward."

"Have you seen Edward?"

"No, I usually see Edward when he comes to town so I know how often he sees his boy. He is stationed in New Jersey. I assume he told you."

"Yes, he does write when he gets moved. He is so far away and gets home less and less. I worry about him being sent overseas. I pray every day."

"I can't think about Edward going to war." The light drained from Grandmother's eyes.

Gertie went to her and took her hands. "I know, Grandmother."

"Mary worries, too. Does William know much about the war?"

"A little, but if he has thought about his Daddy going to war, he hasn't said so to me. William is starting to be protective of me. He might not tell me if he's worried about the war and his father."

"I don't have to tell you how smart William is. He knows what a soldier does. Gertie, maybe you need to talk to him. I am concerned about Edward and I know you are. We have to realize that William most likely, is too."

"Thank you, Grandmother. I'm sure you are right." Gertie had a passing weariness across her shoulders. *Edward, William, War.* It was enough to bring tears if she would allow it. "William loves his father. He's proud and carries a picture of Edward in uniform."

"You've never given William any ill will against his father. I appreciate that."

"Grandmother, I do that for William. It is a small gift I give him so he can completely love his father, and I pray that Edward will accept that love. It is not hard to do what is good for William."

"And, good for Edward, too, Dear."

Gertie glanced up at the clock on the mantel. "Speaking of William, if I leave now, I can be at the school in time to walk home with him. I love you Grandmother. See you after church, if the weather is good for walking."

With a kiss on the soft cheek Grandmother offered, Gertie was gone.

🐌

That same night, in the middle of doing his homework, William looked up at his mother. "What are we going to do about space, Gertie?"

"Space? What space?"

"What are we going to do so we can each have more space?"

"OK, what's this all about?"

William began to tell his mother that it was time for better, roomier arrangements, though what he really meant was that he wanted his own bedroom. It was his cousin who asked him just a few days ago if he slept with his mother. The question was a turning point in the mother/son relationship. William began to see himself as an individual apart from his mother.

"Well, William, it's funny you would bring this up at the very time I was thinking about our space and this apartment. I'm going to see what I can do about getting you your own room."

Chapter 19   1917-1918

America entered the war against Germany in November and was fully involved in the spring of 1917. Gertie's little square town in middle Maryland was not immune to the effects. Families were saying farewell to their men and a feeling of apprehension was in the air. Newspapers blasted headlines of events in Europe impressing on minds that war torn Europe was, black, gray, and white. Only America still had color and that was in jeopardy as an eddy of worry was sucking brightness from everyday life.

The MacGregor family watched Dan leave for the army. Besides Edward, several other Neal men living in the Tenth and Eleventh Street area were gone. Day to day life went on but a nagging black cloud of impending bad news hovered over everything. The town's people could recite the names of every local man serving in Europe—where they were, and when the last letter came. A dreaded yellow-bad-news telegram from the War Department could hardly make it to a family on Tenth Street before food was being cooked and delivered to their door. The complexion of the neighborhood was sad and except for playing children and barking dogs, things seemed abnormally quiet. The newspaper was a harbinger of bad news and never current enough for waiting families.

"He was killed weeks ago and we didn't know," was the often heard lament. The nagging feeling pervaded as if death may have already reaped while life moved on—unaware—widows tending to housework and fatherless children playing. A heavy dose of guilt was weighed upon grief.

It was a bad time for all, except for women looking for jobs. Opportunities abounded but not for Gertie—not in Laurel. Weeks of searching after losing her job in Baltimore were to no avail. Besides the existing attitude, Laurel businesses did not want to hire a single woman with a child, especially when they learned why she lost her previous job. She applied in four Main Street shops and gave up.

"Why do this to myself?"

The town adopted a new prejudice against Gertie because Edward was in the army. They had it all figured out. The soldier's ex-wife wasn't working; she must be living on army checks. Poor *mistreated* Edward. Women couldn't speak the word they had for Gertie, but it went through their minds.

The checks from the army came as Edward promised, but she needed a job desperately.

Mary was not happy either—Gertie was home for her son after school. William did not come to Mary's kitchen each afternoon, although he never failed to come see her every day and visit Clay in his workshop, too.

It had been a long two months searching for a job. Gertie's money was running low and costly bus trips to the city did not turn up a job.

❦

Mrs. Pole came up the stairs and banged on the door early one snowy morning in December. "Come quickly, you have a phone call."

On her way down, Gertie noticed the snow starting to fall. When William left for school, she felt the low, heavy, gray clouds and smelled impending snow in the air. The first day of December was early for snow in central Maryland.

"Hello, yes, this is Gretta Neal. Yes, Yes, I can be there in an hour. Thank you Mr. Morgan." She was so excited she hugged Mrs. Pole and ran up the stairs two at a time.

"He wants to talk to me…" she said out loud to the empty apartment, "…about a job in the bank." When she was a child, talking to herself was a game but, now it was loneliness. There was no one to share her news—only the excited reflection in the mirror.

It was worth extra minutes to dress and groom for this interview as she looked over the two choices she had in dresses. When it mattered her hair refused to be contained and it took extra pulls with the brush to control it. She looked at the stray locks, smoothed the skirt of her dress and commented, "I feel unruly myself."

It took a while to walk to the First National Bank of Laurel at Fourth and Main because sidewalks were slick with the new snow blowing. Gertie was not aware of the cold; she was warmed by excitement she was wearing like a new sweater. She arrived with a blush on her cheeks, her eyes glistened with cold air tears, and a scarf wrapped around her neck and tossed over her shoulder. Gertie looked more like a schoolgirl preparing to go skating than a career-minded woman. After she undid her wraps, Gertie entered the mahogany office of Jesse Morgan. Her dress was exactly right, a warm brown, straight cut, slightly above the ankle, highlighted with a large ecru lace collar. Gertie shook her head to free her hair almost like starting her engine. She felt a strange confidence and closeness to her cameo, just a few feet away in the vault.

"Hello, Gertie." Martha Hanson greeted her warmly; her smile was an apology for their last meeting. This was quite a change from the greeting when she was in this room a few weeks ago. Gertie accepted Martha's new attitude graciously.

"Mr. Morgan, Gretta Neal is here."

"Come in, come in."

"May I call you Gretta?"

"Everyone calls me Gertie."

"Gertie, The board of directors is opening a branch of the bank at Ft. Meade. We have been invited to do so by General Nalley—as soon as possible. It means I have to send two of our experienced people there while we train others here at the home office." He looked into her big eyes and got right to the point. "I'm interviewing for two teller positions for the new branch on Post. Are you interested?"

"Yes, sir, I am interested." She answered without hesitation, sliding slightly forward in her chair. "I don't have experience in banking, but you called me and I'm here—more than willing to learn." She paused before stating her one misgiving. "I would have a transportation problem getting to Ft. Meade, though." She was brought down by the thought. "I don't have a car."

"That's not a problem. We provide a courier service for money, paper work, and employees from the main office to the new branch. That will make your day a little longer but you will be compensated. The biggest problem is time. We have to start immediately—tomorrow. We will begin by training you here while the branch is set up. Then, when you are ready, you'll go there to work."

Jesse Morgan had done his homework on Gertie. He already knew she had a young son. Almost anyone in town was willing to fill him in on her marital status. Mrs. Barnes, his head teller, lived near the Neals and she had a taste for gossip. His investigation on Gertie went farther than gossip. Mr. Morgan contacted the department store in Baltimore. They gave a good report and the reason for her termination—to which he brought his own understanding. Laurel High School provided an outstanding scholastic report and information on the scholarship she declined. He was impressed—and had not been able to get the attractive young lady out of his mind since their chance meeting.

Gertie could not believe this was happening. *Thank you God... and Jesse Morgan.* Her heart was actually beating so hard she was sure Mr. Morgan could see it through her dress. She took a deep breath and stood. "Mr. Morgan you won't regret offering me this job. I'll do my best. I can start today—right now— if you want me to. I can arrange my son's care after school."

That impressed Jesse Morgan, too. "Excellent."

It was almost five when Gertie got back to Tenth Street that evening. The excitement and adventure of her new job had brought her home without memory of walking six blocks from the bank. The winter sky was dark and the snow continued in a fine light dusting that blew and blew and stacked up only in corners. Hardly a half an inch covered the ground. William was reading when she came into the Neal's kitchen.

"Hello, William, ready to go home?" He gathered his books and smiled.

"Thank you, Mom Neal."

"This letter came for you." Mary said, handing her an envelope with Edward's return address. Gertie could tell that she wanted the letter for herself. Although Gertie's heart was softened to Mary's anguish over her son, she was too tired to deal with the letter and her mother-in-law at this moment. In the kindest voice Gertie could muster she said. "We will share the letter with you—first thing in the morning. We have to hurry home now. William has homework and I have to get things ready. I started a job today." News about her job was anticlimactic to the letter from Edward holding center stage. "I promise you, I will share this letter in the morning." Gertie turned at the door. "Mom Neal, William will be coming to you after school again—every day. I hope that's alright. We need you again."

Her silence was taken as assent.

William did his homework at the kitchen table while Gertie warmed the leftovers and opened Edward's letter. "Look, William. Daddy's letter is to you. Can we read it together?"

Dear William,

I wish I could have come to your birthday. It is hard to explain, but I am very busy with my job in the army. It is an important job. If I can come to see you soon, I will but I cannot promise.
Please be a good boy and listen well to your mother. I am proud of the good work you are doing in school.
I think about you every day and believe it or not, I miss Tenth Street. Isn't that funny? I am seeing so many new places and still miss home.
This money is for you to buy something you really like.

I love you very much.
Daddy

The next day Mary Neal got her own letter from her son.

❦

Gertie applied herself to the new job. Her salary equaled what she made at the department store and, she did not have commuting expenses. She felt confident she could take care of herself and William with a little extra for Christmas. She could buy some fabric to make a dress and get William the ice skates he wanted.

Tenth Street was going to have to remain their home for a while longer. Moving was out of the question now that she had a good job in the heart of Laurel. She went down to talk to Mrs. Pole.

"I have a job in the bank."

"That is good news, dear. "Mrs. Pole was a small, quiet woman who put aside her feeling about divorce as she got to know and respect Gertie. She did not want to lose a good tenant. "Are you still thinking of moving?"

"That is what I wanted to talk to you about. I would like to stay here but I need more room. William needs his own room."

"Yes, he does. If we empty out the back storage room upstairs, you could have it for William. It needs some work but if—

"Perfect!" Gertie interjected "He will love it. I will speak to Clay and Sam. They will do the work, and do it as you want. I'm so excited."

"Tell Clay to come over. We will work it out in no time."

"Thank you, Mrs. Pole. Oh… we have to talk about the rent increase." Gertie's practical side brought her down to earth. "I know rent is higher on a two bedroom apartment, so let's talk about that before we go any further with this excitement."

Mrs. Pole brandished a broad smile. "If you and your family make the improvements, your rent will not increase for the next six months. Does that seem fair?"

Gertie hugged her landlord. *Finally, things are going my way.* She took the stairs two at a time again.

Clay did not want Sam's help and he reluctantly allowed Gertie to paint the room when he had finished his work. One week later the old storage room was insulated, the window puttied airtight, a floor vent was cut to allow heat to radiate up from Mrs. Pole's kitchen, and a linoleum floor was installed. William's bed, dresser, and bookcase were moved and he spent his first happy night in his own room.

Mom Neal relished that William would be coming to her for at least another six more months. *Who knows what Gertie will do next?*

The employment of the divorcee by Mr. Morgan was news all over the town's grapevine. "What's Jesse Morgan's interest in her? Gertie, a teller—unbelievable!"

The speculation was deep. The gossip was harsh.

"Jesse Morgan and Gertie Neal."

"I thought he was married."

"What difference would that make to a divorced woman?"

"Imagine—*her* working in our bank. What a travesty."

"Pour Edward in uniform, could be shipped out… "

"Our country's hero… "

Edward was fully redeemed in the town's eyes. It was unlikely Gertie ever would be—especially now that Edward was in uniform.

Sam heard some of the gossip and he headed to the bank to see for himself. He came in, tall, handsome and smiling the third day after

Gertie started her training. He spoke to everyone in the lobby before coming to the teller's cage where his sister was watching him work the crowd. "Sam, you should be a politician. Kiss any babies lately?"

"Only my own. I heard I could find you here. Can we do lunch at Gravilla's today?" Gertie agreed to meet him in the little restaurant across the street at noon. Sam turned with a smile and was out the door.

Gravilla's was popular with Main Street workers. The friendly Italian proprietors greeted everyone who entered with an invitation to "finda seat!" The soda counter was full, all the tables were taken, and bright conversation filled the room. It was the first time Gertie had been in since high school. Sam was deep in conversation when Gertie walked in. She paused in the tall doorway looking for her brother when her name was called from a side table. Although many knew her, no one spoke as she crossed the restaurant.

"Gertie, would you like to share this table?" It was Mr. Morgan. She didn't know quite what to say. After all he was her boss, but Sam was in here somewhere.

"No thank you Mr. Morgan, I'm to meet—"

"Gertie, don't stand me up!"Sam called as he crossed the room to interrupt her last words. "I have a table for us right here and I've ordered your favorite." He continued to ramble on. "I can't wait until the weekend to talk to you, got to see you now."

"Excuse me Mr. Morgan." She hurried to sit down and shut up her loud-mouthed brother.

"Sam, that's my boss, Mr. Jesse Morgan." She said quietly. "He offered me a seat at his table. Monday he called and offered me a job. Isn't it great? I was going to tell you Saturday... I guess you have your own news service."

"So that's Jesse Morgan." Sam looked back at the distinguished man alone at a table. "I've heard a lot about him. Some good—some..." He lifted his hand and made a slow back and forth balancing motion. "Hummm."

"He's fine in my book. I have a job, don't I?"

"So, you do. Where did you meet Jesse Morgan? He didn't just pull your name out of his very expensive hat?"

"I met him on the train one night a while back. He heard me say I needed a ride to Tenth Street because William was ill and he offered to take me. You remember William's fever that cost me my job. I met him that evening and once when I did some bank business. I don't know how he remembered me, but when he needed two more tellers to open a branch at Ft. Meade, he called me. What a wonderful chance. It is a good job and I am trying to learn fast. Most days I leave in time to walk home with William. Of course that will stop when I finally get to Ft. Meade—" she paused her story to voice a fleeting thought, "—I'm glad I don't have to wait on customers on Main Street." Then, she continued her story. "I am finally getting used to handling so much money and Mrs. Barnes, who is training me, says my accuracy is excellent. I have two books to read on banking policy and they are dreary." She drew a breath.

"Slow down, Gertie, you are talking fast and not eating." Sam pointed to her sandwich and continued. "So, you must have knocked old Jesse's socks off. Way to go, Sis." Sam reached across to annoy her by mussing her hair. "I can tell you like your job. That's great. I'm happy for you. What about your plans to move?"

"That's the down side. Grandmother Amsterdam said I shouldn't make too many changes. Said I shouldn't give William too much to handle at once and she is right. I was hoping moving would be the one thing I would accomplish but it will not be. The new job... and Edward could be shipped over at any time. That is enough for William and me, for now. I'll have to stay on Tenth Street for a while longer." She paused to see how she felt about that truth. "I had not expected to get a job in Laurel. Here I am working right in the center of town. And I thought I would have to get out of this town to find a good job..." She stopped to finish her sandwich and think about all the important things she was telling her brother. "I love Laurel—its streets and charm. I love walking over by the river and up Fergus Hill..." She got pensive. "Maybe I *can* make it here in our hometown. What do you think, Sam, am I fooling myself?" She took another bite of sandwich. Sam smiled broadly inviting her to continue.

"Since Mr. Morgan put me in his bank, right up front where everyone can see me; I feel I can look everyone in the eye. I don't have to turn away or lower my gaze. It may be easier to stay in Laurel. What do you think?"

Sam wasn't sure if she was hearing the gossip or not, but he wasn't going to tell her. "You know how I feel about that. I think it is about time you stopped worrying about what some people think." Sam paused for emphasis. "It's not the *whole* town, Gertie." He lifted his Coke as if toasting her. "You and I…we're alike. We can make it anywhere. I like a challenge and so do you. Besides I'm not far away. I might show up for lunch just about any time."

"That's good. At least while I'm here at the main office," she said with a mouth full of tuna salad.

"Edward came by and talked to me about the army. I must say I was surprised to see him. The last time I saw him we basically ended our friendship. Maybe the army is a good move for him. I'd go myself if I didn't have family."

Her sandwich was finished. As she rose to put on her coat, Sam reached up, took her arm, and pulled her back into the seat. "Gertie don't forget, you are good enough to look anyone in the eye. All you have to do is keep your chin up." He curled his forefinger, put it under her chin and lifted with an upward motion that made her laugh.

She rose again and hugged her knight in shining armor. "Lunch anytime, as long as you're buying." She kissed his cheek and squeezed his arm. As she left the restaurant, she smiled at Mr. Morgan.

❦

"I'm almost afraid to say it," Gertie told Sam on a crazy trip to Bear Creek with just the two of them in the car. William had playoff games and stayed with the Neals. Sam's family was visiting in-laws in Virginia.

"Afraid to say *what*?"

"I'm enjoying warm thoughts." She stretched her arms, breathed deeply and continued. "Life is good."

"Why not admit it, if it's true, Silly?"

In spite of concern over the war, the year after getting her job at the bank was a good one. Gertie felt successful. Edward was still on American soil. William continued to succeed in school. Life on Tenth Street wasn't exciting, but it was at last comfortable.

"I guess I don't want to hex it." She leaned back and reflected on her contentment. Sam let her be.

"I like living on Tenth Street. Did you ever think I would say that?" She didn't wait for an answer—didn't want one. "It's a good place, especially after I came to understand the Neals. William is safe and nurtured there. And, I love my job. I'm making it on my own and it makes me feel good." She sat up for emphasis. "Sam, I even put some money in savings. This time last year—"

"Yeah, I know it was tough. Another storm you weathered."

She continued her thoughts. "I'm twenty-five now."

"Your point?"

"No point, just thinking. Do you think I'm old?"

"Sometimes, when you go on like this." Gertie scuffed his head. "Watch it, I'm driving."

"I hope things go on as they have. Almost too good to be true… "

"Let's enjoy this weekend without kids. I'm going to cover the bridge so Papa can rest. What are you going to do?"

"Anything Mama wants… and read a book."

"With Thanksgiving and Christmas around the corner, quiet times at Bear Creek will be rare."

❧

Gertie's warm thoughts were challenged two weeks later when William got a letter from Edward.

> *November 1, 1918*
> *Dear William,*
>
> *The Army is hard work. When I go to bed I fall right to sleep. I'm learning to be a good soldier and I'm glad that Poppa taught me to hunt squirrels because I am an instructor in firearms. Someday I will show you how fast I can take a rifle apart and put it back together.*
> *I hope you are working hard in school and helping your mother.*
> *I will be on board a ship at Christmas so I won't see you. Doesn't that sound exciting? I have been told I will see the Statue of Liberty. I never thought I would see that or cross an ocean.*
> *Tell Gertie to buy a surprise for you for Christmas with the money the Army sends her.*
> *Be a good boy. Merry Christmas.*
> *Love, Daddy*

❦

Edward arrived in Germany after the Armistice was signed. He never lifted his gun or pointed it toward an enemy. Christmas in war torn Germany was drab and gray. Everything was burned, bombed and barren. Edward's duties were to bury the dead, to catalog dog tags and personal belongings. There were assignments to assist with the wounded and sit with the dying. Edward saw human plight such that he had never imagined. He concluded, right or wrong, it would be better to be engaged in battle than to see all this in slow motion. The German refugees from the battle areas were streaming in begging for food or anything to help sustain life. Edward was not sure if he was able to feel anything. Sympathy and empathy caused him to lose sleep. He learned early on that thinking about home didn't help either. When he thought of William, his heart actually ached. When he thought of Gertie, guilt brought a dark curtain and the only tears he shed over losing her.

One terrible night, he was lifting dead men to make room for dying ones. Edward was one second away from relief from all of this and the mess he made of his life. He put his gun into his mouth and had a vision of Gertie in her yellow dress crossing the green lawn on Fergus Hill. The gun fell to the ground. Edward cried and fell shaking on his cot. The next day along with all his grief and remorse, he felt like a coward. He didn't cry anymore but he continued to shake—his hands and then the whole body. He was hot—then cold. Edward had influenza. He died in three days and was counted among the thousands of US doughboys that lost their lives to influenza in Germany that year.

❦

On Tenth Street, the armistice was celebrated. No more dying.

"We only have to wait, William. Armistice means the fighting has stopped. Daddy will be coming home."

"When?"

"I don't know, but we hope soon. Get ready—we are going to church to thank God."

The telegram came to Tenth Street ten days later. Mary went to the door and without a word, accepted the awful yellow slip of paper that took her world away. She held the telegram in her hand and sat on the cold step, covering her face with the skirt of her apron.

Clay could not help Mary nor could he help himself. Years of living an emotionless life had not prepared him for grief that came from losing a son. Mary never got warmth and kindness from Clay and in this sorrow, she did not miss what he could not give.

"Come in the house, Mary. There is no use sitting out here. Please." Nothing Clay said penetrated her mind. She did not talk and she did not cry. "William will be here soon." Those words caused her to move into the kitchen to prepare his snack.

When William came to the door, Mary called out, "Edward!" and finally let the tears flow. "Edward, Edward." She clutched the confused boy who began to cry. William did not want his grandmother holding him and calling his father in such a way. But, he did not understand and he did not know how to make it all stop.

"Mom Neal, I'm William." He looked into her blank eyes and turned to his grandfather.

Clay lifted Mary's hands from William's shoulders and led her to a chair. Then he took William's hands and walked to the work shed to bring him the news that he was fatherless.

"Poppa Clay, she called me Edward. She knows, I'm William."

"Of course she does. We have very bad news from your father. We got a telegram today…"

He did not have to say anything else. William knew about the dreaded telegrams.

"Daddy?" he cried and demanded an answer. "Daddy?"

"Yes."

William embraced his grandfather and Clay let his own arms encircle the boy for the first time. "My Daddy isn't coming home—" He made the statement that did not require validation. William's tongue reached the salty stream coming down his face. "—not coming home again." He drank his own tears. William would not let them drip off his chin. The tears were part of his father and William did not want any to get away.

Clay's head went to the boy's shoulder looking for a place for his grief and his regrets.

"Come son, I see your mother has arrived home. We must take the sad news to her."

Gertie saw Clay walking hand-in-hand with William across the yard. Her first thought was that maybe William had hurt himself on a tool. But, she saw the boy pull away and break into a sprint. He fell into her open arms. "Daddy," he sobbed. "Daddy isn't coming home—" he pressed his face into her stomach and uttered one more word, "—never." They went down together on the ground. Gertie reached down and pushed the heel of her hand against the earth to hold it still, to stop its turning and its shaking. She held William, his tears, his broken heart, and her own sorrow with arms that did not seem strong enough…but were.

She looked at Clay. "Influenza," was the only word he could say.

Gertie's only concern was for her son as he cried the tears of the innocent.

"You told me the war was over? How could Daddy be dead now? Tell me, Gertie." He was making demands to the only authority he knew. "Tell me why is he dead if the war is over. Where is he if he is dead? Momma……"

She took her son home and settled him into the bed, bringing warm soup and milk to him."William, I don't have answers to your questions. We don't know why these things happen or what God's plan is. Your Daddy got sick in Germany. He died of influenza just as people here get sick and die. We're so sad and so sorry that he was far away. It is important to remember that he loved you and you loved him. Let's just believe that he is looking down on us right now—from heaven. Before he died, he couldn't see us—now he can." She yielded to his refusal to let her dry his tears. "It's ok to cry."

William lifted his red swollen eyes to Gertie and asked, "What do I say to God, now? We already thanked him for keeping Daddy safe. What do I say in my prayer, Gertie?"

She joined him on his knees beside the bed. In childlike reverence, Gertie put her palms together under her chin. "William, we ask God to make us strong and take care of Daddy. We didn't know Daddy had died but God did. We can always thank God for taking care of those we love, on earth as well as in heaven." She didn't know if her words helped her son, but they helped her.

Finally William slept. Gertie was left with nothing to comfort or fill the night ahead except the terror of loss and undefined feelings.

The next day, a light tap came on the apartment door. Emily entered the small room. For a few seconds the two women remembered being girls together, but the chasm between them could not be crossed in this brief moment. Emily was Edward's sister, not Gertie's friend.

"A letter came from Edward today—addressed to you. I'll leave it here on the table."

"Thank you, Emily. You know I'm sorry that Edward is gone, don't you? William and I are both mourning."

"Yes, I know. I hope this letter is a comfort and not a hardship."

"How is your mother? Can I do anything for her?"

"No one can do anything for her now."

"She wants to see William tomorrow."

"Of course." Gertie carefully opened the letter as Emily quietly left.

November 20, 1918
Dear Gertie,

It is like time out of life over here. I can't begin to tell you how it is in this beat up country. Germany used to be beautiful, but I don't see anything beautiful. The land is broken and ugly. The people are running in all directions looking for a kind face. The hardest to see are the children. Who is going to take care of them? I give a little but it is so little.

Now I realize how wonderful the United States is. It is the greatest country in the world. I have to believe that my being here is to help keep this from ever happening in the USA, in Maryland, on Tenth Street. My buddies in the Army have fought and willingly died. . . you get that Gertie? Willingly died to save our way of life. Freedom is to a country what health is to the body. Everything!

I have seen so much and I hope and pray that William will never see this. It is often easier to die than to live here. Many are going home maimed, disabled. Do you know if their sacrifices are appreciated? You don't know how many hours each night I wonder about the answer to that question. I wish you could write and tell me if people at home appreciate such sacrifice. When a man gives his life for his country, he should never be forgotten and the man who comes home injured should be thanked every hour of the rest of his life. When I signed on to the Army, I was sure I would come home to Tenth Street again. Funny thing, if I don't, it would be all right because now I believe, truly believe, the United States is worth dying for.

I have seen so much death today and I will see more tomorrow. In the midst of all this, thoughts of you and William save me. I'm not feeling too well tonight and I hope you can read my writing.

I just have to know, do the people back home appreciate what thousands are doing for them over here? I am waiting for your answer. I could always depend on you to be up front with me.

Tell William I love him.

Edward
PS I never told you I was sorry. I am.

"Edward grew up and then he died." Gertie cried the tears of many reasons, no reasons, without reason, and for good reason. She did not know how to feel. Her mind raced back to the early years and the tender feeling she once had for Edward. She realized some of those first-love feelings were still a part of her. Gertie felt a soft pity for Edward. It wasn't a hard pity that had vengeance or selfishness in it. *Pity for me, too*, she admitted during this time of deep mourning.

The shock of Edward's death brought random thoughts and evaluations. Gertie allowed a few moments to question if she could have done anything to save the marriage. *Could we have had another chance? Your letter... I wonder.* "Oh, Edward..." she lamented, not realizing how much she sounded like the young bride of eight years ago.

At a time like this, going back was often easier than going forward.

Gertie read Edward's letter many times before she slept. She still had tears when she finally drifted away to the only relief available to her.

The sun did not show its face the next day. The gloomy clouds seemed appropriate. They were there to hide the sun; they did not water the earth to renew life. They fostered the mood.

"William, I'm walking to Great Grandmothers this morning," Gertie announced as she put breakfast on the table. "What do you want to do? Read?"

"I'm going with you."

"Are you sure?" She would not dissuade him with any of her misgivings. It would be a difficult visit—they both knew it.

"Get two umbrellas, in case."

Elizabeth Amsterdam expected them. All day yesterday family had streamed through her house, everyone but Gertie and William. *Today, they will come,* she thought. "I want to be in the sunroom today. Please freshen my hair and bring a nice robe." She instructed her caretaker.

"Are you sure you want to go there now? I hate to see you wear yourself out for visitors that may or may not come. Shouldn't we wait until we are sure you will have company this morning?"

"They're coming this morning," she replied with compete confidence.

When Gertie and William walked onto the porch, Elizabeth had finished her breakfast and the efforts she made to be ready for them, were accomplished.

"Grandmother…" the greeting was completed with hugs. William sat on the floor at her knee. Gertie tried a chair nearby, but that did not suit. She pulled an ottoman over and sat at Grandmother's other knee. They made a warm circle—a picture Gertie would hold in her memory bank forever.

"We're grieving for Edward and we're concerned for you." Gertie opened the conversation they had to have.

"And, in my sadness over Edward, I'm concerned for you and William," Grandmother replied.

"William and I are talking openly about this terrible way to lose him… in such a faraway place. And, we talk about loving him, too."

"I am happy to hear that. Don't worry about me, children. At my age, I have a good understanding of life and death. Our sorrow is really for each other. I've learned that." She turned her attention to William and took his hand. "You have a long life ahead, William, and each day you are a tribute to your father. Do you understand what I am saying?"

"Yes, ma'am." He looked up at Gertie and Great Grandmother. "Daddy is a part of me and if I honor him all my life, I can be proud of the part of me that is his son—even if I can't see him or talk to him." He stopped to think about his own words. "Great Grandmother, Gertie. . ."

He addressed them both. A deep breath allowed him to go on. "Neither one of you are blessed to have Daddy as a part of you, like I am. Will it be enough for you to look at me and remember Daddy?"

William could not have looked more like Edward at this moment especially when Gertie reached over to him and brushed his hair back into a wave above his forehead.

Tears filled the room.

$$\mathcal{S}$$

Somehow they got through the next few days. Edward's body would not be returned from Germany. The family reluctantly agreed for him to rest with thousands of doughboys in an American cemetery in Germany. A memorial service was planned and it all seemed unreal and in some ways, untrue. Without seeing Edward there was no finality. But it was true and everyone in their own way had to accept that truth.

William grieved outwardly. His eyes were sad and his steps were deliberate. No running or skipping and no cutting up with his cousins. He could not shake his sadness or forget for a short play time the terrible thing that had happened to him and his father.

"Go play, William. Daddy would want you to." Gertie urged.

William had his answer. "I've talked to *him* about it and *we* decided I could wait until Sunday to play again." He had worked out his own mourning period.

"That's fine, William... but that is four more days."

"I have a plan to walk all the paths around Tenth Street where Daddy used to play. And I am going to read two books."

Gertie gave him his favorite foods, lots of attention and let him be. Her confidence in her son grew in this difficult time.

Everyone on Tenth Street found their way. Mom Neal bore Edward's death as if the weight of the world was on her shoulders. She reached out to touch William whenever he passed close. Clay Neal worked in the shed, sun up to sun down. Gertie looked for a mission to give this whole thing meaning. Along with all the neighbors, she cooked and carried food to Mom Neal's kitchen to feed the gathering clan after the service.

"Mama, Papa, I'm so glad you're here. You, too." She exclaimed to Liddy and Lon. The arrival of her family at the church was the only bright spot in this day. "Where's Sam?"

"He'll be along. He couldn't get away this morning."

Gertie circled everyone in a group hug.

"Where's William?" Mama noticed her missing grandson immediately.

"He's acolyte. You'll see him later."

"How's he doing?"

"His suffering is apparent but do not be alarmed, he will be fine."

"How are you, Gertie?' Mama asked quietly as they walked hand in hand to a pew.

"This has been harder than I expected. Oh, Mama…I didn't know I still have feelings for Edward."

"I would have been surprised and disappointed if you didn't."

Her mother's support again prepared Gertie for her next bout of emotion as the organ started the prelude and William walked across the chancel to light candles on the altar.

At the close of the funeral memorial, taps were sounded from the back corner of the church. An army honor guard advanced down the center aisle and presented colors for Pfc. Edward Neal. The stars and stripes were tipped for the life given for his country. Then General Nalley, carrying a folded flag, walked to William.

William stood. Gertie was proud of her son's straight back and clear eyes.

The General first words were spoken softly for the ears of the young boy only. Then in a clear voice for all to hear, he said, "On behalf of the President of the United States and the people of a grateful nation, may I present this flag as a token of appreciation for the honorable and faithful service your father rendered this nation."

William accepted the red, white and blue triangle. The salute from the General was returned with precision. "Thank you, sir."

❧

In the afternoon after the memorial service, the family drifted away, Mary went to rest and Clay headed to his refuge. The amount of food that piled up in the kitchen was staggering. Gertie called Sam and gathered up all the leftover food. She took the bean soup and the biscuits. She took the ham, turkey, and the macaroni and cheese. She took the cakes and pies. Gertie moved around Mom Neal's kitchen as if she were used to working there. Everything was gathered up by the time Sam arrived as she had asked.

"Where are we going with all this food?" Sam followed her directions but still had his questions.

"We are going to the hospital at Ft. Meade. The wards are full of injured men."

"Do they know we are coming... with this?" He asked as he continued to load.

"No, but I figured, how much home cooked food do they get?"

Gertie took time to fix her hair and don a pretty, bright dress. She looked happy and bright by design. Sam picked up on her mood and put on a cheerful air.

The hospital was quiet on this Saturday afternoon. Sam went into the administrator's office.

"Sir, I am Sam Neal. My sister and I have brought food to give a party for patients who are able. Is there a place for us to do that?"

He offered them the recreation center. "Go ahead but I doubt our patients will come. They have dinner delivered to their rooms in another hour."

Sam came back to the car to report to Gertie. "You set up the food and I'll round up the party goers."

She began by searching the cabinets for a tablecloth and utensils. Everything was there, neatly tucked away.

Nurses saw the activity and soon became involved. "What is happening here?"

"We want to give a party for the patients."

"Great. Jane, make coffee. I'll get the patients that need help."

"Thanks. Bring as many as possible."

Sam began leading patients like sheep into the recreation center. Gertie became the hostess. Her natural charm and openness was inviting. Years of dealing with her brothers put her at ease with the men, even those in hospital gowns. Soon the strongest were helping the weakest. A nurse sat at the piano and began to play some old familiar tunes. Singing and laughter filled the big room while Gertie and Sam spread the feast.

When the hospital administrator came to check on the commotion, Sam greeted him, "Join the party, Colonel."

His mouth hung open as he saw Gertie dancing with a young man in a wheelchair to the music from the sing-along. Her cheeks were rosy and her eyes were sparkling. She had repeatedly refused to dance with patients who asked until one in the wheelchair approached her. She accepted the challenge. With his left hand on the wheel and the right one holding tight to her hand, he turned and shifted back and forth to the music. Everyone formed a circle around them and sang.

"Food's ready. All home cooked," she announced. "Line up here if you can or stay in your seat. I'll bring you a plate."

While they ate, Gertie and Sam mingled among them, making small talk and joking. It was hard to tell who was enjoying this most.

Sam noticed that the patients were beginning to tire, and gave Gertie the hint to end the party. She began thanking them one by one for coming. They responded by thanking her, one by one.

A soldier, wrapped in bandages over most of his head, held tight to her hand." Do you have time to talk? You remind me so much of my sister."

"Where is she?"

"Chicago. I wish I could talk to her, but I can't hold a phone to my ear. He pointed to his bandages.

"What's your name?"

"Steve."

"Steve, I can't stay and talk now, but I will come back. And when I do, I will find your room. OK? What's your last name, soldier?"

"Windsor."

"Steve Windsor, I'm coming to see you as soon as I can. I promise. Maybe I can help you call Chicago."

Others heard this conversation and asked for her time. *I'll find a way*, she thought.

There were no leftovers. There were a lot of tired patients who would sleep better tonight. One patient called out, "Sweetie, we don't even know your name."

"I'm Gertie and this is my brother Sam," A cheer went up at the news that the man was her brother.

"Ger-tee, Ger-tee, Ger-tee..." the chant resounded through the hospital as Sam took his sister's arm and led her back to her car.

Gertie climbed in, leaned her head back to rest, and invited sleep from the overloads of the day. "Thanks, Sam."

182

"What for?"

"Everything."

"I'm going to do something else for you... so save your thanks."

Gertie sat up straight. "And, what would that be?"

"I'm going to teach you to drive. If you're going to be coming back here to hold soldiers' hands, you'll have to borrow my car. You don't expect me to sit around like a chauffeur while you do that, do you?"

"I promised them... but I wasn't sure how or when."

"Easy. You can use my car, drive here after dinner. When can we start the lessons?"

Gertie smiled warmly at her irrepressible brother and yielded to the quiet hum of the engine. Sleep was a moment away.

"Edward, the answer is *yes.*" Gertie said under her breath.

"What did you say?" Sam quizzed.

"Nothing, I'm talking to Edward.

Chapter 20 *1918*

Work was the only possible answer to the dark cloud Gertie carried. Immersion in the day-to-day was her solution. *I don't have closure,* she thought. "It's as simple as that," she told the morning air as she walked to the bank." Edward is gone, William and I have to deal with it. I should never have told Sam that *life is good.* It jinxed me. And here I am talking out loud again."

❦

Gertie was grasping the intricacies of her new job. She was rightfully proud as each new banking task was mastered. Mrs. Barnes found her a bright and willing student. Although she originally balked at teaching Gertie Neal, Mr. Morgan ignored her reluctance and made it clear that she would do it. By the third week of training Mrs. Barnes softened in her attitude. Gertie assumed more responsibility and began to take initiative. No matter what Mrs. Barnes' preconceived opinions of the young divorcee were, she admired accurate work and ambition. The business customers liked Gertie, but the ladies of the town avoided her. They only approached her window when it was the only one open.

Jesse Morgan watched over Gertie's work and took every opportunity to compliment her progress. He was observing the lobby when Elizabeth Amsterdam entered the bank. He was quickly on his feet to go to meet the long-time valued customer.

"Good morning, Mrs. Amsterdam. May I assist you with your banking today? Please, come into my office, no need to stand in line at the teller window."

"Thank you Mr. Morgan, but this teller will be fine," she answered pointing to Gertie.

He made a slight bow and smiled. Later as Gertie went to have a cup of coffee on her break, he intercepted her, noticing her pretty dress in the latest two-tone fashion.

"Gertie, I see that you have become a favorite of Mrs. Amsterdam already. It is a compliment that she selected you to handle her business. I'm sure that if you were to remain in our main office, other customers would rely on you also."

"That is very nice of you to say, but I must be honest with you, Elizabeth Amsterdam is my son's great grandmother, by his father, and she is one of my dearest friends. She came to me to inquire about us and how we are doing. I didn't handle any business for her. Actually, she brought me a birthday present. Before she left she told me to tell you of her mission and that she considers me family and cannot, in all honesty, bring her business to my window. I think she thought she had played a little joke on you." Gertie was talking with laughter in her voice and Jesse Morgan noticed that, too. She instinctively tossed her head to make the curls bob up and down as if they were laughing also.

Jesse Morgan joined Gertie and laughed heartily. "I shall be ready for her little jokes on the next visit," he continued with a twinkle in his eye.

"Mrs. Amsterdam is not well. Sadly, I doubt she will be in often but I appreciated the effort she made today. I'm sure she did it for me."

"I'm sorry to hear that. She's a lovely lady. By the way, Happy Birthday. Is it today?"

"Yes, today."

He reached across his desk and made a note on his calendar.

"Do you know when I will be going to Ft. Meade?"

"Next week. I'm thinking—Monday. Mrs. Barnes says you are ready. Do you agree?"

"Yes, sir."

"I was going to talk to you about it before you left today. I think you'll work well with our team. The courier leaves here at eight each morning and returns by four... if you're sure."

"I'm sure," she asserted.

❧

At Ft. George G Meade the new banking facility flourished. Gertie flourished too. The men who came into the bank noticed the pretty girl and tried hard to strike a personal note with her. She was not interested. In her logical manor, Gertie kept the resolve she had made about men a long time ago. *William is the only man I need in my life.* Gertie especially was not interested in military men who would someday return to their home states. There were bets made and challenges offered but the result was always the same. Not one got a date with the pretty teller. In good humor, Gertie enjoyed the banter with them, while safely behind the bars of the teller's cage. At lunch time, she disappeared and returned in one hour. Little did the soldiers know that to make time with Gertie, they had to be recovering in the army hospital just 500 yards away from the bank.

Her promise to the veterans in the hospital was easy to keep now that she worked within walking distance. At noon everyday Gertie entered the hospital. They had one hour of her time, five days a week.

Gertie had a chart of room numbers and a list of patients with important facts about those who would have long recoveries or need rehabilitation. She visited with every patient, room by room, day after day. Her rounds in the hospital were organized so that she had visited every patient by Friday. On Monday she started again at Room 101. The only variance from the plan was to wish farewell to a dismissed soldier or a special visit before surgery or death. Gertie ate her packed lunch in the hospital hallways and got back in her teller cage on time.

When she stopped in the little hospital chapel, she prayed for the recovering men and talked to Edward. "I'm doing this for you," she reminded him.

The hospital was not always a cheerful place, but Gertie did all she could to present a happy face to those she visited. She soon realized that it was a skill that she could polish. She picked up on the situation and entered each room accordingly, with a light touch or a broad shoulder as needed. She carried a large heavy bag filled with magazines, stationery, stamps and candy. After a time, the staff made a locker available to her. From her small salary, she bought greeting cards and other items to help with her effort to keep a promise that the fighting men would not be forgotten. Soon Gertie was thinking of the men in the hospital when she bought a dress—was it a cheerful color?

Gertie read newspapers and magazines, always looking for things that could be shared with patients who could not see. Jokes and bits of humor were gleaned for use on that precious lunch hour. She was willing to give her lunch hours each week, pennies she saved and small bits of herself but she did not take anything away from William or their time at Bear Creek on the weekend.

When she least expected it, on a beautiful day in April, Gertie arrived at room 204 just in time to witness the death of one of her favorite patients. She entered the room and saw a flurry of activity over the young man and started to back out. The nurse looked up, "Gertie, I'm glad you are here. John has been asking for you. Come in."

"Gertie is here, Johnny," the nurse said to the quiet figure on the bed.

She walked to the side of the bed. Her heart was beating way too fast, and her hand began to shake so she thrust it into her bag as if to pack away her feelings.

"Hi." He managed a smile and reached for her. Gertie retrieved her hand and gave it to him.

"Hi, Johnny," she said, but she did not recognize her own tense voice. A smile, warm and loving, was on her face as she had trained it to be. Her dress was way too cheerful but it gave him a pleasant sight in the final moments of his life.

John Logan held her hand in a death grip. It never occurred to Gertie to try to withdraw it.

"Gertie, if I hadn't gotten that letter to Janice…. If you hadn't……." He squeezed.

"But, we did, didn't we, Johnny? You made her very happy."

"Stay with me…please?" Her hand was his life line.

Gertie nodded and smiled. It was a very long ninety minutes— staying with Johnny and answering his gaze each time he opened his eyes.

Finally he said, "Janice…"It was his last word.

She looked down at the young soldier, and then to her hand, which he still held tightly. Her fingers were red from constriction. Gertie froze. At first the doctors and nurses did not notice Private Logan's grip and expected Gertie to step back. In fact the nurse slightly nudged her, thinking she may be dumbfounded by the events at the bedside.

"Step aside, please," the doctor said. Gertie couldn't move. Her hand and the hand of John Logan were locked.

"Excuse me," he said with emphasis

"Help," was all that Gertie could utter as the attending nurse finally noticed her fingers, now painfully crushed in the hand of the dying soldier. One by one, the doctor loosened Johnny's fingers and released Gertie. Her fingers throbbed with her heart. She wrung her hands and pressed them to her breast as if they could steady the pace within. Gertie walked to the corridor and cried with uncontrollable anguish.

"You're fine, Gertie," the nurse said, "… you knew Johnny wouldn't make it." Her explanation for what had just happened did not help. Gertie's heart seemed to be beating in her hand now and she stared at it as if it were not a part of her own body. She swallowed the pill that was offered and as soon as it went down she regretted taking it.

"What was that?" she demanded.

"It will help you to relax."

"Oh, no. I must get back to work." Her protestations were to no avail as she was led to a cot. Sleep came upon her and she drifted off, fretfully. When she awoke, the branch manager was there to assure her that the banking world at Ft. Meade had survived her absence that afternoon.

"The courier is here to take us back to Laurel. Are you ready?"

"Yes." She answered, but it was not totally the truth. The medicine and sleep still had its hold on her. The driver came to guide her to the car. Feeling quite ridiculous, Gertie wanted to get home and have the events of the day behind her. After the heroic death of a patriot soldier, she felt that her weakness had somehow taken something away from him.

Gertie was going to have to resolve this failure with some kind of action. The six short miles to Laurel were especially long today. No one in the car broached the subject that was on all minds. At the same time, no lightness or frivolity was befitting either. Back at the main office, Mr. Morgan was waiting for the car bringing his employees.

"Gertie, will you come to my office, please."

She was not in a mood to talk to Mr. Morgan or anyone. But, she had no choice except to accept the chair he offered.

"I'm very sorry that I failed to work after lunch today, Mr. Morgan. It won't happen again, I promise."

He raised his hand to stop her. "Gertie, I'll drive you home today—as soon as you are ready to go."

"I want to go home and I don't want to inconvenience you." Her effort to get out of the chair was shaky.

He took her arm, helped her with her coat and led her to the car. He did not ask any questions.

She sank into the car seat, realizing that she would have had a difficult time walking home today. She had no strength. The ride was very much appreciated and that surprised the stubborn, independent woman.

"I suppose that is the first time you have seen someone die." He opened conversation. "That is very difficult especially if it is unexpected and thrust upon you. I didn't know until today that you spend your lunch hours at the hospital."

"I had been driving out to visit patients before coming on Post to work. Then I started using my lunch hour." She was telling him something no one knew except Sam and William.

"That is admirable, but you need to prepare yourself for situations like today ... if that is what you're going to do. Not every patient will have a happy ending."

"I know."

"Are you going again tomorrow?" He was talking to her like an old friend and she was surprised how welcome his interest and support was.

"I'm not sure. I need time to think."

"No, you don't." His voice was soft and compassionate then rose slightly. "You don't need time to think."

He took his eyes off the road for an instant and saw her big brown eyes widened by his words.

"You need to resolve that you will be right back there tomorrow. Twelve to one. What else can you do with your time? Would you be knitting or working crosswords or chattering with co-workers during your break time? Not you, Gertie. I think not."

Gertie was startled by Mr. Morgan's animation. He reminded her of Sam. He would be bullying her just like this, if he were here. It made Gertie smile and laugh softly, just soft enough to cause Jesse Morgan to look sideways at his passenger again.

Her quiet laugh made Jesse Morgan happy.

"I think you are right. I'll be at the hospital tomorrow. You know Mr. Morgan…

"Please," he interrupted, "call me Jesse when we are away from the office where I consider myself your friend."

"Jesse… the soldier was Johnny Logan and he wanted to be a comedian on the stage, instead he died for his country. I saw him often. He loved to laugh and make others laugh. He found humor in everything. I remember the letter he asked me to write to his girlfriend. He had never told her he loved her, instead, he always made jokes. In his last letter he said she had his jokes to make her laugh and his love to make her happy. *Laugh* and *happy* are two different things and he knew the difference."

"A wise man."

"A wise, *young* man. Rare."

"Go on with your story."

"Over a year after he was injured, he died for his country—our country. Johnny was a victim of nerve gas; I've seen too many." Gertie shifted in her seat to face Jesse. "Do you think there is any way to show we appreciate what he, and so many others, did? He never complained about his plight, he only continued to dream. There are so many heroes." She hung her head. "Every patient is a hero."

"We can never show just appreciation, I'm afraid. Do you think he was looking for appreciation?"

"No… not really. I think he was looking for some comfort, some help, and relief from his daily struggle."

"And you did all you could to give him those things." Gertie and Jesse fell silent, thinking about the words that had passed between them.

Their conversation was surprisingly easy. Soon she began recounting the day's events in the hospital room. She was animated talking about Johnny Logan, the nurses, the doctors, and herself. As she came to the part about the death grip, her voice was soft. Jesse had to concentrate to hear every word. He pulled the car to a stop at the fire house parking lot on Ninth Street so he could give her story his full attention. He was afraid he would be at her doorstep before she had time to unfold the whole tale.

"Today was not the first time I faced death. I watched a man die when I was sixteen." Then Gertie told of the day that she and her father had raced to save the victims of the accident on the bridge beyond

Fergus Hill years before. Her voice was calm and sure as she talked to Jesse.

"It was not Johnny's death that unnerved me. It was his grip. When I realized he held my hand tightly as his life drifted away, it scared me." She was thinking of the grip that Edward once used to break her arm and the grip that the Neal family and this town still held over her. But she was not ready to confide these things to Jesse. "I was afraid that I might not break loose. Is that strange? Can you see? It was everything that holds and won't let go—everything that holds beyond reason. Am I making sense?"

Jesse Morgan had his own experiences with unyielding grips to bring to her question. It made perfect sense to him. He concentrated on her words. *Someday, I will tell you why I understand so well what you're saying, Gertie Neal.* He put his thoughts aside and paid attention to her openness and vulnerability.

"You are making sense. It was one of those moments in life that puts everything else in perspective."

"Exactly, exactly." she replied excitedly. "Yes, that is what it was. Everyone thought I was terrified by Johnny Logan's death but I wasn't. It was something inside me that was terrifying. You understand, don't you?" She reached over and clutched his arm. He wrapped his hand around hers. She looked into his knowing hazel eyes. Gertie let go and sank back into the upholstery of the seat, exhausted and relieved—not really aware of his hand on hers—not as aware as he was.

"I've got to get you home to that boy and some dinner." Jesse started the car. Soon they were turning onto Tenth Street. "I remember, you live in the last house on the left."

"Actually, that is my in-laws home where William is. We live in an apartment in this house," she said, pointing to 403.

"Jesse, I shouldn't have ...."

"Gertie, you can trust me. We're friends, remember?"

She smiled. "Thanks for the ride home, and for everything. See you tomorrow."

"Are you OK?"

"Yes." She smiled.

Jesse was consumed by desire and the last thing he wanted was to let Gertie out of his car. But, he got out, opened her door, and assisted her to the sidewalk where she proceeded back into her world.

Gertie did not know why, but her evening with William would be so much more pleasant because of her time with Jesse Morgan. Her new friend allowed her to address emotions that she could not share with William. She would not have a knot in her stomach that spoiled her dinner, or a tension in her voice that would puzzle William. Without either occupant in the car knowing why or how, a great void in the life of the lonely woman was filled.

In the quiet of her bed, four hours later, Gertie thought about the time in Jesse Morgan's car. She was surprised that her words had flowed so easily and that friendship seemed so comfortable…so quickly. She had no second thoughts about having him as her friend—in fact, she was looking forward to seeing him tomorrow

"Umm", she said out loud just before drifting off to sleep.

❧

Edward was gone. Gertie would never know if the embers of her first love could glow again. Forgiving him was accomplished a long time ago. She had even to come to enjoy recalling their early courtship and marriage. Her daydreams and fantasies were pointless now. Gertie looked out the window and saw William pitching a ball at the bull's-eye painted on Clay's shed. She listened to the ball hit the target. Thug! *Edward belongs to William.* Thug! *I'll help him love his father.* Thug! *They both deserve that.* Thug!

Routine is often a welcome friend when death changes your life and thinking. Gertie and William needed to rise each morning with work, school, and family obligations. They moved into the phase of mourning when they would *choose* when to think about Edward.

One evening several weeks later, Gertie was clearing the kitchen. William was involved in the history of the B&O railroad when a knock came on the door.

She was surprised by Clay Neal. It was a rare occurrence.

"Come in Poppa Neal." She invited and pointed to a chair. "Is anything wrong?"

"No, nothing wrong." He turned his attention to William. "Hi, son."

William came to his grandfather with the book he was reading. "I'm learning about your railroad, sir—the one you and Daddy worked on."

"I see. That's fine. I have another book you might like to read. Remind me when you come from school tomorrow and I'll get it for you." William went back to his reading.

"Please sit, Clay."

"No, thanks, I'll just be a minute." The tall straight man drew in a breath and began delivering his message. "Edward left William everything. There's some clothing, some jewelry, some money, an insurance policy, his military death benefits." He reached into his pocket and drew out a key ring. "And, his car." He was reading from a list attached to a large manila envelope. She thought she saw his hand shaking as he dropped the keys on the table.

Is he angry? She wondered. *Does he think everything should have come to him?*

"This….," he handed the envelope to her, "is from the army." Clay walked to the door and put his hand on the knob.

"Clay, please sit down for a minute. I'm trying to understand all you have told me." He turned from the door, stepped back in the room and sat down. Gertie took the envelope and withdrew the check and benefit schedule. There was a will, drawn by an Army lawyer, a bank book, and an insurance policy. While she looked at the papers, Clay kept his eyes fixed on her.

Gertie felt his gaze. There was something else—unsaid—in the air.

What's he not saying? She looked at him and sought his gaze.

He was girded with steal and his eyes were not soft when they looked at her. *He is impossible to figure!* She couldn't tell what he was thinking, but she guessed he did not want to be standing in her home giving away Edward's last material things.

"This," she held the papers in the air, "is what Edward wanted to give William. I do not know how you and Mom Neal feel about it. The only thing I can say is this," she paused and drew strength with her breath, "I will keep it all for William. The money will go into an account for his education. I'll do it tomorrow." The old man stood without making any move to leave or to say another word. The silence unnerved Gertie. She wrung her hands and asked, "Is there something else?"

He moved to the door, placed his worn hand on the knob for the second time and, with his back still to her, spoke into the wall.

"Mary wanted to keep the car in the shed until William was old enough to use it. I disagreed. You could use that car to get to work.

Those are the only keys. Of course the car is William's and you are his only parent, you can do as you wish with the car and the money." He turned slightly. "I told her."

Suddenly Gertie saw with perfect clarity what was troubling Clay and Mary.

"I will go to see her right now." Gertie stepped between Clay and the door, moving out ahead of him. She strode toward the house next door thinking that Clay was following her, but he headed for the tool shed instead. Gertie entered the house next door alone. Mary Neal, sitting at the kitchen table, seemed to be waiting for her. She spoke first.

"I know you want to move. Edward is gone forever. Now his money will make it possible for you to take William away, and you have the means and a car to drive to work after you move." She was talking in a drone voice. Despair covered her face. Her eyes were dry. She was convinced that Gertie would climb in Edward's car and drive William down Tenth Street and away. That conviction was beyond tears. Her suffering started now for what she was sure was coming. She would lose William—so soon after Edward's death.

"Mary, William and I are not going to move now. We will stay next door and he will continue to come from school to this kitchen every day. Edward left his son all that he had. He knew I would do right by his son. You need to trust me, too." Gertie moved from standing to a seat at the table across from the older woman. "Edward's car will not sit in that shed for years waiting for William to grow up. I will use it to help take care of us. Edward's last thought was of William. I believe yours and mine will be the same." She paused, exhausted by the decisions she had wrought in this kitchen where Edward and William made Mary Neal's world—each in his own time. "That is something we have in common."

"Good night." Gertie walked to the door, allowing her hand to slide across Mary Neal's shoulders.

The instant Mary felt Gertie's tender touch her face fell into her hands. When her tears came, they were tears of grief and relief.

When she said, "Thank you," Gertie was halfway home.

Gertie had a most amazing thought as she walked home to William. *I love you, Mary Neal.* She stopped in her tracks for another unsought, revealing thought. *Grandmother Amsterdam has been waiting for this— and probably praying for it, too.* The last few steps to her home were light. It would take a while to sort this out. When old attitudes are gone, renewal steps in. She stopped at the porch steps and looked down Tenth Street. The nice, well-kept houses were glowing in the twilight. Porch swings were waiting. Bicycles were dropped by doorsteps. Gertie knew dinners and homework were happening in each. A screened door slammed down the block and a dog barked out back. "That's Blackie." Warmth seemed to drift from yard to yard to her yard. Gertie turned and looked back at the Neal house where the light in the window brought her the same comfort it gave William. *What's changed?* She asked herself. She opened her door, entered 403 Tenth Street, and said, "Me. . . I've changed."

The next day, Gertie dropped William off at school and drove to work. The car was a luxury Gertie could not have imagined. Edward's bequest was the only way she would ever own a car. It took a very short time for her to realize that she could not afford to drive it to work every day and if it broke down she would not have money to fix it. The car spent most of its time parked in a space Clay made in one of his out buildings. She drove in bad weather, on special occasions or when William was ill.

It became like the cameo. It owned Gertie.

The money deposited for William amounted to $365. 00. It was William's nest egg. He often asked Gertie to show him the savings book so he could see what his father had done for him. Each payday Gertie added another dollar to the balance.

❦

1918 was a difficult year and it was not over yet. Fall had colored the leaves and provided a crunchy crisp song with every step for the walking commuter. "I love fall, especially when sunshine lights the colors." She talked to Mother Nature as she walked.

She saw William running to meet her. Before she could suggest raking leaves, he threw his arms around her waist and buried his head into her coat.

"William what's wrong?" She knelt down to his level and lifted his eyes to meet hers.

"It's Great Grandmother."

Gertie wanted to gather him up in her arms, but she could only draw him close and walk him in the house. Clay was sitting at the table alone.

"What's happened, Clay?"

"Elizabeth died today. We got the call five minutes ago."

Even with the short preparation at the gate, Gertie was not prepared to hear *died*. She scanned the room. "Where's Mom Neal?'

"Parlor."

"William, stay here."

Gertie slid open the doors and looked into the dark room. "Mom Neal?" She waited for an answer but none came.

As her eyes became accustomed to the darkened room she saw her mother-in-law sitting in the middle of the settee, her back as straight as a ramrod. She also noticed there were no tears. "Can I do anything for you?" No answer.

"I'm coming in." She began a quiet steady stream of words. "This is hard beyond words—hard for everyone, but you, most of all." Gertie squeezed in between Mary and the arm of the settee. "I'm going to put my arms around you." Gertie did not feel she could do this without at least, a caution. Her embrace circled the older woman; Gertie felt her tension.

Immediately the tears came as her back doubled over. Gertie was prepared with a hankie.

"Tell Clay to call the children." Then Mary said something but Gertie couldn't understand.

"I didn't hear. Say again."

Without looking at Gertie, she spoke again—tears without sobs flooded her face. "I deserve the dark. Mother was the light at the end of my tunnel and I thought she would always be there…holding the light for me…no matter how long it took me to get through my tunnel…but the tunnel always got longer and longer…I deserve the dark." Then she seemed to gather composure. She thrust the soaked hankie at Gertie and said, "Thank you."

Gertie did not know what to do or say as she got the first glimpse into the woman who was circled in walls. Understanding washed over Gertie and put a clear, clean glow in the dark room. She watched Mary dry her last tear on her sleeve and stand up.

"Where is William?"

"In the kitchen with Clay."

She took Gertie's arm and drew her to her feet. "Take William home and help him with this. You both loved Mother…and she you. You'll have each other to get you through this hard time. Clay and I will call the family home; the children will help us through, too. Go—" Mary drew a breath and spoke from her heart. "—but, do not stay away. We need each other in the days ahead."

"I'm very sorry and very sad, Mom Neal."

Gertie was almost out of the parlor when she heard, "Gertie…." Even before she continued, Gertie realized how rare it was for this woman to say her name. "… Edward, now Mother…"

"Yes."

"Make sure William is alright."

Gertie signaled to William. "Come son." They walked home.

"William, we have wonderful memories of Great Grandmother, don't we?"

He nodded.

"And, we will miss her. She did so much to make us happy and she would not want us to be sad very long." Gertie lifted his chin for the second time. "Look at me William. For the next few days we will be sad, but because we loved Great Grandmother, we will not stay sad long. OK?"

"OK, Gertie." In his little boy way and because he trusted his mother, William took her words to heart and believed them.

Gertie had more trouble with her words than her son did. *How can I go on without you, Grandmother?* In the dark quiet of her bedroom, she took reality on and let it rest on her body. It weighted her chest and made her arms useless. *You have been my sanctuary. William and I could not have stayed here without you. I could not have pushed on without the cameo.* Gertie brought her quilt up to her mouth, pushed her head deep into the pillow and let her tears flow. They streamed down on either side of her head, unchecked. The only thing she could do in the dark was call out to her mother, who could not hear her and did not know her anguish. "Mama." It was a whisper. "Mama." It was a prayer.

As sleep drew near random scenes with Grandmother bounced in her mind: Placing the cameo in her hand. Slipping the nightgown over her broken arm. Hugging William. Pouring tea in exquisite cups. Watching Edward and William play in her yard. Smiling…

Well into the night, the blessing of sleep came to Gertie.

Gertie and William left on Wednesday for Bear Creek. They would stay one night, eat Thanksgiving dinner with the family and return for the services on Friday. Bear Creek and the MacGregor clan were medicine to them.

"Mama, we are so glad to be here. We are not far from the sadness on Tenth Street but today, William deserves a big dose of happy and family."

"You both do."

"Grandmother Amsterdam never really recovered from losing Edward. She was fragile before, but after..." Gertie's voice trailed off. "William and I will miss her so much." Their hug was long, strong, and full of understanding.

"I remember Elizabeth fondly, especially when she came to your wedding."

"That seems a lifetime ago." They walked arm in arm into the big house that was already filled with the blend of aromas of Thanksgiving. "What is Papa doing?"

"He has one eye on the bridge, two hands in the stuffing mix and a cup of coffee on the side."

The first smile in days brightened Gertie's face.

Chapter 21

Jesse Morgan was infatuated with Gretta Neal. He liked everything he knew about her and agonized over not knowing enough. No woman, not even his wife in their courting days, infiltrated his mind, took away his concentration, gave him a feeling for tomorrow. He had a sense of helplessness.

Jesse Morgan was a man in command. He stood six foot three and his demeanor was strong. He had been an athlete in school and still prided himself in his muscular, thin physique. Many times he ran a mile course from his house to the paper stand and back just to maintain his speed and strength. Light hair, fair complexion, and hazel eyes came to him from his Scottish ancestry. Hair that was tow-head blond in childhood had mellowed to a true honey color. He took pride in the physical condition he maintained by dedicated effort, but was unimpressed by his own good looks—which were to him, a matter of chance.

His mother was an artist and instilled a love of the arts, but could not make him into an artist too. He took piano and painting lessons and proved proficient in each, yet lacked the passion to excel in either. Jesse Morgan loved business. From his mother he took a color sense that helped him dress handsomely. This same training was apparent in his office where beautiful paintings and rugs gave unusual warmth to the paneled walls of his spacious office on the mezzanine looking down on the lobby of the bank.

T. J. Morgan, Jesse's father, taught him to savor success. But when the younger Morgan graduated from the University of Maryland, he did not go into his father's feed and supply company. He found his passion in the world of finance. Jesse would manage his own future in the banking world.

Jesse rocketed to the top of the largest bank in Washington, DC. He was fair in his dealings, but most of his success was credited to his diligence. He married Catherine Sharp, a woman who wanted him to go high on the ladder of success. The marriage was in a crumbled heap at the foot of the corporate ladder, when they realized the cost of his success. Catherine thought it was worth the sacrifice.

The banking community was shocked when he gave it all up to come to the small bank on Main Street, Laurel, Maryland.

"It is my resignation." He told the board of directors as he slid a letter into the center of the mahogany desk in the board room of the Central Bank of the District of Columbia. "At the end of the month, my office... and my position on this board will be vacant." It was not a matter for discussion. When Jesse Morgan brought his impressive demeanor and steady gaze to those around the table, it was a done deal.

Jesse was convinced the financial structure of the 20's decade was in jeopardy. He foresaw disaster before the decade was over. He would protect his assets, his future and go to a small community where he could not only weather the storm he saw coming, but help others through it, too. It was a wise move.

Then, he had to tell Catherine....

"Catherine, I'd like for you to dine with me this evening—in the solarium."

"Of course, Jesse. I do not have another commitment. Bradley, too?"

Can we start over together? He wondered as she, almost warmly, accepted his invitation.

"Not tonight. I have something important to talk over with you. Seven o'clock. I'll tell cook."

She came into the room, dressed impeccably. He rose, admiring her beauty and perfection, walked her to the table, pulled her chair and slid it gently under as she sat.

Jesse wanted to open the discussion, but a journey of backward steps required a partnership. In Catherine's severely swept, lacquered hair and managed smiles, he saw—there would not be any bending or loosening in her. Across the table he saw a stranger and she saw the same in his manufactured confidence.

He picked up the wine bottle and read, "Pinot Noir, one of our favorites," as he poured.

She sipped and approved with a nod and another taste.

Jesse approached his wife just as he approached the board of directors. The table was different, but the atmosphere was alarmingly similar. With the same commanding presence, he announced his decision.

"Catherine, I have resigned from the bank and taken a position in the bank in Maryland—Laurel, Maryland." Before he could begin details, she shut him down.

"Where the hell is Laurel?" She demanded. "That can't be a step up. You're going to commute?"

"No. I have found a beautiful estate—a wonderful place to raise Bradley."

"I'm not moving." Her face showed the puzzlement she felt. "Bradley is not moving, either. Are you out of your mind?" She began to set her wine glass down and then, before it touched the linen cloth, she lifted it again to drink deeply. "You *are* out of your mind." She proclaimed holding her glass as if it were a toast to his insanity.

This discussion was heading onto the battleground where he and his wife had come to live. Jesse's throat constricted. Communication between him and Catherine had been absent in the marriage for years. How stupid of him to think a quiet dinner in her favorite room in the house could make *anything* different. There were no possibilities on either side of the table.

Catherine had no love for Jesse and basically lived in her own rooms in their town house on Capitol Hill. She was happy with the arrangement that included other men. Jesse's only leverage was his wealth. Catherine liked the advantages it provided. Her only leverage was Bradley. Their four-year-old son was barter for Jesse's compliance to Catherine's will. Jesse wanted to save his financial fortune from impending disaster; he also wanted to save himself from this eternal hell.

"I'm moving to Laurel, Maryland and I would like to have my family with me."

"You made this decision without me; you can go without me... and Bradley, too."

"I realize that my work schedule has left little time for our marriage." It was the beginning of an apology. "I hardly know Bradley. I want more time for you...and for him."

"Frankly, Jesse, *I* don't want more time with *you*." Her eyes were hard and her mind was closed to the appeal of this man for his son.

She glanced at the wine bottle to decide if she wanted to continue this conversation into another glass.

"Tell me how we can work this out." He would not be a fool and beg her to come with him. "Do you want a divorce?"

"Never. I will not live with that stigma."

"But, you *will* have your liaisons?" He failed to see the moral difference in the stigmas.

"Yes, Jesse," She spoke with defiance. "I will. Go live in Hicksville, Maryland. Bradley and I stay here." She pointed down to the marble floor with her well-manicured finger. "Here," she reiterated as she cast her jeweled hand around in a circle as if including all of the Nation's Capital. "You know where to send the checks."

Catherine stood, picked up the wine bottle and walked to the door. "The dinner was great," she shot back sarcastically. Her chin lifted, her mouth closed and she pinched her face with disgust. She no longer resembled the beautiful woman who had entered the solarium minutes ago.

"...for dessert, we will indulge in multi-layered indigestion." Jesse exhaled to the empty room.

Jesse would be generous. And, someday he would search his soul to see if his generosity was because he cared or because he felt guilty, but not while the ice of his wife's eyes was still chilling the room. Jesse Morgan did not indulge in self-inflicted pain.

The dye was cast. Jesse moved to Hilltop Manor. Catherine and Bradley lived in DC and she did all she could to keep father and son from having a relationship. The young boy was never told that his father wanted his family in the Maryland suburbs. He grew up believing that his father left him and did not want him.

🌿

Now Jesse Morgan was in a dilemma. When Jesse was in a dilemma, his right hand unconsciously tapped the edge of his desk like treble piano keys, playing Rachmaninoff. Into the air where imaginary music was dramatic, he whispered, "Gertie."

His business mind and his emotional sense were doing battle. The attractive young divorcee was commanding more and more of his thoughts. He was finding delight in her company and as each feature of her personality unfolded in time, he wanted to know her better. Lately, he played the imaginary keyboard often.

It was not long after Gertie came to work at the bank that Jesse realized his hopes for her success were not entirely in the interest of the bank. He wanted her to succeed for herself. That took him back a step. It was the first time he acknowledged a growing, emotional attachment to Gertie.

Thoughts of Gertie forced him to think of Catherine. After eight years in Laurel, the arrangement with his wife had not changed. He saw Bradley occasionally and never saw Catherine. His cancelled checks represented a marriage that existed on paper only. He had no right to even think of a fine person like Gertie. Women were not easy for him but by the same token, by using the same tactics that he used in business he had had enough female conquests through the years to satisfy.

Gertie was different.

Jesse Morgan didn't want to use tactics and he was not interested in a conquest.

What did he want from Gertie? That question repeated in his mind when he was working, driving, daydreaming, playing the piano or trying to sleep.

Jesse was one of the few people who realized the courage it took for her to get a divorce. He admired her strength, raising a son alone without the resources Catherine had. And, he admired her dedication to patients in the hospital—so selfless. Jesse's mind had never been so conflicted.

The evening that he met Gertie at the train station, stayed with Jesse. He recalled everything about her and surprised himself by making inquiries. Her story was sketchy and contradictory since it came mostly from gossip. It was clear, Gertie needed a job and he had one to offer. It was a good business move. Now she was a good and valued employee and he had to measure his distance.

I have a wife. The thought plagued him as he uncovered the keyboard on his piano. *I can have a friendship,* he thought as Chopin's Polonaise swirled around the room. *Gertie needs a friend.* The last dramatic movement traveled up and down the keys. *And...* his fingers danced ... *so do I,* —accented the last chords. The drama of Chopin's music and his thoughts exhausted him.

Jesse rose from the piano, dropped the keyboard cover and said, "She has a boyfriend." He saw them lunching at Gravilla's, and he saw how devoted they were. "Friends" He proclaimed with relief. The music had worked magic and settled his mind and soul—once more.

Jesse Morgan's heart was lighter. He looked forward to tomorrow morning when Gertie would stop by his office on her way to the Ft. Meade Branch.

He set his schedule to include a visit to the branch every Friday.

Yes, that would be good. I need to go, not to see Gertie—to keep my eye on the new branch. He worked that over in his mind, too.

"Put a visit to the Post branch on my calendar for each Friday at 11:00," he informed his secretary. "And… get the name and number for the officer in charge of the Post hospital. I want to talk to him."

That night, he tapped a waltz on the side of the mattress as he drifted off to a peaceful sleep without his recurring dreams.

Jesse began cultivating his friendship with Gertie. It was easy because she was a friendly person, she has a boyfriend, and within the bounds of the work day, she was comfortable chatting with him.

Life settled in for the two friends. Gertie had left friendships behind when she married Edward. Edward's sister, Emily, moved in another direction after Gertie confided the brutal details of her marriage. Gertie should have known better than to tell Emily and she learned from that mistake. Her school friends were married now and they raised their children far away from the divorcee. Rejection taught her to avoid relationships except within her family. Her social life was at Bear Creek on the weekends. That was the extent of her circle, until Jesse sought her out.

Each morning, she spoke to him with a cheery "Hello." Each evening, before leaving, she stuck her head into his office and quietly said, "See you tomorrow, Jesse."

On Friday afternoons he came to the Ft. Meade Branch. At least once a month, he went with Gertie on her hospital rounds. She had come to look forward to those days—every third Friday. Jesse rarely disappointed her. Soon the patients knew Jesse, too, although they still preferred the pretty girl.

*

Lieutenant Mary Ann Shaw, the nurse in charge, was savvy and knew that Gertie's attention to the patients contributed to their wellbeing. Between noon and one o'clock each day the nurses' jobs were easier and a special healing took place that wasn't entered on charts.

"Gertie, Pfc. Brown in room 215 won't cooperate with his therapy. See if you can convince him." She did.

"Corporal Spencer in room 124 is being transferred. Believe it or not, he doesn't want to go because of you." Lt. Shaw smiled but she was serious.

"What's this I hear, Spence? You're getting fitted for prosthesis at Walter Reed? Great news. I want to see you walk again. When are you going?"

"Day after tomorrow," he paused to give up his resistance. "Yes, I'm going...if you'll write to me, Gertie?"

"I'll write but...I checked your chart. Did you know you are coming back here?"

"I am?"

"You are ours, my friend. So, get over there and get on your feet again—the sooner the better. I'll break my own rule and dance with you, Spence."

The experienced nursing staff was willing to utilize every resource and Gertie was one of them.

A few months after Lt. Shaw came to the hospital, she invited Gertie to call her Mary Ann. It was a great gift from the stern and no-nonsense officer. At times the two sat and shared a restful moment and a cup of coffee. During these rare times Gertie talked of William and the MacGregor family at Bear Creek.

"You never mention William's father."

"Pfc. Edward Neal died in Germany."

"And now you are trying to help every soldier that comes in this hospital." Mary Ann concluded that Gertie's motivation in this work was the tragic event that made her a widow.

Gertie let the misconception stand. It was the first time she hid the truth just to avoid the rejection that it might incur.

"The first time I came here was on the day of Edward's wake. I do this because of him. He wanted to know if we appreciate what these men have sacrificed for us." It was good to vocalize her motivation again.

"Col. Markham wants to see you," Mary Ann said one day as Gertie entered the ward. "Before you go in, let me put a bug in your ear. He wants to talk to you about expanding your work here. He wants the work volunteers are doing to have official status. You are the one to do it." Mary Ann smiled and gave her a sweeping bow pointing to the Colonel's office.

Col. Markham was standing at the window when she was shown into his office. "Ah, Gertie, step over here and look at this," he said pointing across the west lawn of the hospital. "The Post is being expanded. Our population is increasing and this hospital will be serving more and more of our military. We will be receiving patients from the northeast quadrant of the states. Our responsibilities are growing." Gertie stepped to the window and looked at the barrack construction that had been going on all year. The low wooden buildings with rows of windows were all alike. She could count eight under construction, looking out the Colonel's window.

"I have been watching the expansion on the hospital south and west sides, but hadn't paid attention to expansion over there," She said, pointing to the new barracks.

"Big changes." He walked her from the window to his desk. "Sit down, Gertie. I have a proposal for you. We have received funding to set up a volunteer service here. You have been doing a wonderful job for our patients... and we want to make it official. It is time we organized for the future and you stopped being Little Red Riding Hood with a basket of treats. We want you to have a truckload of treats, if you need them." His smile put her at ease. "There is to be an office for you at the hospital. It will be stocked and supplied with many of the things you buy and…. there will be a budget. The funding is generous but it is still a budget. You will have to keep an account of your expenditures. What do you think? Do you want to be Director of Volunteer Services at Ft. George G. Meade Army Hospital?"

"I am flabbergasted. Really…a real service club for our hospital? That is wonderful. I have some questions. Does this mean you want more time from me? Does being director mean this is not a volunteer position any longer? I like being a volunteer and I would not consider leaving my job at the bank."

"No, to both questions, Mrs. Neal. The funding is for equipment, supplies, and services only. We like and appreciate your volunteerism.

In fact, it is vital to the program as outlined in the endowment. We just want to make it easier, and less burdensome as you continue to serve our patients. This hospital is going to be serving a larger population. The need is growing. Some of the officer's wives want to volunteer, too. As for time, we appreciate your daily dedication, but expansion of the program is entirely up to you and the time you have."

"I am really excited, Sir. I'll do my best."

"I'm sure you will." He strode over to her and shook her hand as she rose from her seat. Together, they went out of the office and into the staff room where Mary Ann and her fellow nurses were waiting with applause.

Wow! Very few things in her life equaled this moment. Except for William's birth, she had never felt so fulfilled and obligated. It was almost like a new baby. *This is unbelievable.*

Mary Ann was nearly jumping with excitement when she finally had a private minute with Gertie. "It's grand. How are you going to handle this windfall?"

"I'm going to do all the things I couldn't do before—as soon as I can, too. I forgot to ask how much is in the budget. I guess the Colonel thinks I'm a ninny."

"I know that part," said Mary Ann. "You have one hundred dollars in the working fund and there is two hundred for equipment and supplies. That is three hundred dollars for setting up and services and it is a renewable amount each year. I would suggest you work out costs for equipment, supplies, and services and submit them to Col. Markham. You know he has the final word in this hospital, but as long as you are reasonable and productive, the money is yours to use. It is not military funding. It's a private endowment."

"Wait until I tell Jesse."

He was delighted to see Gertie busy working in the teller office after everyone was gone that evening. He was still at his desk when she closed her books and cleared her work. A light tap on his unlatched door caused it to open slowly.

"Come in, Gertie."

"Jesse, my work at the hospital has been expanded and funded. I'm to be the director of volunteer services...and I have a budget, too. I will always have stationery, stamps, and treats for the patients... and," she was thinking out loud, "...three or four parties a year. We can do so much more, now. I'm so excited." Color flushed her cheeks. Her enthusiasm was infectious. She began telling him of her plans and her concept of the program. He was the only friend she had to share this great news with and she was in no hurry to leave this warm welcoming place. And, he was in no hurry to have her go, either.

She offered her boss this assurance. "I can do this and my job too. I must. There is William's future to consider. You know my job is important and I cannot afford the luxury of volunteering full time for the veterans."

"This is great, Gertie. I'm so happy that you are excited about it. Is there anything I can do to help?"

"Thanks for asking. I do need help. I know what I want, but I've never had so much money to spend and I really don't know how to just go out and buy what I want. Can you help me?" She paused to evaluate the enormity of her task. "And… I have to submit a budget to Col. Markham."

"You bet. I want to help. It sounded at first like you could do it all alone. I'm glad you can't!" He laughed, "We need to list equipment, costs, and operating expenses. That's my bailiwick. As soon as you settle down, we can get started on it." He sounded a little like Sam again. "What about Saturday?"

That slowed her down a bit. Saturday was her day to take William to Bear Creek and they usually got home by three o'clock on Sunday. "No, Jesse. I can't Saturday, but Sunday evening or one evening next week." She was not willing to take from William to give to her patients. They both had needs and she was determined to meet both. Saturday was impossible.

"Sunday evening is good. Can I pick you up at five? We need to do some groundwork and we need a quiet place, how about my home? Or do you have a better suggestion." He wanted to be careful and casual in his invitation to his home.

"That's good. Sunday at five. Isn't it wonderful, Jesse? I am so excited. Just think what we can do." Gertie was already thinking about coffee pots and radios, records and Victrolas.

Jesse was thinking about Gertie and Sunday evening. He was also thinking about her use of the pronoun—*we*.

$
$

At five sharp, Jesse turned the corner onto Tenth Street. A young boy ran alongside his car from the corner to number 403. "You must be Mr. Jesse Morgan."

"And you must be William Neal." They shook hands as Jesse stood beside his car.

"Gertie will be right out. I'll go get her. When I get back, I wonder if you have time to tell me how you can tell counterfeit money." He was gone in a flash and returned as fast.

"She's on her way." William knelt on the running board and looked up at Jesse. "Tell me about money."

"Well, William, the best experts can tell by the paper quality and the printing. Some counterfeit money is very well done, but the special process used to make the paper and the expert carving of the printing plates gives it away. The best counterfeit fools the casual eye but the expert can spot it right away. Someday, come to the bank and I will show you some examples we keep there."

"Neat-O." He turned to his mother approaching the car. "Gertie, Mr. Morgan is going to show me some counterfeit money at the bank as soon as you take me there." He hugged his mother and stepped back so she could get into the car. "Thank you, sir." He waved at Jesse.

"William, stay in the yards until your Grandmother calls you in. I will come in to tell you good night when I get back."

"OK."

"A fine boy. Good mind." Jesse was impressed with the boy and his conversation. He took a moment to mourn the time and opportunities lost with Bradley. "Bring him to the bank soon. I made a promise."

"I will... and, hello, Jesse." She popped into the car and straightened her skirt and blouse. Her fresh smell filled the car. Jesse looked at her as she waved to William, unaware of his gaze.

They traveled to the large manor house that nestled back from the road. The large circular portico was supported by six white columns. The trees on the drive were large black locust trees, so common in Maryland. She could imagine their beauty when they were full of fragrant yellow flowers in summer. The third story had four dormers across a black tile roof. Two wings spread out on either side of the symmetrical Georgian house. The expansive front lawn was a level carpet of green. The back fell away to the rolling hills of Howard County. Down on the left was a horse stable and paddock. On the right up a slight rise was an apple orchard, dripping with fruit.

They were greeted at the door by Bertha, a tall black woman. "Evenin' Mr. Jesse."

"Bertha, this is Gertie Neal. We will be working in the study. Bring us—" he turned to his guest, "—will it be tea or coffee, Gertie?"

"Evenin', Miss Neal."

"Bertha" Gertie nodded. "Coffee, please."

Jesse guided her into the library on the left of the foyer; but Gertie pulled back so she could take in the beauty of the square stairs rising three stories above her. It was the widest, most beautiful staircase she had ever seen.

"Beautiful isn't it?" he noticed her eyes following the staircase. "This entry and those stairs are why I bought this place. The rest is just rooms and windows but this is the personality of the house. I named it Hilltop Manor. Wait 'til you see the view from the back."

"Let's sit at this game table to work." They went into the library where a work table was set up in front of the wall of book shelves with a sliding ladder held to the shelf with brass fixtures. She tried to pay attention to his words, but was totally involved in looking at her surroundings. Gertie was embarrassed when she realized that she had made a 360 degree turn in the center of the room. Suddenly, she saw Jesse laughing while he stood waiting for her to come around to him again.

"What do you think?"

"How many people live in this house?" Was her only nosy question, asked innocently, not meaning to pry.

"Just me... and Bertha and Jed. They take care of me... and it. Do you want a tour or do you want to work?"

"It is all beautiful but I want to work. We came to work. Maybe I can tour another day." He did not miss the possibility of another visit to his home and he was energized by the thought. Jesse had prepared note pads, pencils, a good light and lists of items and ideas. Gertie drew her notes from her bag and they set to work on the project that had captured her heart and enthused Jesse Morgan, too. Time flew by as they worked on her dream service club for the hospital.

Bertha brought in coffee, cheese and hot apple muffins. On the side was soft creamy butter. Gertie enjoyed the food and the very thin china it was served on. She noted everything, the embroidered cloth on the tray, the matching napkins, the shell shaped sugar spoon as well as the delicately shaped cream pitcher. She was sure that the apples for the muffins came from the orchard on the far hill.

"This beautiful cup makes the coffee taste better." Gertie said, in her habit of talking to herself—except this time Jesse heard her.

"I agree." He replied, surprising Gertie with his response.

All too soon they were finished and Jesse drove Gertie home. She was feeling good about the plans they made and the outline she had ready for Col. Markham tomorrow.

He felt good about the evening, but for him it was over too soon. "Let me know as soon as the plan is approved and I will begin ordering the items," he said as she left the car. "See you tomorrow."

"Perfect. Good night Jesse. Thanks a million." She disappeared into 403 Tenth Street and he had never felt so lonely in all of his life.

✍

Three days later Sam came into the bank right after noon looking for someone to help him find Gertie. Mrs. Barnes directed him to Jesse Morgan's office. "Mr. Morgan," he began immediately upon spotting Jesse as he entered the doorway. "Will you give me directions to the Ft. Meade office; I have to see Gertie Neal as soon as possible."

"Is this an emergency?" Jesse asked. *He lunched with Gertie that day.*

"Yes sir. I must get to her right away. I am Gertie's brother, Sam."

Jesse heard nothing after the words *brother, Sam.* His head and heart were reeling, but he came to his senses quickly.

"Pleased to meet you, Sam." He extended his hand. "Tell me the problem."

"Our father has had an accident and we must go home as fast as possible."

"I know that she will be on her lunch break right now. Can you wait until she returns to this office later?"

"No sir."

"Let me take you to Ft. Meade myself."

"Thanks, but I want to take my car and leave right from there. We're going northeast of Baltimore—Bear Creek. That is where our parents live. We must hurry. I'm not sure when we will return but I'm sure she will not be at work tomorrow…and, maybe not the next day, either."

"Sure Sam, I understand. I'll call Mr. Mitchell and alert him to your arrival. Tell Gertie her absence is approved in this emergency and she's to call each day to let us know how your father is doing. Does William know about this?"

"No, Sir. I hate that he will have to learn it from his Grandmother Neal when he gets home from school but I could not take time to stop at his school."

"I'll go to Tenth Street and make sure that William understands."

"Thanks. Tell him Gertie will call after dinner."

Sam got the directions and left in a flash. Jesse called the branch office and told Mitchell to expect Gertie's brother, but not to mention he was coming. He directed Mitchell to provide a private place for them to talk. Then he turned his mind to the important information he was digesting. He could not help himself from saying over and over again in a whisper, "Sam is Gertie's brother! Her brother," he let his relief out with a long exhale. All this time he had been mistaken. He was not her boyfriend. His fingers danced along the edge of the desk.

Jesse was on the porch at 403 to flag William down as he went past to go to Mom Neal.

"William! It's Jesse Morgan. I have a message from your mother and Uncle Sam."

"Hi, Mr. Morgan. Where's Gertie?"

"She had to go to Bear Creek with Sam today at noon. Everything is alright, I'm sure, but your Grandfather MacGregor had an accident. Sam said he will be fine. I promised them I would come and tell you about it since your mother will not be home tonight."

"How long will she be gone?"

"Maybe a couple of days. I'm not sure. She promised to call Mrs. Pole tonight and talk to you. Will you be alright?"

"Yes, sir. Gotta hurry, Mom Neal is waiting for me."

"Is there anything you will need while your mother is gone?"

"I have a bedroom over there." He pointed to the house next door. "My grandparents will be glad to have me. Gertie was going to help me with my book report tonight."

"I'll tell you what. You go on to your grandmother's and I'll come back at 6:30 and help with the report."

Jesse rearranged his evening and was back as promised to meet William. They went up to Gertie's apartment and set up for work on the kitchen table just as William was accustomed. They had hardly started when Mrs. Pole called to William. "Your mother is on the phone, hurry."

"Hello Gertie. Yes, I'm fine. How is Papa? Are you sure? I'm working on it now...and Mr. Morgan is helping me. I didn't ask him; he offered. OK. I will. I love you, too."

"Papa will be OK but his leg is broken. Uncle Dan is going to tend the bridge. Gertie and Uncle Sam are coming home day after tomorrow."

"That is good news."

Then he remembered. "She said thanks for helping me."

They went back to the book report. Jesse was relieved to learn that the book was Huckleberry Finn, one of his favorites. Jesse offered to come back tomorrow evening at 6:30 if Gertie was detained another day. "We won't let your homework fall behind."

"Bye," William called back to Jesse as he went to his car.

Jesse came the next evening.

"Thanks for coming Mr. Morgan but I don't have any homework today."

'Well, why don't you ask your grandmother if you can go down to Eighth Street field for the game? I'll bring you back by 8 o'clock even if the game isn't over." Mary Neal did not like the idea, but she could not tell the boy, *no,* so off they went to watch the Laurel Volunteer Fire Department team play White's Cab Company.

It was impossible to tell who enjoyed the game more— Jesse or William. Talk flowed easily between them and they managed to keep up with the game, too. As they walked back to Tenth Street, Jesse resolved to find a way to spend more time with his own son. They would never have times like this, doing homework and walking to a ball game. He didn't even know if his son liked <u>Huckleberry Finn</u>, but he knew he didn't like baseball. It was bittersweet for Jesse because this was just a sad attempt to make up for what he would never have with his own son—and he knew it.

After two days Gertie returned to work with news that her father was recovering. She stopped at Jesse's office to thank him for arranging her days off.

"It seems I am constantly indebted to you, Jesse. I'm glad to be home and feel things will be fine at Bear Creek until I can go back this weekend. I'm glad you got to meet Sam, and thanks for taking time with William. He really enjoyed it."

"William and I have plans to go to the Smithsonian."

"He told me of that plan. He's excited."

"I'm glad to meet Sam, too." His smile was much broader than that statement warranted, but Gertie did not analyze it.

Chapter 22   1923

After the 4th of July celebration, William wanted to stay at Bear Creek. He and Sam, Jr. wanted to stay the whole month and even talked of staying all summer. Gertie did not have any reason to say no, except that she would miss him. She immersed herself in work at the bank and the hospital but the evenings were long and lonely. She walked to the Eighth Street field after dinner to watch the city softball leagues play. Sam and some of the Neal brothers were on teams and members of the MacGregor and Neal families were usually in the bleachers. This evening the crowd was thin as a storm threatened. She considered it a nice walk and not too far to run to Tenth Street if in fact, the storm came. Gertie had hardly settled in her seat on the bottom bleacher when Jesse called to her and moved down from his seat high on the riser.

"That's my nephew playing third base," he said. "I promised to come to one of his games. Do you come often?"

"Yes, when William wants to. He stayed at Bear Creek and I came out for a walk. Looks like it is going to be rained out." She pointed to the dark western sky.

The flashes of lightning ended the game in the fourth inning.

"Let me take you home." Jesse offered.

"I can make one block quickly," she said beginning to descend the bleachers.

"Or… we could ride to Seibel's Dairy for ice cream," he invited, as he took her arm and rushed them both to the car under a flashing sky.

The rains never came. They sat in the parking lot eating cones and watching the lightning. Finally the clouds circled to the east.

"Good ice cream and good company." Even the quiet of a departing storm was comfortable for Jesse and Gertie.

"Yes, both are unexpected treats," she agreed realizing how very pleasant it was being with Jesse. They sat and talked, both enjoying the evaporation of loneliness. "I knew I would miss William, but it's harder than I expected. I keep busy with the hospital service club and bedside visits."

"You give the impression that you can handle it all."

"Oh, it is going great, but I have to bring some work home—accounting and scheduling the volunteers." She worked on her cone and continued. "Not complaining."

"Thriving on it?" He was genuinely interested.

"Yes, I am. I love the time with the patients—that's the best. Then I see more accomplished, more visits—all because we have more volunteers. I feel good about that, too."

"So, what do you do for fun?"

"I have my weekends at Bear Creek."

"Your parents are there, right? So, what's the fun?"

"My brothers and sisters gather there most weekends. We used to go every week but it is harder and harder to get away. We're lucky to get there twice a month. It's a great time. How about you, what do you do for fun?"

This was new territory for the friends—small steps into their personal lives.

"I like to run...and I exercise." He laughed. "That doesn't sound like much fun, does it?" He paused to think and she let silence wait on him. "I like to go to theater and to concerts and I love the beach... but must admit I didn't get there once last summer and not yet this year."

"William and I love the beach, too. We go each summer without missing. That is how I use my vacation time."

She looked at Jesse to see the laugh lines around his eyes that she had noticed many times before. The light from the neon sign danced on his blond hair. She noticed his strong knees stretching his pant legs. Gertie admitted to his handsomeness and contemplated his appeal. Jesse's closeness invaded her mind. *Touch me.* Gertie remembered desire.

The last bite of cone was gone and Jesse started the motor, surprising Gertie. She wasn't ready for him to start the car and head down to Tenth Street. *What's wrong with me? I can't think. Whose brain is in my head?*

As they traveled Sandy Spring Road, Jesse's hands were playing an imaginary keyboard on the steering wheel. Gertie's attention was brought back from her feelings. "Are you playing music there?" she asked pointing to his hands.

"You caught me. I have a habit of playing piano without a keyboard. A little ridiculous, eh?"

"I just couldn't make out the tune," she teased. "You play the piano?"

"Yes, when I have time… and sometimes to clear the cobwebs from my brain."

"And, that works for you?"

"Sometimes—but not all."

They reached Tenth Street and her hand was quickly on the door handle.

Jesse reached over, and took her hand and the handle to stop her. His touch came into her hand and into her psyche. It was all she thought it would be.

"Gertie, can we continue this conversation over dinner?"

She did not pull her hand away.

"At Hilltop?"

She leaned back in the seat and looked at him.

"Tomorrow at seven?"

She smiled.

"I'll pick you up?" Still questioning with his voice; holding his breath.

"I'll drive myself to Hilltop." She had to have some control.

Gertie knew what she had done. She let Jesse arrange a tryst. She accepted his invitation and she was scared. "How ridiculous," she said as she walked to the door, looking at the hand that was still burning from his touch. Gertie dropped to the sofa and spoke to the empty apartment. "I want to, Jesse… more than you know… and that is why… I can't… shouldn't…*can't*…." She prepared for bed, but was drawn to the mirror on the dressing table. "Mirror, mirror, it is hopeless." Before her hair was all brushed out, she decided to correct this mistake. *Tomorrow I'll tell him, I can't come.* "Tomorrow morning, first thing," she reaffirmed.

Gertie relaxed and went to bed. The light was out and she began to recall the feeling she had when Jesse started the car to bring her home. That pleasant time was over. *Over and done.* She hoped that would be her last thought of Jesse Morgan tonight, but it wasn't.

She saw his smile, the shine of his hair under neon lights, heard his laugh and watched him play piano on the steering wheel.

Oh dear, there goes sleep. She would have another sleepless night thinking of the man who was making her less contented with her life.

No point in wrestling the pillow. She got up.

Gertie warmed a left-over cup of coffee, spiked it with extra sugar, and went to the porch steps. The black sky was lit with a thousand stars. The air was charged with extra humidity. "I wish I could play a piano and clear some cobwebs," she told the summer night.

By the time she finished her coffee she knew what she would do. *I don't want you to know how I feel about you, Jesse.* Gertie stood to announce her decision. "No dinner, no date. Nothing can change for us. The bank and the hospital—no more. You will be at Hilltop; I will be on Tenth Street." Gertie touched the house numbers on the door jamb. "4—0—3," was recited into the dark night as she went in the house.

The next morning she was prepared.

Jesse did not come to work. She checked his office in the morning before leaving for Ft. Meade, and again in the afternoon. He was out all day. As soon as she got home, she called Hilltop. No answer.

Gertie made a plan. She drove to Hilltop, arriving at six o'clock. That was plenty of time to stop Jesse from preparing dinner for her.

I'll just tell him. "We're friends." Her thoughts burst into the air over and over. "Friends. Friends."

She didn't dress; she wore a plain cotton housedress, bobby sox and tennis shoes—definitely not date attire. Her hair was pulled back with a silk head band. She looked more like a teenager than a woman on a date. "It's the right decision," she announced to the mirror which agreed—she was dressed perfectly to break a date.

Jesse answered the door with a surprised look on his face. Puzzled, he asked, "You're early. Did we say six? Come in, come in."

"No, no, Jesse. We said seven…. I came early to tell you…."

"Don't 'no, no' me, Gertie. You are here and I don't care if it is six or seven." He took her arm and gently pulled her into the foyer closing the door behind her.

"This is a bad idea…. ."

"This is a good idea! A great idea! Yes! I stayed home from work today so you couldn't back out. I even gave Bertha and Jed the day off—no one to answer the phone. Now you are here and we will have dinner. I'm not wearing this apron as a fashion statement. You're going to help fix the dinner. Might as well put the apron on yourself." He whipped his apron off and put it over her head. He reached around her to tie it and suddenly kissed her. His lips found hers and as suddenly withdrew causing a vacuum of emotion which could not be attributed entirely to the surprise of it.

She didn't move; she didn't breathe. A tear came softly from her eye and he kissed that, too. Gertie's knees went to rubber and she folded down to the Persian carpet. Jesse went down with her—his arms still circled her waist, his hands still on the apron strings. It was a smooth ballet movement. They rode the moment to the carpet.

"Why are we on the floor?" he asked.

"I'm holding on...," she said, without looking at him. "Jesse, do you remember the story I told you about the man dying in the bridge accident when I was sixteen?"

"Yes, you told me that story when the young soldier died."

"That day—the day of the bridge accident—I had to reach down and hold on to the earth. I felt it move."

Jesse knew Gertie was about to open herself to him. He took her hands and waited for the rest of her story.

"Two times in my life since, I have felt the earth move." She finally lifted her big brown eyes and looked at him. "And then... you kissed me."

Jesse thought his heart would burst.

"I had to come down here—" She pointed to the floor "—and hold on again." In one breath, Gertie allowed Jesse to fill the vacuum in her life.

He kissed her again and she kissed him back. She wrapped her arms around his neck and allowed her feelings; she did not deny them. Unspoken promises from hungering lips fired their passion and passed from her to him—and back again.

Gertie got up before Jesse, always the gentleman, could offer his hand. She reached down to pull him to his feet. He got up smiling.

"Gertie, I have waited so long...too long."

The realization that she had wanted his kiss for a long time took her by surprise.

"Jesse.... Jesse." She searched for words."What has happened to us? Can we do this?"

"Can we kiss and have dinner? You bet. All we have to do is hold off the kissing for a while. I've got a steak to cook." He smiled and laughed and guided her to the kitchen, his attitude light and contagious. "It is called happiness, darling, happiness."

When he tried to reach the untied apron strings again, she stepped back. "Maybe I'd better tie them myself."

It had been a long time since Gertie felt so light and gay—so young and alive. With new eyes, she watched Jesse as he moved around the kitchen. She saw the back of his neck and checked his hairline, the neat cut and slight curl right at the bottom. She saw his easy movements and strong arms. She made note of his confidence in the kitchen. Most of all she saw how he looked at her. His eyes glowed with adoration and she was overwhelmed and near tears when she saw it. He was unabashed in his feelings. When he saw her studying him he moved his lips mutely saying, "You are wonderful."

She could not bear to be across the room. She went to him. He drew her to himself. Gertie felt his arms circle her body and his hands caressing her arms. They were strong arms and hands with power and she knew they would never bring her pain. Jesse Morgan did not use his strength *on her*; he gave it *to her*. Gertie softened to him and gave into happiness. The next kiss came from her to him.

Nothing in his life had prepared him for this moment of submission from Gertie. The world was his.

"Jesse, I tried and tried."

"Me, too."

"You got into my life and suddenly I looked back and realized. It wasn't your attention to William, or your support at the hospital, or your friendship. It was you. And, I cannot believe I am standing here with my heart on my sleeve." She walked away from him to say one more thing. "I am afraid—"

"Two things matter—you and me. There is nothing to be afraid of." He let her have her distance while he carried dinner to the well-prepared table. "First we eat, then we figure all this out." They walked together to the dining room. They were hungry and food did its usual good job of bringing comfort to those sharing the meal.

"I have wanted to tell you something for a long time. I fell in love with you that night at the train station. I remember everything about that night—w hat you wore, your sad face, the curl in your hair.... and, those beautiful dark eyes." He reached over and touched Gertie's face.

"William was sick."

"Yes."

"I could not even remember your face until I saw you at the bank." Gertie paused as a very heavy shield was lowered. "I lived for the days we were side by side at the hospital." They laughed and talked of past times. The ease of it was amazing to both.

Jesse carried a coffee service to the living room where they settled in the over-stuffed sofa. He allowed her silence until her coffee cup was half-empty.

"We have some important things to talk about." He didn't want to, but he had to open some troubling topics. "You know... I am married."

As honestly as possible, Jesse told Gertie about his marriage and his son. He gave her all the facts he could without malice to Catherine. She was easy to describe in unfeeling facts. It was harder to explain Bradley. His troubled look tugged at Gertie's heart. She could feel his struggle and thought of her own. He did not spare the details.

Jesse wanted Gertie to understand. She had to know he shared some blame for his failed marriage.

"I know you and I are not talking about marriage... but for the first time in ten years, I want to be free. I'll begin divorce proceedings right away."

She was quiet and did not interrupt. Jesse's heart stood still. He knew her next words would make or break his dreams.

"Jesse, your love means the world to me, but I have to be honest with you." She sat up straight and moved inches back from him. She could not say her next words while his breath was in her hair.

Gertie was pulling back. Jesse looked away. He would not look into her eyes while she dashed his hope.

"I've protected my reputation in this town for almost a decade. I've lived so that William would never be subjected to gossip. I'm not the reason for your failed marriage... and, I *cannot* be the reason for your divorce."

Jesse lowered his head. *I'm losing her.* Cold shivered down his spine.

"Let me think, Jesse." Gertie stood up and started for the door to the porch. "I'm going to walk around the lawn."

He watched her cross the porch, go down the steps and turn the corner. Jesse went to the foyer and watched her cross the front lawn. He went to the library and kitchen, saw her on the side lawn and wished he were out walking with her. Jesse stood at the window as Gertie went to the back yard and squared the last corner of the large yard. When she came back to the north porch, Jesse was seated back on the sofa—waiting—not at all patiently.

"Jesse, when we were at Seibel's eating ice cream I admitted to myself... I've loved you for a long time. As the lightning was flashing in the sky, I was in my own storm..."

He took her hand and pulled her closer.

"You started the car to take me home.... I didn't want to go." She looked into his adoring eyes. "I wanted to stay there.... forever. I was sure the love I was feeling for you would not survive if we came out of the storm cloud into the sun. As I walked and squared the corners around Hilltop I was thinking about my life... and you."

"I know."

"It would not make any sense to go off in a tangent away from the square. Where would I go if I am not connected to where I started? I kept turning toward you. I don't want to go away." He slipped his arm around her waist. His strong gentle hands caressed in a hug that was so gentle that a catch came to her throat. "I know what love is, Jesse. For the first time in my life, I know who I am and where I belong. I thought about how happy I have been since six o'clock." She charmed him with a soft laugh. "I've been getting happier by the minute."

"Tonight is a dream come true for me."

"It's been a long time since I've allowed myself to dream."

"How does it feel?"

"Wonderful..." Gertie let a serious note come into her voice. "I've decided."

Jesse's fear came back and he looked down again.

"At risk of losing your respect for me... I...," she paused. He looked up. "I..." It was hard to say. "I... want to be with you... but... without marriage."

Jesse couldn't speak. She was giving him back the possibility he thought was lost. She took his hands. "I've been falling in love with you, Jesse. I tried denying it but I can't. Do we deserve to find some happiness, now? We cannot marry. Does that mean we can't be together?" She moved as close as possible to him. "Can we keep it secret? No one—not even my family can know."

"Oh, Gertie, are you sure—no doubts?" He reached over and pulled the head band that failed to hold her curls. Her hair spilled forward as his kisses warmed her passion.

"I have not allowed myself to dream… but, I want to dream. I'm totally happy at this moment. Can I be this happy tomorrow, or the day after? I don't know, but I have no doubt. I want to be… I want to be with you."

"We do not need to rush things, let's enjoy our moments together. I love you, Gretta Neal."

"I love you, Jesse Morgan."

He pointed to the second floor. "You can take me upstairs whenever you want. I am yours, Hilltop is yours, all that the stairway leads to—is yours."

It only took her a moment to decide. Her pent up feelings were burning. "I want it all and I want it, now."

Jesse picked her up and started up the winding staircase. At the first landing, he put Gertie down. She followed his lead to sit on the next step.

"Gertie, I don't want to give the wrong impression. I have been in love with you for a long time and as much as I want to take you up there—," he pointed up the staircase, "—your wellbeing is precious to me. We are not here for only one evening. It is not enough for me. My feelings for you cannot be measured or expressed in one night." It sounded like a vow.

Gertie sat wide eyed, listening and waiting. "I'm sure of one thing, Jesse. This one evening will not be enough for me, either. My commitment to you is so much more than marriage promises that were not fulfilled before." It was her vow.

She stood up on the landing, looked down into the distant foyer and up the winding staircase. "We have come so far…," she said, "… and there is so much ahead of us." The beautiful winding staircase seemed symbolic of her life of small steps to some distant height. "Take my hand." For the second time this evening, Gertie pulled Jesse to his feet.

"You are my *forever*." Jesse was as positive as Gertie.

They walked, in perfect accord, up the stairs to their future.

❦

Beginning on that first night when they climbed the beautiful staircase, Jesse and Gertie claimed a love that was deep and profound. It quickly became more than those early feelings of excitement and fire.

They spent one long evening evaluating their situation, prompted by Jesse's concern for her. "Gertie, I'm worried. It would not go well with you if it were known we were spending time together here at Hilltop." Jesse knew and hated the irony—discovery would destroy her and leave him unscathed. Society never condemned the man.

He had to present the idea again. "I will clear the way—get my divorce."

Gertie had anticipated this conversation and was prepared. "Catherine is a socialite. She associates with politicians and celebrities. Her divorce from you would be a public matter. We couldn't marry after that. It is easier to be together as we are, than it would be after your divorce hits the papers. I can't go through that again." If she would relent, he would get a divorce and endure any negativity it caused, but she stood firm. "In my heart, we are married, but... " She could not endorse another divorce. " Jesse," she moved closer, "we have carved a beautiful life here. A marriage ceremony would not make me any happier."

"I want to give you more—my name—my protection."

"I have you. That is all that matters." She sealed it with a kiss. "Stop talking; we have better things to do." Gertie switched off the lamp and threw the loose pillows off the sofa.

He gave up.

✿

Jesse concentrated on his banking career and the rare, but wonderful times, with Gertie at Hilltop. That was enough for him—and it seemed to be enough for her, too.

Because they were determined to make this work they disciplined themselves with the reminder that all waiting would be worthwhile. They were loyal to their resolve. That was the easy part. The hard part was keeping their happiness hidden. So often she wanted to tell William or Mama or Sam or Liddy how happy she was, but she didn't. Only Jesse knew how hopelessly in love she was.

At rare times when she thought of Edward, it was for William, never for herself any longer.

Paradise was claimed at Hilltop when they were together—unexpected by others to be at other locations. Gertie slowly came to trust her emotions. Jesse's total devotion built a new kind of trust—trust in a man other than her brothers. He was patient and wise not to push her.

They maintained a more distant relationship in the work place. She did not stop at his office every day, now. All of their public time together, outside the bank, was working with the veterans at the hospital. Gertie kept the patients and staff happy. Jesse took care of her cost and expenditures ledgers.

Jesse recognized Gertie's independence. He knew the boundary where she would accept help. She let him keep her car in good working order. He could not pick her up on Tenth Street. Her car made it possible for her to come to his doorstep at unexpected, but always welcome, moments.

After the first few months, Gertie took the bedroom adjacent to Jesse's as her own room and set up her personal items. All gifts from him were kept here. At first she discouraged his gifts, but realized that it gave him such pleasure. She never carried them away from Hilltop.

He brought marriage up to her once more. "I want to marry you."

"I know, Jesse, but I can't. I have not changed my mind. I don't want to be the instrument of your divorce and give validity to attitudes I have lived with for many years. I must think of William. We are as one, aren't we? With great care, we can keep this just for us to understand." She leaned over and kissed him. "I never imagined I'd ever be this happy."

Living separately worked for them because each was entirely dedicated and neither felt taken advantage of, or taken for granted. Jesse understood that there could not be any competition with William for her time or attention. She gave herself entirely to William when it was right and cleared her mind for the time she would have with Jesse.

And thus, they formed their own special arrangement. They lived each moment as if it were a lifetime.

Gertie concentrated on her work and when she was promoted to manager at Ft. Meade, it was because she deserved it. She was a natural for the exacting nature of bank business and working with the military community. She refused all suggestions that she come back to the main office in Laurel. She would not abandon her obligation to the hospital and service club. There were too many reasons to stay at the Ft. Meade branch. Jesse was one of them.

Opportunities to be together at Hilltop were rare but special. Once each summer they were able to slip away to the beach at Ocean City for a weekend and get lost in the crowds. Even then, they took separate rooms and frequented small concession stands. There was no holding hands in public and, if they saw someone from Laurel, they could seem to have just met on the boardwalk. Gertie never contrived, she left that to Jesse. She never lamented on the small amount of time they had. She never hesitated when it was time to go. Jesse always hoped his lover would contrive or lament or tarry but she never did. Gertie's discipline was grounded in her love for her son and her conviction that they could keep their secret.

What she did do was set him afire. Gertie immersed herself in Jesse whenever she could. At Hilltop nothing else mattered to her, only Jesse. As soon she entered the door she began to unwind and relax into the most desirable woman he could imagine. Her wiles and ingenuity were boundless. Her mind matched her body for erotic stimulation. Gertie was surprised for she was sure that these feelings had been lost in her disillusionment. To prove the town wrong about her morals, she had allowed herself no leeway and denied her own sexuality for years before Jesse aroused old needs within her and she realized she could share herself with a man again.

🍎

The months passed quickly as happiness propelled their lives. Gertie and Jesse managed to live and love with their secret for almost a year. Both agreed—it was the most wonderful year of their lives. They talked about everything except the future. Neither saw reasons to change—anything.

They celebrated the intimacy they enjoyed this morning. The weekend had been perfect and the morning lit their world.

"Gertie, wake up. We are planting apple trees today. Jed is already in the new orchard and here I sit, waiting on you, my love."

"What time is it?"

"Ten after six."

"So early..." She stretched and came into the moment with him. She would not get out of bed, much less go to the orchard, without her morning kiss.

"Do we have to go plant apple trees now?" She asked as she threw the cover back and invited him to her bed. "Apple trees… or me?" Gertie knew she would win this decision.

The greater her pleasure, the greater his thrill. He took her to marvelous heights with slow and easy lovemaking. He explored her body and loved every part. His hands explained nature, they defined life, they promised tomorrow and they made her universe. This morning, he was the maestro, she was his concerto. In climax Gertie knew why she was born and why her life was here at Hilltop.

Jesse knew he would never have enough of this woman. His voice had remained soft and reassuring even as he reached the physical epitome. "I love you more than life." And then on a lighter note, "I love you more than apple trees, too."

"I suspected that."

As they lay together spent, she asked if she could go back to sleep. "For a little while?"

"Sure, my love."

"Stay with me or I will think you lied about how much you love me compared to apple trees."

While she slept, he watched her and loved every wild curl that was loosened out of control across her forehead and around the nape of her neck.

She felt his fingers on her neck and leaned into them with a sigh.

Her sleep was dreamless in the big white bed. Her strong features were relaxed and the blush of color on her cheeks complimented her lips, reddened by his kisses. When Gertie awoke a short while later, Jesse was still holding her.

Chapter 23   1924

Clay and Mary Neal were gone. So quickly, they died, one after the other.

Today, weeks later, Gertie was still trying to come to grips with the irony or was it coincidence…or something mystic? Over a cup of coffee, this Saturday morning, it all came back with a sweep of emotion. *Maybe this caffeine makes things intense again.* Even with that thought, she went for another cup of coffee.

The whole town was abuzz about the surprising death of Mary so soon after Clay was laid to rest. His grave in Ivy Hill was barely smoothed over when another had to be dug right beside it. Six days of rain after Clay's funeral made the whole scene one of mud and desolation. The small amount of new grass that had emerged was trampled by people at the graveside services for Clay. Now, not one blade of spring grass stood up to the returning grave diggers.

Maryland clay-mud made it nearly impossible to walk to the site again. But, the pallbearers and family ignored the mud to go to the graves containing a whole generation of Neals.

Gertie and William stood holding on to each other. William wouldn't allow her to wipe his tears so they ran down his handsome face and dripped off his chin. Friend and neighbors stood in the rutted unpaved road through Ivy Hill—that was close enough and muddy enough.

A week ago Monday, Mary found Clay dead in his workshop. His tools were beside him and a new trellis laid out, ready to be nailed and painted. He was face down on the sod floor. His limp hand, with a dirt filled fingernail, was stretched out. An *M* had been scratched in the dirt.

"Clay! Clay…" There was no pulse. She sat down beside him and with all her strength turned him to his back so she could press her ear to his chest. "Clay," she whispered one more time in farewell.

Mary put his head in her lap and wiped the dust from his face with her apron. Her gentle hand and soft cloth cleaned his eyes, nose and mouth. Her fingers combed his thinning hair back from his brow. This was precious time with Clay. He did not pull away from the touch of her aged hand nor did he object to her fingers in his hair. The words she spoke to him were accepted as she kissed his forehead. "I love you." The words came from her throat like square bricks that smashed against her ears. "I love you," she repeated, this time coming easier. She had not uttered them for a long, long time, and they were strange to her ear. When she uttered the words, "I forgive you," her inner being shuddered and she begged, "Clay… forgive me, too." Like all married couples, these two aged partners needed love and forgiveness even in their final hour.

Mary looked again at the scratching in the dirt. *M* Her heart leapt in her chest and she cried for her husband. She reached over and finished his effort, *a r y*, filling her finger nail with dirt, too.

For the first time in many, many years she let her mind go back to the day Clay Neal picked her to be his wife.

❧

Mary was not a striking beauty but her manner and smile were enchanting. She was short and shapely, more like the figure in a Renoir painting with plain brown hair and green eyes. She was not a slim, fragile looking girl, but rather one of solid stock. Clay had never met a girl like her. She was the first girl that didn't act smitten with him and he hated girls who went all giggly and silly around him.

Mary thought he was handsome, as did most people who met him, but she did not fall all over herself to impress him, as most girls did. She knew she was not beautiful so why set sights on a handsome man? It was that simple.

John Mitchell was courting her and it was certainly a pleasant courtship but often after they had been together for an hour or two, she was anxious for him to leave. Not once did she wish for him to kiss her and after their first few months, they didn't hold hands unless crossing a street or climbing into a carriage. They had come to assume they would wed one day and Mary could see their life together stretched out before her. John would make a fine husband and she had no other prospects except to attend Academy after graduation.

Mary would be a student for at least two more years. John was agreeable to this plan. They were both very patient about it.

Clay Neal had been watching Mary at school and at church and he was drawn to her by her shy, standoffish way. He set about replacing John Mitchell.

"I will walk you home from school today." She looked around to see if he was talking to someone else. No one else was there.

"Walk me home?" she shrugged. He smiled and his eyes lit in his handsome face. It was a fantasy she had entertained many evenings after John went home—a fantasy where Clay Neal replaced John Mitchell in her life. And now, he was here and wanted to walk her home.

"I don't talk much and we don't know each other very well. Why don't you talk and I will listen," he said. It was easy for her because she had talked to him many times in her daydreams.

"I heard that you were going to quit school. Is that right?"

"That's right."

"Don't you like school?"

"I like it well enough, but there is no point in me staying any longer. I have a chance to work on the railroad so this will be my last year. I have a life to begin. School can delay your real life."

"My parents want me to go to the Academy…. and, I will. But, that's because I don't know yet what my real life is."

"Are you going to marry John Mitchell?"

"Probably." She could not believe she was having this conversation with Clay Neal. How easy it was to answer his direct questions. Maybe I had better get right to the point myself, *she thought. "Why did you ask to walk me home today?"*

He reached out and took her hand, which nestled warmly into his. It was good that he had decided to talk because she could not think, much less talk, as his hand burned into hers. Redness traveled up her neck to her ears.

"I was afraid if I waited too long, you might be committed to John. So today was the day and I will do it again if you will let me. Which house is yours?"

"Here we are." She pointed to the lovely home behind an ironwork fence. "Would you like to come in and meet my mother?"

"Not today, tomorrow. Bye." He was gone.

Her limp hand could still feel his grip. Her head was spinning. She was shaken to the core. He called back from up the block, "Tomorrow is Saturday."

What does that mean? *She wondered. That night she tried to figure out her feelings. Mary could not make herself even picture John. Clay filled her brain. She could only think of how he made her feel. Her crush was becoming chemical and there was electricity that she did not understand. She dreamed of him touching her, kissing her, taking care of her. It was passion and it was totally new to her, although John had touched her many times. Mary could not wait to see Clay again.*

The next day she was sitting on the porch when he came down Prince George Street. She did not wonder where he was going—she was not surprised to see him stop at the gate, open it, and come up the walk.

"I'll take you to the ball game at McCullough Field tomorrow," he said without greeting her. "It would be good to meet your folks before we go to the game. They need to know me, too. One o'clock." He finished reciting his prepared speech. Mary was still trying to find her tongue when he turned to leave the porch. He had one more line to recite. "No one would make a better husband for you than me. I'll see you tomorrow." He stepped off the porch.

Mary was astonished. "Wait, Clay Neal, I don't know you myself. You cannot come here and make such an announcement."

He turned and took the few steps back to her and reached for her hand. Once again, heat went up her arm to her face and she thought she would faint.

"Mary, I just did. So don't tell me I can't. You might say 'go away' or 'don't come back tomorrow', but don't tell me I cannot tell you right out what is on my mind. It's the only way I know." The silence may have been long as each listened in their hearts to what the other had said. The two young people standing in the yard, holding hands, had an instant of looking into each other's eyes. Mary felt the earth shake and Clay listened hard to the silence, which he took as assent. He drew her hands to his chest and she felt him breathe through her fingertips. He stepped forward and planted a swift kiss on her cheek. Mary was lost in her feelings for this dream come true that had rescued her from nothingness and led her into passion.

Tomorrow, right after dinner, they would go to the ball game and, he would meet her parents first.

At the appointed hour, he marched up the Amsterdam's front walk without a doubt that Mary would be ready. He was sure that her parents would be ready to meet him and he knew—he was ready. Like a warrior who is well prepared and sure that right and might were on his side, he rang the bell.

Mary did not come to the door to greet him. Mr. Amsterdam did.

"Come in young man and have a seat." Courtesy was thick.

Clay could not breathe and he definitely could not sit.

"I am Jonas Amsterdam." Her father extended his hand.

"Clay Neal, pleased to meet you, sir." Clay noticed his grip was strong and powerful.

"Mary will not be going to the ballgame with you, but it was kind of you to ask her. Could we offer you something to drink, you have come so far?"

Clay tried to take this in. It was difficult when breathing seemed to take all his concentration.

"Is Mrs. Amsterdam at home?" He took a deep breath, drew his strength. "I had wanted to meet her, also."

This took Jonas Amsterdam by complete surprise and took control of the situation away from him. He had expected retreat and the boy/man sitting here had outflanked him. The courtesy that had worked so well for him just moments ago, now worked against him. He had to respond to the boy's polite request.

"She is upstairs. I shall ask her to come down."

Elizabeth Amsterdam came into the parlor with a quizzical look on her face. "Yes, Clay, how do you do? I have met your mother and aunts at the Sisters of Mercy. I hope they are well." She extended her hand which he accepted with a nod.

"Mr. and Mrs. Amsterdam, I told Mary of my intentions and they are honorable. It is sometimes hard to accept the direct approach, but you and Mary will always know where I stand. I want to get to know Mary better and I want her to get to know me. Frankly, I need to know if Mary does not want to see me."

Mrs. Amsterdam pushed the awkward moment aside with a smile. "Clay, if you would like to come to see Mary after church tomorrow, we would enjoy your company for dinner. Mary would too," she added with a twinkle in her eye. She left the two men standing like statues.

Clay started for the door. "I will see you tomorrow, Sir."

"Yes."

❦

Mary learned to cook and sew because it was the custom of the day. The Amsterdams had help at home; Mary did not have to do these things as chores. She was a flower, groomed, and nurtured without the competition of weeds. Her feet were planted firmly by her mother who instilled a sense of responsibility to what was expected of her. Her father expected her to excel at every task. She had to excel at school, at the piano, and at the constant testing by her father. He seemed to be most proud of her when he saw her persevere at unrewarding tasks. He often assigned a job knowing that it was going to take that extra measure of tenacity. She would never be a quitter. Neither parent tolerated a quitter.

The plan to send their only child to the Academy and possibly to the university was gone with the appearance of Clay Neal. She was not the first, nor would she be the last to fall into a love fantasy—driven by a handsome face and unfamiliar passion. It hit especially hard on this shy young lady who did not have a clue about anything other than facts gleaned from books or presented by her parents.

Clay formally proposed two months later and Mary, head over heels in love, made her mind up. Clay would be her life from now on. They would be married as soon as she graduated in June and he started his new job at the railroad.

❦

Mary began to chill, sitting there on the ground with Clay's body cooling in her lap, while she traveled back over the years.

She recited the 23rd Psalm and an old poem she had written to him many years ago.

> Come sit with me again
> And tell me of the things
> We will do together.
> In your sure tone
> Brighten the day, and
> Feed the dream again.

Finally, she pulled herself from under the weight of him and rose up to summon help.

The passing of Clay Neal had a profound impact on William. That was expected, but Gertie was taken by surprise by the depth of her own grief. In his stoic way, Clay had been a benefactor to her. She had always given and received respect from him, and was truly upset at his death.

Gertie stood against the wall in the kitchen while the Neal family made plans for Clay's funeral. She stepped forward to pour coffee and served in any way she could. William waited on the porch with his cousins. After a while they walked home hand in hand.

"Wash up, William, while I make sandwiches."

When he came into the kitchen he saw her tears and gave up the brave stance he had maintained. He cried and she did not try to stop him. "How do we go on without Poppa Clay?"

"In the same way we learned to go on after your Daddy and Great Grandmother died."

"But, I saw him every day."

"It may be hard but you are strong."

"I don't feel very strong."

"You are, William. I promise."

"Where is Poppa Clay now?"

"He is at Nickerson's Funeral Home, but will be brought home tomorrow. After everyone comes to the house to visit the family, we will go to the church and then, to the graveyard."

"I loved him."

"He knew that and he loved you. He still loves you, but you can't see it… you just have to remember it. He will love you forever." She wiped his tears from his face. "Ready for your sandwich now?"

"I'm *afraid*… nothing will be the same." Finally the young boy voiced his biggest concern. Change—now that his grandfather was gone. Gertie had to address that fear.

"You're thirteen. Nothing stays the same. Life is all about change— one way or another. Your grandfather will not be next door any more. That is true. But, what he taught you and all he stood for can never be lost. In the days ahead, you will see him in many ways and in many places. In a few days you will begin to understand what I am telling you. There is nothing to be afraid of. I will help you and you will help me."

William would not raise his head or look at her.

"Is something bothering you?"

"I don't want to go in the parlor."

"Don't worry about that tonight. It's up to you; you don't have to go in."

Gertie knew that the best thing for William was to follow tradition and go into the parlor and see his grandfather, but she was not going to force it.

The next day William got up early and went to Clay's tool shed. Gertie heard hammering and tinkering noises, but stayed away. By early afternoon, Poppa Clay's unfinished trellis was complete. While the paint dried, William walked around the yard trying to decide where his grandfather had intended to put it. Then he made his own decision. "Here," he proclaimed as he selected a spot on the sunny side of the porch. Then William went back to the work shed to wait for the paint to dry and think about his grandfather.

When he came in to eat, he was ready to talk. "I made the trellis exactly as Poppa Clay taught me—maybe not as good... but, pretty good. Look Gertie, you can see it from here." They stood at the window together. "I was surprised how much I knew." He smiled at his mother. "I surprised myself."

"You will find your teachers in everything you do. I told you, son, your grandfather was a good teacher. In that way, he will never leave you."

Early on the morning of the funeral, William waited for Gertie at the kitchen table. "I fixed coffee." He poured the strong aromatic brew and pushed the sugar bowl toward her. "I've decided. I want to go visit Poppa Clay as soon as you finish your coffee."

It was not easy to walk into that room and see Clay in death. He looked so alive. William reached out his hand and drew back at the cold touch. But he stood a moment and touched his grandfather again, this time, not in horror, but in love.

"Poppa Clay is not here anymore. I see that he's already gone."

"Yes."

"I'm not afraid anymore, Gertie."

"That is because he left you so much. He knows tomorrow and all the days after, you will be fine. Won't you?"

"Yes, ma'am."

Gertie was busy with the family preparing food for all who would gather on Tenth Street. A Neal relative lived in all but three houses on this street. On Eleventh Street many houses also had Neal family members. To a person, everyone in the two blocks came to the funeral—and many, many more. Mary looked tired and sad, but showed no tears. Tears came mainly from Edward's sisters.

Gertie kept her eye out for William and was relieved to see him sitting with Sam on the porch next door. The other grandchildren made quiet play—no running or shouting. They were made to understand.

Along with the adults, the children were overcome when Clay was lowered into the ground. Then, even the grown men cried.

"Momma, I hate leaving Poppa Clay up there, in the ground, in the dirt."

"I know son, it is the hardest part." She took his hand, refusing Sam's offer to ride, and walked down the hill to Tenth Street as if they were the only two people in the world.

"Someday Mama and Papa MacGregor will die. Mom Neal, too." They were statements not requiring answers. He was learning to compartmentalize facts of life. "And you... and me, too."

Gertie stopped walking and turned to stand in front of William. "Would it have made a difference in Poppa Clay's life if we had spent any of it contemplating his death?"

It was a strong hard question.

"No."

"Would we have loved him more... or differently?"

"I see." His eyes brightened and they resumed their walk.

"Will I forget Poppa Clay?"

"No, William. You will remember, but as time goes by you will recall the good memories. That is how it is supposed to be when we lose someone we love."

"It hurts."

"I know dear— it hurts. But it won't hurt forever."

"I didn't want to tell you, but I can't remember Daddy; I have to look at his picture."

"I'm glad you told me, William. I'll help you. I'll help you remember your father and all of us will help you with the hurt you feel today. That's what families are for."

That night William had more questions.

"Why does God take away someone we love?"

"In the Bible, God tell us his plan. It may be hard to accept but as much as our loved ones miss us when they leave, they are happy to be with their heavenly Father until we are united again in heaven."

"Do you believe that, Gertie?" She didn't think this could get harder, but now he did not want the philosophy or religion—he wanted what she believed.

These few minutes, standing in the door to his room, did not give her time to think—only time to take a big breath. She crossed the room and sat on the foot of his bed. "I have thought about death and God. I was about your age when I asked these questions and it has taken me many years to bring some sense to it. You too will have to think about it and find answers that are acceptable as you grow up."

She turned toward William, meeting his gaze, choosing her words with care to comfort with hope rather than to grieve with despair. "You ask what I believe. God has a plan for us and we cannot know what that plan is. We can live keeping our hearts and minds open because our beliefs and understanding change over time. I believe that God gives us life and He would not let a beautiful life end without hope. There is more and it is a mystery." She paused to release tensions building from his questions. She knew her answers were important to his young soul.

"Nature shows us renewal every spring and that is a big clue to God's love and plan. Just as the trees do not need their old leaves and a butterfly does not need the old body of the caterpillar, Poppa Clay does not need his body. Poppa Clay has passed into renewal. Because I see the wonder of God's world, I believe he and your father are content and patiently waiting for us. Can there be anything better than our world and being together here? Yes, if we spend our life appreciating God's gifts in it."

He was tired and ready for sleep and she had left him with a good image to take into the night. She was exhausted and sleep came easily to her, too.

Neither Gertie nor William knew, as they gave into sleep, how important her words would be in the ensuing days.

❧

Mary Neal stayed in bed the next day. A steady stream of children came and went. Emily urged her to come to the table to eat and finally accepted her resistance and took her meal up to her. The family was unnerved to see her in bed at midday and agreed that the only time she had done that was the day she gave birth to one of her children. When Gertie came over after dinner time, the uneaten food was still on the tray at her bedside and she would not look at her or talk to her.

All agreed that Mary needed this day and maybe tomorrow to rest. Gertie told William good night and told him she was sleeping in Mom Neal's parlor. He would be fine with Mrs. Pole downstairs.

Mary did not get out of bed the next day. The steady parade of family continued up the stairs. She did eat a small offering of food. "Is it still raining? We must plant grass over Clay." It was the only thing she said that day.

All were encouraged that tomorrow she would be better. Gertie crossed the yard with her pillow again that evening.

The rain continued. Mary stayed in bed. After work Gertie came in and called her name.

"Mom Neal."

"Gertie, before you take William home, send him to the workshop to get Clay. Dinner is ready." The rest of the night she talked to Edward. "Your father wants the grass cut Saturday, no excuses." Looking at the wall, she held a long conversation with Edward, mostly about William and at times confusing the two.

Dr. Bryant was called. He tried to get Mary to respond to him but her eyes were glassy. Each of her children in turn was sure he or she could get her to engage in conversation. By ten o'clock, even the mention of Clay, Edward, or William did not illicit a response.

"I've seen this before. Her mind has shut down rather than accept Clay's death. The key is to get her to eat and drink until she comes around. She can will her mind to close down, but she can't will her body to die unless she stops eating and drinking. Give her liquids and this tonic." He paused and took Gertie's hand. "She must drink—water, or any liquids. It is vital. I'll stop on my rounds tomorrow."

There was no improvement the next three days. Mary refused water and food. Dr. Bryant prepared the family for the worst.

Gertie told William that Mary was very ill. "William, she doesn't want to live without Poppa Clay."

"But, we need her."

"I know, but she's feeling very bad."

He was frantic to go see her.

"Please, Gertie. Don't say I can't go see her. I gotta." Gertie and William arrived at the house as Dr. Bryant was leaving.

"Doctor, can William and I go in to see Mary?"

"Yes, of course. William you must understand, your grandmother may not talk to you. She is much too sad. It won't be your fault. OK?" William nodded as the doctor patted his shoulder and walked toward the gate. He stopped and took Gertie's arm.

"We must get her to drink. If not..." The doctor shook his head and went out the gate.

Mary was lying with her face turned to the wall. Gertie pulled up a chair for William and lifted Mary's hand toward him so he could hold it. It was soft and warm and he could not help but rejoice that it wasn't like Poppa Clay's just five days ago.

Gertie went around to the far side of the bed and looked at Mary's blank face. "William is here." There was no response but she let Gertie gently turn her head toward William.

The dimly lit room looked sad with long shadows from the lamp and the drawn shades. Even the flowers on the wallpaper seemed wilted and tired, as if they had marched across these walls too long. The edges on everything, even the finely carved mirror, were fuzzy. William was the only thing in the room that was defined.

He declined the chair that was pulled to the side of the bed. Instead, he knelt beside his grandmother so his face was level to hers. It was a heartbreaking scene—the young boy holding the deeply veined and age-spotted hand of the elderly lady while he stared into her unseeing eyes with great expectation. Without any urging or coaching from his mother, he began to tell Mary what he came to say.

"Mom Neal, it's William. Are you very tired and missing Poppa Clay?" He paused to let her think about what he said. "Me, too. He should be planting beans and you should be fixing dinner, but that is not God's plan for you today and that's alright with me. You can rest if you want to and you don't ever have to do that anymore if you don't want to do it without Poppa Clay. That's alright with me, too." He paused, not wanting his thought to come at his grandmother to fast. "I wonder how much God loves us—you and me and Gertie. Does he love us as much or more than we love each other? If it is more...that sure is a lot. If God is going to take you where there is more love than here...

and Poppa Clay and Daddy are waiting for you," he paused, "that is alright with me, too." He kissed her forehead and felt her hand tighten, ever so slightly, in his. "Goodbye, Mom Neal."

William was amazingly composed and even managed a weak smile for her glazed eyes.

Gertie saw the tear slip out, trail down Mary's pale cheek to the lace on the pillowcase, and then disappear into its beauty. No one on this earth would know if the tear was for the life she had or for the life she did not have.

For the first time in the last seventy-two hours, her glassy unseeing eyes closed and sleep came to Mary Neal. Sometime in the night, she went to get more love than she had had on earth.

Chapter 24 1925

"I'll get it." William ran to the door to answer the soft tap.

"Hello, Aunt Charlotte, come in. Gertie, we have company."

Gertie came in the room with dish cloth still in hand. Visitors were rare and welcome, especially from the Neal clan. A large box, tied in a blue ribbon took her attention.

"Hi, Charlotte. Is it someone's birthday?"

"Harley and I found this in Mom's attic today. Look William, it has your name on it."

It was just short of a year after Mary's and Clay's deaths that Charlotte brought the box to William. She and Harley had moved into the house at the end of Tenth Street and set about making the home place their home. William was glad to have his aunt, uncle and little cousins next door. He did not want strangers in the yard, in Poppa Clay's shed and Mom Neal's kitchen. That was how it was on Tenth and Eleventh Street. Homes were passed to relatives. Strangers did not usually move in to the Scotch-Irish west end.

Charlotte and Harley replaced the wood burning cook stove with the latest gas range, put a Frigidaire on the enclosed porch and installed modern plumbing that allowed the toilet to be a part of the house. She brightened the wallpaper and paint. Best of all, the yard was as it had always been. Harley's garden wasn't as perfectly maintained as before, but that imperfection was comforting to William.

"We were going over things in the attic and found this." Charlotte explained as she went to the sofa to sit beside William placing the box between them. "Look." She pointed to his name written in Mary's fine and recognizable hand. Charlotte was curious and hoped William would open the box, it was a personal treasure. He would not open it here.

241

"Thanks, Aunt Charlotte." His voice was excited. As soon as it was polite to do so, he excused himself to go to his room with the box. He wiped the dust away and saw in small print—*Edward's Things.*

"Thanks, Mom Neal," he uttered, as a prayer, to the empty room and magic box. He blew the dust off—the only thing he was willing to discard from his gift. Thoughts of sharing with Gertie were put away—at least for now.

William cleared his bed and with great ceremony slid the bow off the box. He lifted the lid and paused as his feelings moved from excitement to sadness.

His father's army tag was on top. William picked it up gingerly, turning it over and over in his hand. He slipped the chain over his head and fingered the round tag with 'Edward William Neal' impressed in the metal. William repeated the numbers—001563441—until they were his to recall at will. Pins, ribbons and medals were fastened to cardboard. Each had significance and he would have to research them. In a little brown sack, labeled buttons, he found and counted his father's dress uniform buttons.

Edward's wallet was explored. Every compartment opened. Two pictures, faded and worn, as if they were handled many times, fell out. "Me," he said aloud to one. Gertie and Edward looked back at him from the other. He was sitting in a chair; she was sitting on the chair arm. William noticed her arm lovingly draped across his father's shoulders.

William ran to the front room to look again at the chair in the picture. "Daddy and Gertie," he said aloud. It was the first time he had ever linked his parents in so many words and it was the first time he saw his parents together in such a caring way. In fact, William had no memory of them together and the picture gave him a new vision of his parents. The picture went on his night stand.

The telegraph from the War Department caused William to halt his rummaging in the box. This fragment of his father's life reminded him of the day it came. William walked to the window and sat where he could look out to the house next door."I remember the day this came," he spoke aloud again. *I cried and so did Poppa Clay.* His thoughts continued. *We were in his tool shed. Mom Neal must have been in the house crying, too.*

He open the letter that detailed exactly where Edward's grave was located: a map of Germany, a diagram of the military cemetery, and the Army regulations detailing the services his father received. "I'm going there some day," he promised himself. Then William read aloud the condolences expressed on behalf of the United States Government.

"Ten days." William spoke again with even greater sadness. The date on the telegram and the date of his father's death were a span of ten days. William took time to count it out. "Thursday, Friday, Saturday, Sunday, Monday, Tuesday, Wednesday, Thursday, Friday, Saturday." They had gone about their lives in Maryland while his father was already dead in Germany—for ten days. He took a deep breath with the paper clenched in his hands.

William took time to mourn those days. He could not possibly remember what he was doing ten days prior to learning his father had died, but he knew that it wasn't fair that this family was eating and laughing and going about their lives while his father was cold and dead in Germany. *With dirt shoveled over him.* The young boy took heavy thoughts to heart for his father.

Maybe if he sat still with these memories that Mom Neal had put in the box, his father would somehow know how sorry he was that it happened that way.

William carefully placed everything back where it had been for many years and where he knew he could find them again—whenever he wanted to. There was more, but he closed the box for now and went to find his mother. He could come back to it later; right now he needed to not be alone.

The Good Housekeeping magazine Gertie was trying to read could not keep her attention and she turned the pages while waiting for her son to come from his room.

"Gertie, the box is Daddy's things. It's a wonderful box. I haven't looked at everything. I want to take my time. It's wonderful but sad."

"Aren't you lucky to get such a box of treasures?"

"Yes, I am."

"Let's go for some ice cream. We can get some at Slater's but it is such a warm evening, I challenge you to walk to Katherine's Shoppe for some homemade ice cream. What do you say?" Katherine's Shoppe was on Fourth Street and a six block walk would be good for talking. If he said Slater's, around the corner, she would know he was not ready to talk.

"Slater's."

The box was tied up with the bow when she went to make his bed the next morning but all the dust was wiped away. He knew with complete certainty that his mother wouldn't go into the box unless he invited her.

She could see that he was greatly moved by the contents. Her desire to go into his feelings was overruled by her wisdom to let him have his time and find his peace with it.

Right after church William went straight to his room and closed the door. He found a smaller box inside the big one. It had things not related to the army. There were school papers and report cards. He looked carefully at the photos—Daddy in a ball uniform and sliding into first base were faded, but he saw his father's face almost like looking at his own. The baseball with 'Edward' written on one side and 'Curley' on the other, finally gave the boy something tangible to hold on to. His hand was not the only one around the ball at this moment.

"It was your ball, Daddy and, now it's mine." the boy said out loud, a habit picked up from his mother. The ball was turned and turned in his hand to have the stitching just right for a pitch to an imaginary catcher. His arm made the circle several times but there was no chance that the ball would leave his hand.

In a quick motion, William brought the ball to his nose and drew in his breath. Beyond dust, he smelled leather, sweat and the man he missed so much.

He found his father's baptismal certificate and grade school diploma. "I'll ask Gertie for mine so I can save them together in this box."

Finally in the bottom under Edward's primitive artwork he found his father's book of jokes each written in his own hand with comments on how effective the humor was. The book had a date on it and when William counted up he saw that his father was the same age when he wrote the joke book as he was today.

Gertie heard sounds coming from the room and was puzzled. Was William crying? She walked to the door and listened. *Is he crying?* "Laughing," she said as she walked from his door.

The mood was much lighter when William came from his room for dinner. He began telling his mother about the small box within the larger one. She enjoyed his animated chatter about Edward's youth.

"Did you ever call Daddy, Curley?"

"No, I never did, but some of his friends did. I'd forgotten about that nickname."

"Did he mind being called that?"

"No. Every boy in west end had a nickname and some of them are beyond understanding. Your father didn't have a problem with his nickname. Usually as the boys grew older it was seldom used. I think it was mostly used in play and always on the ball field."

"Tell me some of the nicknames." William leaned forward, anticipating the smallest bits of enlightenment. He hadn't realized until now that he and his mother shared his father—a profound connection that created yet another bond between them.

"Let's see, your Uncle Sam was Skeeter. Uncle Dan was Shorty. Uncle Clifton was Campy. Bob Tasker was River. I can't remember all of them. Ask your uncles."

"I'm glad Mom Neal made the box for me. Someday I will show you all the things that are in it."

"Are you finished going through it?"

"I think I've seen everything once but I am going to go through it again. Do you have a chest or something I can keep everything in? The box Mom Neal used is falling apart."

"I'm sure Mama has one. We'll ask her next weekend."

A small wooden chest was brought from Bear Creek for William's treasures. It had a latch lock but the key was lost. He thought it was perfect. Gertie was invited to come in as he transferred everything from the dusty box to the chest. He lifted items and told her what they were, but did not offer to put any of them in her hand nor did he give her the parts that were so dear to him—like the date on the telegram or the signatures on the ball or the date on the joke book. When he lifted the last item out he noticed something that had been overlooked.

"There is more. Look." Something fit snugly into the bottom of the box, giving it a false bottom.

"What's this?" Gertie said as she noticed what appeared to be writing on the bottom of the box. Actually the writing was on a manuscript cover and it said, <u>My Journal by Edward Neal</u>. William pulled to get it from the box encasing it. It was large and thick. As he got it in his arms, Gertie got up from the floor and announced she was going to get a cup of coffee, and left her son with the last piece of Edward.

Before she sipped from the cup, she paused to pray. "Dear God, Help me to say the right things to William. We need help with this special piece of Edward. I don't want him to read that manuscript now. Please, dear God." She was worried. Edward's story would be a very difficult one for their young son. The story of his stormy life and his war experience was not the same as sandlot tales, nicknames, and joke books. She felt her chest tighten. *Should I keep him from reading it?*

Gertie was startled to see William standing beside her with the manuscript pressed to his chest.

"I want to read you something, Gertie—the first page."

She smiled weakly and invited him to sit with her. She took her first taste of coffee as William opened the cover and began reading.

Dear William,

I started writing my journal when I was seventeen and left Tenth Street. I tried to write about events as they happened but sometimes I wrote as I looked back. It wasn't until after you were born, and living with Gertie, that I decided that my journal was for you. A man wants to be understood and to have a chance to explain himself. Sometimes it takes a while to figure that out. Life isn't all baseball games and happy times. It is often mistakes and wrong decisions. I want you to read this journal when I am an old man or maybe when I am planted in Ivy Hill. I am leaving for Germany tomorrow. The next pages should be very interesting from the small town boy going into the big world at war. Mom Neal will add them to the box. By the time I get home, I should understand myself.
Do you understand yourself? When your answer is—yes— you are ready to read this journal.

Love,
Daddy

"I don't understand his question."

"Then you can't answer it with a *yes*, can you?"

"No, I don't have the answer Daddy wants…so I guess I should't read the journal now."

"You are a very fortunate boy. You will have a chance to get to know your father even though he is gone. I don't think he wrote it thinking you would have it while you are so young. He probably wrote it for you when you are an adult. We have to think about what your father intended when he wrote the journal."

William was delighted with his chest full of his father's life. He polished the wooden box and seemed content to wait to read the journal. She saw him lift everything out and fit the journal into the bottom of the chest just as it had rested in Mary's attic.

Gertie asked Jesse to come and talk to William about the manuscript. She went for a walk and left them together. After a short talk Jesse left Tenth Street with the problem resolved and Gertie breathing, easier.

A safe deposit box was opened in William's name. Jesse took the manuscript to the bank and safely stored it there until the boy would be ready to read it. Then Jesse brought the key back to William and took payment from him for the rental. It was a contract between William and the bank. Jesse and Gertie were very deliberate. They did not want William to think that his mother was locking Edward's writings away from him.

Chapter 25 *1926-1927*

Gertie was happy. Life with Jesse became so much more than the acceptable life she had settled for. They were perfectly synchronized dancers moving through their new life as if it were a waltz. It was not long after the day of their discovery that she gained perspective and began to believe in her right to happiness.

Jesse and Gertie remained true to their resolve to keep their relationship secret. Both were dedicated and they were amazed at the ease of it.

"It's our anniversary," Gertie announced as they sat on the porch overlooking the apple orchard.

"Anniversary?" Jesse tried to think fast.

"Our first date at Hilltop. Six years ago—and this is the first July 8th that we have managed to be together since."

"And, you are springing this on me?" he asked as he picked an apple from the basket on the coffee table and lobbed it to her. "Was I supposed to know that?"

Gertie caught the apple and took a bite—talking, not too well—with apple in her mouth. "But—," chomp, chomp "—the apples we had that night were Golden Delicious, not Macintosh."

"And I'm supposed to remember that, too?" Now he was laughing, enjoying her game and the sparkle in her eye that he had come to love more and more.

"It's the woman's job to remember these little details. I came home from Bear Creek yesterday so we could celebrate our anniversary."

"We could have done something special…like go to Washington for dinner."

"I'm doing exactly what I want to do—right now." She moved closer to him and put her arms around his neck. "Almost… " was punctuated with a kiss.

Nothing in the outside universe could come into Jesse's world when Gertie was there. They were in perfect agreement—quiet dinners, enjoying Hilltop and each other.

"Next week Jed and I are going to whitewash the stables. If it works for you, come help. I'd like to see you spattered with that watery mix."

Gertie looked at him with a smile that told him without words, *I will, if I can.*

His returning look said, *I know.*

"Shall I call William? Maybe he would like to do it."

"Yes. Call him—but he has games on Tuesday and Thursday."

"I'll call him for Wednesday and if any other day works for you, you know where I will be," he said, pointing over the lawn toward the stable.

Their gazes, in unison, traveled across the summer-painted hills beyond the porch. Neither had to, nor wanted to, pass quickly over the scene grounded in lush green and sparked with blue bachelor buttons and white daisies—dotted deliciously like eye candy.

He broke the reverie. "Penny for your thoughts."

She pulled her eyes away from the scene to her love. "You and Sam. I don't know how William and I would have managed…." She gathered her thoughts, pulled her knees up under her and went on. "William has good male role models. You and Sam have filled important roles in William's life. How can I thank you for that?"

"I can't speak for Sam, but don't thank me…, please Gertie. I care for William. He's a great kid."

With Jesse's interest in her son, Gertie could relax about providing everything for him. William was growing strong and Jesse's masculine touch was important. During these school years with careful planning, William became convinced Jesse was more his friend than Gertie's.

❦

The country's impending financial disaster did not take Jesse by surprise. Starting in mid-decade, he cautioned his customers and took his own advice as a hedge. He dissuaded loans or at least convinced his customers to borrow less. If at all possible he avoided giving home mortgages. By summer of 1927, Jesse refused to finance real estate purchases and advised customers not to move if at all possible. He feared many fortunes, jobs, and homes would be lost.

Salaries at the bank were frozen as inflation ate away at the country's economy. Gertie's car stayed next door parked in its space—the space the Neal family still allowed after her in-laws' deaths. She budgeted carefully and thanked God for William's small stipend from the army.

"Let me help. Please Gertie, let me help." Jesse pleaded. "Can I at least buy your gasoline?"

The look on her face answered his question. "As long as William and I have what we need… no luxuries." *And I have the cameo*, she thought.

"You need gas to drive to Hilltop. That is a luxury I'm not willing to forego."

"I agree… that is a necessity, not a luxury." She crawled into his arms. "It feels like a luxury," she said as she started her kisses.

He did not ask again, but watched carefully for signs of financial struggle in her life. And, he checked the safe deposit registry to be sure she did not go into the box and remove the cameo.

Ft. Meade's hospital population had leveled out, but she was still tending men who needed prolonged care and rehabilitation. Exposure to mustard gas left many soldiers with long term problems. Respiratory disease and lung cancer from repeated exposure kept two wards open long after the war was over. Death was not a constant now, but her presence was still important to patients in the wards.

Gertie and Jesse had their world while William had his. School and sports took his time and effort. The happiest times were when William could bring his friendship with Jesse naturally into his world with Gertie.

William did not talk about going to college. Who would he talk to? None of his cousins on Tenth and Eleventh Street wanted to go to college. Even at Bear Creek the talk of youngsters going to college was non-existent. Sam's son left school to work at the racetrack. Lon's two boys were going to Loyola College in Baltimore to study business, and that was it. None of the girl cousins aspired to careers that required higher education.

William would be seventeen this spring and graduate in June. Most boys left school at sixteen. William's class of 1928 was overwhelmingly female—ten girls and four boys. Just one year ago the boys outnumbered the girls. It was common for parents to brag a bit when their child finished high school and that was all the pride anyone could afford in these hard times.

William did not want to quit school when he was sixteen, and Gertie would have been disappointed if he had.

"I can go to school and get a job, too," he insisted.

Gertie did not discourage or encourage the idea. She waited to see how important it was to him.

"School's important, William."

"I know, but I can work and keep up my studies. Most boys are helping their families; I want to help, too. You know I can keep my grades up."

Although he had a paper route, he repeatedly brought up getting a *real* job.

"I'm only making change with the paper route." He opened his hand to show the two quarters and three nickels. "I could make dollars—if I had a real job."

"School is your real job."

Gertie tended her money carefully, but the reductions at the bank made things tight. William looked for a job. He never gave up.

"Gertie, Mr. Slater will hire me at his store. It's right around the corner and he would not expect me during school. If I work after school on Wednesday and every other Saturday now, he will use me more when school is out." His pleading was persistent and he made every argument.

"Let's talk about when school is out. You would not be any more suited or settled for a job like that than Sam was when he got out of school. I hoped you would want to talk about going to college."

"Sure, but we can't afford that—can we?"

"Do you want to go?"

William looked at his mother with pleading eyes.

"Of course you do. Come into the kitchen, I have made some notes." They went to the place where William usually did his homework. Gertie had her bank book and William's spread out—along with papers with figures and notes.

"Your father's money... and look what I have set aside. I'm sure we could do one year... and then there are scholarships. They looked together at the facts Gertie had prepared. "I was thinking...University of Maryland. Live at home. Bus fare is a lot less than living on campus."

William leaned back and pushed his hair off his forehead. "If you get me in for the first year, I can earn that scholarship." William looked up. "I will," he asserted.

Gertie smiled. He was grinning from ear to ear.

"I feel better about you taking a job now that we agree it is not your life plan. What will you be doing for Mr. Slater?"

"Cleaning, stocking, and unloading. Please, Gertie. If my grades go down, I'll quit—but, they won't."

"What about the Saturdays we go to Bear Creek?"

"I told Mr. Slater—every other Saturday. We don't go every week." He was right. They had been skipping weekends and Mama only expected them every other week. "And he knows I play ball on Tuesdays and Thursdays." She had to agree as she looked at the boy who was becoming a man.

William took the job and Gertie planned that Saturday for time at Hilltop. On occasion, Gertie would drop William off at Hilltop to spend time with Jesse. They were important *man* times, which never included her. They were special to a boy who lost his father and a man who lost his son.

In the summer Jesse and William hiked down the Little Patuxent River toward Savage collecting Indian arrowheads or digging around for native artifacts. They called it their archaeology lab. Gertie did not mind being unwelcome during those times. A good book filled her day while she savored the thought other two men together.

In winter Jesse and William did some historical research in the library on topics of interest to William. He loved to study old maps of the world, especially the sea. He borrowed books, fiction and non-fiction, about the navy and the sea—read them quickly and went back for more.

❧

"William talked to me about college." Jesse began after a meal in the study on one of their days together.

"He wants to go and I am going to do all I can to see that he has a chance."

"William's a natural student but he doesn't think you can send him. He's trying to figure how he can go without being a burden to you."

"I've been looking in to it. He would have to stand competition or go to prep school to get a scholarship. Unfortunately our school doesn't prepare students well for college. William would do well in scholarship competition but might need a tutor or prep school for scholarship competition. That costs money. It seems more feasible to send him to college and let him compete for the sophomore scholarships that are offered only to freshmen who excel. I can send him for the first year, but he will need a scholarship to continue. It bothers me that we might not afford the rest. That would be terrible."

"You know I would love to pay for… "

"Stop, Jesse, don't say it. I know, I know, but, William and I have to do this on our own." Whenever he had tried to help her she shut him down—his stubborn, stubborn love.

It was clear in her mind. She might be his mistress, but she would not accept any favors that could be misconstrued as payment for their relationship—not in her mind or the world's.

"Consider a personal loan from me. It is an option and also a resource for you. He must finish what he starts, and, he must believe when he goes for the first day that graduation day will be his, too."

"You are so right—again." She kissed him. "He can't start college unless I know he will be able to finish. How thoughtless of me. There is always the cameo…" Gertie went quiet and he left her with her thoughts.

"You need to consider my offer… for William's sake." Jesse knew what the cameo meant to her and, if at all possible, he would keep her from parting with it.

"He wants a military career."

"Yes, not surprising. He started studying WW I, wanting to know all about the war that took his father. He has been especially interested in the fact that Edward chose to go. Then he studied Napoleon and the Civil War. I don't know when he got so interested in the navy."

"We did a lot of talking about British sea power, the Spanish Armada, and the sinking of the Maine. He's interested in it all."

"I'm going to help him with whatever he chooses." Gertie stretched out her knees and pushed closer to Jesse so his arms could circle her while she told him some special thoughts. "You know, the cameo has been my anchor. At times my life and livelihood hung by a thread and determination to keep the cameo got me through. At the deepest, darkest challenges I fought to keep that beautiful brooch. I feel differently now. If I have to use it for William's future, I'd gladly part with it." She looked up at Jesse. "I believe Grandmother Amsterdam would be pleased. If I sell it to pay tuition, it won't be because I failed." She paused to think over the words she had just said. To reiterate the truth in them, she patted Jesse's chest and lifted her gaze to him. "I don't think you ever saw the cameo."

"No, but I'd love to see it." He kissed her lightly.

"Someday when we have a moment at the bank, I will open my box and show it to you. It's lovely beyond words."

"Gertie, you are lovely beyond words… but I'll look at your cameo."

She ignored his compliment and went on with her thoughts. "William's worth it, that's for sure. He has one more year at school then four years at college. Those five years will fly by." Jesse gave Gertie a hug knowing that this conversation was taking a toll on her.

Gertie turned her attention to him. She would wait to get home to think about William and college again.

❦

William dreamed of the Naval Academy but doubted he could get an appointment. He put Annapolis out of his mind and, turned his attention to the University of Maryland.

If Gertie can send me to Maryland that will be fine, he thought. *Maryland has ROTC and, I'll get a commission in the navy.* William was a realist. He would find a way without putting a burden on his mother.

"If Gertie says it has to be Maryland…." he said to the book he was reading on ROTC history. "I can go to Maryland and make it into the navy." The book went back on the shelf. "Never the Army." He spoke aloud to the almost empty library. William knew that his father hated sleeping on the ground and he did not want to sleep on the ground either—or live in a trench that could be his grave. William never forgot how he felt when he saw freshly dug dirt shoveled over graves of his loved ones in Ivy Hill. "The sea," he proclaimed to the navy blue summer sky as he walked down the library steps that night and headed home.

William loved to go to the parade grounds at Ft. Meade and watch the platoons march. He could look at a soldier and tell if his uniform was perfect, his medals pinned right, his hat at just the right angle, his salute precise. On Memorial Day he was at the corner of Tenth and Montgomery Street to see the annual parade honoring military heroes.

"Hurry, Gertie, it's almost time."

"We have never missed it, have we?" She replied as she tied a red, white and blue ribbon on her straw bonnet.

"I'm going to walk to Ivy Hill to hear the gun salute, Are you?"

"I always have, haven't I?"

The only thing better than this parade was watching a battleship come up to Sparrow's Point. There was no way this boy would leave the water's edge as long as it was in view from the beach at Bear Creek.

Each summer Gertie took him to the ocean and he was awestruck by it.

"I love the ocean," he declared.

"Me, too. I am not sure why, but I look forward to the beach each August."

"There is something here that makes me feel important, is that silly?"

"No son, actually that is very perceptive of you. Here we can connect with God and know, although we are as numerous as the grains of sand, we are still one with God. I feel the same."

"And, when I leave... I begin to want to come back."

"Is this conversation to tell me you don't want to go in for lunch?"

William smiled at his mother as she pulled out the peanut butter and jelly sandwich from the beach bag. Even as the sun was setting he did not want to leave and, first thing in the morning, he was back at the edge, marking the tide all day.

"We're at ebb tide. Give me twenty minutes to see it change. Please?"

He could not put it into words, but he knew he was complete there—even without a father. He would work hard and maybe, just maybe, when he grew up, he could go to sea in the navy. The only boats he had ever been on were the ferry across the Chesapeake Bay and a rowboat at Bear Creek.

Jesse wanted to pay for William's college, not only for Gertie, but because he cared for William and saw his potential. She would not allow him to pay and it pained him greatly. His resources, which were formidable, were an abomination if he could not use them for the ones he loved.

On William's next visit to Hilltop, Jesse had a special book in plain view: <u>From Maryland Ramparts to Sea Power - The United States Naval Academy</u>. William noticed it immediately, and sat down with it as if Jesse were not even there. William did not aspire to the Academy, but he knew that it sat about fifty miles south in Annapolis where the Severn River flowed into the Chesapeake Bay. Jesse left the boy alone with the book for an hour.

"William, would you like to go to Annapolis and visit the Naval Academy?"

"Sure."

"Call your Mother and make sure it's alright with her. Tell her I will bring you back to Tenth Street." They headed to Annapolis with William holding the book tight under his arm. It was heaven for the young man. From the moment they checked in at the front gate and got permission to enter, William was ecstatic. He couldn't keep from running to the ramparts where he could see the water and look back toward the resident halls and chapel. He opened the book to find the scenes on the pages. He read aloud to Jesse each picture caption.

Suddenly doors opened and midshipmen poured onto the parade plaza for the noon formation. A sea of white uniforms covered the soft grey stones. William was beside himself watching these men only a few years older than himself. He imagined being in the line with these fine, uniformed students.

Jesse looked at William and noticed he was standing at attention while all the platoons were called and answered. The midshipmen were dismissed to lunch and William stood at ease.

"We have time to walk around, and we can go see the chapel. No visit is complete without seeing that." It was the biggest church William had ever seen and the sun lighting the beautiful stained glass windows illuminated him.

"I wish Gertie could see this. I wish she could see it all." he whispered. They sat quietly in the chapel as do all who enter. The rotunda and altar commanded respect. Jesse guided William to the stairs that led down to the marble crypt of John Paul Smith. William read everything that was on the wall commemorating the life of service of this naval hero. "I'm ready to go home," he said as if he had absorbed all he could. He was deep in thought and quiet on the trip home.

William had a dream, but he was a realist. Midshipmen at the Academy came from families of position and power. He would stick to the possibility of attending Maryland. That was a big enough dream for him. Still, the United States Naval Academy at Annapolis was awesome and he was in love with it.

As he climbed out of the car he turned to Jesse, looked him in the eye, pausing a moment to connect with the older man. "Thank you very much, Jesse. It was a great day." Then he saluted Jesse with precision motion.

By the time he got back to Tenth Street William had worked through his many thoughts and was ready to tell Gertie about his day at Annapolis. The only impression he wanted to give was his conviction that a naval career was for him. He did not want her to think he entertained thoughts of attending the Academy. William would not give Gertie that heartache. He knew she would give him the moon if she could and he was careful not to ask for it.

Chapter 26

Jesse was more realistic about the moon than William. It was not part of any of his faraway dreams. The moon was only a backdrop to purpose, work, and expectations. He had his own thoughts about William's education. William's reaction to the Naval Academy gave Jesse a mission of his own.

The next morning, Jesse walked into his office and handed his secretary a note.

"Make this call for me. I want an appointment to talk with Senator Perry. If he isn't in his Baltimore office, I will go to Capitol Hill to see him. Try for next week." He started for his office and paused, "And, get me an appointment with the principal at Laurel High as soon as possible."

Jesse needed time to gather William's grades and get his resume ready.

"Mr. Morgan, the principal's name is Clarence Boyette. He can see you today at two. Senator Perry will see you next Tuesday in his Baltimore office. Here's the address, sir."

Mr. Boyette endorsed Jesse's efforts to get an appointment to the Academy for William. He would not only write a recommendation, he would ask William's teachers to write recommendations.

A week later with resume, grades, and recommendations, Jesse headed to Baltimore armed with his briefcase and the confidence that there was no better candidate for an appointment to the Academy than William Neal. What he, in his enthusiasm, had forgotten was that there were other young men across the state with fine credentials. It was a mistake to think he would come home with the appointment and be able to go directly to Tenth Street with good news.

"I will look this over, Mr. Morgan, but I can't promise you anything. I have nineteen others on my desk to read and evaluate." Senator Perry pointed to the files stacked on the corner of his desk. "They represent at least twenty interviews—and I am not the only congressman taking recommendations. Thank you for bringing William Neal to our attention but I can tell you that although his records are impressive, we cannot appoint him right out of Laurel High School. Unfortunately his curriculum does not prepare him for the Academy. There are math and science requirements he will have to get at prep school. He would be vying for a spot for a year after he graduates."

"The appointment is not promised when he enters prep school?" Jesse had to be clear when he took the message back to Laurel.

"Not promised, but he would be notified that he passed all the entrance requirements except the required advanced math and science classes. This appointment would be for entrance in August 1929; he would be eighteen then and ready for the life of a midshipman. Mind you, he would not get the appointment if he failed to excel in the required prep school courses. We still have interviews and competitive exams." He thumbed through the papers Jesse brought. "His record is impressive." The senator flipped the pages, Jesse waited. "One other thing, Mr. Morgan, if William Neal has a family history of service to United States military, a letter telling us about it could be important. I don't see anything in his papers."

Jesse was elated. He thought of Edward and of Gertie's dedication at Ft. Meade. The requested documentation began to form in his mind. "Senator Perry, you will have that as soon as I can get back to Laurel. The Neal family, both his father and mother, have served well and it will be documented for you."

"Excellent. I will be expecting that. Send it to my attention. I will ask my secretary to put William Neal on the list to be interviewed." The senator glanced back down at William's file. "Mind you, I am accepting this application and answering your questions—not making promises."

Senator Perry rose, the interview was over. "Mr. Morgan, my secretary will give you a list of acceptable prep schools."

"Thank you, Senator. We are most hopeful and have confidence in William Neal's scholastic abilities."

There were stumbling blocks but not insurmountable ones. Jesse saw the dilemma Gertie would face. She would be spending the money she needed for his first year of college to send William to prep school. Jesse knew Gertie and her logical, independent mind. The next problem was telling Gertie that he did all this without consulting her; now he was really on shaky ground. He decided to take a round-about approach.

"Gertie, let's talk about getting married. I want to take care of you and William."

"You want to pay for William's education. I can see through you. Now, in order for you to get William his degree, I have to get me a MRS degree." She was making fun of him for being so transparent, but he saw anger behind her eyes.

"I've always wanted to marry you."

"All it takes is *another* divorce. Don't throw the impossible in the air." Her voice rose with frustration. "I won't talk about this."

"But why, Gertie. Why all the anger?" Jesse was stunned by her drastic stance and the look of despair on her face. He knew she would be difficult, but her reaction hit him in the gut. She had a look on her face that he had never seen before, one that chastised him for insensitivity.

Gertie moved toward the door without looking back. "I have to go."

"Gertie…" he pleaded.

"I thought this was settled. You have put William and his education in this discussion, Jesse." Her final glance was defiant and charged with defenses. The door latch resounded in the foyer and bounced off his chest. She was gone, leaving only the scent of her perfume to make his emptiness more profound.

"Stupid. Stupid. Stupid." Jesse spoke to himself as he watched her taillights go slowly out of the drive. He hoped she was considering turning around. *Come back, Gertie. Turn around.* He was wrong; she wasn't turning around. She was taking time to dry her tears before reaching the main road.

Out of sight of Hilltop, Gertie pulled over. The mention of marriage put her in a tailspin. "Marriage," she said aloud looking up to see her reflection in a mirror as she often did. There was enough light to reflect. The word in the air stung but, she looked undamaged. "Did he expect a *yes?*" she demanded of herself.

Then she shouted to the night air, "Another divorce. Divorce so I can get married." She put her head down and broke into sobs of despair. She cried until she recalled her mother's admonition about emotional crying on the day Liddy got married. Gertie pulled herself together and spoke once more to the girl in the mirror. "Jesse, I love you but…" she placed her palms over her eyes, drew her hands across her cheeks, pulled her hair back and looked at the bare unadorned, red splotched face and shouted, "…. *no*." Her head dropped hard against the steering wheel putting a perfect square shaped bruise at her hairline. The stinging pain was welcome; she knew what it was and where it came from. Much better than the pain she had coursing through her being—undefined and all encompassing.

Gertie put the car in gear and drove home to Tenth Street.

Jesse hoped, but knew better—Gertie would not stop in his office the next morning. He stayed late, but the Ft. Meade workers came and left for the day and no one came to his office. His fingers tried to play on the desk but could not. It was stupid to drive to Tenth Street, but he did. Even as he turned on her street, he knew he would not go to her door. The window where William did his homework shone bright with light. Jesse circled the block and headed to Eighth Street field. The only person he saw was Sam.

"Hey, Jesse. How are you doin'? Is your nephew playing tonight? I don't see him."

"I wasn't sure. Thought I would stop by in case." He wasn't in a mood to chat with Sam and kept moving while they had this short exchange.

There was nothing to do but go home. As soon as he turned in the driveway, he saw her car and a tear of relief escaped his eye. Jesse put his head down and prayed. "Please God, help me say the right things."

It took a while to find her. The library was empty, the great room dark. He went to the kitchen and saw the door ajar. She was sitting on the top step of the back porch. Still not sure of his words, he silently sat beside her.

Gertie took a deep breath, and so, he took one, too. She reached over and took his hand.

"Look at the summer mist coming from the hills. Every time I see night fall on these hills, they are different and more beautiful."

"Never more beautiful than tonight, Gertie."

"The changes tonight do not take away from the way they were yesterday. And, tomorrow if they are dressed in rain, fog, or snow, they would not lose anything they had today."

Jesse knew exactly what she was saying as he took her in his arms. "You are my hills, my valleys, my morning, and evening mist—my love."

"And, you are mine."

His kisses were soft and needy; hers were yielding and wanting. The silence bound them into a tighter unit. Understanding fell over Jesse and Gertie like the early evening mist. They lost the world in each other and came back to it with clear minds after a while.

"Maybe someday, Jesse, maybe. . . but..."

"But, we will not talk about marriage," he interrupted.

She nodded her head.

"I love William." He spoke with conviction.

"I know you do."

"Can you stay for a cup of coffee? Is it alright for me to talk about William?"

"Yes. Yes—to both questions. You know what I can and cannot do, Jesse. While I am facing changes in William's life, I must keep mine on an even keel."

He pulled her to her feet, led her to the coffee pot, poured her cup and waited for the aroma to work its magic on her. "I'm so sorry, Gertie. It was thoughtless. Am I forgiven for wanting too much without the right to ask for it?"

"I want a lot too, Jesse...but I am accustomed to a lot less of what I want."

"Will you at least lend an ear to my advice on William's education?"

He couldn't pull that fast one on her, either.... even though he was very close and hard to resist. He blew in her ear and laughed.

She laughed heartily and pushed him away. The air and atmosphere was lighter and embraced by both of them. "I'll listen very carefully. Is that good enough?"

"OK, if you don't interrupt or run away." He held both hands and turned her to look straight at him. "I accept that I cannot pay for William's schooling. William needs to go to prep school after he graduates. I know it costs tuition and transportation, but it is a good investment in his future. I have met with Senator Perry and submitted him for an appointment to the Naval Academy."

"Jesse..." She was astonished by the thought.

"Don't interrupt; you promised," he reminded. "If he is selected it will be for the fall of 1929 and he has one year after high school to get ready."

"The Naval Academy? I don—"

"Wait, Gertie, I'm not finished. If he doesn't get the appointment he will be more than prepared for Maryland. And, he will be eighteen—another year to mature. Not a bad idea in itself." She started to speak, but his finger went softly over her lips."I know it will be money you have saved for college tuition. I realize that. I think we have to have confidence and faith in William. At worse, you will have to *borrow* from me or sell the cameo...and you already accepted those possibilities. Senator Perry recommended a school in Baltimore. He can ride the Greyhound bus everyday. At best, you will spend your money on prep school, William will get the appointment, and it will not cost you a cent for his college years. Mmmm...let's see have I forgotten anything?" He paused to allow her to speak, but all she could do was pull her hands from his and grasp her face in disbelief. Not a word came from her lips

"Sweets, you should have seen the light in his eyes when we went to Annapolis. I am so sorry you were not there. You would be selling your soul to get him there, if you had to. Oh, one more thing—I know I did all this without talking to you first, but you are always reminding me of your MacGregor stubbornness. I lived with that last night and all day today, and frankly, I don't want to go through that again." He kissed her soundly. "Before you get upset about any of this remember that I did it for William." Jesse was a smart man, ending on that note.

Gertie climbed on his lap and sat there thinking. Jesse knew her move to his lap was a sign that she was not going to get angry with him. Now he had to give her time to think things over. In her usual manner, taught to her by her mother, she began to arrange the problematic issues in order.

"Prep school would benefit him no matter which school he went to."
"Yes"
"William would be a good midshipman"
"Yes,"
"Either way, I don't have enough money to pay for four years."
"Yes...but remember, we have faith in William."
"There is no promise on that appointment to Annapolis."
"That's right."
"I can always sell my cameo if I he doesn't get the appointment."
"Leave your cameo off the list for now and put my loan on the list."
"I don't want to."

"You have to. And, add—William deserves the chance. Wouldn't you do everything possible to give it to him?"

"William deserves the chance," she repeated with a nod. A kiss sealed the deal.

"Jesse, tomorrow evening call William and tell him you want to talk to him and you want me there. Let him arrange our meeting."

"Good idea. I'll suggest Hilltop, though. I've never had both of you in this house at the same time."

$\mathscr{S}$

William and Gertie walked up the steps to the beautiful mansion. William had entered here so many times he did not knock. Today, he opened the door and welcomed his mother in. Symbolically it was very emotional for Gertie. She always thought she would someday open this door for her son.

Jesse greeted them—first William with a strong manly handshake, then Gertie with two hands to totally encapsulate hers. The mission and intent of the meeting was lost to him for an instant. "Come to the breakfast room. Bertha has something special for us."

Together, Gertie and Jesse told William of the plan to send him to prep school and help him secure an appointment to Annapolis. He could not believe he actually had a chance to be a midshipman. His mind raced to all the possibilities that presented. He shook Jesse's hand and gave his mother a big bear hug.

"Ahh, here's Bertha with homemade ice cream."

$\mathscr{S}$

Later that evening, back at Tenth Street, William tapped softly on Gertie's bedroom door.

"Come in, dear."

"I will save all my wages; I will pay bus fare and buy my books. You'll see Gertie. The prep school year will go fast." He sat at the foot of her chair where the lamp light highlighted his hair. She resisted temptation to run her fingers through his curls, instead, patted his head.

"I'm sure of that, but I don't want it to go too fast."

William felt his father in the events of today. "I think Daddy would be happy to know our plans. Don't you?"

"Absolutely, Son."

When he returned to his room, William went to the closet and pulled the wooden chest from the high shelf—Edward's box. It went on that shelf when he was eight. On rare occasions he brought it down. This day, with the possibility of going to the Naval Academy, was a perfect time to go to the shelf and take down *Edward's Things* again. He brushed his hand to push the dust aside and unlatched it.

William could, in some small way share with his father the exciting news by visiting the box. "It's not a sure thing, Daddy. But, since it is all up to me—one way or another, I am going to have my dream." The boy/man took a deep breath and put into words, for the first time, exactly what that dream was. "I want to go to the Naval Academy and make you and Gertie proud. A boy from Tenth Street, west end can go to Annapolis, can't he?" He replaced everything—with one addition. Before he closed the box, he laid his hopes on top of the old, faded, yellow telegram from the war department.

Chapter 27 1928

If Gertie was going to make it to William's graduation on time, she needed to hurry. A hot day was forecast and she did not want to be sweaty and mussed when she got to the schoolhouse. It was the worse time for the hospital to call for her.

"Pfc. Sykes is asking for you, Gertie. His time is short, very short."

"4:15," she absentmindedly read the clock aloud after writing a quick note to William.

The sun would not be up for hours. The cool, quiet, dark morning was calming as she stepped into the car and began the drive to Ft. Meade. The town was still asleep as she traveled east on Montgomery Street under the canopy of maple trees, lined with the homes of Laurel's doctors, lawyers, and merchants. Gertie never failed to admire the lovely homes and well-tended lawns. She looked down Fourth Street to the turn to Grandmother Amsterdam's house and allowed herself a moment to mourn the lovely lady again. Maybe in her busy life she failed to think of Grandmother but, often in quiet moments like this, she thought of her wonderful benefactor.

To pass the dark miles, she put her thoughts in the air. "You would be so proud of William on his graduation day, Grandmother. He's going to college. I'll find a way." She listened to her own words and added, "If he doesn't get the Naval Academy, I'll sell the cameo. He *will* go to college." It was an acceptable resolution.

The young soldier at the gate waved her through."Mornin', Mrs. Neal, awful early."

Gertie started down the dark corridor toward the ward where she had spent so many hours. She passed familiar doors and nurse's stations that held so many stories, hopes and tragedies. Tonight every feature was dark and sad because she knew what was going to happen in room 302. She drew her strength and pushed the silent door open.

The dying soldier looked very small in the bed and his sweaty forehead glistened as light filled his space. She wiped his brow and listened to the sound of the almost silent footsteps of the nurse and the quiet whirl of the fan, trying to cool the stuffy place. Gertie had learned to concentrate and focus so as not to hear the death rattle in the soldier's throat.

She tried not to look at her watch as she sat with the dying soldier. "Time isn't marked here, Warren. You are not alone." she said to herself in a whisper. Her heart was with her patient, but she had trouble keeping her mind from racing ahead to this special day in her son's life. Contrasting this young man and her son on this day tore her heart and she cried. She took his hand in hers and tried infuse mother love to him.

As always, the things she said were very personal and comforting. Yesterday, she spent hours with Warren and talked on the phone to his far away family.

"I talked to your Mother. She sends her love. Willy and Bryan are working at the service station this summer. The carnival is set up at the vacant lot next to the firehouse and watermelons are good this year." Her seasoned ability to say just the right thing took the deep lines from his face just as his hand fell away from hers. She paused a moment while his death took precedence over the universe.

Her first thoughts screamed out to the deadly gas that was trapped along with our soldiers in trenches—sometimes killing quickly and other times putting beautiful young lives like Warren Sykes' in a long struggle. Gertie softened as she saw his torn, broken body accept peace. Then she turned her thoughts to his soul.

"Our Heavenly Father, have mercy on us. Take your beloved young servant, Warren. He gave his full measure to you and to his country. Give his soul rest and his loved ones comfort. Abide in us. Amen." It was the prayer she had said too, too many times.

The sun finally poured long slanted beams across the foot of the soldier's bed, announcing the new summer day. Its brightness seemed a sad contradiction.

Gertie spoke to the nurse in attendance and went to her office. She took time, sitting at the desk, to hold services for Pfc. Sykes in her mind. Her Bible fell open to the ribbon marking John 14: 1-4. She read the verses aloud and closed the book.

After a few quiet moments in this place, where death pushed her life aside, she was ready to go back home.

She hurried toward the car, graduation day, and the picnic planned after the ceremony.

Gertie looked at her watch. *Eight-twenty. I have some time.* "Thank God. I need every minute." She stepped out in the bright sun of this perfect June morning. She ran across the parking lot, and saw Jesse, standing at her car waiting. He stepped toward her and put his arm gently around her shoulder. "William called to invite me to your picnic. He told me where you were. I decided maybe you should not drive back to Laurel. You would not have been called unless it was urgent."

"Yes. I lost another one today."

"I'm so sorry. Get in my car; we can come back for yours after graduation."

"My bag is in the back seat," she said as she lifted a hanger from the front. "I brought my dress in case I ran out of time." She climbed in and waited for Jesse to get behind the wheel and reach over to hold her hand.

"Jesse, what would I have done if he had hung on past noon?"

"No point in thinking about that now."

Jesse understood her anguish. Today was no easier than the first dying soldier she attended years ago.

"You know, Jesse. We don't lose as many as we did in the war years. How did we do that day after day—so many gravely ill on each ward?"

"By celebrating those we helped to heal and send home. Keep that in mind."

"I do. But, one lost is too many." She heaved a sigh. "Let's think about William now."

"You have plenty of time to change and be at the school on time. Bertha will be delighted to fix you some breakfast."

"I'll call William. He's going to the school early to help set up."

As soon as Bertha opened the door at Hilltop Manor, Gertie flew up the stairs and began drawing a bath while holding a conversation with Jesse.

"I'll be mixing the Neals and MacGregors at my place today. William has been the catalyst for the families. We have many reasons to celebrate this day. Mama and Papa couldn't come, but we are going down home tomorrow." She rattled on; he listened.

It was pleasantly cool in this room with the westerly breeze holding the chiffon curtains from the open windows. Gertie stood barefooted, holding her dress and stockings when she noticed Jesse watching her. She took one look at her watch to calculate the time and dove into his chest, taking him flat onto the bed.

"Wouldn't you like something cold to drink before your bath?" he asked with her face nosed against his.

"I would like some of you before my bath."

✍

Gertie pulled herself from under Jesse's heavy arms, from under his chemistry and started for the bath.

"I'll get us a bite, Love. Hungry?"

"Starved."

A small breakfast was on a tray when Gertie returned to the room, dressed and ready to go. She could hear Jesse in his bath. She hadn't realized how famished she was until she started eating the fresh fruit and cereal.

Gertie had matured into a beautiful woman of thirty-five. Her hair was fashionably short and her clothes becoming. She treated herself to a new dress for the occasion. It dropped below her knees, barely, and the flowing skirt drifted over her calves exuding freedom. There was no waistline, but her slim hips invited a lovely white belt that matched her shoes.

"Peach," she explained the color to the mirror girl. "Lovely." she allowed herself. The sleeveless fashion was perfect for such a warm day. "I'll carry the jacket for effect." Gertie's modesty was surprised when she noticed how well the color set off her dark chestnut hair. Her curls had relaxed since girlhood and soft waves embraced her ears.

Peach rouge on her high cheekbones, Vaseline glossed her lips and her slightly tanned face created a stunning porcelain look.

This was the day she would wear the cameo for the first time. "It is a happy day, Grandmother," The cameo pin slipped easily into the center of her collar and made her dress complete. She patted the brooch. "You got us here." The lock on the pin turned smoothly to secure it. She ran her fingers over the ivory image and longed for the touch of Elizabeth Amsterdam's soft cheek. "Today is our day, Grandmother."

"I've never seen you wear the cameo before." Jesse walked in to hear her last words.

"I never have—before."

"It truly is the day for it." He took the mood higher. "You look wonderful. I guess we *have* to go." Jesse returned to have some breakfast with her. He could have stared at her all day and the thought crossed his mind.

"Jesse, we have time to go back for my car. I can drive to the school and meet you there."

"Yes, we do have time, if that is what you want to do."

"It is the best plan. Give me a moment to call Mrs. Pole and make sure all is going well in her kitchen."

❦

Graduation was held on the high school grounds, weather permitting and today was a perfect day for the ceremony on the lawn.

The beautiful Georgian style school stood on a knoll overlooking Montgomery Street filling the block between Seventh and Eighth Streets. The tall brick building had two stories with a cupola on the top. The windows were tall. The white dental trim around the roof gave it a classic look. Six huge granite steps led to the double wooden door. Above the door, bricks were arched to give added architectural detail to the building. Mayor Fergus had been justly proud of this school. The staff and students shared his pride, as did the whole town. The terraced lawn invited students to sit and study. Shade trees lined the circular drive making it a truly lovely campus. Today the lawn had a dais and podium, faced with rows of chairs.

Gertie was seated with the family when Jesse arrived and joined them. He greeted Sam first and then Gertie who made introductions to Sam's wife, Dan, Liddy, and Lon. He took each hand as he was introduced and shook it warmly. Gertie's hand was taken in a formal handshake. "How proud you must be of your son," his words smiled. "The bank is giving a scholarship to the outstanding young woman in the class. I must go to my seat." He pointed to the dais. "Glad to meet your family, Gertie."

Sam leaned into her shoulder. "He looked at you as if you were his ice cream cone on a hot day." He lightly punched her arm. "Don't tell me you didn't notice."

"Sam… *behave.*"

"Well, you and Nora both look delectable." Gertie smiled at her irrepressible brother with one eye brow raised and a slight blush on her neck.

The MacGregor's talk turned to family matters and watching for William's appearance from inside the school.

The doors opened and the graduates, in caps and gowns, lined up on the granite steps for the class picture and then took their seats on the dais facing the audience.

Gertie thought her heart would burst with pride. *Edward? Are you seeing this?*

"Oh, my?" She let the words quietly slip from her lips.

"What?" Sam whispered. "What's wrong?"

"Nothing… he looks *so much* like Edward." She took a deep breath and smiled at her brother. Nothing was wrong—nothing at all. "I wish he could see his son today."

Gertie turned her attention to the formalities of graduation. Platform guests were introduced and speeches were made. Before the diplomas were awarded, special recognitions were announced for perfect attendance awards and good citizenship. Jesse presented an award to the outstanding girl. William spoke as valedictorian and received the school medal.

"Before we award the diplomas, I'd like to invite Mr. Jesse Morgan to come to the podium again. He has a special announcement." Mr. Boyette, the principal, sat down as Jesse came forward.

"Graduates of Laurel High School, Class of 1928, families, and friends." He fixed his gaze on Gertie. "I have been given the privilege of announcing that a member of this class has been selected for an appointment to the United States Naval Academy. I am sure you will agree that this young man has worked hard and set a fine example for excellent scholastics—as well as good character. His accomplishments and commendations were presented to Senator Perry and he recommended and secured an appointment for William Neal to the class of 1933. He will enter the Academy in August 1929 after successful completion of one year at prep school."

William couldn't move or speak. Jesse walked to him, took his arm and brought him to his feet. The applause was loud, excited and long. William's grin spread across his face as he was congratulated by his classmates, teachers and Jesse. His eyes searched the second row, looking for his mother.

Gertie was so surprised she could not join in the applause... and she could not see William. His classmates surrounded him, but she knew the look that would be on his handsome face and the joy that would be in his eyes. She gave him to the celebrants and waited patiently for their time. Tears spilled and useless hands lay passively in Gertie's peach lap. Sam laughed as he used his handkerchief to dry her cheeks and take away some of her rouge. Gertie looked past Sam's busy hand and caught Jesse's eye. They held a long gaze, unnoticed by anyone. Gertie saw the glistening of un-spilled tears along his eyelashes.

William emerged from the crowd on the dais, his face and eyes exactly as she expected. As he moved toward her, the Neals and MacGregors stepped aside to give him a path to his mother. Gertie stood and regained use of her arms. Gertie also regained the universe she had yielded this morning when Pfc. Sykes died. She held the universe in her arms, as he lifted her off the planet.

"Gertie, can you believe this? Did you know?" If William had not wrapped his arms around her, Gertie would have needed to reach down to touch the ground to hold the earth still.

Graduation proceeded with the awarding of diplomas and William's school days in Laurel were over.

The happy groups of MacGregor and Neal family members walked two blocks to Tenth Street for the lawn picnic Gertie had planned for them. Everyone was hungry and thirsty as they walked and talked about the exciting news of William's appointment.

"Boy, Sis. You sure kept *that* secret."

"It wasn't hard, Sam. I didn't know he was getting it."

"Really?"

"Really. I knew he had been submitted and I saw the resume that went to Senator Perry. He was interviewed months ago. But I was as surprised as you to learn today that he got the appointment. I'm all flustered. Hope I can get the food on the table."

"You better. Nothing worse than hungry MacGregors."

"Or Neals," William chimed in.

As soon as they arrived Gertie made a little speech. "William and I are so happy to have you here today to help us celebrate his graduation and as it turns out, his Naval Academy appointment. Many of you are missing the Sunday school picnic to be here so, with Mrs. Pole's help, we've duplicated the menu. We are bringing out fried chicken, potato salad, deviled eggs, baked beans, sliced tomatoes, watermelon.... and when you are ready for dessert—don't miss Liddy's chocolate cake. Ladies let's go in and get the food. Ice tea and lemonade are on the porch. William and I could not celebrate without you." She raised her hands to her mouth and threw a kiss to the gathering.

There was a soft summer breeze. The temperature was trying to get to eighty, but the shade of the huge cottonwood trees kept the celebrants comfortable. Croquet was set up on the side lawn and chairs were grouped around. Neighbors were called to join the party and William mingled and accepted the best wishes of everyone.

Jesse timed his arrival carefully giving Gertie's family a chance to enjoy their special graduate. William saw him coming around the yard and went to bring him into the family circles with an introduction. "Everyone, this is my friend Jesse Morgan. Find him a seat and feed him. Treat him well because he has been a great help to me and because, as I said, he's my friend...and by the way, he's Gertie's boss, too." William looked at Gertie to share a smile. "Jesse, make yourself comfortable. If you need anything, remind them you are the special guest of the celebrity of the day—me." The spirit was light and happy, just the right touch for everyone to welcome Jesse.

Gertie floated on a cloud of happiness. This day was perfect. Her life was perfect. *It's the greatest day of my life.* She sat in her Adirondack chair, which forced her to lean back, relax, and think about her life on Tenth Street where she had managed to raise her son, take care of her tiny family, and build a life within the Neal's enclave. She thought about Bear Creek where Mama and Papa would give William another party when the family gathered this weekend. To complete her reverie about her life and her son's life, she turned her head so she could see past the backyards to Eleventh Street and the house where William was born. The labyrinth of her life flashed quickly from there, to here, to Hilltop. Her thoughts took her to Fergus Hill. She saw Edward walking up the lawn on Sunday, many years ago. And, she realized the same feelings when Jesse came around her house today. Struggles and joys mixed.

A dying soldier and graduation chopped together. Mom Neal and Mama, Poppa Clay, and Papa, flashed though her mind. Grandmother Amsterdam and the cameo slid in and out of view. Finally she looked at Jesse, standing beside William, and she had to bring her hand over her chest to be sure her heart was remaining where it needed to be.

Jesse's voice brought Gertie back to her chair on the lawn. She looked up at his handsome countenance and came back to the happy realities of this day.

"William, thank you for inviting me to your graduation celebration. Congratulations. We have great faith in you and the path you are on. Good day." They shook hands before Jesse turned from William to look at Gertie. "Thank you for this lovely picnic. I leave you now to continue with your families." He smiled broadly to the scene and turned to leave.

She wanted to run to him and say, *don't go*. But, she didn't. Gertie waved and smiled just before he walked around the house.

William came to where she sat and they had their first minute together all afternoon.

"Isn't it great, Gertie? I can hardly believe it. Jesse helped get this for me, didn't he?"

"Yes. I think he must have done a lot to get it." William sat on the grass beside her chair contemplating the day and the events.

"You did a lot, too, Momma."

"William, you did it. You worked for it. Nothing Jesse Morgan or I did would have meant anything if you had not worked hard and kept focused. You did it and you have to do it in the future. It is, and will be, your challenge."

"Today I have been thinking about Dad, Mom Neal, Poppa Clay and Great Grandmother. So much—why?"

"Because you want to share this day with them. I was thinking about them, too."

"Why is it, on one of the happiest days of my life, I get so sad thinking of Daddy?"

"You want to share this with your father, and, honestly, so do I. But we can't and that tends to make us sad. But, think of this—the last thing your father would want is to have any sadness today. Son, be happy *for* him. You can do that, can't you?"

❧

274

It had been a long day since her pre-dawn call to go to the hospital and Gertie was tired. The men cleared the yard and the women squeezed into the little kitchen and did the dishes, talking all the while. It was a day of ups and downs and she was determined to review it no matter how tired she was.

William went out to meet with his friends and at last she was alone in the quiet with her thoughts. Gertie went to her desk to write a letter to Pfc. Sykes' family. She never put off this task. It had to be done on the *day*.

Dear Mrs. Sykes, Willy, and Bryan,

I stayed with Warren during the last hours of his life. He was comforted by your love and the words we shared on the phone yesterday.
His passing was peaceful and I am confident his last thoughts were of you
and the home he loved and missed so much.
Thank you for sharing his favorite cookie recipe with me. He enjoyed
the peanut butter favorite on Tuesday. I have included in this note the prayers
and scriptures we shared today.
I would like to personally assure you that Warren's sacrifice is well noted
and appreciated. His last days were passed in loving comfort, dignity, and honor.
It was my privilege to know your son and be with him today.

Most sincerely,
Gertie Neal
Director of Volunteer Services
Ft. George G. Meade Army Hospital

It was her privilege to serve this soldier and that line was included in every letter she wrote to grieving families. There would not be a hint of a government form letter—not from Gretta Neal.

At midnight she stamped the envelope and closed her desk.

It was after midnight when Gertie broke her rule and called Jesse. "Hi."

"Gertie!" He was alarmed to get this late call. "Is everything alright?"

"Everything is fine. Did I wake you?"

"No. Sleep isn't coming easy tonight. It was a lovely picnic."

"Today was glorious. I want you to know that William told me he was inviting you."

"So… you wanted me to come. I looked for approval on your face when I came around the house…and I thought I saw it."

"You did, my darling. I was expecting you."

"Can you come over here, now?"

"No. I wish I could—but not tonight. We are leaving for Bear Creek tomorrow."

"I forgot. Wishful thinking."

"William had a great day. How can we thank you?"

"Don't say a word. If you thank me, it will be as if I didn't love William enough to do it for him. I didn't do it just for you."

"I know."

"Besides, he did it. He worked for it. I really don't have any political pull; you know I don't do politics. I turned the papers in and they spoke for themselves. I think his interview must have been awesome." Jesse did not mention the letter he secured from the post commander about Gertie. The General wrote a glowing epistle documenting her service to the hospital and its veteran patients. He cited Edward's death and the reason for her dedication. He was not sure which carried the most weight because both the interview and letter were important. They brought William to the top—above many other fine student applicants.

"I love you, Jesse. More today than yesterday and will, even more—tomorrow."

"I love you, too, Gertie."

She hung up the phone and cried. She cried because she needed to be held and she didn't know why she needed that so desperately—at this moment. She was having trouble with the fuzzy reason she was at Tenth Street and Jesse was at Hilltop Manor.

Chapter 28   1929-1933

1929 was a good year for Gertie and William in spite of the financial terror the country was experiencing. Gertie couldn't fill her car with gas but she could put in a gallon or two and William had bus fare to go to school each day. She cut every corner and made sure William had lunch, books, and supplies. He worked at Slater's store and brought home groceries when Mr. Slater could no longer pay wages. Jesse watched their circumstances very closely.

Few citizens of Laurel, and none in the west end, were in the stock market. When the crash came in October, 1929, it filtered down and hurt small businessmen in his town and even the man who wanted to add one more bedroom to his home. A mortgage to add seventy-two square feet to a home could cause it to be lost by foreclosure in hard times.

Jesse worked to keep himself solvent and handled the bank's assets carefully. No one in the bank lost a job, though salaries were decreased. When his work force was reduced by natural attrition, Jesse could not hire a replacement. Employees who still had a job gratefully worked hard to pick up the slack. He would do all he could for families from US 1 to Fergus Hill in his square soda-cracker-like town. He did not know how long it would take, or how long the money would hold out. That was the worst part.

Laurel was a very conservative and modest pocket of survival. Jobs with the railroad, the nearby federal government, civilian jobs at Ft. Meade, and the government farms only ten miles south, gave residents some security. Pay was low but came in on a regular basis. Many young men went into the military, leaving one less mouth to feed at home. Every backyard was planted in vegetables and every housewife canned the harvest.

Tenth Street survived. Families, mostly Neals, pulled together. No homes would be lost. No one would go hungry. No one would be cold. Everyone adjusted to the new realities of life.

"Gertie, See you in an hour or so." William dropped his books on the table, grabbed a cookie and headed back out the door.

"Where're you off to?"

"Coal delivery day." Gertie had forgotten what day it was.

"Dinner will be ready when you get back."

William and his cousin, Jerry would make the rounds to every house on Tenth and Eleventh Streets as they did every Thursday. Pieces of coal that fell unnoticed during delivery would be retrieved. Pieces of black gold that fell from the truck would be saved from the streets. At some homes two or three pieces of coal would be placed outside the coal chute as a quiet donation. Their dirty gunny sacks were filled with the treasure. Every neighbor in the two block area agreed that the boys could take the bits of coal to the firehouse where it would be given to those who came begging.

William came to dinner, late, hungry, tired, and blackened. Gertie wiped a smudge of grime from his face, and put it on her own so she could share his service and show her pride, too.

"Wash up for dinner."

"You, too, Gertie," he said, his voice laughing at his crazy dirty-faced mother.

§

William loved prep school. He worked hard and brought home excellent grades. It was good for Gertie, too—she still had him at home. Nothing seemed different. William went to school and he came home. Gertie went to work and she came home. Weekends at Bear Creek cemented their lives.

Time with Jesse, although never enough, made Gertie's life happy. She was deeply in love and even more deeply contented and committed. Hilltop became Gertie's other world when she could arrange to be there. She was at home in the large rooms and inviting surroundings. The lovely manor was her home on a different scale and definition than Tenth Street. Loneliness and alone-ness were erased at Hilltop. Jesse's manor became an oasis in her desert.

Opening the gate at 403 Tenth Street and walking up to that door brought another kind of comfort. The small upstairs apartment was a symbol of her accomplished life. Sixteen steps up the staircase were high enough. Every time she climbed them she thanked God for this place where William grew tall and strong. The truth was, Gertie grew tall and strong here, too. Every evening she and William spent together on Tenth Street was precious. Next summer would be William's plebe summer, and after he left, he would never again be solely hers.

"Gertie, the letter I got today is from the Academy's admissions office. Let me read you the first line." He stood for the reading making it very dramatic. "The United States Naval Academy," pause, "is happy to inform you," pause, "that *your*," he pointed to his chest, "admission requirements have been fulfilled," pause, "*successfully*." His voice boomed. William picked Gertie up and swung her around. "...fulfilled successfully," he repeated. "I'm really going," he whispered in her ear as she circled the room.

"OK, I'm feeling a little dizzy." She took to her feet and made it to a chair. "Shall we celebrate?"

"I want to call Jesse. Maybe he can celebrate with us." William had the phone in his hand.

Gertie enjoyed the moment while William made plans with Jesse.

"He'll be here to pick us up in half an hour. We are going to Baltimore—Little Italy. Spaghetti for me."

"Sounds wonderful."

❦

The Academy years flew by. *What is it about school years?* She asked herself. *What makes them go so fast?* It was late and she should be asleep but, when Gertie did some evaluating of her life at bedtime, she could not turn it off. "Why did I ever start thinking about this?" she fussed at herself. It was too late. Once William's future came to mind, sleep was postponed.

The small picture on her night stand was the six-foot-three-inch midshipman. The same picture, enlarged, hung in the living room. The white uniform highlighted his handsome persona. Gertie looked at this picture and saw the confidence and assurance that exuded from him. William also told the camera that he was who he should be, where he should be, and why he held the future. Gertie often picked up the picture, ran her finger down his cheek and across the wave in his hair before turning off her night light.

The Naval Academy was the right choice for William. The demands of the curriculum and regime were taken in stride. He never looked back at Tenth Street as if he were *getting away*. Instead, he thought back over the neighborhood with affection and connections he did not want to escape, but rather take with him wherever he went. That enhancement of the past into his future kept him grounded and allowed his mother and family to be a part of Lt. William Neal, Commissioned Officer, United States Navy. His world was definitely getting bigger and grander, but William would not exclude the wonderful worlds on Tenth and Eleventh Streets, as well as Bear Creek.

In four weeks, William would graduate and have his commission. Gertie was not the only one proud. Everyone was—Mama, Papa, the MacGregor and Neal families, the west end, the whole town, and Jesse. Gertie was surprised when citizens congratulated her and inquired after William. After all these years it seemed fine to acknowledge his life. He was a shining light for his generation in this small town. He was proof, walking down Montgomery and Main Streets in uniform, that the Naval Academy was an attainable dream for any boy. If Gertie Neal's son, why not mine? Yes, they could acknowledge William and speak to Gertie. But they did not have to look back and make amends because Gertie was happy for the attention to her handsome, successful son's handsome uniform and highly polished shoes.

"I have a special request for my graduation," he announced when he was home for the weekend. "I want to have my party at Bear Creek."

"That's a wonderful idea. I wish I'd thought of it. It's time for us to go to the MacGregors instead of them always coming here. I'll get the invitations out quickly so the Neal family can make plans." She went to William with a happiness hug. "Make your guest list."

"How much time will you have after graduation before reporting for duty?"

"Ten days. I will get my orders with my commission."

"Ten days...," she repeated aloud as she lay in bed that night. That started her reverie and robbed her of sleep. It had been hard enough during these college years, but the future was going to be much emptier. "I'm spoiled—forty miles to Annapolis—now the world."

Her next thought was a common one that often ended her nighttime journey. "I need to see Jesse tomorrow."

❦

Bertha met her at the door. "Hello, Miss Gertie. Did Mr. Jesse know you was comin'? He not here."

"That's fine, Bertha. I'll be here when he gets home."

"I'm fixin' him a late dinner. Gonna set two plates."

"Thank you."

Gertie went up to her room and spread out on the big bed. The Academy years had made trysts with Jesse very easy. Gertie came more often and stayed longer. She pulled a pillow under her head and kicked her shoes over the side. With a quick glance to the orchard, Gertie stretched her arms out and invited sleep to replenish the hours she lost last night. Anticipation blanketed her and sleep was pure.

The room was dark when a sound brought her awake. At first, she did not remember where she was or why she was here. "Jesse?' she questioned the confusion.

"I'm here," he said as he entered the room.

Her anticipation turned to joy. "Jesse," she repeated. "I wanted to see you this evening."

"I want to see you every evening." His kiss was tender as she came to him but it quickly turned to passion. Her head fell back into his hands as uncounted kisses traced her neck. "How long can you stay?" Jesse whispered as he took her back to the bed. Gertie waited to answer his question until they were side by side and breathing softly.

"I have to go home tonight. Sam will pick me up at 8:30 in the morning. William is going with us to Bear Creek this weekend. We're picking him up."

"That's great. I know you love that. Bertha has our dinner ready. Hungry?"

"Very."

They talked as they walked hand in hand down the stairs. "William wants his graduation party at Bear Creek."

"I know; he called me."

"It will be both families and a few friends. Will you come?"

"Gertie, I can't imagine not being there. I was afraid I might be un-invited."

"Oh, Jesse, you are a part of William's success. We could not celebrate without you. Please be there."

"Wild horses could not keep me away. But, I may have to restrain myself from kissing you at Bear Creek." He stopped on the landing and kissed her to make his point.

"Do your best," she smiled. "It is time you saw Bear Creek. It's a special place."

They sat in the breakfast kitchen. "Bear Creek's not just a place, it's a feeling. I hope I can explain."

"Try."

Gertie took a few seconds to savor her thoughts about the MacGregor home. "You'll love Mama and Papa, everybody does. They are genuine people. Bear Creek is home to all of us because of them. It is acceptance, warmth, generosity, support, from wherever any of us are. Stranger never came to their door and I know they will welcome you, Jesse. The MacGregors know how special you are to William."

Gertie's words hurt Jesse. He hoped this party would their coming-out party. He reached across the table and took her hand.

Suddenly, she knew what she had said. Her eyes grew big with apology but she did not say anything.

"It's alright, Gertie." He squeezed her hand. "Alright, darling." How could he—a married man—chastise her for holding so tightly to their secret.

❦

On graduation day, Hilltop seemed to be glowing with excitement—or was it Gertie's infusion of anticipation. She walked to the veranda from her bedroom and took in the beauty of the day lilies lining the far fence. "Jesse, come quick."

"What?"

"A rabbit. Walking the fence line do you see him?"

"Yes, amid the day lilies. Look at his cotton tail.

"Oh no! There's a fox coming out of the orchard as if the world was his."

"I want to warn the rabbit. Oh, Jesse. The fox is going to get him."

"We can't interfere with nature. The fox will get the rabbit. The only thing wrong with this picture is—we are witnesses."

"It's Mr. Fox's day."

"But, Mr. Fox, the day's not yours. It's ours."

Gertie was visibly shaken. "That rabbit went about his day. Happy in the lilies. He didn't know that the beauty of the day could be lost in an instant." Suddenly the fox pounced.

"That's right, Gertie. On the other hand, the fox is most likely feeding pups. His day was perfect because he had a meal to take to his den. Let's not make too much of the tragic play Mother Nature had for us today."

Jesse turned her around and kissed her soundly. "You're right," she said but a touch of reality dampened the spirit of the morning. Gertie looked once more across the lawn. The breeze moved the lilies in perfect unison and brought sweet apple blossom perfume from the orchard. She regained her delight in the morning although a nagging sadness lingered for the rabbit.

"Don't start anything, Mr. Mor-th-gan," she laughed and spoke while he continued to engage her lips—messing up her words and her mind.

"Later," he replied. They walked away from the color and the intrigue down by the fence row.

"Do you know it has been nine days since we were together?"

"Yes. I count them, too."

"William was a great help last weekend. We got two cords of wood stacked and ready for cozy fires this winter. I was happy to have a few hours of his time Saturday while you were at the hospital. By the way, how are things at the hospital?"

"I don't know how to answer that. Do you think we're going to war, Jesse?"

"That is everyone's question. Why do you ask?"

"Well, the meeting Saturday was about scaling back at the hospital and we are told there will be no scaling back. In fact, we are directed to build up services."

"Politically, the answer is no. But, the military is not going to let our guard down. There are a lot of drums beating in Europe."

Gertie did not like this talk. "Enough about the world situation. Let's get on with today."

"It is hard to believe William is graduating."

"I told you the years would fly by. It seems like yesterday that we watched him graduate from high school." Gertie pulled at her curls, straightened her collar and moved the cameo one more time.

"Stop fidgeting." Jesse took her hands and smiled. "You look perfect."

"I can't help it… I'm so excited."

"William told me that Roosevelt is speaking."

"Amazing. I'm going to see my son graduate from the United States Naval Academy and a president, too." Gertie was overcome thinking about it. "The nerve of Mr. Fox and his bushy tail thinking this was his day."

"Yes, Gertie, put on that straw bonnet and show the world whose day this is."

She picked up her program with the Navy seal and read again.

Eighty Third
Commencement Exercises
The United States Naval Academy
Dahlgren Hall
Annapolis, Maryland
Sunday May 21, 1933
Eleven O'clock

"What time is it?"

"Nine o'clock. Plenty of time."

She did a recitation of plans. "I'm going to Sam's and ride with him and Nora. Lon and Liddy are bringing Mama and Papa to Annapolis. Dan and Mabel will meet us all. The Neals have their own plans to get there on time."

"And what about me?" he asked.

"You, my dear, will meet us at the entrance."

"Will I sit with the MacGregors?"

The Neals and MacGregors have seats in the family section. You have your seating ticket?"

"Yes."

"Our seats are together." She went to him with a gentle kiss. "The soon-to-be commissioned naval officer expects you to be seated next to his mother, with his family."

"And you—"

"I would be lost without you next to me… if you behave."

Jesse walked her to her car and leaned in the window with a last word. "This is a great day for you, Gertie."

Her smile was broad as she left Hilltop.

It was a great day for the Neals and the MacGregors. Their boy from humble background, raised on Tenth Street, was graduating from the United States Naval Academy today. The weather was perfect, the sky was cloudless and the temperature—seventy-four. Everyone would look as fresh and sharp as the midshipmen.

The freshest, sharpest, handsomest midshipman would be William Neal.

Gertie's excitement was tempered by the knowledge that William would never live with her again on Tenth Street. Although his time at home had been very limited during the past four years, he did come when he could. That was about to change when the world became his home.

No telling where he will be. She let her mind wander as she drove. *Thank God, I have Jesse.*

The route to Annapolis from Laurel included passing through Ft. Meade. Gertie let Sam and Nora carry the conversation while her mind wandered to the many hours she spent at the hospital. "Sam, remember the day we took the food after Edward's memorial service?"

"Yes. How many years have you been doing that now?"

"Sixteen."

⚓

Gertie could hardly breathe when the MacGregors took their seats in Dahlgren Hall.

Franklin Delano Roosevelt was seated on the dais with several naval and civilian dignitaries. His presence demanded soft talk among those taking seats. A hush of whispers pointed to his presence.

"Sis, everyone is proud of William, and rightly so. I'm proud of you, too."

"You aren't going to mess up my hair, are you?" She asked as she removed her hat and put it on her lap.

"Not now, you're too prettied–up but, probably before the day is over." Then Sam leaned over and whispered. "Did you see how Jesse Morgan looked at you when you arrived?"

Gertie shushed him and pointed his attention to the Navy band filing in the hall.

Nothing could match this day. When she saw William enter in his dress whites, tears spilled despite every effort she made to hold them in. Her tears of joy were delicious, they were delightful, they were delectable, and they were beyond description. Gertie only knew if she did not let them course down her cheeks, she would burst. Try as she might to concentrate on the musical prelude, her mind hopped, skipped, and jumped to images of her boy running to see his father, sliding into third base, comforting Mom Neal on her death bed, sharing science with Jesse, diving from the trestle bridge into Bear Creek, reading the acceptance letter from the Academy. Gertie did not sort her thoughts, but if she had, she would see they were all visions of William's independence. Now she put the next vision in her memory as he took his seat with the midshipmen in the class of 1933.

After the invocation and introduction President Roosevelt rose with great effort on the arm of his aide and advanced to the podium. He paused and looked at the graduates, sitting straight with caps and white-gloved hands. His gaze went down each row, engaging individuals. He would not hurry. Time stood still.

"I am not going to talk to you of the many heroic examples that have been set by those who in past years have received their commissions on occasions such as this…" FDR's strong New York accent sounded through the hall. "I am not going to give you a lecture on the uniqueness of your position as the first line of the nations' defense against aggression."

The young men were ready to hear what their president expected from them.

"You have an advantage over many other young men…having survived the tests requisite to receiving your diplomas, especially in that you have learned discipline, responsibility, industry and loyalty—the very elements … upon which success is founded. Others may have to demonstrate their reliability; yours, because you have graduated from the United States Naval Academy, is taken for granted."

The charismatic leader gave every word as a gift to those who had sacrificed for this day.

He was ready to challenge the graduates.

"...don't overestimate the importance of understanding and sympathy with what might be called the average citizen. You will find very few successful men and women who do not take into consideration the effect of their individual efforts on humanity as a whole."

William and Gertie both thought of their humble beginnings and embraced President Roosevelt's focus.

"So I ask you...to cultivate the friendship of people—the average run of folks, the same folks you have known and liked. You, who become today, officers of the United States Navy, are not set apart as a clique. You have pride in graduation from our splendid, historical, Naval Academy. You inherit the tradition of honor and efficiency. You inherit the tradition of service to the people of the United States. You will think of all the people on sea coasts, on plains and among the mountains, in the city, village and farm, rich people, poor people. You are not above or below them. You represent them all. They have given you a glorious opportunity. Make good. Keep the faith. Good luck to you in the days to come."

Gertie had not expected her president to use this speech to assure her and William that they were worthy—but he did. There was no point in continuing to compare their humble beginnings in Laurel to this place.

Roosevelt was tired from the effort to stand, but he was determined to remain standing for the awarding of diplomas. Aides supported him on either side. Finally, Admiral Benedict announced, "Lieutenant William Edward Neal." William stood, came forward with a precise salute to the Commander in Chief, and accepted his diploma.

Gertie felt hands from her family grasp her shoulder from behind. They all wanted to touch her and share the moment. Jesse was the only one in the reserved family section who took and held her gaze.

🦀

The graduation party at Bear Creek was reminiscent of lawn parties at the caretaker's house on Fergus Hill. The crab pot steamed over an open flame by the back door. Food was plentiful and spread out in the kitchen, dining room, and on the porches. It all seemed to appear magically and without effort. Papa cooked hams and turkeys last night. Liddy brought many cakes. The Neals brought pies and cookies.

Three generations mingled without formality. Gertie was busy working with her sisters and sisters-in-law. Only the MacGregors had chores. All others were guests. Sam put William to work dipping crabs from the live-box tied to the pier. Gertie made sure plenty of plates were washed and re-circulated. Papa closed the bridge span and watched for high-mast boats whose captains did not know that his grandson had just graduated from the United States Naval Academy.

Gertie had only a moment with Jesse as he arrived.

"Hi, Jesse." Her gaze said so much more. "William will show you around. He and Sam are down at the water." She pointed across the back yard to a well-worn path to Bear Creek.

"Go, do what you have to do, Gertie. You don't have to take care of me. I'll be fine."

"He got his orders—Newport." She looked at Jesse with sad eyes. "I was hoping he would get Philadelphia or Norfolk."

"You will have to get used to the distance between you. And, we have the perfect reason to go to New England." He wanted to take her hand and give support with his touch, but he didn't. "It's a wonderful party." He beamed. "We are going to have great fun with our boy, today."

"Yes, we are. I will be seeing you around and about and when we sit to eat crabs, I want you next to me."

"It's a date and, when you come back to Laurel, I want you at Hilltop."

"It's a date."

They exchanged smiles and went their separate ways.

At times, Gertie felt she was a voyeur at the party. She watched William move from group to group, engaged with everyone. Jesse seemed to be enjoying whoever was close at hand. Mama and Papa were having a wonderful time. It was such a different feeling from this morning and the formal glory at the Academy. She stored each tableau as she scanned the festivities over and over.

She was on a mystical journey to each quadrant of the party when Sam came up and tousled her hair. "I warned you I would do that before the day was over"

Gertie kissed his cheek. "I feel very benevolent today—even to you," she laughed.

"Whoa. People will think our sibling rivalry is over."

"Not a chance," she said as she punched him lightly in the stomach and watched him double over. Their smiles were identical MacGregor grins.

"So much for benevolence." Sam pulled her to the step. "Whatcha thinkin', Sis?"

"Too much perfection. Think what we've been through to get to this day. I have so much happiness, it scares me."

"Ahhh, never too much. I felt that way when little Sam was born but after three more children, I decided happiness is allowed, even in mass amounts." He rocked toward her and bumped her shoulder. "It's your turn now, Gertie." It was a profound declaration, but she let it go.

Instead, she turned to him and required him to get serious. "William belongs to the United States now. Actually—to the world. He leaves next week and after that, he will be only a visitor here and on Tenth Street."

"That boy," Sam pointed at William who was helping Mama to a seat at the crab table, "will never leave you, no matter where the United States Navy sends him."

At that moment, William caught Gertie's eye. He waved and then thought better. He saluted his mother off a tanned forehead and under one unruly curl dancing in the breeze.

"Sam, I see Jesse Morgan at the crab table. I'm going to go join him."

"You do that." Sam watched her walk away from him and approach Jesse. He saw the look on Jesse's face. "You do that," he repeated, but she was long gone.

Chapter 29   1938-1940

There were many excuses for Gertie to run to Hilltop but none as compelling as a letter from William. Today's letter was dated October 20, 1938. Gertie sat on the step at 403, read it and checked her watch. "Five o'clock. I have time, if I hurry." Although she had a commitment at seven, and plans to see Jesse tomorrow, she decided to go to Hilltop now. "I can tell him my news and William's, too."

"Where's Mr. Jesse?" Gertie asked as she stepped into the kitchen at Hilltop.

"Orchard, Miss Gertie. He and Jed pickin' apples. They's got a crew today. Apples ready—lots o' work dis week—apple jelly, apple butter, apple pies." Bertha loved the apple harvest. "Want me to make coffee, Miss?"

"Yes, thank you." Gertie went out the back door to find him.

The trees were bent with fruit. Gertie passed through the Jonathans shining like rubies on the limbs and went into the rows of Golden Delicious, her favorite. She reached up and took one.

"Poacher!" Jesse called. "Stop stealing my apples."

"I'm helping, aren't I, Jed? One less to pick, carry, sort, and take to market."

It was obvious that Jed was not going to get into this debate as Jesse scooped Gertie up and set her on the back gate of the pickup.

"Are you here to help, make trouble, or eat up our profits?"

"All of the above."

"Actually, we are about finished for today. Sun's hanging low." He climbed up and sat beside her on the truck bed.

"It's beautiful out here. I love the orchard, especially when the fruit hangs like jewels. Looks like a good year for apples."

"A good year for us, too. Can you stay for dinner? I'm sure Bertha set you a place as soon as she saw you."

"I only have time for coffee. Come on to the house. I've something to tell you." Suddenly Gertie's countenance became serious and Jesse saw it immediately.

"Go ahead. I need to talk to Jed. I'll catch up."

Gertie started the long walk across the lawn looking up at the beautiful white mansion that she had come to love. Jesse's quick strides caught up with her before she got to the steps. He took her hand and they went in together. "Please stay. I'm not above begging. You look wonderful. I've missed you this week." His kiss was distracting but failed to derail her from her purpose.

Gertie wanted to crawl into his embrace and clear her mind of debris and clutter, but instead she suggested they have coffee in the library as she picked up the coffee tray. He followed.

"Don't drive me crazy, Gertie. What's on your mind?"

"Mrs. Pole is selling the house. She's going to live with her son." Gertie took a deep breath and said, "I've decided to buy it. Calvin Pole is coming over tonight to talk to me. Seven o'clock. That's why I can't stay."

Jesse got very quiet. Gertie knew the thoughts running through his head. He drank his coffee and left it to her to speak again.

"William—"

"Wait, Gertie," he interrupted. "William has nothing to do with this. You know it and so do I. You'll never ever come to Hilltop to live, will you?" There was an unusual edge to his words.

"Jesse, William has everything to do with it. He wants to own a house on Tenth Street. But, he can't afford it now. I'm going to buy the house that has been his home. Don't make more out of it than it is. It doesn't mean—*never anything*" She pressed her hand into his chest. "It simply means that Mrs. Pole won't live there any longer. That is all."

"Gertie, I hope that is all it means."

She got reflective. "Please understand. I work very hard to keep things right for me and you. I don't want anything to change in our lives. If I move from 403, well…" Gertie looked at Jesse waiting with expectation, "I can't have a decision forced on me. Support me in this, Jesse. Please."

"I think buying the house is good. What a wonderful opportunity to give William what he wants. The boy seldom asks. I was selfish, and I apologize." He kissed her tenderly. "I won't give up the dream of

Hilltop being your home." He paused just a moment to let the thought drift away. "Of course, I support you in this." He kissed her again to prove his sincerity.

"Tenth Street means something to me that is hard to explain. It's my home place. We MacGregors have a tradition of coming home. William is a MacGregor—Tenth Street is his Bear Creek. Does that make sense?" She looked pleadingly at him. "I love Hilltop. I come gladly, happily to Hilltop. And I am happiest when I am here with you, but Tenth Street—" she paused to find the words. "— defines who I am." Jesse leaned back and put his head against hers. "If I had to choose, Hilltop or Tenth Street, I would choose Hilltop and you. But the greatest gift you give me is that I don't have to choose." She turned her head and put her nose firmly against his. "I have the best of both of my worlds." Her lips sought his. "Don't ever forget—I'd choose you."

They finished their coffee and yielded to tender moments before Gertie went to the car. Jesse went back to the orchard to walk among the trees and think. Gertie's decision to buy the house bothered Jesse more than he let on. Each time he thought things were lined up for them to move toward marriage and making Hilltop their home, she tied her life on Tenth Street into a tighter and tighter bundle. Jesse kicked a fallen apple, watched it soar to the far barren field and burst into red and white pieces. He was looking for another apple to kick when Gertie ran into the orchard and called to him.

"Jesse. Jesse! I forgot to tell you...William has new orders. He is going to San Diego." She pulled a letter from her slacks pocket. "I got a letter today."

"That is great news. His ship is leaving Norfolk out of the Atlantic."

She took his hand. "I'll tell you what...let's go back to the house. We will read William's letter and look at the picture he sent. I'll call Calvin Pole and reschedule our meeting while you tell Bertha I'm staying. Good thing I remembered the letter before I got far. I would have had to turn around."

"But, you would have."

They raced back to the house. He tempered his speed so she had hopes of beating him.

❦

There was a picture with William's letter.

Gertie gave Jesse the picture. "This an official picture of his ship. William wrote on the back."

USS Arizona Battleship
Commissioned 17 October 1916
Pacific Fleet San Diego, California
Here I come.

❧

This was good news. Jesse wanted William transferred to the west coast. A naval base in California was a long way from the problems increasing in the Atlantic. Germany was harassing commercial shipping. Their submarines and warships were looking for a chance to engage ships plying those waters. There were rumors that submarines were invading territorial waters. Jesse worried that it was just a matter of time before the US Navy would have to defend American interests against aggressive actions in the Atlantic. If Germany attacked an American merchant vessel by design—or by accident—ships from Norfolk would be the first ones in the fray. A transfer to the Pacific coast would delay any chance that William would immediately be in the European war.

Gertie read the papers. She saw the news reels about the march across Europe by ominously strong German troops. Concerns about another war were waylaid by editorials and political speeches focused on *staying out of it*. She followed the news that was reassuring to the mother of a young naval officer and tried to ignore news that frightened her.

Jesse read *everything* about the growing war machine in Europe and the threat to England. He did not seek opinions that were comforting to him; he sought the truth and it alarmed him. William was in danger of being in a major war. He was trained to defend and Jesse believed that he would have to use that training before Hitler finished his rampage.

He was careful not to discuss with Gertie what he read about the situation in Europe. They shared their concern for William but always with confidence in his training and in the strength of the United States.

❧

1939 was not a good year for the world and Gertie's disappointing birthday was dwarfed by events. Her hopes for non-involvement, dimmed when Canada declared war following the invasions of Austria and Poland. She knew the United States and William were moving steadily toward conflict. The changes at Ft. Meade underlined the war probability as she watched the base double in size, the hospital expand, and almost unlimited funds made available for services. Gertie did not celebrate her birthday this year. A snow storm closed roads and Jesse could not get back from a business trip to New York. The cake at Bear Creek was enjoyed by Mama and Papa. The phone was a poor substitute for being with her loved ones.

But then the telephone rang. Anxious to hear another voice on such a gloomy day she rushed to answer.

"Hello, Gertie. Happy birthday."

"William, how wonderful to hear your voice. Thank you."

"Are you going to Bear Creek?"

"No, darling. The roads are snow covered. My birthday will be very quiet this year."

"How are you?"

"I'm fine. How are you?"

"Good. California weather is great but the weather in Hawaii is even better. You got my letter and picture of Louisa?"

"She's lovely. Serious?"

"Could be. We are shipping out and it's the first time I hate leaving for a new port even if it is paradise. Must be the girl." She could hear his happiness. "How is everyone?"

"Everyone is fine. Always asking about you."

"Jesse? How's Jesse?"

"He's fine too. I share your letters with him."

"Tell everyone I said *hi*. I miss Tenth Street and Bear Creek and Hilltop, too. My two minutes are about up. I'll write when we get to Pearl Harbor, and I'll send a pineapple. Would you like that?"

"You send it—Jesse and I will eat it."

"I love you, Gertie."

"Love you, too. William."

Their good-byes were in unison. As always the joy of his phone call left her blue and lonely.

❦

At the end of a long pleasant evening before Gertie left for Christmas at Bear Creek, Jesse took Gertie up to his room where Bertha had set a dessert table and Jed lit a fire for the December chill. Fine linen cloth, delicate china, silver service worthy of the hot apple pie and coffee were spread for them on a low table between the settee and the fireplace.

"Aren't we spoiled?" Gertie remarked as they entered.

"Bertha loves you. She'll do anything for you."

"Not just me." She took charge. "You pour, I'll cut."

"I'm to ring for her if we want ice cream, too."

"No ice cream. Tell her she's done enough. We'll clean up."

Talk was sparse while they enjoyed the food and ambiance. Finally, Jesse took her cup from her and pushed the table away so he could hold her close.

"Now, Gertie, something is bothering you. Are you going to tell me what is really on your mind? I don't know how long you can stay but, I'm not going to let you go until you tell me."

"I can stay tonight." Gertie looked at him with total honesty. He felt her love and devotion and it caused his heart to skip a beat. Jesse turned off the light and returned to Gertie and the glow of the fire. He waited. He knew he did not have to push. He only had to give her time and invitation.

"William—" He pulled her closer. "—Edward." He put together all her thoughts between the two men and saw fear in her eyes.

"Gertie, start somewhere. You have got to say it. We can face it, together."

"The *war drums* as you call them are terrorizing me at night. A new decade starts in eight days—1940 ... and all the news is scary. William is going to fight in a war, isn't he?"

"I'm not going to lie to you, Gertie. There is no point. Without a miracle Roosevelt is going to help England. Hitler has to be stopped."

"Is there some predestination for my son to meet the same fate as his father?" She started to cry. "There Jesse, I've said it." Now amid sobs, she said it again. "Are we going to lose William in this war?" She buried her head in his chest and cried for all the unspoken and unacknowledged fears for her son. "I can't bear the possibility." She began to shiver and shake. "All the excitement of William going to the Naval Academy, all the pomp and circumstance, all the pride in his accomplishments, all the distinguished uniforms, are not worth losing him." She cried with abandon. "Nothing is worth that. I wish…" She stopped short of lamenting William's going to the Naval Academy.

Jesse held her and gave warmth but he knew she wasn't shaking from a chill. Instead of stopping her quaking, his body quivered with compassion. "William will be fine. He will come home to you…to us.

Jesse lifted her face and forced her to look at him. "Gertie, if we go to war, William would be in it along with every other able-bodied man. It is much better that he meet the challenge well prepared as an officer. His father did not have that advantage. William expects us to keep the faith. He *will* come home to us." Jesse leaned back and looked at Gertie. "Say it." He demanded.

"He *will* come home to us."

Jesse sifted his fingers through her curls and caressed her head. He could not say anything as he pressed his cheek to hers. Jesse could only blend his fears and tears with hers.

Purging was good and when they spoke again, fear had been shelved. It was not conquered. It would stare down from that shelf for a long, long time.

"William is young, strong and alive—today. He will be tomorrow, too. We will live in today and tomorrow. We won't rob today's happiness for something, unforeseen, in the future.

I believe in the power of thinking positive. William will have children and he will have grandchildren who will hear from his lips stories of their remarkable great grandmother."

"Yes, Jesse, he will. And, he will watch them play in the yard at 403 Tenth Street. I bought that house because he will live there again—some day."

"Yes, Gertie. He will—he has to."

They sat quietly until Gertie took Jesse's hand and led him to the bed. She began to unbutton his shirt while he kissed her neck. He sat on the bed's edge while she pulled his shoes and socks off. "I'll be right back."

Jesse got in the bed. His desire grew as he waited. He knew she would soon return to him, showered and beautifully attired in a satin gown. Her hair would be brushed, her face scrubbed and her body lightly fragranced. There would be no hint of sadness, no divided attention. Gertie returned to him fully prepared—not unlike the ripe jewels he plucked from the apple trees for the 1940 harvest.

Lovemaking was wild and intense, the way it had to be for these lovers who were frightened. They fought for each other. Jesse lifted Gertie up; she pulled him down. He used all his strength and Gertie matched him muscle for muscle, sinew for sinew, bone for bone. Gentleness would have been too soft, too easy, and too mild for this night of facing possibilities.

❧

News of the London blitz was headlined in the papers, on the radio, in every conversation and heavy on the American hearts. World leaders were meeting and citizens were wondering exactly what war in Europe would mean here at home. Worse was speculation about tyranny spreading to our homeland. Could there be an invasion? Here?

A strange trembling started at Gertie's core. She began to live with a national worry that she shared with people she passed on the streets of Laurel. For the first time since she was a young girl, Gertie had something in common with everyone in her home town.

❧

It was time. Although Gertie wanted to talk to William face to face, it could not be put off for many reasons. It took her three days to write the letter and she started it off just like that.

Dear William,

It is time. I want you to know all there is to know about Jesse and me.

William read with a broad smile. "Did she really think I don't know about her and Jesse?" He found a quiet spot on the aft deck to read his mother's confession.

Jesse and I are in love and have been for a long time. For us to marry he would have to get a divorce and I am opposed

297

to that. In deference to me, we have kept our relationship secret and forged a wonderful life together at Hilltop. I want you to know we are totally dedicated to each other. I am not alone and I am happy beyond my expectation. Take care of yourself and don't worry about me—not one minute—while you are fulfilling your duties. Jesse will take care of me and I will take care of him. I believe you will be happy with this news and maybe, not too surprised. Ours is not a very acceptable arrangement in Laurel so I will continue to live at Tenth Street and go to Hilltop often. Jesse and I will keep the home fires burning for you in both places.
We live for the day we can all be together again.

Your loving mother,
Gertie

William smiled again as he folded the letter. He knew it was hard for Gertie to write and admit that she did not follow all the rules. Through the years he watched her punish herself for rules that society dictated—rules that he did not understand until he was a man.

"War is coming, Momma." He spoke the deadly probability and the seldom heard name. William spoke to the blue Pacific splashing against his ship. "Things are changing. Rules don't apply. While the Navy and I struggle to save the world in coming days, you are going to find a new path." He pushed Gertie's letter into his breast pocket. "God, I want to go home again. Please..." he continued his prayer in silence before going on with the conversation he started. "When I get to Tenth Street, this..." he patted the pocket and the letter, "... goes in the box with Daddy's things." He looked across the deck to the Big Island on the port side.

Meanwhile back in Maryland, Gertie put aside the fear that William could die before he knew she loved Jesse, too.

Chapter 30   *1941*

The settled, comfortable life Gertie and Jesse enjoyed since William graduated from the Naval Academy was in jeopardy. But theirs were not the only lives that faced the unknown and unsettled.

William's assignment to the Pacific Fleet gave him a lot of sea time plying the waters with an eye toward a new menace—Japan. In a matter of months his port was changed from San Diego to Pearl Harbor, Hawaii.

Events in Europe made it a scary time. Jesse was sure the United States would come to the aide of its allies. Visions of Nazis in Paris affected the staunchest isolationist. Each day, he read the morning paper and muttered, "Just a matter of time." Jesse knew when the United States entered the conflict, William would be fully engaged and Gertie would not be living alone during the war, if he could help it.

❦

Jesse had a plan for their annual beach weekend in July.

"I want to get married," Jesse announced to Gertie as she lifted her eyelids from a nap in the late afternoon sun.

"What? What are you saying?" Gertie wiped her face, forgetting the sand on her hands. She sat up to brush the sand off her face with the beach towel. The sun sat low in the western sky and the Atlantic seemed to roar louder as he repeated his words.

"I want to marry you, Gertie," He would risk all and go into the abyss that had been forbidden.

Gertie was mixed in emotion and sand. She couldn't think and she couldn't get the sand away from her eyes.

"Now is the time... the right time to get married." As he talked, he wiped the sand off her face and away from her eyes. "See, you need me."

"I know, I need you, Jesse." She took his hand and stopped its busy work around her face. "Marriage? I really thought this was settled for us." She was puzzled. "You want to talk about this again? What makes it the right time?" She sat up straight. "Why now?"

"Why not now? We could be together all the time. William is half a world away. You worry about him all the time. You have your work and your duties at the hospital…and you have me. But your work and duties and, even your time with me, leaves a lot of down time. Let's turn the priorities around. How about—me—work—hospital? And I will help you worry about William, too, even though you know he is fine—doing what he was trained to do—and loves."

She got very quiet. Doubt rushed in as Jesse forged ahead. "Why go on living alone on Tenth Street?" He used every tactic except the inevitable war.

Over the years he had tried to talk marriage to Gertie, but hated to spoil their time together with a disagreement over this topic. Jesse remembered well the first time he brought it up and what a staunch stand she took against it. Gertie set the rules and Jesse willingly lived by them. Their years together had been wonderful, but pending war caused him to look beyond stealing time together. Jesse's mind worked over the possible implications of his proposal. He would try this last time. *You are strong, my sweets, but you cannot carry our secret and bear your concern for William. You are going to be cared for even if William is…* Jesse could not allow the worst possibility into his thoughts. The only way he could assure Gertie's security, no matter what jeopardy William faced, was as her husband. The time was right and the beach would be the place. Jesse's plan was not a spur-of-the-moment thing. He spent the last three months putting the wheels in motion to clear obstacles to their marriage. Jesse rightfully believed the biggest one would be the potential bride.

Gertie leaned forward. Her countenance darkened as she started to speak.

"Wait. Don't say no." Jesse put his raised finger across her pursed lips. "I want to tell you some things before you say a word."

She relaxed back on to the sand blanket. "My proposal is different this time. I have taken care of all my problems first so you can't use them as excuses." He took her sandy hands, pulled her upright again. "I divorced Catherine. It was final two days ago. Just paperwork and, unbelievably easy. The lawyers handled it and I never saw her or went to the court. Neither did she. It's done and we're both relieved. Her status is secure and financially she is better off than I am, right now, but I will recoup." Jesse took Gertie's chin to raise her eyes to him. "I am free. Can you set yourself free?" His voice pleaded.

Her eyes were soft, as a deep furrow plowed into her brow.

"I want to take care of you every day for the rest of my life. I want to be sure you are secure no matter what the future holds." He added, "Please marry me, Gretta MacGregor Neal." and sounded like a child begging for another piece of candy. "I love you."

She smiled at those three little words, even as her mind went in a different direction.

He took heart in her smile.

Things were changing on the global scene, but socially nothing changed in the little town of Laurel. Gertie would always be an outcast and in truth did nothing to foster better acceptance. Some had forgotten the divorce; some never would. The ladies of the town kept their attitudes and Gertie said, "So be it" Her checks were appreciated at church, her support of local charities was acknowledged, but she was never invited into the inner circles. She had respect, yet no respectability. Gertie knew she was often the topic of gossip—gossip about possible male companions; even gossip about her and Jesse. They gossiped about her possible sexual persuasions. She decided to live above reproach. To live on that high plain, she had to keep her long relationship with a married man in secluded, secret places. Tenth Street was where she needed to get her mail and keep her image. She needed a hard outer shell. That hard shell became an integral part of Gertie Neal. The only time she softened was at the hospital and Hilltop Manor. Through the years she learned not to dwell on what people thought. Most of all, she protected William. Her guard never went down. There was nothing to hold against her except her divorce and decision to live a single life while raising her child.

Not marrying again had become a credo, a requirement—a validation, a vindication.

Jesse thought she was considering marriage in her silence, but she was reviewing what life's experience had taught her. She looked at him. *My love, we have so much but, we can't have it all*, she concluded. Gertie gently shook her head from side to side.

"You're saying *No!* You... are... saying, *no*... Oh, Gertie," he said with despair. They sat together watching the surf tug at the shore. He put his arm around her and they were alone on the beach in Ocean City. She leaned against him with the weight of the world on her chest and he held her as if she were never going to fit into his embrace again.

Jesse found some words. "If this is how you want it – it's how it will be. Just remember, I didn't choose this road for you and the high and mighty in Laurel didn't choose this road for you, either. You chose it. Many years ago you decided to stand tall but, unfortunately, you never demanded the same from the people of the town. Both you and Laurel are locked in a nasty habit. Gertie, it is just a habit adopted over the years and hard to break." She felt him squeeze tighter. "Isn't it time to do something just because it is what you want?"

Gertie pushed against his chest. She wanted to run but he held tight and would not let her rise. She pulled against him. Jesse held on.

"Run," she whispered. Then, she wondered, *where to? From what?*

She gave up the struggle and began to cry the wail of years and years of holding it in. With total abandonment she let a tide of emotion rip from her core. Waves of tears washed down her face. Her issues, like the sand that could not be counted, blasted her psyche. And, the reality of it all broke over her barrier reef and tore at her shell. She continued to cry as he lay her down on the blanket and pulled the edge up and wrapped her like a clam.

Jesse lay beside her until she slept on the beach as the ocean roared its song. He felt as useless as a piece of driftwood.

It was twilight when she stirred and Jesse was still holding her cocoon. She looked up at him and smiled. Her eyes were swollen, her cheeks blotchy and matted curls surrounded her face. She was not her usual beauty but he looked at her through eyes of love. Lit by the light filtering onto the sand from the boardwalk, he read her lips mouthing the words, "I *do* love you."

Jesse, in the same way, said, "I know."

"Aren't we hungry?" He asked. "Let's go eat a soft crab sandwich and some boardwalk fries. Sound good?"

"Sounds delish." They gathered their things up from the beach and headed for the Atlantis Hotel entrance and their separate, but adjoining, rooms. In no time they were refreshed and back on the boardwalk strolling toward their favorite food stands. Ocean City bustled. Hundreds of tanned and sunburned strollers were walking the boardwalk on this beautiful summer night. The penny arcade provided a carnival of music and the chatter of children wafted across the crowd. A juggler entertained a group and beside the boardwalk on the sand's edge in the reflected light an amazing sand castle was under construction by a college fraternity. Gertie remarked on everything and put each scene in her memory to treasure another day. They had never walked hand in hand in public—never walked arm and arm away from the grounds of his home. So, Jesse was surprised when Gertie reached over and put her arm around his waist as they walked. Without skipping a step, he draped his arm around her shoulder. Gertie laughed out loud.

"Does this mean we can get married?" he quipped, as they took a booth in Thrasher's restaurant.

He was picking up the menu when she said, "It's too late today.... but maybe tomorrow or the next day."

"Don't tease, Gertie." Jesse dropped the menu and stared at her. Scarcely above a whisper he repeated, "Don't tease."

"I'm not teasing. I'm practicing keeping my head up and doing what I want." She raised her head to kiss him right there in front of the sun baked crowd eating crabs and fries by the Atlantic Ocean. "I will marry you, Jesse. I want to tell William first. Any day after—"

"I told William. I needed his permission to ask for your hand."

"Really?"

"He gave it."

"Did you tell William when?"

"William can't come home. So...we might as well get married tomorrow. Does that sound like a good day?"

"That's Mama's birthday; a good sign. July 7th." They kissed again.

"I have something for you." Jesse opened a small compartment in his wallet. Wrapped in a piece of tissue paper, a gold ring emerged with two perfect diamonds and several small aquamarines—set in a swirl of gold. "I thought I would never be able to give this to you. I've had it a long time. Back in my room are two matching wedding bands with the same pattern—one in my size—one yours. I had them made after our first trip to Ocean City. It is to remind you of the sea and surf. I brought you back here this week because I thought everything would come together for us. Like it?"

"Oh, Yes. I love it." He slipped it on her finger and focused on the happiness on her face.

"I am anxious to get started on our new life. I have a marriage license and we can be married by the Justice of the Peace in Salisbury. Our appointment is ten, tomorrow morning unless you want to go home and be married in the church there."

The waitress approached with pencil in hand, but she could not get their attention. She heard their conversation and turned away with a smile thinking she had seen and heard everything on the boardwalk at Ocean City. This was the first proposal with elopement plans.

"Let's already be married when we get to Laurel. I know William will be happy for us."

❦

They left the hotel and headed west early the next morning. Even in the bright light of day, the glow of the night before shone in their eyes. She was more beautiful than ever in her white floral dress and dark tan. Her hair was streaked with highlights and a few strands of grey. She scrubbed her face to a shine and lightly oiled it to keep the glow.

Jesse also had a dark tan and his naturally light hair sparkled in the sun. His broad shoulders and strong gait were more animated on this wonderful day in his life.

He's beautiful. Her eyes took him in and adored him.

It took forty minutes to get to Salisbury and another thirty minutes to say the "I do's. The matching wedding bands were slipped on and the papers were signed. Gertie and Jesse were married. The Justice invited him to kiss the bride and then extended *best wishes* to Mrs. Jesse Morgan.

"I cannot believe how excited I am, Jesse. I feel like a school girl."

"You aren't a school girl, Gertie. You are the most wonderful, beautiful woman in the world and I want to give it to you."

"You have already. I will love you forever."

"That's exactly what I want—*forever.*"

Gertie and Jesse walked across Court House Square where he paused just long enough to drop a letter in the mailbox before he led her to the lunch counter in Woolworth's for a sandwich. He pulled the small vase and single carnation on the counter and set it in front of his bride.

"You didn't have a bouquet. I'll make it up to you. When I get home you will have many beautiful flowers and we will have food and a cake and invite all the family and friends to Hilltop. Would you like that?"

"Yes, I would." She could have the flowers, cake and party and greet her guests as Jesse's wife.

Jesse drove to the Bay Breeze Inn in Cambridge, Maryland, owned by old friends. A special suite was ready for the bridal couple. Their hosts were delighted to have them and offered a drink and a toast to their future. Gertie added to her store of memories the view of the Choptank River, the beautiful traditional furnishings highlighted with many bouquets of roses scattered around, bringing beauty and fragrance to her wedding day. She relaxed and enjoyed the glass of wine. Jesse's thoughtful friends were first to know Jesse and Gertie as a couple.

"I have reserved the whole inn and with my encouragement, our hosts decided to take a short vacation this night. They filled my grocery list so I can prepare our dinner and breakfast…if we have time to eat. And now, I want to take my wife to bed."

Gertie's happiness was boundless. Her smile—constant and radiant. "Nothing is better than this." she spoke aloud to herself in the shower. And she did not know if the feeling came from the marriage ceremony or the new freedom she had claimed. The rest of the day and night was a true honeymoon. They alternately ate and made love—each bringing appetite for the other.

"Would you like a honeymoon trip to Hawaii to see William?"

She answered by diving into his chest with her pillow. He grabbed her and rolled until they fell off the bed, laughing. "Yes, yes, yes. Don't tell me you already have tickets for that."

"I wasn't that confident. Although I thought if you didn't marry me, I'd go see William alone." She raised the pillow to hit him and start the fighting and rolling again.

They laughed, played, and planned. Years of pent-up dreams were spread on the bed, on the breakfast table and on the future. There was newness in their relationship simply because of the fresh air of openness. Just as the new breath of spring brings on the flowers, their love produced new buds of hope and optimism. For the first time their love was blessed with a future. Many times Jesse took her hand and moved his fingers to feel the ring on her hand. Just as often she fixed her gaze to study the matching ring on his hand. The rings circled the lovers' fingers in matching perfection.

Gertie could not believe how light she felt. The corner she turned was complete and she tackled the new territory with the same vigor and determination that she had used so often in the past. Tomorrow she would begin to show her little hometown her rebirth.

In the car on the way home the next day they talked of concrete plans. "Gertie, we will go straight to Hilltop today. Are you ready to move to Hilltop immediately? What about Tenth Street?"

"Didn't I always say I would live at Hilltop with you? I'm ready to move." She got quiet and Jess knew what she was thinking.

"Thinking about Tenth Street?"

"Yes. It has been my world for a long time." She paused and added, "And, it's been a good place for me and William. I'll rent it to soldiers until William comes home."

She turned to him with a bright, happy smile. "I cannot believe how easy this is for me. I'm ready, my love. I just didn't know it."

The next afternoon, they were almost home, rounding the curve on Governor Highway outside of Annapolis when the tire blew out and the car careened out of control and off the highway. Jesse threw his right arm across Gertie's chest to keep her from hitting the windshield. She bounced off the dash instead. He had nothing to protect himself from the steering wheel, which crushed his chest and killed him instantly.

Gertie climbed out of the wreckage and began walking in the direction they were traveling. She was going to Tenth Street. When the police found her she had walked several miles, one shoe on and holding a blood soaked beach towel to her head. She couldn't answer the simplest question. "What's your name?"

The closest hospital was on the army post so she and Jesse were transported to Ft. Meade Army Hospital and a call to the address on her driver's license was futile. No one answered the phone. An officer went to Tenth Street to find Gretta Neal's family. A call to Hilltop Manor was answered by Bertha. In response to their question, she gave the police Catherine Morgan's name and number in Washington, DC.

Gertie stared off into space. They decided to medicate her and x-ray for possible head injury although no external injuries were seen except a cut on her forehead, a goose egg bump and a large bruise on her right shoulder. Medication brought sleep. Jesse came in her dream.

"I took care of everything, Gertie." Jesse walked toward her. "Good bye, my darling." He walked away through a strange doorway lit from behind. His hair glistened in gold perfection.

Sleep was so easy and a small voice inside kept telling her not to wake up.

$$ \text{❦} $$

Catherine Morgan came to Ft. Meade soon as she got the call. She talked to the police and identified Jesse. While the Duty Officer prepared paper work for her signature, she called Winslow Nickelson the only funeral director in Laurel. Jesse would be moved in the morning.

"No, officer, I don't know Gretta Neal." Catherine allowed a look of relief to cross her face when told that Jesse's companion was not seriously hurt. She declined going to see her.

Nurse, Joyce Palmer, making rounds, let out a gasp when she saw Gertie's chart and looked in on the familiar face. She hurriedly called the doctor who had worked with Gertie so often at the bedside of soldiers. News traveled quickly through the hospital and everyone knew of the terrible accident, Gertie's plight, and the tragic loss of Jesse Morgan.

Nurse Palmer requested assignment to sit with Gertie, and waited for her to wake up. Many times she had sat with Gertie waiting for a soldier to rejoin life. Now she would do that for her friend. She wiped Gertie's brow and whispered soft words of encouragement.

Nurse Palmer sat up when she saw Gertie stir and let out a whimper. Gertie opened her eyes; Joyce was ready. "Don't move, don't think. Just listen to me. Gertie you are all right. You are not hurt. The worst thing you could do now is panic or go to pieces. Hold on tight and use all your strength and reserve. William is on his way here. He will be here soon. Don't move; don't think. William is on his way right now. William will be here soon. Don't move, don't think. William is coming." Joyce continued and Gertie repeated with her, "William will be here soon."

Toward morning, the voice she waited for called to her.

"Momma."

"William. William. I can't face this." Gertie began to cry, ever so softly.

"I'm here. We'll make it."

"I think Jesse is gone. Is he …gone?"

"Yes, he's gone."

She tried not to cry to no avail. "He came and told me good-bye."

"It's OK. Go ahead and cry. I know how much you love him. I love him, too." William cried with her.

"We're so fortunate that you were not hurt. A bump on the head and bruised shoulder. You were stunned and in shock but they will only keep you here a couple of days. I'll stay right here with you."

"William, call Sam. I need Liddy. Tell him to bring Liddy. He'll call Bear Creek and tell them where I am and what happened. Where's Jesse. I must see him."

"Not now, Gertie. Not yet."

"Now, William. Please, now," she pleaded.

"Alright, I'll go find him and be right back. Can you hang on while I am gone?"

"Yes, go."

"Close your eyes; let the medicine help you." He did not let go of her until he felt her relax. He went to find Jesse as Joyce stepped back into the room.

"Gertie, it's me, Joyce Palmer. I have medicine for you."

"Joyce, I don't want medicine. I must be clear-headed. If I stay calm and you and William help me, I will not need the medicine." All the while a steady stream of tears poured from her eyes with no crying.

"I will put the pills in my pocket and give you a chance to pull yourself together."

"Tell me what you know about Jesse. Where is he?"

"I am not sure if he has been transported by Nickelson's Funeral Home yet. William has gone to see. I sent him to the Information Officer. He should be able to find out. Now if he is gone, you will have to recover enough to go to Laurel to see him again. If he is still here, I will do all I can to get you to him. I promise."

"Thank you."

"Jesse suffered a terrible blow to his chest and his heart couldn't continue. His face was untouched. They called his wife and she came and signed..."

Gertie sat up, grabbed Joyce, and shouted, "No, No, she can't do that. I—"

Joyce retrieved the pill from her pocket. Gertie's screaming and crying alarmed William when he re-entered the room. "William, help me get your mother to take this pill." Gertie could only shake her head and look pleadingly into William's eyes.

He took the pill from the nurse and sat on the side of the bed, throwing his arms around his mother to enfold her. He showed Gertie the pill with a questioning look on his face.

Gertie answered with a firm "No, William. No medicine now." She sobbed to catch her breath.

"Gertie, Gertie, take a breath. Take a breath." He took her in his arms and spoke into her ear. "Jesse is still here."

She settled right down.

"He will be moved at eight this morning."

"What time is it?"

"0-five-ten. The staff will call us when it is OK for us to go see him, but you have to be in control to go into the halls. You wouldn't want to disturb other patients." She nodded her understanding.

"I'll be ready. Stay with me, William. I want to tell you about our wedding day." But, she found she could not talk about yesterday, and only fell back on the pillow for more silent tears.

"There will be time for that, Momma. You did get married, then?"

"Yesterday." William slid his arms around her. "Or, was it the day before? The 7th."

"Give me a minute. I can do this." She pulled herself together and prepared to go see Jesse for her farewell.

"Joyce, help me. I need to wash up... a comb, mirror, and some Vaseline." Gertie put herself back together—outwardly.

William pushed her wheel chair down to a private room, especially prepared for them by the staff who loved both Gertie and Jesse. Rules were broken. Jesse was brought back to a room. She would not have to go to the emergency room or morgue to see him, not in this hospital where she had softened so many blows for so many over the years. A low light and a small bouquet of garden flowers sat beside the bed. Jesse lay peaceful and still. Dressed exactly as he was yesterday.

He's so beautiful, she thought for the second time in twenty-four hours.

William took her in and then at her bidding, left Gertie alone with her husband. She found that she did not have to give any final thanks or explanations to him. "Jesse, you and I are the only ones who know what we mean to each other. You asked for *forever* and I give it to you.

Now I know what *forever* means." She spoke only of her undying love. They had lived so honestly and their love had been so complete even the last hours were done right for them. "Our wedding was perfect, my love." Gertie knew, just as he had known, they had used every hour well. They had had more than most. "You gave me everything, Jesse."

No one saw her slip off the wheel chair and climb on the bed beside him. Gertie picked up his hand and slid the golden band with aquamarines off his finger. She kissed his hand and slipped the ring on her thumb. No one saw her press her shoulder under his arm so she could feel his weight on her one more time. She pressed her hip against his hip and her knee into his knee. She rubbed the top of his foot with hers.

"Jesse, I promise I will keep my new freedom for you. I'm proud to go through the rest of my life as your wife. I'll be all you want me to be. I promise." No one saw her get down and in the wheel chair again. Gertie did not want William or Joyce to come and tell her to get out of Jesse's bed. Decision to do what she must do would be her own starting right now. She pushed the chair toward the door and stopped. A quick hand on the wheel turned the chair back to Jesse. "Find a way to stay with me, Jesse. Be at Hilltop when I get there." Gertie's fingers went through his golden hair. "Hilltop, darling—the orchard."

William tapped on the door.

"Come in, son." She turned the chair around to face the door. "Jesse is gone. He's not here. The sooner I get to Hilltop, the better I will be."

"The doctor said a couple of days."

She looked up at William with all the control she could muster. "Today, William, today. Take me to the administration office now. I have business to tend to on Jesse's behalf."

As she waited for the Duty Officer, Gertie could not help but think about the accident. She couldn't remember anything after Jesse put his arm across her chest. She didn't know how she and Jesse got to the hospital. Then she looked down at the rings on her fingers. She took hers off and studied it. It was so like Jesse—solid, thoughtful, extraordinary, beautiful. She caught sight of the inside and saw an inscription but couldn't read it in this light. Slowly she put it back on her finger.

Instead of the Duty Officer, the Post Commander, General Kellogg, came in the room. William saluted; Gertie tried to stand.

"Please, at ease. Gertie. . ." He encouraged her to remain seated. "I am so sorry to hear of your accident and the tragic loss of your friend and fellow worker. We shall all miss Jesse. Not many know what he did for this hospital and your service program, but I do. Did you know he was the benefactor that supported the service program from its inception? A real patriot. I guess we don't have to keep his secret any longer. Jesse Morgan made the renewable grant."

"No, I didn't know." She took a deep breath and reached for a tissue.

"General Kellogg, Jesse was my husband. The police made a mistake when they called Catherine Morgan and I'm sure that she didn't know that Jesse had remarried. An honest mistake, but a mistake nonetheless."

"I am doubly sorry, Gertie. I didn't know. I offer my sincere condolences and my assistance in every way. What can I do for you?"

"All paper work must be redone so I can act on my husband's behalf. Would you call Nickelson's Funeral Home for me? They must be instructed to do nothing until I meet with them. I need to inform Catherine Morgan of the situation. Meanwhile, if you should hear from her, please feel free to tell her that I have taken charge. I'll make every effort to inform her as soon as possible." She brushed her exhaustion aside and continued. "I'm worn out, but tests show no injury to me. I'm leaving the hospital now with my son. If you need to reach me, call this number. I will be at Jesse's house near Laurel. Thank you, Sir."

"We are at your disposal." He turned to William, "Lieutenant, please let me know the arrangements."

Gertie would make the final miles into Laurel as Mrs. Jesse Morgan without Jesse.

§

Gertie and William were met at the door by a weeping Bertha. For the first time on this terrible day she found herself consoling someone else. The old black woman cried with the passion of years of suffering and praise of her forgiving Almighty.

"Bertha, I know you are upset. We all are."

"I be alright, Miss Gertie." She dried her reappearing tears. "What can I do fo' you and Mr. William?"

"First, I want you to know that Mr. Morgan and I were married. We were coming home to Hilltop together."

"Oh dear…. " Bertha wailed.

"Don't cry Bertha. We need you."

"Yes'um."

"Fix a room for William, please. And make sure he has something to eat. A sandwich. I'm not hungry."

"I bring yo a sandwich, in case, Miss Gertie."

Gertie went to her room with her memories. She settled down for the evening, but when the lights were turned down the black horrors swept over Gertie. She inwardly cursed fate and stopped short of cursing God for allowing this to happen. The thing that got her through the night was the ease with which she could conjure up Jesse's memory. She could picture him in many favorite settings—at work, at the hospital, in the car, at home, on the beach. She could see him doing some of the things that meant so much to her—giving flowers, tending the garden, cooking meals, swimming, picking apples, relishing food, playing golf, enjoying William, and slipping a ring on her finger. Without sobbing, a steady stream of tears flowed from her eyes across her cheeks down to her ear lobes, to her neck, to the pillow. It was an amazing amount of tears and the flow seemed endless as she recalled Mama's words. *Don't use up all your tears when you are young, Gertie. You might need them later.* Soon the pillow was soaked as was the curly hair at the nape of her neck. And still they flowed.

Gertie got out of the bed and went for Jesse's robe. She crawled into it and breathed in the aroma of him. Almost as if he was there. Almost.

Then she went to the window seat and looked out on the Howard County hills they loved. "Jesse. Jesse. Jesse…" She pulled the long sleeve of his robe and made a resting place for her head on the window sill. She kept her eyes on the misty distance where the sun would be up in a few hours. Gertie called his name until sleep came. "Jesse. Jesse… Jesse… Jesse. . ."

❦

A light tapping on the door forced Gertie to open her eyes to the sun. The clock blasted reality—8:30. A raging headache and stiff neck begged her to go to her bed. The tapping came again.

"Yes?"

"Miss Gertie, I's hate to bother so early. I gots coffee."

"Come in." She was a bit surprised Bertha would risk waking her to bring coffee, but she was glad to have it. She lifted the cup to her nose; she didn't need to drink it, she needed to smell it. *Bear Creek.*

Bertha made no move to leave.

"Bertha?" Gertie questioned.

"Yo' all mus' come down, Miss Gertie. Der's someone here."

"Who is it?"

"It be Missus Catherine Morgan."

Gertie took a draft from the cup.

"Give her coffee in the solarium. I will be there in fifteen minutes. Please find William. Tell him that Catherine Morgan and I are in the solarium. And, Bertha, thank you for bringing my coffee. It helps more than you know."

Chapter 31

Catherine Morgan sat at the huge glass top table in the bright sunlit room at the back of the house. Through the window the rolling hills made a lovely backdrop, but she looked too fashionably contrived to fit the pastoral scene. Her cup was lifted with confidence in her mission.

Impeccably dressed and coiffed Catherine knew the strength of her appearance. Her dress was navy with white details and the navy and white shoes were designed to complement the dress. Her high heels and bouffant light brown hair made her almost six-feet tall. *I hope Gretta Neal is a shrimpy woman,* she thought as she drew her hand up her calf to make sure the seam in her hose was perfect.

The sharp edges of her face kept her from being pretty, but she had enough manicured beauty to turn heads. Her manner of lifting the coffee cup and holding her elbow just above the table gave her a theatrical air.

She looked formidable to the woman coming into the room to greet her.

I hope I'm up to this, Gertie said to herself, as she approached the table.

"Catherine Morgan, good morning. I'm Gretta—"

"I know who you are Mrs. Neal. This is quite awkward, but it is best to get right to the point." She sat her cup down as if to accent her words. "I know you were…uh… close to Jesse and I am sorry for your loss and your terrible accident yesterday." She rose as she began her address to Gertie. She rose up, up, up and Gertie had to tilt her head back to look at her. "I am appalled that you would come here…," she swept her arm around to point across the room and rolling hills, "…. to Hilltop, and put yourself in this compromising position."

Gertie looked up at the towering woman. Her mind saw Jesse and Catherine, like tall matching candlesticks. With her coloring and size, they could have been mistaken for brother and sister. Gertie had trouble taking in this person and the words pouring forth from her mouth. She felt dwarfed by the woman and the immensity of her message. The table was large; walking around it to her chosen seat gave Gertie a few seconds to think about the words spewing from the bright, red, angry lips. She began to comprehend the point Catherine Morgan was making.

"I will be happy to provide my driver to take you wherever you want to go." Catherine continued.

"Let's sit down." Gertie started with these words. "I will call Bertha for coffee—a fresh cup for you and one for me, too." She needed a minute to think, but Catherine did not allow it.

"I've had enough coffee. This isn't a social call. I am finding it very difficult to be here with you and I am doing my best to be civil and ask you to leave. I'm not interested in your relationship with Jesse; I couldn't care less. I'll be receiving our families and Jesse's friends and business associates here before the funeral and I would expect you to be discreet and absent."

Then Catherine turned her face toward Bertha, who had just entered the room with a coffee tray. "Bertha, tell my driver that Mrs. Neal will be right out." Bertha responded with the biggest eyes Gertie had ever seen.

"Please sit down, Catherine. I have a few things to say before anyone leaves." It was almost a command and because Bertha had not made a move to follow her orders, and because she found herself awkwardly standing alone, she sat.

"Bertha, is William coming to the solarium?"

"Yes'um. On de way."

"Prepare our breakfast. We will eat shortly." Her strength was coming from deep within her. William would soon be here to give support.

Gertie gave her attention to her coffee and let Catherine's outrage brew. Slowly, she turned her head from her cup and looked directly into Catherine Morgan's eyes.

"Catherine, my name is not Gretta Neal. It is Gretta Morgan. I am Jesse's wife, and I am not leaving Hilltop."

"It's a lie. You can't be Jesse's wife—our divorce was just final. You are a liar."

"No, I am not a liar. I'm going to ignore your insult and take this one occasion to tell you what you need to know. I am Jesse's wife. And,

I will be arranging the funeral and receiving our family and friends here in our home. You, your son, and family are invited to join me as we celebrate his life and receive guests. If you cannot do that in the spirit Jesse would want, I invite *you* to be discreet and absent." Gertie carefully put the emphasis on the word *you*.

Catherine Morgan leaned back in her chair, but as soon as she felt the rungs of the chair touch her back she snapped forward again. She was stunned. The strong set of her mouth was gone. There was a hint of confusion in the narrowing blue eyes. She unconsciously straightened her skirt.

Gertie continued. "Mr. Nickelson has been informed of the mistake made last night and he is expecting me at ten today to make the arrangements. All the death certificates and pertinent papers have been redrawn with my name and signature. You are Catherine Morgan, but you are no longer Mrs. Jesse Morgan, no matter how recent your divorce."

William's footsteps were a welcome noise as he entered the breakfast room.

"Ah, William. Dear, this is Catherine Morgan. Catherine, my son, William Neal. She is just leaving. Would you escort her to the door? Bertha should have our breakfast ready." Gertie smiled at her son and looked gently on Catherine, inviting her, with a look, to do the proper thing and leave.

Unable to voice Gertie's name, Catherine stood and began walking toward the door away from the sun and the beauty of the rolling hills. Halfway across the floor she turned to voice the questions that were racing through her brain. "Are you so sure this house is yours? Did Jesse have time to change his will between our divorce and his death?"

It was the word *death* which stung Gertie and she collapsed as soon as the woman took three steps and disappeared from view. No one heard Gertie's words, "Jesse. Jesse. How much harder can it get?"

Gertie was drying her tears when William returned. "Momma, is there anything I can do for you?"

"Yes, sit and we'll have our breakfast together. Tell me what Jesse would say to me today."

"He would say…. you can do this, Gertie. He would say that because he knows you can." He spread his napkin and put eggs on her plate.

❦

News of the marriage spread through the town like wildfire, especially interesting to everyone because of the tragic accident that took the groom's life. The story moved quickly through the business community and the quiet streets of the west end. Tenth Street mourned for its daughter. Up and down Main Street, in the restaurants and at the Laurel Race Track, the marriage and accidental death were the items of the day. Old friends came to console Gertie. There were people from the church and those who hadn't spoken or come close to her for years. All came to say how *very sorry* they were. The whole MacGregor clan, except for Papa and Mama who could not make the trip from Bear Creek, were there in a small gathering in the library, within eye and ear of Gertie. They were poised to rescue if they saw a need.

William stood at her right hand every minute. Sam, Liddy, or Dan took turns on her left. Every person was greeted by a trio. The visitation started at two. At exactly that time, William took her elbow.

"Prepare yourself, Momma, General Kellogg, officers, and nurses are getting out of cars and army transports at the portico." He pointed out the window.

"Oh, look William, enlisted men are marching up the drive." She began to shake with emotion. "My soldiers." A few were in casts and bandages—each determined to be here for Gertie and to honor Jesse. "Go greet them, William. I'll wait here." She could not walk; she clutched Sam's arm.

Each man and woman in uniform had a moment with Gertie. At last, General Kellogg took her hand again. "Gertie, so many wanted to come. There are some in the hospital that would have been here if they were able, you know."

"Yes, sir. I know. I will see them next week."

"Palmer and I will be with you for services tomorrow. We'll represent the Post."

"Thank you, sir."

"Thank *you*, Gertie. You and Jesse." He stepped back and saluted her.

Gertie went to the window and watched them leave. William put his arm around her waist. She was smiling through tear filled eyes. "I love my military men." She kissed her sailor.

The sight of the military mustering at Hilltop caused a buzz through Laurel citizens who had no idea of the commitment Jesse and Gertie shared at Ft. Meade Army hospital. This amazing display of military at Hilltop would be the new talk of the town about Gretta Neal...eh. . . Morgan. It was display of patriotism that the town could claim as the whole country was looking for flags to wave. Some had to agree, "Gertie is as red, white and blue as they come."

Gertie, William, and Sam walked back to the receiving line bolstered by the last hour. She reached out to those who cared for and would miss Jesse. She received and gave comfort. Others she knew meant well, but really had no connection to the man she loved. These people were greeted warmly and she allowed them to be comfortable in the midst of her grief. Even to the spectators who came, she was gracious. Sam stood beside her when two friends from her girlhood came and took Gertie's hand. He did not offer his hand to them but Gertie offered hers.

"Thank you for coming," she said and relieved them of their shame. "I hope your family is well."

As they stepped away, Sam could not help but say to his sister, "You are a bigger person than me, Sis."

Gertie warmly greeted the Neal family who came to genuinely embrace her in her grief. They stood by William and received for nearly an hour.

It was after seven when the last person left.

Gertie was up early on the day of the funeral. The beauty of the day belied the black cloud on her heart. "How could the sun shine so brightly?" Gertie said aloud to herself as she looked at the early sun. Her composure had amazed everyone, but it was easier for her because her intimate relationship to Jesse had just become known to those who came to the services. It was almost as if those gathered thought her ties with Jesse were brief. She could be composed.

The services were held at his church in Washington DC. Many from the town, especially the business community came. Sam, Nora, Dan, Mabel, and Liddy sat with her in the front pew and William held tight to her arm and hand to get her through it. Edward's brothers and sisters sat in the next row. Emily gave Gertie a hug and expressed condolences. It was all a blur for Gertie until William rose to give the eulogy.

"Jesse Morgan was a good man. I am so fortunate to have known him. He became my friend so many years ago when I learned to trust him as a boy. He kept his word and treated others as he wanted to be treated. Nothing can touch a young life as much as knowing an adult who consistently walks the higher ground, year after year when you are growing up; knowing an adult, who never disappoints you, never lets you down, and never lets you be less than you can be. That was Jesse Morgan to me. He was just too big in my life to be just a memory from now on—he will be an influence in all I ever do. My mother and I will miss him so much, but he will always be with us." He paused to be sure he had Gertie's gaze. "Our small family—Gertie, Jesse and me, shared all the love we could in the time we had."

Jesse's family came to the church services. It was the first time Gertie saw his son and grandson and she noticed how much they looked like Jesse. Catherine never came forward to speak to Gertie, but she didn't expect she would. Catherine was not big enough to forgive herself the mistake she made following the accident. She felt she would have to apologize for something and she could not find words for that—so there were no words she could say.

The reception at Hilltop Manor was done with great taste. The food was abundant and it was served by Bertha in a gentle and plentiful manner. The tables were dressed with arrangements of white and green. Gertie quietly received everyone at the door and invited them to refresh and enjoy the provisions. She knew everyone except some of Jesse's classmates from the university and some business associates from Washington. It was difficult to know what to say to this grieving woman standing at the door, but Gertie made it easy for them. She spoke first of her husband and then offered condolences instead of waiting to receive them. She was gracious and strong. As she spoke the same words over and over, "Thank you for coming," she thought of the times she had come to Hilltop. "We know how Jesse was loved and admired," she thought—*no one knew him as well as I did.* "I know you will miss him so much," she thought how much she had to keep him alive in her memory.

During the last hour, the people of Laurel came in a steady stream. Almost by design people from every quarter of the town waited to go through the receiving line. They saw Gertie with new eyes.

The whole exercise of receiving was wearing on her. *Leave! Everybody! Just go.* Her heart began to scream. *No more words, please. No more assurances of Jesse's goodness. His generosity. His passion for life. Please. Go.* And still she smiled. Gertie came to understand that she was standing there to console. Nothing happening in this room was consoling to Gertie.

William saw Gertie's demeanor change. He took her hand and drew her aside. "Momma, do you need to sit down for a minute? Something is wrong."

"Walk me to the library. I need to regroup."

They crossed the foyer, past the imposing staircase and went into the quiet library. Amid Jesse's books, Gertie embraced the silence. William gave her the minutes she needed.

"I'm better. How does this parade relate to our loss?"

"I don't know the answer, Momma. Jesse helped save this town during the recession. He never wanted thanks. I think they are here to say it to you."

"Will this soon be over?"

William looked at his watch. "Thirty-four more minutes."

"I can do that." As they passed the stairs again, Gertie whispered. "Soon, Jesse." If William had heard that, he would have been concerned. They returned to the receiving line.

Gertie could not wait for everyone to leave so she could talk to Jesse and tell him what she had discovered for herself on this day of his funeral. She now knew the secret of mourning–loss is personal and no one can make it different, easier, or less devastating than it is. And, she had discovered the truth about loss—right there at the door of Hilltop Manor. —on the very spot she had found her love.

When the last person had left, Gertie went to her room to freshen her hair and face.

"William, I'm going to walk in the orchard."

"Do you want company?"

"Not this time." She crossed the side porch and down the long lawn, a diminutive giant dressed in black. William took a seat on the porch to keep his eye on her. The contrasting dark figure on the vibrant green grass moving toward the orchard, pregnant with fruit, imprinted on his brain.

Gertie went into the trees and sat on the rustic bench Jesse placed there for times when a visit to the orchard did not include work. She straightened her dress and wiped an errant tear from her chin.

"Jesse—"

"I'm here. You asked me to be here and I am." His hand went gently around her waist. "Close your eyes, Love; this will be easier."

Gertie looked up into the trees, closed her eyes and leaned into his arms.

"The summer green apples that you see in our orchard will be a rich harvest... even if I am not here." He tightened his arm around her. "And, each year thereafter."

"Jesse—"

"Hilltop is yours. Look for me in the mist on the hills. I will see you in the orchard."

"Jesse—"

"I have one last gift for you." His arm tightened around her waist. "William will not die in battle. He will come home to you and his children will play on Tenth Street." He lifted the familiar curl from her neck. "You will live in the glow of two more generations."

"Jesse—"

She felt his hold lessen and tried to move closer.

"Gertie, don't try to hold me. You can't. That will be too hard. Hold our memories they will never be heavy; they will be joy."

"Jesse—"

"Listen...," his breath entered her ear, "I love you."

"I love you, too."

"I can't talk to you again, but you can talk to me anytime. From now on, when you talk to yourself, as you always do, I will be listening."

Gertie smiled as Jesse left the bench.

§

William met her as she returned from the orchard. They joined hands without a word and joined Sam and Liddy in the drawing room.

"Gertie, sit here. Do you want anything to eat or drink?" her son asked.

"I'd love a cup of coffee... and I'm hungry. A sandwich would be fine." The family and especially Bertha took heart with her appetite.

"Well, Sis, this was a hard day, the hardest of your life. What can I do for you? What are your plans?"

"Will you call Mama and Papa for me? Use the phone in the hallway. They need to know I am OK but I don't have the strength to call myself.

Let me know when you get them on the line. They need to hear my voice…and I need to hear theirs."

"Liddy, can you stay the night or longer?"

"Yes, Gertie, I can stay."

"I will tell you it is easier to be here in Jesse's surroundings than any place else. I really don't feel so alone here. William has two more days of leave and he has to get back. I will sure hate to see him go."

"Do you want to go to Bear Creek? When are you going back to work?" Sam asked.

"I am going back to work on next Monday. It will be good for me. I will get back to the veterans in the hospital one day later this week. I almost forget what day it is. Today is Wednesday, right? Yes, I will be able to get to the hospital in a couple of days and back to work next week. I don't know when I can go to Bear Creek. Do I sound as confused as I feel?"

"You sound fine, Gertie," Liddy assured.

"Jesse's ex-wife said I might not have this house or be Jesse's heir if he did not change his will after the divorce. Jesse's lawyer left his card with a kind note saying we should meet later this week. You know it is not the big house I care about; it's the presence of Jesse in this house that matters to me. Meanwhile I will only use my car and not disturb anything in the house." Then she said something that surprised them all. "Hilltop will be mine."

"What about Bear Creek? You missed the 4th celebration to go to Ocean City with Jesse."

"Isn't it strange how things work out? I want to go see the folks as soon as I am comfortable leaving the house for a few days. It is not inconceivable that Catherine would feel she has a right to come in here and take possession or carry off some of Jesse's things. I will stay put."

"I'm glad you have Bertha with you. She is a gem and seems to know what you want before you ask. Here she comes now with the coffee. Am I ever ready for a cup, too. I could get spoiled," Liddy exclaimed with a smile for Bertha.

"Miss Gertie, I brung sandwiches and apple pie. Y'all needs to eat somethin' and what's better n' that?"

"Thank you, Bertha, I will." She replied as she lifted the dish from the tray.

The tray had some of Gertie's other favorites, apple muffins and cinnamon coffee cake. The first taste reminded her of her hunger and gave Bertha her first happy thought of the day.

The three siblings sat until the wee hours, long after William had gone to bed. They talked about so many things that had led Gertie on the path to today. She told them of the many years she and Jesse had shared. She told of their common interest in volunteer work with veterans and how it had brought them together. She told of her time spent here at Hilltop Manor and of Jesse's care of William. It was a purging for Gertie to go over these secrets with her brother and sister. Now they would understand what had really sustained her through the years. Liddy was glad that Gertie's life had not been as lonely as she had imagined. Sam felt all along that Gertie had found a place somewhere and respected her right to keep it to herself for so long.

When they finally said good night, Sam left and Liddy was led by Bertha to a guest room. Gertie looked at the clock and figured only two and a half hours of darkness to pass through until dawn. William heard her door close and he listened to hear her cry but he heard nothing. Gertie had turned her sorrow inside out today. The public sadness was over; her tears would be private from now on. She began with a long conversation with God and then turned her thoughts to Jesse, knowing he would be able to understand all she had to tell him. There was some sleep before dawn.

Chapter 32

The next morning Catherine's lawyer called for a meeting as Gertie and Liddy drank their first cup of coffee. After his first condescending remark, calling her *the new bride*, Gertie referred him to Ernest Black, Jesse's lawyer, and hung up the phone. It was good to have Liddy with her as she dealt with the unexpected call. They had just started eating breakfast when the second call came, this time from Mr. Black.

"Mrs. Morgan, I hate to bother you so soon, but I have already gotten a call from Catherine Morgan's lawyer and they are pushing some issues. I'd rather be on the offense than defense so I think we should meet soon. Are you up to seeing me this afternoon? Say, One?"

"Fine, one o'clock. I will be there. Do I need to bring anything?"

"Yes. Your marriage certificate and any letters you may have in Jesse's hand that gives you anything. Do you have anything like that?"

"I have the marriage certificate, but nothing else that I can recall."

"Check your desk and his. At one."

Gertie went to Jesse's desk but it was locked and the top was cleared. Then she went to her desk in her own room. There in the corner was an envelope with her name on it that she had not noticed before. "A letter from Jesse." she cried aloud. The tears started before she got it open. She very carefully undid the sealed flap, not wanting to tear the precious parcel. Finally the wonderful, manly vellum was in her hand and she thought she could again smell him. She laid it down and went for a handkerchief. The tears seemed endless, but she was determined to stem the flood before reading Jesse's letter.

Gertie,

I just wanted to tell you I love you in case you in case I am not standing there with you as you read this. Where could

*I be? It doesn't matter because I will be happy knowing
you are at Hilltop. You have made my life worthwhile.
This home on the hill is alive when you are here and the
rest of the time, it is waiting for you. Nothing can keep me
separate from you. Nothing. You are a part of me
wherever I am. Here is the key to my desk in the library. Go
to the bottom left drawer and find a large envelope with
your name on it. I hope this makes you happy. That is all
I want to do in this life.*

Love always,
Jesse

The letter was dated July 1, 1941. "The day he got his divorce," she
said to herself. A small key was taped to the bottom. She looked around
the messy desk and found two more short love notes from him to her.
They were tucked in among papers over two years old. He had been
doing this for a long time and she had never seen them. One gave her
the tea service she had admired on her first visit to Hilltop Manor and
the other gave her the apron he was wearing the first night he kissed
her. Each was dated at the time the events occurred. Gertie began a
methodical search among old papers and cubby holes. She found a total
of eight notes. Each one warmed her heart and brought her bittersweet
joy. Each gave her a present, mostly small things, but very meaningful
in their relationship. He wanted her to have the clock on the mantel
in the bedroom because it was his mother's and he wanted her to have
his coin collection to give to William. That touched her most of all. He
loved her son. Gertie crawled onto the bed and reread every note until
finally hearing Bertha announce lunch. It must be noon and she had
to dress and be in town at one. She hurried and forgot about the key
to Jesse's desk.

"Bertha, please bring my sandwich up here. I have to eat while I
dress to go to town. Please tell William that I will meet him out front
when he brings the car. I'm running late."

Mr. Black's office was right behind the bank on Fourth Street. It
was a converted out building of the old Stanford Mansion on the corner
of Fourth and Main. The colonial looking building was unique and had

low ceilings. They were high enough for Mr. Black and William, but made you feel it was necessary to duck.

"Pleased to meet you, Mr. Black. This is my son, William."

"Have a seat. May I call you Gretta?"

"Gertie, everyone does, Mr. Black. Here's our marriage certificate."

"Fine Gertie. It will be returned to you later. I have Jesse's will, which he executed recently. I am the executor. Back in April when he decided to file for divorce, he began to write a new will and we were finalizing it at the time of his death. Unfortunately he didn't get to sign it. It would have made a difference to you because he wrote it based on his hopes of a new marriage. The will that is effective was drawn up earlier this year when he found out that he was ill and he made provisions for you then."

"Jesse was ill?" Gertie was visibly shaken.

"Yes. He had the same heart condition shared by the men in the Morgan family. He was under the care of a doctor. As he approached the age when his father died, he became anxious to tie up all loose ends. Jesse was a fine man and I was proud to help him with his legal work."

"I never knew. If only I had known…"

"Don't do this to yourself Gertie. Jesse had faith you would understand his motives," William comforted his mother.

"I'll try."

"Basically he made five provisions. First, there are endowments for his son, his grandchild and your son." He paused to note the surprised look on William's face. "They are in equal amounts to be administered by the bank. Second, there is a lump sum payment to Catherine Morgan, equal to one year's alimony. Third, there is a generous endowment to the service clubs at Fort Meade. It is set up so that the principal isn't used, and the interest will provide a good monthly income to the program. Jesse has been supporting that program for many years. Fourth, he left you his bank stock and also the contents of the house. You also have what is called a life estate, the use of the house as long as you want to live there. Finally, there is provision for the estate to maintain the house administered by our law firm. We have power of attorney for Hilltop Manor."

Gertie was trying to remember all that was being said, but what stayed in her mind was inclusion of William. How generous. "I'm overwhelmed," Gertie muttered.

There are some problems and I will try to explain. At the divorce he made a generous settlement with Catherine Morgan…. really more than he could afford. That is one of the reasons he needed to change the will, which gives her another payment equal to one year's alimony. The money is just not there for all the bequests he made when this was written seven months ago. All the amounts in the endowments will have to be reduced unless we as executors sell the mansion. That is the only variable left to us. If he had bequeathed it to someone we could not sell it and the other endowments would have to be reduced proportionately, according to the value of the estate. Because you were bequeathed a life estate in the mansion, we cannot sell it without your consent and, if financially feasible, you will be paid the value of your life estate. We are in the process of evaluating the estate now. He gave you the contents of the house so those items are safe and cannot be sold. Have I made it clear?"

"You are saying you *may* have to sell the house. It is possible that you won't?"

"I have a pretty good feel for the assets in this estate and it is most likely that the house or at least some of the property will have to be sold. Catherine will push to have it sold to satisfy the endowments, since she can't have the house. She was sure that he had left the house to her and had not had time to change the will since the divorce just days ago. The truth is when their son turned eighteen Jesse changed the will in respect to the house. Catherine Morgan would not have gotten the house even if Jesse had not remarried. I expect she will probably contest the will in court and will try to force the sale of the house. She has a lot of resources and the generous divorce settlement; no doubt she has the money to buy it. She is shrewd and she wants that house."

"She will not get it."

"Not if we can help it. I'm going to do my best."

"Is there any problem with me staying in the house now? Can I keep Catherine out?"

"You may stay in the house. Remember you have a life estate in it. It is your job to protect the contents, which will be yours when the estate is settled. Change the locks and be careful to protect your interests."

"I have several letters from Jesse that may be important to you. I didn't bring them this afternoon because I am not ready to part with them. Give me a chance to think about all you have told me. Can I call you as questions come to mind?"

"Of course, Gertie…. anytime. Tell me a little about the letters from Jesse."

"The things he gives me in the letters are part of the contents of the house and I guess, covered by the will."

"Umm. Yes, that is probably so, but I would like to see them. Come by and let me read them and you won't have to leave them. Could you do that soon?"

"Yes. Thank you. You are very kind."

Gertie went home and sat staring at the coffee in her cup. So much. "Jesse, what shall I do? Sometimes I feel like walking away and letting the vultures in, but I know you don't want me to do that." The chairs and walls listened, too. "I've got to get busy with something. Can't just sit here," she said aloud as she often did. As she started across the floor something fell from the papers she was carrying. It hit the floor with a small jingle. It was the key to Jesse's desk drawer. "The desk key. I forgot." As Gertie knelt to pick it up, the breeze pushed open the french door that was slightly ajar.

The lower desk had only one envelope in it – a large manila envelope with her name on it. She opened it to find the deed to the property and house, properly executed in her name. All the transfer taxes were dated July 2, 1941. A small note from Jesse tore her heart.

Gertie,

I got the marriage license, arranged this deed and these envelopes because I am so sure you will accept my proposal and become my wife while we are in Ocean City next week. This is your wedding present.

Love, Jesse.

Her joy and sorrow was interrupted by the ringing of the phone. "Please answer that Bertha and take a message."

"It's Mr. Black, Miss Gertie. He say impo'tant."

"I'll take it." She ran down the stairs. "Yes, Mr. Black."

"Gertie, I received a letter by post today and it is from Jesse, mailed in Salisbury on July 7ᵗʰ. Do you know about it?"

"No, sir. That is the day we got married and I remember he mailed a letter outside the courthouse, but I don't know anything about it."

"Well, it's the darnedest. He is telling me you are married and that he gave you the house. He wanted me to remove all reference to the house from the will I was drawing up. Said it is not his house any longer. I will have to go to the courthouse in Upper Marlboro and get a copy of the latest deed to Hilltop Manor."

"Mr. Black, I have just found the deed that he executed in my name. It was locked in his desk drawer. It was transferred on July 2nd."

"Well, Gertie, I'd say we need not be concerned about who owns Hilltop Manor."

I was never concerned, she thought remembering what Jesse said in the orchard yesterday.

Gertie hung up the phone and went to find William.

"Mr. William at da stables, Miss Gertie."

She grabbed an umbrella against the warm summer rain and went to find him. The smell of summer was heavy in the stables where she found William mucking out a stall.

"What are you doing, William? Mucking the stable? Jed has someone to do that."

"Jesse and I sometimes did this. He told me that it was *leveling* work. I didn't quite know what that meant when he said it, but I came to understand. One day I came here in my summer whites. He told me to go to the house, change, and come back here for some *leveling*. Believe it or not—that lesson has served me well on board ship. Today I felt like doing this." He pushed the pitchfork into a pile of straw and manure and laughed.

Gertie's mood lightened.

"Go over there in the tack closet and get a pair of boots, Gertie. You will be surprised what this job will do for you, too."

Mother and son worked side by side and finally found time to talk.

"I have been waiting for the right time to tell you about Louisa. She is a wonderful girl. You saw her picture—beautiful, too. She comes from a nice family and they seem to like me."

"Of course, they do—Laurel's finest."

"I requested and received a special intelligence job with the Fleet. I go back to the Fleet Office in San Diego every six weeks or so. I like the job, but to be perfectly honest, I wanted the job so I could see Louisa."

"Tell me more about her."

"You will love her, too. She's fun and smart. She finished at USC and works in naval intelligence, too. We play tennis and she is teaching me to dance. The most leave I can get now is three days and that isn't time to come to Maryland. Her family welcomes me."

"I am happy for that" Gertie always hoped William would find a welcoming home away from home. "Jesse and I were planning on coming to Hawaii for a honeymoon trip."

"Why not come yourself? Louisa's family would welcome you in California and then you can come on to Hawaii. Maybe a change would be good for you."

"Not now. I came to find you to tell you about Hilltop and new information since we saw Mr. Black."

"Really?"

"Jesse deeded Hilltop Manor to me before we went to Ocean City."

"It's yours? Hilltop is yours, Momma?"

"Yes, but Catherine Morgan will contest everything. I can't travel now. I've got to stay here."

"I wish I could stay, too."

"I am happy to have one more day."

"This afternoon I am going to Tenth Street to visit the Neal families and walk around 403. Tell Bertha I'll be back for dinner. There isn't a cook to match Bertha on Tenth Street since Mom Neal died. My last day will be here at Hilltop with you."

The stall was looking better. The workers were looking messy and loving every dirty, smelly minute. They were leveled.

Chapter 33

Somehow Gertie got through the first week without Jesse. Then she faced the next.

Small things that keep daily life going filled the hours, while searching for memories at every turn. She needed to recall each moment she shared with Jesse and duly file it in its proper slot. During the hardest times his favorite books, his clothes, and his pillow comforted. Gertie sought his aroma in the car and drove his favorite lanes around the manor. Jesse's muddy boots stood by the stable door—untouched. When it was time to eat, she chose his favorite foods and when it was time to sleep she picked a time they shared and relived it. No one saw her cry, though tears were there every night. She went to the bench in the orchard often.

How many tears do I have? Mama always cautioned her not to waste them. *Don't cry over spilt milk, child. Save your tears for when they are really needed.*

"I saved too many tears," she said to the picture of Jesse on the nightstand.

She did not know going back to work would be so difficult. She woke up dreading it. It was hard to dress for the day and her breakfast was pushed around the plate.

"Miss, not hungry?"Bertha asked. Gertie offered a weak smile as Bertha placed her hand at the nape of her neck and massaged down the shoulder. Gertie leaned into the stroke like a puppy asking for more. Bertha smiled down at her. "Plenty of time fo' eating. You won't pass Bertha's cookin' ere long. Mind."

Gertie looked up to her with sad puppy eyes.

"Go 'long, Miss Gertie. It be fine. I says, today be one day, tomorrow be 'nother and dis day be's behind."

It was one of those hot July days in Maryland where the temperature did not drop overnight and the first rays of sun seemed to set a fire burning. It was hot driving, and even hotter walking across the parking lot. Gertie glistened with perspiration. It was a relief to step in front of the giant fan blowing across the lobby. She stood at the door not knowing where to go. To the teller cage and check out her work or to Jesse's office as she usually did every Monday morning?

Walter Noble stepped forward and offered her his arm. "Good morning, Gertie. Kitty Ward has been at Ft Meade as acting manager for you this past week. She will go again this morning so you can stay here and work in this office today. The board has asked Charles Hamilton to act in Jesse's place in the interim.

Why does it hurt to hear his name? It only belongs to me, now.

"Come, I'll take you to Kitty's office for today." He was a savior to the moment and she let her breath out in relief while her brain screamed—*no*. Gertie was glued to the floor as if her body knew that was not what she wanted to do.

The fan made one more pass across the stifling scene.

"Mr. Noble, I want to go to Ft. Meade today. I don't want to change my routine. Would you check with Mr. Hamilton and see if he insists? Meanwhile, I will prepare to check out my work so I can be ready with everyone else. Where is Kitty? I want to thank her for sitting in for me." She looked pleadingly at him. She would face Jesse's office at a later time and she did not want to see Charles Hamilton, or anyone, sitting at his desk... not yet.

❧

After the first one, the days back at work were good for her. They helped almost as much as returning to the hospital did. Everywhere there were hugs of welcome and support. She wondered if the attention was harder than merely being ignored would have been. Immersion into the trials of the patients gave her mind a rest from the feeling of deep loss she was burdened with. The smile she put on for them lifted her for an instant, and those instances added up to keep her spirits high for five minutes, then ten minutes, and soon she could spend her whole hour smiling for her charges. Their smiles gave her joy. She felt better. There *was* a road to recovery and she had made the first step.

Sam fell in with her crossing to her car on the third day back. "Hey Sis, got time for your brother today?"

"Are you useful or just a handsome face?"

"Depends on who you ask ... and why you ask."

"I'm on my way to get some things from Tenth Street. I could use some help and I don't object to your handsome face."

"I listed furnished apartment in the post paper and got a tenant right away. I really can use your help."

"You're beginning to think like a business woman and running Hilltop is a business."

"So is 403 Tenth Street."

Gertie's chatter with Sam made moving personal things easier.

"What about this place?" Sam asked as he crossed the front porch for the sixth time.

"I bought it because William wanted it. I am depositing the rental income for maintenance on the house and I will keep it in good condition. The possibility remains that I might return there to live. Jesse's will is in probate. I am not positive that I can afford to live at Hilltop. This old white house with the green shutters means a lot to me and William." She looked back at the house that fit so perfectly with the others on Tenth Street.

As she walked down the pavement with an arm full of items too precious to pack, Gertie looked over to the house where Edward's parents had watched over her for so many years. It was easier to move knowing they were not there any longer. She remembered her promise to stay on Tenth Street and not take William away. Now Mom Neal, Poppa Clay, and William were all gone from Tenth Street and she was the last to go. The irony of that did not escape her and she smiled. "I kept my promise," she said aloud.

As she started the car and drove away, she recalled the years of devotion Mary Neal gave William and the support Clay gave her when life with Edward was so hard. There had never been much softness between them and she wondered what she could have done differently. Gertie did not recall the hurt she had had from the Neals; she only wondered if she could have done more, loved more, or been more tender. Her feeling here on Tenth Street gave her insight. She admitted that she loved them and she missed them. But she could not dwell on that, there were too many things for today that required her attention. When she turned off the corner to Montgomery Street, she admitted—*I don't live on Tenth Street any longer.*

✿

Mr. Black filed the will in probate and advised Gertie that it could be six months before everything was settled. He had several meetings with Catherine Morgan's lawyer and revealed all the conditions of the will and the facts concerning the title to Hilltop Manor. He did all he could to make the issues clear and point out that the will was fair to all and the manor was not part of Jesse Morgan's estate. At his death, Jesse did not own Hilltop. Catherine was furious, but Jesse had done a perfect job of attending to the deed. On advice of her lawyer, she did not contest. Gertie was secure in the house and content among Jesse's things. On advice from Ernest Black, Gertie did not return Catherine's phone calls and after several attempts, blocked by Bertha, the calls stopped.

It was simple mathematics to deal with her income and the monthly expenses that wiped them out. Meetings with Ernest Black were clear on one point—the estate was sizable, but would not be available for some time. She could appeal to the executor and get funds against the estate if needed. That seemed not quite right to this working girl, who did not spend ahead. Gertie simplified it and made a decision. She would continue to work and to live on her income, changing nothing except her address. If she needed more funds she would use the rental income from the Tenth Street apartments and replace it when things were settled. Let the legal and financial minds worry about the rest.

Her busy, interesting day was not over. A note from Ernest Black was waiting for her as she returned to the main office. She went straight to the phone and called his office.

"Hello, Mr. Black."

"Gertie, I need to sit down with you and go over some things. When would be convenient?"

"I am going to my parents for the weekend, but if you like you can come out to Hilltop this evening."

"Good. That would be fine. Time?"

"I'll call Bertha and have her set you a plate. It can be over dinner if that suits you. 6:30?"

"Yes." Mr. Black lived alone after his wife of fifty-two years died last spring. He was delighted to extend his day in this way. Going home was the lonely part of the day for him. The highly respected lawyer was a fixture around town. His life's work was providing good legal advice to his friends and neighbors. Nothing delighted him more than to be on first name basis with everyone he met. He was quick to loosen his tie and walk to Denny's Tavern with a client, or opponent's lawyer, to take the edge off of the work at hand. This casual manner often misled his opposition and underestimating Ernest Black could be a big mistake. He was a skilled and imposing figure in court always well prepared and polite of manner.

He was faithful to Edith Black's insistence that every court day he wear a suit, fresh from the cleaners, a starched shirt and spotless tie. It had been her mission to send him out thusly. After she died he hired it done. He respected her advice by coming to court with all his edges sharp. He missed her admonition to stop at Vet's Barber Shop and get a trim and now his white hair often turned up around the edges. Ernest was not a man to look closely in a mirror. Edith had been his mirror. He made one change after she died. He decided to grow a moustache after finding an old picture of his father with a fine moustache, curled in the fashion of 1920. When it was full and done in that way, he looked just like his father and he was pleased. He doubted Edith would have been pleased. "Sorry sweetie," he said one time to her picture. "I wish we could go head to head over my moustache today. Nothing I'd love more."And he touched the picture while curling the moustache with his fingers, as was his new habit.

Excited about his work for Gertie Morgan, he looked forward to seeing her at Hilltop Manor tonight.

"Bertha, Mr. Black and I will have dinner in the library on the small table."

The game table, spread with a tablecloth and set beautifully, was ready. Gertie thoughtfully set a floor lamp beside the table to provide good lighting for her guest. Ernest Black arrived right on time.

"Ah, Gertie, what a treat to join you for dinner and call it work."

She took his arm and led him into the library. Gertie had dressed down to gabardine slacks and a blouse. She was at ease with her first guest since she became mistress of the manor."It is good to see you Mr. Black. Let's have a glass of wine first."

"I thought I told you to call me Ernest, or Ernie, if you like."

She smiled at the distinguished gentleman, "Chardonnay, Ernest?"

He smiled back at the rule of address Gertie adopted. He was a seasoned barrister and he eased into the issues at hand as smoothly as the wine went down the throat to remove the weariness of the diners.

The problem he had for Gertie was maintenance of the manor. "By giving the manor to you, Jesse took the responsibility away from me, the executor—all well and good. But, how are you going to take care of the expenses of the manor? You have the furnishings and you have the bank stock, but they are not liquid assets. It takes money to take care of this place. Money that will not be available until the probate is complete."

"I had just begun to contemplate this problem last week when the insurance bill arrived. I've cut utility use considerably and have managed to pay Bertha and Jed but I am stretched to the limit now. I'm researching Jesse's household accounts. He kept exacting books on every cost and detail of this place." She paused to look out the window. "I'm overwhelmed with the expenses involved. The pastures should have been cut before now—the orchard needs attention as do the stables, roads, and fences. The stables and horses are very expensive. I'm going to see if Sam would be interested in moving in that empty farmhouse on the back lot. It would solve a problem if he took care of the horses and stable. Jesse gave the roan to William when he was a teenager and the other was Jesse's pet. I am not prepared to decide what to do with them and, with Sam's help, I wouldn't have to decide right away."

Gertie was fatigued over these issues, but she went on. "Jesse used the income from the tenant farmer to maintain the lanes around the place. The apples were a hobby to Jesse. Income from them often did not cover costs of maintaining the orchard. I love that orchard as much as Jesse did. I can't let it go."

She paused to enjoy some dinner and gather steam to go on.

"I see that a stock dividend check should come to me for the last quarter and that will help. In the past it has been about five thousand. Will it be the same this year?"

"Yes. It will be about that. Have you met with a CPA yet? You know taxes have to come from that, too."

"I have an appointment next week with Mr. Shaffer. He worked for Jesse and he knows the accounts."

"He's a good man and that's a good, first step. The dividend money will help here in the immediate, but there is more to consider. Any major repair or expense could wipe out the dividend."

"I know. Jesse has notes about some major renovations he was planning—one on the portico roof. He estimated that at twenty-five hundred—must be structural."

Gertie dropped her fork and gathered her chin in both hands. "I don't know anything about pastures, fences, and roads. That scares me. You met my son. He is an officer in the navy and his career will keep him away most of the time. It'll be a long time before he can take an interest in Hilltop. I have thought a lot about *why* Jesse left this place to me." Gertie relaxed as she spoke of Jesse. She picked up her fork again. "He was a smart man and he knew the challenges. I'm sure he thought he had time to recoup from his divorce settlement and to teach me about managing this home as a team. He must have thought a long time before he deeded it to me because I am finding notes everywhere with information. Notes that I believe he prepared to remind himself to tell me about this or that. They have become my *how-to* directions. I'm collecting and cataloging them."

"Let me interject this, Gertie. At the time, I wondered about Jesse giving Hilltop to you. But, looking over the possible alternatives and getting to know you… I can clearly see *why* he did as he did." This personal observation was rare for Ernest Black. He was surprised at himself.

Gertie poured coffee and put a generous portion of bread pudding in dessert dishes. "Jesse wanted me to have this manor because we loved it—together. But more than that, he expected me to keep it and live here, no matter what happened to him. I've got to do all I can to fulfill that wish, but I will tell you, I have my misgivings, and I'm scared."

"I understand. I got the same indications from Jesse when he talked to me of the manor and of you. At the time I thought it was a lot to expect. I remember clearly the day he said to me. "Do all you can to help Gertie, even if she doesn't ask. Jesse faced his mortality wiser and more forthrightly than most. He was a remarkable man."

Gertie lifted the napkin to catch a tear before it could escape. She was pleased that Ernest didn't notice the tear; he only saw the soft smile Gertie managed.

"That is why I called you today. You haven't asked, but I want to help and offer a possible solution. The answer may lie in the stocks."

"Yes, I know they are worth a lot and I thought I might have to sell them."

"No. My advice is—don't sell. Think about what they mean. You own 55% of the bank's stock. You can vote yourself President of the bank—take Jesse's position, which will automatically put you on the board—as chairman, if you want that, too."

That astounding suggestion almost caused Gertie to choke on her last bite.

"I'm on the board myself and I know for a fact that the other board members are about to approach you. They will want to buy some of your stock. One that I know of could gain majority by buying a portion of your stock. You may even receive an offer to sell all of it. I know they will be fair market offers, but you need to be prepared by deciding what you want to do beforehand. "

"I must say Ernest, I hadn't thought of holding the stock and using it like that."

"The point is, by taking Jesse's position at the bank, you will receive a salary that will support Hilltop and you. You must be smart about it—smart enough to secure your basis. Selling the stock would support you here for a while, but you would be exhausting that asset. If you sell stock and drop below majority, your opportunity is gone."

The rest of the evening, Gertie asked questions and took in all the information that Ernest Black could provide. He found her questions astute and probing. Earlier in the day he had misgivings about offering this advice to Gretta MacGregor Neal Morgan. Now he felt confident. He came because of his long association and abiding respect for Jesse. His misgivings disappeared as they talked. Gertie would not be the first wife of an executive to step into corporate shoes. Ernest Black was convinced after this evening that Gertie would do better than most.

"Gertie when you get to work tomorrow ask Sandra to get you the corporate records. The first thing you need to study is the bank structure. Salaries and board stipends are all listed. You need to know. Boring, but important to you."

After coffee and mints, the evening ended. Each felt rewarded by the give and take they shared over dinner.

Gertie walked him to the door and tendered one last question, "Which would you suggest I do, Ernest, vote myself on the board or take Jesse's job as president and get on the board that way?" Even as she heard her own words it was incongruous to her. *Gertie MacGregor, caretaker's daughter—west end—bank president, board of directors... landowner.*

Ernest was pleased that she was not dismissing the concept. "Why don't you do your homework and think about it for a few days without my input and see what conclusion you draw. Give me a call next week and ask me the question again... if you want."

"All right, I will. Thank you. It has been a pleasant evening."

"And, we called it work," he replied, and left with a smile on his face. "Anytime."

She took the stairs two at a time, unable to contain her excitement. "Jesse, do you think I could do it?" She asked aloud as was her old habit. This time the silence that answered hurt. She slowed and took one step at a time until she reached the landing. Her mind was so busy that she had trouble falling to sleep and she knew she had to pack and get on the road to Bear Creek early tomorrow. She wound the alarm and crawled into bed and went right to her nightly prayers, forgetting to cry.

Chapter 34

It had been two weeks since she had been to Bear Creek and she looked forward to the riotous activities of her family. By leaving early, she could have time with Mama and Papa before Sam, Dan, and Liddy and their clans arrived. Before dawn she was on the road, driving the familiar route while letting her mind wander into unknown territory. Hilltop and the bank twisted in her brain.

The day was warm and the morning sun had just broken the horizon. Lights from the kitchen window could be seen from way down the lane. It made Gertie cry aloud, "Bear Creek."

The aroma of coffee and fresh baked bread filled the house with comfort. Mama stood at the door to welcome her to the kitchen where her cup of coffee was being poured by Papa. "Sit down child and tell us how you are doing and what you hear from William." As Gertie brought them up to date on her life and adjustments, she saw her parents with new eyes. Mama seemed shorter—still pretty but, with greying hair. Papa—how old he looked. No, no he couldn't be seventy-eight, but he was. The twinkle was still in his eye, but she saw how he had to struggle to rise from his favorite chair. A broken leg many years ago made moving more difficult as time went by. She didn't remember seeing that before and she chastised herself for not paying closer attention.

"William is doing fine. The navy has him back and forth—Hawaii to California. He has a special girl in San Diego. I think, very special."

"So far away." Mama lamented.

"Seems far to me too, but to young people going from coast to coast is just a good adventure. He speaks of me coming to see him in Hawaii as if it were just around the corner. Can you imagine?"

"I sure can. You'll go, Gertie. If I were a betting man, I'd bet on it," her father teased.

"I'll bet on it—here's twenty." Sam entered the room. "I'm a betting man, especially on a sure thing."

The family weekend began. There were hugs all around and voices filling the rooms at the big house on Bear Creek. The kitchen seemed full with Sam's family, but soon Dan's family, Liddy, Lon, and children poured in, too. Patsy would arrive with her new husband. Shirley hadn't found the right man yet although Sam was scouting hard for her. Gertie enjoyed it all the while keeping her eye out for the chance to talk to Sam alone. Finally she had to tell him that she needed to talk.

"Gertie and I are going to ride out to Creek Market to get some ice and some soft drinks. Anyone need anything else? Mama?"

"Can't think of anything."

"Nora, I'll be right back. Shall I bring Tootsie Pops?"

A chorus of *yeses* came from the children who hadn't seemed to be paying attention.

He winked at his wife and she knew that Gertie needed to talk to Sam and she would hear all about it later. Nora had long ago learned not to be jealous of the bond between Sam and Gertie. She was such a romantic and Gertie's life gave interest and intrigue to her life as a mother of four. She was lucky to get time to read a newspaper. It was fine because she genuinely liked Gertie.

Sam draped an arm over Gertie's shoulders. "It's only six miles out to Creek Market. Is that time enough to spill the beans? How is it goin?"

"I'm doing better. The work at the hospital is really a challenge. The post is growing and the post commander wants to talks about another service club. It could be a full time job. There are people coming from many military installations across the country to see what we are doing at Ft Meade. My program has become the hallmark. In some circles I'm famous."

"Here at Bear Creek you are just *Gertie*. Maybe I should announce in the kitchen that our famous sister deserves special treatment."

"I'm sure that'll work for me in this family," she responded wryly.

"I asked you to spill the beans. Ready to get serious?"

"If I have to." She glanced away from her brother. She knew he had taken off his three-pointed red and gold joker's hat. She couldn't look into his concern.

"You have to."

"It was one thing and then another piling up—Hilltop, the bank, Ft. Meade. I don't know where to start."

He wanted to help. "Start with Ft. Meade. Changes in the clubs?"

"There are rumors that the USO is going to take over the service clubs at Ft. Meade. I maybe out of a job with the service clubs, but meanwhile I'm still running the clubs and managing the volunteers."

"USO? Is that a bad thing?"

"Not if it is better for the soldiers. I can step aside. Ft. Meade has almost tripled in population. With a bigger population, more patients and more demands at the hospital—and, the hospital is my priority. I want to be there every week day." She finally looked at Sam. "I'm on call every day, around the clock, Sam."

"Are you afraid you can't keep up at the hospital? Is that what's bothering you?"

"I'm training some great women to help me. It is so hard to let go… but, I have to. I will not be at every bedside now that the new wing is open. What's bothering me is the bank."

"You always managed. So?"

"I was the manager at the Ft. Meade branch. That is going to change. I have to be at Main Street, now."

"It's only six miles. Right?"

"Right…" she let her answer trail off.

"So?"

"There's more."

"William is ok. You are not sick. And tell me Bertha continues to bake cakes and Jed is going to keep the fireplaces going." He had to put humor in the situation. "'Cause, if those things are good, all else can be managed."

She ignored Sam's rationalization and continued. "I wish I had more time for Ft. Meade but right now I'm settling Jesse's estate and actually have less time."

"Save the thought." Sam parked the car and went into the market, emerging quickly.

Sam unwrapped a Tootsie-Pop and shoved a red one in her mouth. "Cherry. Go on. You were telling about the changes at Ft. Meade."

Gertie took a stronger attitude with the infusion of sugar and brotherly care. "I've learned to be a boss and tell everyone what to do. There are plenty of volunteers and I can quickly tell who can lead others.

I have to be careful—some volunteers are only there to find a husband. I come awake at night, worried that some need is overlooked."

"Maybe Shirley should come and volunteer."

"Be serious. Shirley has plenty of time to find a husband and get married."

"Do you remember what you did at seventeen?" her brother retorted.

For a fleeting moment, she remembered Edward and she hadn't thought about him in many months. She changed the subject. "Sam, I have something else on my mind."

"Go ahead. I have a dozen Tootsie-Pops to see us through."

"I've got to decide what to do about Hilltop Manor."

"Do you want to live in that big place all by yourself?"

"Bertha and Jed are there and it has been good for me to be there among Jesse's things and our memories, but I know I don't want to live in a museum and he would not want me to. He did want me to have it and to keep it. All that luxury is frightening, too. I am a wealthy woman, at least on paper. Did you know that?"

"Really? I suspected so, but I thought Jesse might not have had time to redo his will before he died."

"He was writing a new will when we got married but he had deeded the manor to me and put me in his old will. Isn't that amazing?"

"Hilltop Manor is yours?"

"Yes it is. Jesse has loved me for a long time and did all he could to take care of me. I regret I did not agree to be his wife earlier."

"You know, I suspected that, but decided a long time ago to let you have it your way. I didn't think Jesse was anything to tease you about."

"I should have told you, but I couldn't tell Mama and Papa. They would not have liked the shame of my being with Jesse while he was married. I regret not bringing him down home some weekends."

"Hey, we are not the kind to look back with regrets," Sam reached over and mussed her hair.

"I know, I know. Anyway, the manor and the furnishings are all worth a lot of money. He left me his bank stock, which is also worth a great amount, more than I ever imagined. But, it costs a lot to keep the manor up. I have been going over Jesse's accounts and he spent five to ten thousand every year on that place. I can hardly imagine those amounts except in a teller's drawer. Right now I'm paying the utilities and staff out of my salary from the bank. Soon taxes and insurance will come due. I'm about broke."

"Wow." Sam was impressed with her high finances. "If you start selling the stock, you will be a poor woman living in a rich house."

"You got it. Eventually it would eat itself up, literally. I guess you get the picture. And that *picture* robs my sleep some nights."

"Let me see." He said cocking his head and scratching his chin, looking so much like Papa at that moment."You can live high on the hog for maybe ten years and the house would go on the block anyway."

"I have been advised on another course by Ernest Black."

"Ernie's a good man. I've shared a beer or two with him at the track. What does he suggest?"

"He said I should use my 55% stock majority to elect myself to Jesse's job as president and/or chairman of the board. I've researched and the board job will not support Hilltop and I believe Jesse intended for me to take care of it. If I want to keep Hilltop, I have to take the bank president's job. That would give me a salary big enough to support me and the manor." She took a deep breath. "Sam, I cannot believe the words coming from my mouth." She took Sam's forearm in a vice grip. "I'm not kidding, I'm scared."

"It is scary." Sam agreed and took a deep breath with her. "Gertie, can you do that?"

"Are you asking if my stocks can set me up like that or are you asking if I can do those jobs?"

"Oh, I know with your majority you can take the jobs. I'm asking if you know how to be a bank president or a board chairman? Do you know how to do that?"

"Ernest Black seems to think I do… but, I haven't the foggiest." For the first time since her dinner last night with Ernest Black, she laughed. It was so incongruous. She leaned back and laughed until she cried. And, the sobs came.

"Let me cry for a while."

Sam stopped the car and put his arm around her, drawing out his folded handkerchief. "Blow." he ordered. She took the handkerchief to her face and did a loud raspberry into it causing it to flap into his face. Laughter resumed at this old childhood prank the MacGregor children had played on each other for years. He held her and they laughed together.

"There is a fine line between laughter and tears." Gertie recited Mama's words.

"Both help."

"I'm going to do this. I'm going to get Jesse's estate straight and I'm going to take the job at the bank so I can save Hilltop. I say it, but it is the first time in my life that I have decided to do something and didn't know how to go about it."

"Not so. You decided to get a divorce without a clue on how to *get* it or how to *live* after you got it. Remember, Sis, you met that challenge." He took her forearm in a vice grip. "You will do it again. No doubt in my mind."

Gertie could not argue the point well made.

"Any advice?"

"Same advice I gave before. One day, one problem at a time." Gertie opened her mouth but Sam spoke fast. "No gushy stuff, now."

It was time for a bit of silence and some thinking. Gertie's voice was brighter when she spoke again.

"For my peace of mind and to fill the emptiness in my life, I am going to pour my care on the men and women in uniform. I started when Edward died and now that Jesse is gone, I have new dedication." She paused. "So help me, God." She spoke past her brother to a greater power.

"The first thing I have to do is decide on which job in the bank."

"I think you know." Sam said as they parked at the house.

"I'm going to stop thinking about it until I'm home again Sunday."

"Good decision and I am sure your next one will be just as good. Just let me know if you need anything from me."

Then she looked at her brother very seriously. "Wait Sam, before we go in I have something for you to think about. There is an old farmhouse on the estate. It is boarded up. I'm not sure of its condition but it has four bedrooms. Would you like to take a look at it as a possible home for the Sam MacGregor clan? I need someone to care for the horses and stable or I will have to get rid of them."

"Really, a house?"

"You can live there if you fix it up yourself and take care of the stables. You could even stable other horses for income. There are three empty stalls and plenty of pasture. Interested?"

"Sounds great. I'll talk to Nora about it tonight and take look at it this week."

"It would be wonderful to have you all at Hilltop."

The adults gathered at the table for the meal and the children were given plates to carry to the stairs. Each child was given two steps; one to sit on and one to hold the plate. There were three high chairs pulled to the table for the littlest grandchildren. The menu was meatloaf, gravy, noodles, carrots, lima beans and applesauce. The children were admonished to clean their plates so they could have a Tootsie Pop. At the stairs there was much trading of carrots and beans to get all the plates clean. It worked every time.

Liddy announced that she and Gertie would do the dishes if everyone got out of the way. The table and stair steps cleared out quickly. All the dishes were stacked and the entire family found other places to be. Gertie poured two cups of coffee while Liddy ran the warm soapy water. Now the two sisters could have time to visit, too.

Liddy needed to know how Gertie was doing."Did you do the right thing, moving from Tenth Street?" It was her first question to start the conversation.

"Yes, it was the right thing." It was easy to explain to her sister how she felt at Hilltop Manor and she knew Liddy would understand.

Liddy was not one given to introspective thinking and she looked to her little sister to get insight. She marveled at the independent way Gertie handled things. Gertie was Liddy's hero. Edward's brutality had not kept her down. The tragedy of Jesse's death would not defeat her sister, either. Liddy could not speculate on the truth, especially if it was unsavory or even sinful. She had faith in her sister and believed she could make everything come out right, just as she did when Papa was under the steam tractor many years ago.

"I know you will be fine, Gertie. If it was me, and I lost Lon…well, I just couldn't make it; but, you will. I have thought about it and I just can't think about losing Lon. I'm not like you. I wish I were."

Gertie found herself comforting Liddy. "There, there, Liddy. We never know what we can do until we have to. You are not going to lose Lon."

"I'm a silly goose." Liddy recovered and threw suds from the dishes into Gertie's hair.

The two kitchen maids resumed their task, each with her own thoughts. Gertie found the right time to get some deep thoughts out in the air. "I thought about things a lot since I found myself married and single again. You know it isn't right that single women are thought to be unable to take care of themselves or raise a child or several children alone. Families feel they have to find an old bachelor to marry them or at least bring them back home to live off their parents. How pitiful. How wrong. There will come a day when women can choose to stay single and raise children."

"Gertie, you really believe that?"

"I do. I believe it could, and should, be a choice. We can work and make a life without a husband if that happens. Divorce was better for me than just being sure I had a man. Look how much I have achieved. Look at how well William turned out. Look at Edward—growing up and going in the army instead of putting his problems on me. And Edward's death would have left me alone anyway. If we go into this war in Europe, many women will be raising children without husbands. Sad fact, but true. It's the children that matter. Good jobs for women will make the difference. Jesse gave me a good job. Where would I be if I hadn't gotten a job at the bank? I can't imagine."

"Gertie, do you really think other women could meet life as you have?"

"Of course."

"Well, I can't believe that. I think you are a rare exception."

"I absolutely believe women do not need to stay in a bad marriage. I saw in our family how a good marriage should work and Edward and I were 180 degrees away from that. You'll never know how many people advised me to stay with Edward knowing I would be battered." She paused for a sad recollection. "No one deserves that corner. There has to be another choice. Liddy, mark my words, some day there will be many, many women who will lead lives as I have. My life is not so special. Except for finding Jesse—that was special. I can't say that many women find a man like Jesse to love them. We had it all—Jesse and me. Enough to last me the rest of my life. I will never marry again. My greatest happiness will be in my memories and William. It may be a while before my heart is light again. Thank goodness for Bear Creek, and coming down home on weekends. The most important time in my life is opening a letter from William and sitting by a soldier praying that he will open his eyes."

Liddy went to bed sure that Gertie's thinking was flawed by her tragedy. Gertie went to bed thanking God that He gave her strength, and before she slept, she asked Him for more.

֍

Mama came into Gertie's room after the house was quiet. Her light was still on, waiting for her mother. As she lay tucked under that deep comforter, she remembered the days she and Liddy shared a room in Laurel and all their secrets.

"Gertie, how are you doing with your sadness?"

"Sometimes, it is like a heavy dark blanket, so wide that I can't throw it off. I'll make it, but I have a ways to go. I try to think of what Jesse would want me to do. He would not like to see me unhappy."

"One thing I am sure of—you can do anything you put your mind to. Always have. Just make up your mind to deal with your loss and do it. Make up your mind about anything and just do it. Simple as that. I love you, child."

"I love you, too Mama. And, Thanks."

"Thanks? For what?"

"Making it simple."

֍

The next week Sam came to Hilltop to look at the old farm house. He called Gertie at work.

"Hi, Sis. I called to talk about that farmhouse. Busy?"

"I've got time. Does Nora like the idea of moving?"

"She liked the idea of more room and plenty of running space for our little monkeys."

"Have you looked at it?"

"Yes, Jed and I looked at it this morning."

"How bad is it?" She was almost afraid to ask.

"Surprisingly good. Walls, floors, windows are fine. No signs of leaks. We'll have to check out the electric and plumbing. Heat is coal but I'll take care of that before we need it," he quipped. "I insist on paying rent."

"Keep account of the repair costs and after you have been there long enough to offset that, we will talk, but you know I'm not concerned about rent. You will be doing me a favor at the stables. And it'll be a comfort having you there. I talked to Mr. Black and he agreed—it's a good solution for that empty house and I won't have to make a decision about the horses. I don't think I could do that right now."

Gertie hung up the phone and took a moment to relish the idea of having Sam, Nora, and the children at Hilltop. A slow happy feeling crept over her and she allowed it without guilt for her sorrow's sake.

Chapter 35   1941

On Monday, Gertie called Ernest Black before he got into the office." This is Gretta Morgan. Please have Mr. Black call me at 725W extension 40."She hung up the phone, but was still connected to the thoughts she had to share with her attorney. They remained foremost in her mind as she walked from the teller cage to pour a cup of coffee. The clock was at nine sharp. Her thoughts needed to be directed beyond her personal concerns as the branch opened for the day. The next time she looked at the clock it was two o'clock—time to close the bank and head for the hospital.

Sandra handed her a message from Ernest confirming an appointment when she got back to Laurel.

Mr. Black will be in his office this evening, awaiting your convenience.

She stopped to check her hair and straighten her dress. The usual curl had escaped to her forehead and she tucked it into her bouffant hairdo. A touch of powder brought back her soft glow. Pleased with the reflection, she picked up her purse and began her walk around the teller cages making sure things were put away without exception.

She could see and smell and feel the ending summer season. "I need an apple," she thought as her steps picked toward her car.

Ernest was leaning back in his chair, resting his eyes, when she entered calling his name in the apparently empty law office.

"Hello, Gertie. Come in, I'm at my desk. Are you here to ask that question again?"

"No, sir"

"Good, then you are here to tell me what you have decided."

He led her to his back sitting room where coffee was brewing. "Have a cup and let's get to it."

She waited while he set a cup of coffee before her and she inhaled the aroma that always took her down home. "Ernest, I've decided to take Jesse's job—president. That will make me a member of the board, but I will not be chairman."

"Well done." He replied, slapping his hands on his knees. "Well, done." He showed his delight and hid the smugness he felt. Ernest Black had been sure she would not make the mistake of turning aside this great opportunity. He loved judging human nature and he loved being right. It was a small game he played in his mind. Gertie was not going to disappoint—neither him nor herself.

"I'll be at the board meeting Wednesday and I look forward to your announcement. Are you ready?"

"Not hardly, but I will be."

Gertie slipped into the driver's seat for the ride home and quickly fell to dreaming that Jesse was waiting for her. She shook the dream off and embraced her disappointment. No one was waiting for her at Hilltop except Bertha.

❧

The bank was buzzing with the news that Gretta Neal Morgan was about to take the helm. News traveled along the grapevine to those who could not believe and to those who claimed they knew this would happen. Often secretaries who typed the memorandums fed the rumors about Gertie and her stock. This time it was Ernest Black, himself who wanted it known. He knew the members of the board needed time to digest her intentions and realize they had no option but to support her majority. It would make her move into Jesse's office go more smoothly.

The second Wednesday of September arrived—the regularly scheduled meeting of the board of directors. The day Gertie dreaded and anticipated was here. Gertie closed her branch at Fort Meade and drove to Laurel in time to enter the room with the members of the board. As soon as the meeting was convened Ernest Black called for an election to fill Jesse's post. The men, gathered around the large mahogany table, hid their feelings, and took the action in stride. Clued that she intended to fill the position and realizing she had the votes to elect herself, J R Preake moved that Gretta Morgan assume the place vacated by Jesse Morgan. It was swiftly seconded and passed unanimously. It did not matter what these men thought about Gretta Morgan. It did not matter that she had only been married to Jesse Morgan for two days. It did not matter that she probably did not know how to run the bank. She had the stocks; she had the power—thus, she had the job.

Gertie drew notes from her briefcase.

"If you please…Gentlemen, I am honored to assume Jesse Morgan's place as President of First National Bank. I look forward to working with you. I am challenged to meet Jesse's standard of excellence, fairness, and good business policies. It is my goal to do everything I can to learn this business from this perspective and take an active part in the growth and success of our bank. I am mindful that this turn of events is unusual and could be awkward. With your help we can keep our mission of serving the community and continue to build a good profit base. I know that I am inexperienced, but the majority that I hold behooves me to come right in. Each of you came to your position on this board from other businesses and without knowledge of banking. At least I have had many years in banking and several as manager of the Ft Meade Branch." She did not want to pause in this announcement. She barely took a breath. "None of you would fail to grasp this opportunity that tragedy has brought my way. The officers on the board and in the bank should remain the same. The most important thing we can do for this institution is continue to work and fill our positions. Mr. Hawkins you have been acting chairman of this board. Please continue with that job for the next six months, after which, you will return to vice chairman." Gertie had done her homework. She knew Mr. Hawkins was happy to return to his former position since running his hardware business was his main priority.

"With your approval, Mr. Hamilton will continue as acting bank president while training and preparing me to serve in that position. At the end of that time Mr. Hamilton becomes chairman of this board—in recognition of his service to the bank. Unlike, Mr. Morgan, I will not assume that position."

Gertie looked to see if her executive announcements were being well received, but she could not read the faces around the table.

"I need your support; I expect it. I hope you will be as clear and open in what you expect from me."

She had carefully thought through her plan. With Ernest Black's help she was building compromises into her actions. Mr. Hamilton's elevation to Chairman of the Board would bring him into an equally important position and a very secure place. He knew his appointment, as acting president of the bank the day after Jesse died, would not be a permanent position. Now the power of Gertie's majority was allowing him a lateral move instead of downward one. His loyalty went straight to the young widow.

Gertie did not aspire to be both president and chairman. She only wanted to use the advantages given by Jesse to do what he would want her to do for Hilltop and herself. *Oh, God. Help me.* Her shaking hands were controlled, but her knees were bouncing against the chair. *Thank you God—for plush cushioned chairs in this lofty place.* She had enough to deal with trying to fill her husband's shoes without worrying about her knees making strange battering noises under the huge mahogany table.

She looked around and saw questioning looks, maybe doubting looks, but no hate or animosity in the eyes of the men assembled.

"One last thing I would like to propose. A new office—to be outfitted for Mr. Hamilton. There has never been an office in the bank for the Chairman of the Board. Since we will continually be working together, I propose his office in the space at the top of the balcony opposite Mr. Morgan's office. With your approval it will be done immediately."

Charles Hamilton and the members of the board were impressed with this suggestion and knew it was another compromise to assure them that power was not taken from the hands of the experienced. That was one motivation for her suggestion; the other was that she wanted Jesse's office vacated as soon as possible.

"Mrs. Morgan, Jesse's office will be available to you tomorrow. I will find a space until my new office is ready."

"Thank you Mr. Hamilton. And, gentlemen, when we are meeting—just us—please call me Gertie."

"We officially offer our condolences, Gertie. Jesse was a wonderful business partner and friend." Mr. Hawkins closed the meeting.

Gertie stood. "I would like to invite you and your spouses to dinner at Hilltop Manor on Saturday, October 16th, at 7:00. I hope you can come."

Ernest was the first to accept and all the others followed. She would host her first party and it would be all business. Gertie began immediately to plan the menu and fall decorations for her dinner party. Since fall was in the air—she decided on cornucopias with fresh fruit on each table. The menu would be roast pork with cranberry glaze, green beans, wild rice, apple compote, and pie. Bertha and Jed were quick to put her at ease with their expertise. They would have plenty of help and after making the menu selections, Gertie was dismissed from the planning. Later when she went back to them to suggest canapés, they again assured her that Jesse had a file of selected favorites; she needed only to select one. She concentrated on seating and seeing to the drinks.

Gertie knew that the men on the board ran the meeting on a first name basis and she made sure that she attained permission to do the same before they left Hilltop.

It was a wonderful party. The guests departed and Gertie took her good feelings up to bed. She was happy with the social success but was not foolish enough to believe that her party would assure her smooth transitions at the bank

She would have to prove herself to Jim, Howard Charles, Laurence, Conrad and Phillip. But, she was already proven to Ernest.

❧

Gertie's work with the veterans at Ft. Meade fulfilled her passion and gave her an emotional outlet while she worked through her own tragedy. A message from General Kellogg appeared on her desk one Friday afternoon in November. He had written in his own hand a request to see her at Hilltop—almost a reverse invitation. She went to his office at Headquarters.

Crossing the parking lot, she noticed the leaves scrunching under foot and the glow of twilight filtering through almost bare maple trees. She paused, and said aloud, "Fall's almost gone." The changing seasons always brought joy but since Jesse died she hadn't taken notice. Summer had vanished and soon it would be Thanksgiving. She wondered when the first crisp air had blown."When did it happen?" she asked herself in her habit of talking to herself.

"When did it happen?" she repeated and then she reached down, took a handful of leaves, crunched them and lifted them to her nose to take in the aroma and continued to the Headquarters' building.

"Hello, Gertie. I didn't expect you to come here, I thought you would call...Well, I guess my request was a bit unusual. Come in; please sit."

"Thank you, sir. I'd be delighted to receive you at Hilltop. When would be convenient?"

"It is official business, Gertie, but of a nature that an informal setting would be great. Any evening this week. Name a day."

"Tuesday will be fine. After dinner—seven? We will have coffee and dessert, if that suits."

"Perfect. Tuesday at seven. Two gentlemen and one lady will be with me. We want to discuss USO and Special Services."

"Now that we have business finished, tell me, how are you doing? You are looking well."

"Thank you, sir. I am taking one day at a time, but I will admit that my work here is a big help."

"I am glad to hear that. Good for you."

The meeting was over and Gertie's interest was tweaked.

❧

On Tuesday evening at seven, Bertha greeted General Kellogg and three other guests at the Hilltop foyer. Their eyes were on the impressive staircase. "Good evenin'. Please come this way." She led them to the great room where Gertie waited.

Coffee and dessert were set on the gate-leg table. Small tables sat at three wing chairs that had been pulled to the sofa. Obvious planning made a comfortable setting for five people to enjoy an informal meeting with refreshment.

"Thank you, Bertha. I will serve."

"Good evening, General Kellogg."

"Gertie, I'd like to introduce Major Bruce Collins, Guy and Lorraine Mills." He extended his palm upward to her. "Gertie Morgan."

Gertie knew Major Collins was coordinator of USO development on the east coast. Guy Mills was well known as a leader of a swing band that set the tone for virtually every nightclub and supper club in the country. The band and its leader also took an active part in entertaining the troops and growing the USO.

The excitement of having Guy Mills in Gertie's home was contained by courtesy.

"General Kellogg."

Please call me Bob. This is informal, as I said."

"Bob, very well—" she smiled, "—while we are off post. I am Gertie here as well as on post." The ice was broken. "It is a pleasure to have you all in my home. Please come serve yourself coffee. After we are settled, I'd like to cut you a piece of my Bertha's wonderful chocolate cake.

"Gertie, we have spoken on the phone. It's nice to finally meet you. I'm Bruce." He looked across to the sofa. "Guy and Lorraine, first names?"

"Absolutely," they spoke in unison.

"The Mills' need no introduction."

Bob Kellogg took the lead and got to the point. "Gertie, you know that your service clubs at the hospital and rec-center at Ft. Meade have gotten a lot of attention on military installations across the country. Bruce called me last week asking for this meeting. Guy just happened to be here this week."

"I'm delighted to have you all."

"Big changes are coming to Ft. Meade. Our services to our personnel will have to change, too."

Gertie paid close attention. *What does that mean to me? Is my simple little service program, started for Edward, obsolete?* She had an uneasy feeling that she would be replaced when USO became official at Ft. Meade. She looked at Bruce Collins. He would be the logical person for the job. And, Hilltop was a pleasant place to get fired—if you can be fired from a volunteer position. To give her mind a rest, she served cake.

"The population on post has tripled. There will be greater increases by the end of this year and in 1942, too. Ft. Meade wants to take good care of our troops and morale is a big part of that. The Third Service Command is opening a Special Services Unit Training Center here. This is the place where soldiers will be trained in all phases of the entertainment field. The army is recruiting talent as we speak. In other words we are going to produce morale, not haphazardly, but with professional help and a developed plan. Guy is very interested in plans we have here at Ft. Meade to support the Special Services with USO activities." He paused and looked at the celebrity about to eat chocolate cake, inviting him, with his gaze to speak.

"Wow, this cake is wonderful, Gertie." Guy used his napkins to be sure no crumbs distracted his words. "We are on our way to Maxwell Field, Alabama. I stopped to see Bruce and he thought I would be interested in Ft. Meade's USO development. After all, a terrific band needs a place to play for our troops. Bruce and I are old friends. We went to school together in Missouri." He paused for another bite of cake. "I haven't had chocolate cake like this in forever. Lorraine doesn't have time to cook—or an oven—when the band is on the road." Gertie accepted the compliment for Bertha. Guy Mills did not rush his enjoyment. "I hope I don't intimidate this meeting. I'm a voyeur—a very interested one. I will be leading a service band soon maybe playing at a USO at Ft. Meade, too. I have heard a lot about the work you have done here. I fear the future will require so much more from us, even those who are not carrying weapons."

"I'm flattered, Mr. Mill... Guy." Gertie still did not gather the facts logically. More questions were presented than answers.

"Gertie, I see a puzzled look on your face. Forgive me; I never said... this meeting is about USO development at Ft. Meade. You are pivotal in this discussion. We want you in on the ground floor. It is my hope and Bruce's too, that you want to be part of the future of special services on our post with USO units. What do you think? Will you be director of volunteers for the USO programs at Ft. Meade?"

"I thought you were here to relieve me and gently fire me. This is not that, is it?"

"No, it most certainly is not that! We need you more than ever. If you will take the job your staff will include army personnel as well as your corps of volunteers. There is much to work out. We need the right facility and direct coordination with the Special Service Unit Training Center. It is a paid position."

"I have to think. I didn't expect this. It's a relief to know I am still needed. I cannot imagine my life without serving at Ft. Meade. But, I want to remain a volunteer. I would like to have a paid position as an assistant. That will give you two for the price of one and I can spend time at the hospital and of course, you know, I am a working woman. The time I spend at the hospital is not negotiable. She paused to think over what she had said. *I'm getting bossy.* "Goodness, it sounds like I accepted, didn't it?"

"Yes, it did. And I support all your stipulations. In fact I endorse them." Bob Kellogg took her hand, drew her to her feet, and gave an unexpected hug before he told of her many hours at the hospital and the admiration of everyone at Ft. Meade. "This lady is one of a kind. She has turned one afternoon party for patients at our hospital into a lifetime dedication. She has been an angel to countless men and women." Gertie was truly embarrassed. "—and, she was worried that she wasn't needed any longer." General Kellogg laughed heartily.

More coffee was poured and the meeting melted into a social exchange with the Mills sharing many fascinating stories. Guy was so passionate about forming a service band to entertain troops at home or wherever they are stationed. He felt the world would be his stage. His patriotism was contagious.

Before they left, she reached into her husband's briefcase and drew out a piece of music. "Guy, sign this for Gertie. She would never ask."

To Gertie, Angel of Ft. Meade
Thanks for your hospitality and inspiration,
God Bless America.
Guy Mills
November 12, 1941

Gertie pressed the copy of *God Bless America* to her chest.

❦

When she woke up Sunday morning, her first thought was uttered aloud, "It was five months ago today, July 7. Now it is December. I guess I'll remember the 7th of every month."

Bertha was busy setting coffee and juice on the table as Gertie entered the sunny kitchen. It was a glorious December Sunday. "You goin' to church, Miss Gertie?"

"Yes, Bertha, are you?" They exchanged the morning greetings. "After church, I need to go to Ft Meade and check on some things at the hospital. You and Jed take the day off."

"Thank yo', Miss. I'm leavin' a nice plate in the ice box for dinner. Be careful, now, hear."

Yes, Bertha, I'll be careful."

It was quiet in the hospital and Gertie headed to her office, made coffee and turned on the radio to WTOP for background music. She was ready to get some work done without interruption. It was a perfect time to inventory supplies and prepare orders to restock for the Christmas season.

A lot of patients; a lot of tears; a lot of smiles. Gertie continued her reverie with thoughts about the changes coming next year when the USO officially took over *her* clubs. Meanwhile she worked to meet the need of the growing army post. The town of Laurel was beginning to feel the impact of many young service men without activities on their time off. Gertie had a dance floor installed and provided non-alcoholic drinks and snacks. From her budget she managed a good sound system and a second-hand pool table. The club averaged 20 to 30 men every evening. On Saturday the churches from the surrounding communities brought their young women and chaperones to the dances. She needed more volunteers and always more money.

Gertie spent part of every weekend in her office to keep up with needs. This meant that she didn't get to Bear Creek as often, though she rarely missed three weekends in a row. Often she came here on her way home on Sunday evening. This weekend she didn't get to Bear Creek and she was at the hospital in the afternoon—Sunday, December 7th, 1941 when WTOP broke into their regular programming.

"We interrupt this broadcast to announce that the Japanese have attacked Pearl Harbor by air. All Naval and military facilities and activities have been attacked. There is no doubt that these attacks mean war. We will bring information from the White House as soon as it is available."

Gertie uttered, "William!" and lay her head down and wept just as mothers all over the country were doing. "Please, Jesse. You have to be right. William must not die." Even with perfect memory of her time with Jesse on the bench in the orchard, doubts and fears flooded her. She began to gather papers and clear her desk. *Hilltop. I must get to Hilltop.* All over the country people were hurrying home to be with family and wait by the radio.

The sentry at the gate usually waved her through, but today he stopped her. "Mrs. Morgan, be careful." He saluted as each saw the other was crying.

"You, too, soldier. God bless."

The tranquility at Hilltop was eerie as she opened the door with a trembling hand.

Gertie was surprised to see Bertha and Jed in the foyer.

"We hurry back to Hilltop—soons we got the terrible news. Miss Gertie. What's we gonna do?"

"Bertha, we are going to pray. Please bring my dinner to the library at five. I'd like for you and Jed to eat with me, we will listen to the news together. I am going to call my family now and tell them to keep the faith that William is fine." She spoke with authority and confidence that came from some unknown place.

She asked the operator to get the Bear Creek number. "I'm sorry. All lines are busy. The national emergency will take all the lines. I don't know when I can get your call through."

"Thank you, operator, I understand. Call me when you do, no matter the time." She was isolated from family. No calls would go through not even to Sam who was probably on the road coming from Bear Creek.

Gertie closed the library door and went to her knees in the room lit only by the fireplace. She prayed for William, for all service men, for all the men and women who would be in the war, for the United States. Then she prayed for all the families torn apart on this day, for all the families who did not know if their loved ones died at Pearl Harbor. "Oh God, we implore your mercy. Grant us strength for the days ahead. Give our leaders wisdom. God bless the USA." Her supplications were recited as they came to her. "Please take care of Mama and Papa, they are so worried. They don't know that William will be fine. Help me to hold to that, too." Gertie paused and took a deep breath. "Show me, guide me, help me be your hands in the lives of our brave service men and women." She started to get up, but instead went back to her knees. "I am yours, Lord. Use me."

The radio gave the news and introduced President Roosevelt. A slight pause in the broadcast gave her a second to remember the beautiful day FDR spoke at William's graduation.

"No matter how long it may take us to overcome this premeditated invasion, The American people, in their righteous might, will win through to absolute victory. With confidence in our armed forces and the unbounded determination of our people we will gain the inevitable triumph, so.... Help... us... God."

Gertie looked at the clock. "Four thirty." She knew she had a half hour to tremble, weep and give into her fears. She had thirty minutes to call William's name in every prayer she knew.

At five, she had to pull herself together and be ready to eat, without appetite, with Bertha and Jed—the only family she could gather.

Chapter 36

The apples fell from the trees and went into baskets scattered in the orchard. The kitchen was full of apples. They bounced down the staircase and decorated tables in the foyer and great room. The abundance was amazing. Jesse's rough wood bench sat under the Red Delicious tree. Who is that on the bench? Jesse? I'm coming Jesse. . . but the phone is ringing. I can't get to the bench; I have to answer the phone. The bench! The phone!

"Ring! Ring! Ring! Ri ..." The demand brought Gertie from the red and yellow apple painted dream back to her dark bedroom.

"Hello."

"Gertie, it's Bob Kellogg."

His name brought her awake. "Yes, sir." *Something is wrong at the hospital*, was her first thought.

"I talked to William."

"William, William? Oh God...praise the Lord." Gertie could not think and hardly breathe as she swung her feet over the side of the bed and sat upright. "You talked to him?"

"He's fine. He was in San Diego on Sunday."

"Oh, thank you. Thank God." She dropped the phone and held her head together with both hands.

"Are you there? Gertie?"

"Yes, yes, tell me... "

"I know, I woke you, but as soon as I finished talking to William, I had to call. He's going back to Hawaii as soon as possible. His call was limited to military business. He traded targets for his intelligence contacts to call Ft. Meade. He knew we would let you know and it is my pleasure to awaken you with this news."

"General Kellogg, I can't thank you enough. I am going to call every MacGregor and Neal. No one in this family is going to spend the rest of this night sleeping."

"I'm not sure how soon he can talk to you. As you can imagine, things are chaotic there but at least you know—he is fine."

"Yes, sir. I know it, now. Thank you, sir."

"Good night, Gertie and pleasant dreams." It was one of the happiest chores of General Kellogg's military career.

Gertie fell back on the bed and cried tears of relief and joy. It was not until this moment that she admitted, despite Jesse's assurances, fear for William had taken over her life. Chills wracked her body and still she cried.

She cried tears and names. "William…, Jesse…William…, Jesse…," Anguish for Jesse poured over her again. And then, from deep in her gut she cried another name, "Edward."

Purging began to unburden as lightness and happiness enfolded her. She wanted to run and skip. At the closet she put on her warmest slacks and sweater, wool socks, and boots, coat scarf, and gloves.

She ran and skipped across the lawn to the orchard in the cold December predawn. The barren trees against a soft black sky drew veins of life. The orchard would bloom again in three months; her life would bloom again, starting right now. She wrapped her arms around a tree trunk and swung herself, like a child on a playground ride. The strong, unmoving tree gave her lift as her feet rose off the ground. "Who planted you?" she asked. "Was it Jesse? William? Or me?" Her foot stepped on an apple nestled under a heap of leaf mulch. She picked it up, amazed at the color and freshness. "Ah ha, little apple. You were lost; now you're found." She shined the apple to a high gloss with her gloves.

Gertie sat on the bench holding the apple. "Jesse, William is safe. Thank you for watching over him." It was a prayer, a praise, and a thanksgiving. She wanted Jesse to put his arm around her waist as he did before, but she had to rely on her memory to feel the pull and the pressure. She slid farther to the right but the void remained. She closed her eyes. "Jesse, I know you are not here, but I feel so close to you in the orchard. Go, my love. You have a big job looking after William. I'll tend to Hilltop." She opened her eyes to the glowing eastern sky. "I will always love you."

Gertie placed the shiny red apple on the weathered wooden bench, in the winter brown orchard and smiled. She took three steps away and looked back. The apple seemed to glow—a symbol of life in a dead setting. "Found!" she called back.

Gertie returned to the house, made coffee, and started making phone calls.

❦

A week in slow motion passed with routine filling hours until evening, when the radio became the center of attention. Dreading the news and yet unable to ignore it, citizens gathered for the latest war stories. The next day the Washington Post and Baltimore Sun reiterated the news delivered the night before, often with pictures. Gertie invited Bertha and Jed to join her in the library; she did not want to listen alone.

How many times must I listen to the air raid on the Arizona, she wondered. Sometimes she ran for a coat and started for the orchard before both arms were in and buttons were secured against the cold December wind. Bertha hurried to hand her a hat before she bolted.

❦

On December 16th, Bertha met Gertie at the door. She had an odd expression on her face.

"What is it, Bertha? Is something wrong?"

"Oh, no, Miss Gertie. You's got a letter." She was holding back the biggest smile possible, which pushed her cheeks to the sides of her broad face.

"A letter!" Gertie dropped her coat and purse, kicked off her wedge shoes and took the stairs two at a time to get to her favored place in Jesse's room.

"William… at last." She kissed the envelope before she tore it open.

December 10, 1942
Dear Gertie,

If only I could talk to you. A letter, at this time, is the only way. I trust Ft. Meade told you we had communicated through official channels. I am so glad that you did not have to wait for this letter or sweep for my name when the list of casualties came out. Many families are doing that right now. It will be weeks before official telegrams to

*bereaved families arrive. Many of the over two thousand
dead were my mates on the Arizona. I have a great portion
of guilt over that.*

*My monthly TDY to San Diego was to start on Monday,
December 8th. I got a pass so I could spend time with
Louisa. I left Hawaii on Saturday December 6th.*

*Momma, I have very important and wonderful news for
you. News that I wish we could at least, tell you on the
phone. I came to San Diego with a ring in my pocket and
every confidence that Louisa would accept my proposal. On
Sunday morning, in her parents back yard. I proposed and
she accepted. The family was so excited for us. We did not
have a radio on. When I went to the phone to call you with
the news, the lines were down for civilian calls. That is how
we learned something terrible had happened. We turned
the radio on and got the horrible news. The attack at Pearl
Harbor took precedence over our lives—over everybody's life.
My flight back to Pearl was at noon on Monday. Louisa
and I went to the court house and got married at nine on
the morning of December 8th. We are so in love and so
scared. I would never have suggested it…but she did and
I love her for it. We had a two hour honeymoon at the
Hilton. I am a happy but sad bride groom.*

*I hope we have not disappointed you too much. This week
is the beginning of a new set of life's rules. I love having
Louisa waiting for me. She is truly wonderful. Can't wait
for you to meet her. You are going to love her, too. It is not
how we wanted to do this, but I have no regrets.*

*We agreed that Louisa would give me time to get a letter to
you before she contacted you. You will get a call on the 18th
and I hope you have read this letter before then.*

*I don't know why it was my fate to be away from Hawaii on
Sunday. God must have another plan for me. As soon as the
attack was over, the navy rushed me back to Pearl. It was a
black, devastated world, different from the paradise I left
four days ago. But, I can see beyond this disaster—Hawaii
will bloom again. I'm grateful that I have survived, for
you and for the job I want to do for our country. I'm more*

*than ready to get back on a battleship and go for the black
hearts that did this—it cannot come too soon.
I know you are praying for me and for our beloved United
States of America. God will sustain us against the evil that
is sweeping over the world. Our faith only needs be as big
as the mustard seed, remember?*

Gertie lowered the letter with a gentle smile as she recalled that after a Sunday school lesson William wanted a mustard seed to see how big his faith had to be. She fished a mustard seed from the pickling spice and placed it in his small palm. "Not that big, is it?"

With a sigh, she raised the letter again.

*I have no expectation of seeing you soon. But, I will come
home. I promise. Louisa and I will walk the hills and
orchards at Hilltop and the familiar sidewalks on Tenth
Street. Believe it!
I love you and I live in the love you have for me.*

William

"Bertha!" She called over the railing. "Dinner will be a little late; I have some calls to make. William is fine. Just fine."

"Yes'um." A wealth of happiness flowed from that simple reply.

❧

Two days later, Gertie hurried home. December 18, was circled on her desk calendar at work and at home. All day she counted the hours and figured the time difference to the west coast. She couldn't wait to talk to William's wife.

"Bertha, I will eat in the library near the phone."

Before Gertie had taken one bite, a knock came on the door. She went to the foyer, waving Bertha off. "I'll get it."

The lovely young lady framed by the massive door could be only one person.

"Hello, Mrs. Morgan. I'm Louisa."

Louisa may not have been ready for a bear hug, but she got it. Gertie could hardly pull back from the girl to see her pretty face, blue eyes, and softly curled blond hair. The truth was—Gertie could only say one word. "Louisa." She locked into Louisa's elbow and led her to the library. Bertha stood by.

"Bertha, *this* is William's wife, Louisa." Gertie presented her with pride.

"How do, Miss Louisa." Bertha's grin was ear to ear.

"Can you please reset the table for two?"

"Oh, yes. I's can." Bertha turned to the kitchen muttering, "Young Mister's wife...."

Gertie took Louisa's hands. "Louisa. Louisa... welcome to our family...to our home." Tears of joy welled up in her eyes. "I'm so happy to have you here. It's a wonderful surprise."

Louisa had worried about her welcome and what she would say to her mother-in-law. She came on William's insistence that Gertie would be happy to see her. He was correct, but even he could not imagine the joy Gertie experienced at having his bride at Hilltop.

"I began to think surprising you was not a good idea, even though it was William's. He kept saying, 'Gertie will be in the library waiting for your call on the 18th. Knock on the door instead.' Half way across the country I decided to call you. We had a short stop in Indianapolis, but service men tied up all the phones. I couldn't call—it was going to be a surprise after all."

Gertie smiled broadly to reassure her that William's surprise was more than welcome. It was life invigorating.

"Forgive my manners. Before we eat, I'll show you the guest room and you can freshen up. We can start our visit over dinner. And, Louisa, as soon as you are relaxed and comfortable here at Hilltop, I hope you will call me Gertie, everybody does."

Gertie noticed the small bag, which prompted the question. "How long can you stay?"

"I have a return ticket for Monday. Naval intelligence has been crazy, especially now. Those of us who worked double shifts every day since the 7th were forced to go home for four days. I got right on the train, but luckily the navy is flying me back on Monday. We have the weekend. I want to see Tenth Street and Bear Creek."

"Yes, indeed, you can see Tenth Street and Bear Creek and meet as much family as possible."

At the guest room, Gertie embraced Louisa once more. "Dinner back in the library as soon as you are ready. I'll be waiting for you. You can tell me all about yourself and we can talk about William."

"I am so happy, Gertie."

"I'm happy, too."

❦

While Louisa was upstairs, Gertie thought, *Friday, Saturday, and Sunday. Mmm.* When her daughter-in-law returned she had a plan to share over dinner.

"I'm going to take the day off tomorrow. Would you like to walk over William's hometown?"

"Oh, yes, I would."

"We'll start at Tenth Street."

❦

The stroll started in the yard at 403. They walked around the house. Gertie pointed to William's bedroom window and his grandparents' house next door. Aunt Charlotte had gathered several Neal family members who were not at work.

"Come in for coffee. We want to say hello."

Louisa was delighted to be in the kitchen where William had spent so many hours with Mom Neal and Poppa Clay. She felt she was stepping into a picture her husband had drawn.

Louisa was very pensive, imagining William in these settings. "This is very exciting. William said we'll live here someday."

The walk down Montgomery Street and past Grandmother Amsterdam's house eventually led them to Main Street and a quick visit to the bank. Gertie introduced Louisa to everyone in the lobby, behind the cages and in her office.

"This is William's wife," she announced with pride and pleasure.

Louisa asked questions about William's childhood and school years, Gertie answered her questions and relived the happy memories while quietly rejoicing that William had found this lovely girl.

367

The next day they drove to Bear Creek to meet the MacGregors. Gertie lost control of the situation as Louisa was immersed in the bosom of her family. Coffee was thrust at her—which she accepted as if warned by William.

"Here comes Sam. Be prepared. He is going to pick you up." Gertie hurriedly whispered.

Louisa smiled the whole time she was at Bear Creek.

On Sunday after a typical MacGregor abundant and boisterous noon time meal, they headed back to Hilltop.

"Glad yo' back, Miss Gertie and Miss Louisa. Coffee set up in da solarium. Snow so be-utey-full out dem windas."

"I wanted to walk over Hilltop with you, Louisa, but the snow is falling fast and piling up."

"Do you have some boots I can borrow? William said I must walk not only in the yard on Tenth Street, but over the hills at Hilltop and in the orchard—for him." She was on her feet, ready. Her eyes sparkled and her cheeks flushed. Louisa looked so young—like a school girl—and yet she was a woman waiting for her man to return from war. The thought stabbed Gertie.

"We will go out into the storm together." Gertie's meaning was profound and understood by William's youthful, sweet wife.

"Let's." Louisa took Gertie's hand.

William was right. Gertie loved Louisa, too.

❦

The Pearl Harbor casualty list was in the papers on Monday. Laurel saw that William Neal was not listed and they rejoiced. Gertie never told anyone—family or friend—about Jesse's promise that William would be safe, but when she saw the pictures and news reels, she knew—that Jesse knew—William was not destined to go down in USS Arizona's inferno. A small amount of confidence slipped into her being. There was only one way to be sure, absolutely sure that she would deserve the blessing of William's safe return. Gertie had to dedicate her life to her country and all that William was *willing* to die for.

"I must do more."

It was a common theme as patriotism mushroomed in every quadrant of the United States—a country at war. While many people spent time wondering exactly what they could do, Gertie was fortunate, she had a place and a mission to do her duty to serve God, country, and the never-to-be-under-appreciated person in uniform.

She got two star flags, signifying William was serving his country in the war. One *had* to hang in the house on Tenth Street. Her tenants were happy to do that. They were also given the stars and stripes to fly from the porch post every day, observing proper flag etiquette. It was a beautiful walk down her old neighborhood street where well-kept modest homes, mostly white, were ablaze with red, white and blue flags blowing in the breeze.

At Hilltop, without Gertie asking, Jed installed a standard holder in the middle of the circle drive. He installed lighting so Old Glory could wave day and night. She put the second star flag in her bedroom window where the sun could illuminate a red, white, blue, and gold light every day until William came home.

❧

Each morning, Gertie's feet touched the floor running. The hospital, the hospital service club, and the new club she was running at the post recreation center, were expanded. The attack at Pearl Harbor brought more and more volunteers and resources to support her efforts. She became the go-to person for morale at Ft. Meade.

Gertie went to headquarters to thank General Kellogg personally for his call, and took the opportunity to address something that was on her mind.

"General Kellogg, the USO is organizing. How soon will you bring them into Ft. Meade."

"Frankly, Gertie, I wanted to talk to you before any changes were made. I'm glad you brought it up, let's talk."

"If we can do more…. I'm for it. I want more for our men and women. Don't worry about stepping on my toes. I will continue to serve, even if it is not my program."

"The USO will not sit at bedsides, as you do. Nothing replaces that. But in the war effort, USO will offer great organization and uniformity throughout our military installations. Major Collins is ready to talk to you about conversion of your clubs to USO. I wanted to talk to your first and give you a heads-up."

"It will be good to talk to him again. Things are moving fast and I don't want to be in anyone's way."

"Believe me, you are not. In fact, Major Collins is incorporating some of your ideas into the USO program. Shall I set up a phone conference for you?"

"That will be fine." Gertie rose to go. "I have taken enough of your time. Did you know about Corporal Gladden, the possible double amputee that came in this morning?"

"Yes, an ordinance accident. How is he?"

"Very grave. He should be out of surgery by now. I'm on my way."

$$\text{\textbf{\textit{S}}}$$

Gertie went straight to the nurse's station on the surgery unit. While she walked down the corridor, she prayed her usual prayer.

"Dear God, Help Robert Gladden through these hard hours and help me be an instrument of your love in service to him. Give me the words and means to serve this patriot. Amen."

"Hello, Gertie. I thought you would be here." The nurse in charge turned to greet her. "Corporal Gladden did well in surgery. His left leg was amputated above the knee, the right has been saved for now…but could still be lost. His left arm is severely damaged. Fortunately there are no internal injuries and no brain damage. He has been in recovery for an hour and should soon rejoin us."

"Thank you. I will sit with him until he comes to. Do you have his personnel file?"

"Yes. I knew you would want to know about his family. Come with me to recovery."

Gertie read Corporal Gladden's family records while she listened for his first sounds. He got married three months ago. His bride, Marilyn, lived near his parents. Gertie suspected they were high school sweethearts. His family—mother, father, two sisters, and wife—lived in Beaufort, North Carolina.

"Help me…"

Gertie put a wet cloth to his mouth, knowing that anesthesia caused a dry mouth that felt like cactus.

"You are fine, Robert. The surgery is over. Sleep."

"No..." He was going to fight sleep and struggle to know what his new world was like.

"I'm your connection to Marilyn and your family. Lay back now. Rest. Sleep." She knew hearing his wife's name would help.

"I want..."

"I know. Lie quietly and listen for a minute. I have Marilyn's number as well as your parents. A call was already placed. They are on their way from North Carolina. My name is Gertie and I am here to help you."

When she brought cool water to his lips, she won him over. He accepted her as his friend because she answered his immediate need. "Do you need the nurse?"

"No nurse." His voice was weak. "You... stay?"

"Yes, Bobby. I'll stay. Now, sleep."

Corporal Robert Gladden was the same as every soldier Gertie had ever tended. And, he was different from every soldier she had tended. She went to his heart and gave him the basics of comfort. Then she offered support that would come from his family—if they could be here now. Finally she made sure he knew that she would stay for as long as he needed her. Gertie relieved his anxiety and got him to give in to his medication and take the first step toward healing.

The road ahead is long and hard, but you do not have to travel it alone, she thought as she looked at his square jaw and laugh lines around his mouth. *You are handsome and I think, fun,* she assessed.

"You will recover," she whispered to his sleeping relaxed face. "And, you have a future. The war is over for you, soldier."

Gertie stayed until Robert Gladden's family arrived from North Carolina. He did not need her any more tonight. He was not alone

The drive home was calming for Gertie. The roads were familiar and deserted. It didn't bother her that hers was the only car on the road. But, when she walked in to Hilltop, her spirit crashed. It bothered her greatly that she was alone. So alone.

Chapter 37   1942

The idea came to Gertie in the middle of the night, waking her from a fitful sleep full of dreams of Jesse, with Edward in the background. She reached over and turned on the light to see the clock. "Ten of three," she spoke to the lamp as she pulled the chain to put the room back into darkness. Gradually her eyes became accustomed to the dark again and she could see the room was lit by a setting moon shining from the western sky. She gathered the extra pillow and tucked it under her head so she could see the moon better and wait for the thought that had brought her out of sleep, and it did—immediately.

Gertie lay there for a while, making sure she was awake. Her thoughts became organized and she was happy with a contentment she hadn't felt for a long, long time. She stretched her legs and arms to take in a big fresh breath of air. "This is too good to sleep on," she said as she grabbed both pillows and rolled over until they made a full circle and were again under her head. "Might as well start right now!" Her excitement grew. She turned the light on again, threw the pillows to the floor and jumped from the bed. The big clock in the library chimed three times.

At the desk she wrote on the first sheet of paper, *Hilltop USO*. "Jesse, you are going to love this idea."

Thus began the conversion of the beautiful estate into a haven for service men. Gertie's thoughts came so fast that her notes were a jumble.

"Let's see. The rooms?" She said as she began renaming the rooms to accommodate activities like those going on at the USO at Ft. Meade. Soon she realized that Hilltop could be so much more than a canteen and social hall. Her excitement grew with the list forming on the paper.

Ballroom with room for a bandstand—the great room was perfect. Billiards, *Jesse's pool table hadn't been used since*— she let that thought go.

Gertie's mind traveled from room to room. The Library could double as a parlor/sitting room for those wanting quiet times. The large butler's pantry would be the coffee corner. The kitchen and breakfast rooms were perfectly situated and the dining room would be a perfect place to serve meals or snacks buffet style. The bright solarium would be the quiet visiting spot and perfect for patients from the hospital. As soon as the weather warmed, both porches would give the men and women room for more dancing or fellowship.

"Perfect. Perfect. Perfect."

Hilltop had it all. She knew without a doubt that Jesse would be delighted with this amazing plan that was pouring out of Gertie like a fountain.

The next sheet she titled *Problems to Be Solved* but quickly erased it and wrote *Issues to be Addressed*. She listed transportation, parking, hostesses, insurance, overhead, operating expenses, volunteers, wheel chair access, backers, advertisement, and promotion. She didn't write money, but she knew that a big dollar sign went with everything on this list.

"I'll come back to this list." It was daunting but she would not let her dream be diminished at this time of birth.

Gertie took another sheet of paper and headed it, *Personal*. Here she noted hers and Jesse's adjoining bedrooms, furniture and furnishings, household items, security for areas not open to public, as well as wear and tear.

We will need shuttle buses from Ft Meade or the many stations in Washington DC and Baltimore. Gertie knew that would not be a problem as there was a system already in place—just another stop on the route, that already included the movie theater on Main Street. The proximity was perfect. She said, "Perfect," again.

For every possible problem, Gertie saw a solution.

The amazing and almost complete picture of her plan formed quickly. Gertie may have been over confident, but in the flush of early excitement, she needed all the confidence she could muster.

"What about me?" she asked herself while standing in the middle of the room and making a complete turn. She walked through the open door that went into Jesse's room and realized her big idea required giving up parts of Jesse. His room was dark, lit only with the light from the doorway. Gertie sat on his bed in the dim light. "Help me with this,

Jesse. Hilltop USO is a great idea, but what about me?" She asked again not sure what was troubling her at this moment.

The answer came to her, "Tenth Street." *I need to go back to Tenth Street.*

Her military tenant turnover was high in her house in west end. Every three months or six at the most, her tenants left. By the time she got everything arranged at Hilltop, Tenth Street would, most likely, be vacant. She would not have to ask a soldier to move.

"Jesse, please love this plan. Our rooms at Hilltop will be sanctuary to me, but I am going home to Tenth Street to live so I can make Hilltop into a USO."

Gertie listened to her own words as they comforted her.

Her spirit was not daunted although the job seemed immense. The USO on post had grown out of her small service club—she knew what had to be done to bring Hilltop into the USO camp. And, she knew where to go for help. Like a General with a new mission, she was ready to assemble troops and march toward this goal. "General Gertie." she called herself and laughed.

As dawn broke, she was exhausted. Gertie put aside her notes and sat in the window seat in Jesse's room. The eastern mist in the dawning day invited dreams. She imagined military men and women enjoying the beauty of Hilltop. She envisioned swing music across the huge living room and out on the porch along the north side of the manor.

"Come back to Hilltop, Guy Mills!" she exclaimed.

Her reverie continued. On the wide square staircase men and women would enjoy a cup of coffee, cookies, and conversations. Fine lounging chairs for recovering veterans would line the wall in the solarium and dot the summer lawn. Her patients would take in the peace of the hills surrounding Hilltop. A game of badminton, volley ball, or even baseball would be boisterous on the level lawn toward the stable. The long table in the dining room would be laden with sandwiches, cakes, and cookies. Gertie even saw uniformed guests pitching in, carrying trash, making sandwiches, cutting cake, greeting newcomers. Perhaps couples would enjoy picking apples together as she and Jesse had.

Her vision was complete by the time the sun broke the horizon.

❦

The country was in the right frame of mind for supporting the war effort after Pearl Harbor and the declaration of war. The tiny town of Laurel, Maryland was no exception, and Gertie was going to tap into that fervor. The war effort became part of everyday life. Patriotism flourished and everyone searched for ways to help. Families kissed loved ones good-bye and counted ration stamps. New brides wrote long letters, held precious memories, and prayed diligently. Mothers knitted socks. Children bought saving stamps at school each week. The stars in Hollywood led campaigns to buy war bonds. Children gathered scrap metal in their wagons.

Through the cracks fell the older men, many World War I veterans. They were feeling old and under used as their sons and grandsons went off to war. They needed to feel needed. They wanted to do something important for the war effort. Gertie went to them first—she called a special meeting of the Board of Directors at the bank.

"Gentlemen of the Board," she began as soon as they were seated in the board room at the bank. "There is a great need we can fulfill right here for the war effort…." Her eloquence in presenting Hilltop USO came from her passion for troops that she had been serving for almost two decades. The words poured forth. She painted a picture of service, she outlined difficulties, and she defined the task, and clearly stated the cost. "I am willing to give Hilltop Manor to the cause and bear some of the expense, but I can't do it alone. Mr. Shafer prepared this financial basis. His cost estimates and overhead are here." Gertie passed out the prepared report. "I am taking this to every church and to the Laurel business community as well. The United Service Organization, known as the USO, will help with programs after we are up and running." She was pleased that, to a man, each one around the big mahogany table eagerly looked at the proposal.

"Most of us have a family member far away in the service. Let's take under our wing the young men and women who happen to be right here and give them a place to enjoy and be family with us. Hilltop USO will be a place of beauty and peace where they can relax before they face God-only-knows-what. Jesse's home will be a place where the injured can come and feel whole, where the homesick can find a friend and the fearful can build camaraderie. I hope Hilltop USO will be a place where they can believe the world is not lost to them. Let's do it for sons and daughters who come here. And I hope and pray, wherever our children in uniform are, someone is doing likewise for them. I don't know of any better service we can do directly for our own—than this."

To a man, they became her army in this mission.

Next she went to Laurel's churches. This was not an easy step for Gertie since she had felt the sting and stigma from them years ago but she did not let that deter her. She decided to go to the Catholic parish first. It may be easier to deal with one person of authority in the Catholic Church than the democratic make up of a protestant church board.

Father Sheegan, the senior pastor at St. Mary of the Mills Catholic Church, was more than happy to talk with Gertie. She carefully chose her dress and shoes to look subdued, yet attractive. She wanted to give an impression of organization and purpose when she approached the impressive stone church on Eighth Street.

"Gretta Morgan. Come in my dear and have a seat."

"Thank you, Father. Please call me Gertie, everyone does."

"Gertie, this may be our first introduction, but I know about your work at the army hospital. You have called the parish secretary on many occasions to ask Father O'Neill to come to Ft. Meade to tend one of our flock. He told me about you. I am well aware of the important care you have given our service men. Before you tell me what is on your mind, my housekeeper is bringing tea. A cup?"

"Yes, thank you. That would be lovely."

The rectory parlor was a beautiful setting. Gertie took in her surroundings as tea was poured. The traditional furniture and Oriental rug were a sunset of color in gold and burgundy. Gertie's gaze traveled the walls, noting paintings, and a curio cabinet full of figurines and glass. Beautiful vases adorned the tables. Father Sheegan noticed her interest.

"We use this room to display lovely gifts given to the parish priests over the years." He picked up a beautiful cobalt blue vase. "Here is an Italian art glass piece from Florence dated early nineteenth century. There is a story that says it once belonged to Cardinal Venuccia and he gave it to the Archbishop of Baltimore. Supposedly it once sat in the Vatican and was rediscovered in the rubble of the great Baltimore fire." He handed the beautiful blue glass vase to Gertie. "Look at it. Perfect in everyway—such a beautiful thing. It was tossed aside covered with ash, rescued in the reclamation by a worker who happened to belong to this parish. No one saw the beauty and value in it until he cleaned it up. Then he said it was too beautiful for him to keep. I think there are many great lessons in that story." He returned the vase to the table beside Gertie. "I never fail to remember them when I look at that vase."

"I will remember the story, too, Father." Gertie placed her cup in the saucer.

"What brings you here today? Is there something I can do for you, Gertie?" father Sheegan replaced his cup and gave her his attention.

"I have something too beautiful to keep to myself, too." The whole story of Hilltop USO poured forth as she told of her steps to achieve her dream. As before, it was easy for her, just as it had been before the board of directors. Father Sheegan listened intently, smiling occasionally and even nodding once or twice.

"Hilltop is a grand house destined for wonderful things. I believe my husband, Jesse Morgan, knew I would find a way to fulfill that destiny." Finally she drew a breath and put her overactive hands in her lap.

"Commendable." The priest was pensive. "Commendable. I know you are not here just to get my endorsement. What exactly do you need from the Church?"

"We need community support. Not just from St. Mary's, but from all the churches in Laurel. We need volunteers to help with the programs, chaperones to attend, cakes and cookies baked, and as always, we need money. We need to let the community know what is happening at Hilltop. It is my dream to have Laurel embrace the project as if it belonged to everyone. I think the best way to get that community-wide support is through our churches."

Father Sheegan fell very quiet. He drew out his pen and pad and wrote a note or two without looking up. Then he sat with his eyes on his lap.

Gertie wondered what she was to do. Should she leave? Was the meeting over? Then he raised his head and made the sign of the cross at his chest, uttering, "Amen"

"Your project has the blessings of St. Mary of the Mills Church. I'll find a person to spearhead our effort and gather a committee of parishioners to work with you. Maybe six or eight. They will help you gather volunteers and come back to me and the church with specific requests as the program gets off the ground. I am certain all the families with loved ones in the military will be anxious to be a part of this. This same group will sponsor fundraisers." He smiled. "We are very good at that." Gertie smiled back.

"War time is a challenge to the Christian community. We must be in the forefront meeting needs. I think you have come here with the answer to the question we have been asking—what can I do?"

"Father, I am overwhelmed. It is more than I hoped for."

"Child, do not hold yourself back with small hopes." He smiled generously and Gertie responded.

"There is an ecumenical lunch meeting at Gravilla's," he said. "Will you come to the next meeting? First Monday of the month at noon? We will put this proposal to all the pastors. You are a very eloquent spokesman for your mission. I can almost guarantee support from every quarter."

"Thank you. Thank you so much. I'll be there."

"My dear we are all instruments of God. There is no doubt; He woke you up that night. Inspiration like that is not random." He walked her to the door. "One more thing, Gertie, I offer my condolences on the loss of your husband, Jesse. He and I were friends and I miss him. You may not know that he donated the land on Eighth Street behind the church so we could have more hallowed ground for burials. Wouldn't take payment, just asked for prayers for his family. And, that includes you, my dear." She took his hand and held it.

As she stepped out the door a quick breeze blew and she thought she smelled salty sea air. How ridiculous! Salt air here in central Maryland! But, she enjoyed the thought and kept her heart light as she thought of Jesse and the beach. *Our love and memories are in the air tonight, Jesse*

❧

Two days later the chairman of the committee for Hilltop from St. Mary's called to introduce herself. "Hello, Gertie. This is Maggie Chapin and I'm your St. Mary's person for Hilltop. Is this Gertie MacGregor?"

"Yes, Morgan, now."

"I'm Maggie Deaken—Chapin, now."

"Maggie, Maggie. How are you? I haven't seen you for such a long time." Gertie recalled long ago school days with Maggie.

"I went to college in North Carolina and married there. My parents moved down to Winston Salem, too. Now my parents are gone and when Rob died, I decided to come back to Laurel. My two sons are in the army, on their way to England right now—as we speak." She hardly drew a breath. "I'm coming out to see Hilltop and find out what's happening. I'm excited to be a part of a USO at Hilltop in Laurel. We'll make it the very best."

"You bet we will, Mag. Come out Saturday morning about 9:30. I'll have brunch ready and we can catch up and get started."

"I'll be there." Gertie felt this was a wonderful connection to girlhood that had been denied her for too long.

§

Maggie was right on time. "Come in. We're eating in the sunniest room in the house." Gertie led her to the solarium.

Maggie was an open book. She did not hide her amazement at Gertie's home. "I remember this house... and now it is your home?"

"Yes."

Maggie was ready and willing to recite her history without asking Gertie too many questions about hers. "Rob died suddenly and did not plan well for me. The boys send me something every month. I got a small apartment off Main Street. I moved in three weeks ago. I am so appreciative of this job. The salary will pay my rent and put food on my table."

"Salary? Maggie, I cannot offer you a salary."

"Oh, Lordy, no. Gertie. St. Mary's is paying me a salary. I work two days a week there and three here. Plus, I am free on weekends and can fill my empty evenings here as a volunteer. It's perfect. I need a lot to fill the void I live in."

Maggie did not realize that Gertie shared her void and her hope for filling it. *I am trying to fill a void, too,* she thought. *I can't go into a black, blank nothingness like Mom Neal did.*

"Maggie, let's fill our hours working for men and women who are sacrificing for us. We'll wave the red, white and blue, serve coffee and snacks, and pray for our sons on both sides of the globe".

"Sounds like a perfect plan and I am ready to get started."

General Gertie was sure Maggie's enthusiasm for Hilltop USO was the second divine intervention in this plan.

"Tell me about you and Hilltop."

Gertie shared some details of her life—that she had lost two husbands, and William's story. She told about Edward's death and a few facts about Jesse's. Maggie's ears were sympathetic and totally without judgment. She was not too interested in the past. She wanted to know about the plan. Maggie listened intently to Gertie and became totally dedicated to Hilltop USO.

"It will take a lot of work and community effort but if we prove our worth, USO will bring their program and support to Hilltop. That's our mission." Maggie was wide-eyed with enthusiasm. "Come Maggie; let me give you a tour of the house. I hope you can see my vision and offer some new ideas."

"I'd love to see it."

After going from room to room on the main floor Gertie took Maggie up the impressive staircase. "I have a new idea for this floor, too."

"I need an office and you do, too. Look at these two rooms." She took Maggie to the two bedrooms on the front. "Those two rooms," she pointed to the back, "I am keeping personal although I don't plan to live here when the USO is operating…at least not in the foreseeable future."

"An office for me? Great. This is getting more wonderful by the minute."

They began laying out the plans to make Hilltop USO the finest service club of its kind. Maggie brought even better news than Gertie expected. Father Sheegan called each member of the Laurel Ecumenical Council and presented the Hilltop USO to them after his meeting with Gertie. Not wanting to be outdone by their Catholic counterparts, the Methodist, Baptist, Presbyterian, Lutheran, and Pentecostal churches all picked up the banner and joined the army under General Gertie.

On Monday at noon, Gertie went into Gravilla's. She was greeted warmly and she did not have to ask for support; before this Ecumenical Council meeting, each church had called her.

Chapter 38

The work to make Hilltop Manor into Gertie's dream began on a hot day in May 1942. And that same day a moving van came to take some furniture and personal items to Tenth Street where Gertie had converted two apartments back into a single home. Upstairs the galley kitchen was converted to an additional bathroom. Gertie was not concerned to redecorate immediately. She would move into 403 just as it was. She got rid of the furnishings that had been used by her tenants. Old favored pieces and some lovely ones from Hilltop filled the rooms.

The movers passed back and forth across the porch while Gertie sat on a wicker chair and watched. At last the move was accomplished, but something was holding her back. The house was empty—no family was in there. Only memories walked in the rooms. Gertie had trouble believing that possibilities waited inside. Here on the porch, she was between worlds.

"Just me," she announced as she grasped the large brass door latch. She twisted the door bell and heard its familiar jingle. Zingleee. She did it again. Zingleee.

"MacGregors always come home." Gertie moved inside and stepped over the boxes stacked in the front hall. In the kitchen she found a basket with a note.

Gertie,

Welcome back to Tenth Street.
Here is coffee, cream, sugar, and
a percolator, in case you can't find
yours right away. Enjoy a cup of coffee
and sweet rolls. The Neal family is happy
to have you in this house again.

The gift, the coffee, the note brought tears. Not tears that interrupt life, but gentle, soft tears that enhance strong feelings. Gertie found her cups, made coffee, and ate the still warm cinnamon rolls with sticky fingers. Her spirits rose with each delicious bite. *Life is a circle.*

"Gertie! Gertie!" a wonderful, familiar voice broke her reverie.

"In the kitchen, Sam." He picked her up for a hug. "Coffee?" She pointed to an open box. "Get a cup."

"What ya doin'?"

"Mostly thinking. Life is a circle."

"A circle, eh? What about this circle—I live at Hilltop; you're back in the west end." They laughed together at the irony of it.

"I still have my rooms at Hilltop, but you are right, I *am* back here." She took a breath. He let her have the moment. "It feels good." She paused to look around and out the window. "The conversion work at Hilltop is going well, but if I lived there, it would consume me."

"I like Maggie. She is a dynamo—even bosses me around." Sam's opinion made Gertie smile.

"Thank God for Maggie. Everybody likes her and she gets things done. Maggie was so enthusiastic on her first day at Hilltop and her enthusiasm has only grown. She is worth her weight in gold. Not running like clockwork yet, but it will."

"Gertie, your plate is full."

"Yes, I still keep my daily visit to the hospital, but it isn't on my lunch hour. Now I go at two, after the bank closes. Of course, they can call me at any time. My responsibility at the USO on post is scheduling volunteers. As more boys join up, more mothers, sisters and wives volunteer."

"And…you have time to make Hilltop into a USO?" Sam was playing devil's advocate. "How many hours are in *your* day? Mine is still twenty-four."

"That's my baby. It is marvelous. And, like I said, thank God for Maggie."

"OK, Sis. You are wonder woman. You can do it all."

She interrupted. "Sam. I need to have my days filled. Busy is the way I do it. I can't miss Jesse every minute, every hour is enough, and worry about William. You know he is on the Battleship North Carolina somewhere in the Pacific, now."

"Yes, I try to keep up with that situation. His battleship is attached to the Enterprise and that's good. The Enterprise is the greatest carrier."

"The Japanese claimed they sunk the North Carolina twice. General Kellogg called me both times to tell me it was propaganda. I'll die a million deaths before William gets back to Tenth Street. I'll be right here waiting for him."

Sam put his hand on her hair and she thought how long it had been since she had been touched. He changed the subject. "The war isn't going to last forever. Hilltop won't be a USO forever. What then?"

"Sam, I haven't the foggiest."

❦

Gradually transformation took place. Hilltop buzzed with activity as USO officials, volunteers, Maggie, Gertie, and even Bertha, pulled the plan together.

The two bedrooms she kept at Hilltop gave her a retreat after many hours she spent working for the cause. Besides offices for herself and Maggie, a room was set up for volunteers to refresh and relax. Another room was set up for private counseling or as a place where fond farewells could be exchanged. On the third floor two huge rooms were a dormitory with military cots lined up like a barrack. The nightly ticket was twenty-five cents and it provided a layover for those times when a soldier, sailor, airman, or marine had nowhere else to go.

"Hello Private. Did I see you cutting grass yesterday?" she asked a particularly happy young man.

"Yes, ma'am. I got a three day pass and I can't go all the way to Oregon. I'm staying here. I met your brother, Sam. He's keeping me busy."

"Really?"

"Yes, Miss Gertie. I love it. I hope I'm earning my keep."

"You are, soldier."

If a serviceman preferred, he could pay for his cot by doing a chore. A chore list hung by the door and often the fee was paid and a chore was done, too.

The library was expanded to include the latest paperbacks, which could be taken away. There were two cubby corners with desks, stationary, pens, and stamps. The butler's pantry housed the very popular coffee pot, Coca-Cola cooler and cookie trays. There seemed to always be someone to make a new pot or fill a tray.

The dining room became a buffet and once a day sandwiches, vegetable, and fruit trays appeared. The First Baptist Church decided something hot had to be offered so they initiated a soup of the day. It became an instant hit, especially in the cooler months. Lemonade was a real treat, though sugar was a rationed item.

"Jed, do we still have bee hives on the property?"

"Yes'm. Over, pass the orchard."

"We need that honey. Let's harvest it. And Jed, take care of those bees."

Gertie found Bertha in the kitchen. "Tell me, Bertha. Can our cakes and cookie recipes be converted to use honey?"

"I knows how to use honey fo' sugar."

"And, Bertha, I don't want you to wear yourself out in this kitchen. You're up awful early."

"I be up, Miss Gertie, but I's love bakin' fo' our troops. No worry."

✽

Hilltop was known for apples. From the basement cool storage room, Jesse's wonderful apples, in all varieties, filled baskets for every room in Hilltop. A sign on the wall by the steps to the basement gave directions for finding the storage and filling baskets. Gertie never had to go down herself.

A serviceman might come on the shuttle for three to five straight days, learning the ropes, chipping in to help—then he was gone, never to be seen again. Gertie never got used to that and found the only way to deal with the sadness of a missing smile was to turn her smile on for a new face.

The grand foyer did not change. It made such an impression on anyone entering the mansion that Gertie wanted it to remain the same. She placed a huge arrangement of flowers on the side table in front of the mirror as long as there were fresh flowers from the garden. In the winter a colorful arrangement of wax flowers greeted the guests. A huge guest book lay open on a podium ready for everyone to sign and leave comments. She loved to pause before going home at night to read what was written in the book that day.

The wide stairway became the favorite sitting place just as Gertie had imagined. The laughter filtered up and down the staircase and sometimes the whole group broke into song as one of the favorite Bing Crosby songs came from the Victrola. Gertie always stopped what she was doing if the song was, *Don't Fence Me In,* her favorite.

The living room with its two fireplaces became the dance floor. The rugs went into storage and the aged oak hardwood floor developed a patina only dancing could produce. Most of the time music came from the record collection that mysteriously grew and grew. A soldier, unbidden, appeared to tend the records and make sure carelessness did not scratch the precious disks. Dancing was lively and fun. Off in one corner dance lessons were given by several hostesses. On occasion a small dance combo would come in and play. Usually they were service bands who were traveling the bases. After appearing at the club on post, they came to Hilltop. Then the place would swing to the big band sounds done with just a few instruments—but wonderful just the same. Gertie loved it when the weather was warm and the french doors could be opened to the porch and the music and the dancers drifted into the summer's night air. She often sat on the porch to listen and watch.

"A man on the phone says he is Guy Mills." Maggie ran toward Gertie.

"I'm sure he *is* Guy Mills." Gertie took the call in the library.

"Hi, Guy. How is Lorraine?" Maggie stood by with her mouth hanging open. She wanted to hear at least one side of this conversation.

Gertie listened and smiled at Maggie. "I'm good. You should see Hilltop now."

"Can't wait."

"Just say when…perfect…that's wonderful…thank you…I will… you too. Goodbye Guy."

"Tell me, tell me. Are Guy Mills and his band coming to Hilltop?" Maggie was nearly dancing as she talked.

"He'll be here a week from Saturday. And, yes, he is bringing his orchestra. His team will come that morning to set up. We don't have to do anything except have extra food for the crowd."

"I can't believe it."

"It's true, Maggie—believe it. Call a volunteer meeting. You can bet we will have plenty of volunteers and young ladies that night. Let the churches know. The word will spread."

"Will they all stay overnight?"

"No, they will stay at the BOQ on post. But, we need to have food in the volunteers' lounge for Guy and his people. My room will be available if his wife and lady singers come, too." Gertie's mind began working on logistics as they climbed the stairs. "Let the post shuttle know we will need extra trips that night and late ones, too."

Maggie took notes as she followed Gertie.

❦

It was a magical night. Hilltop was filled. The crowd spilled off the porches on to the lawn. The music drifted through the house, out to the solarium and up the beautiful staircase. The dancing was energetic and often romantic. Every favorite was requested and played. Guy Mills looked dashingly handsome in his captain's uniform.

Maggie and the girls from the church youth groups were spellbound.

"Come I'll introduce you." Gertie pulled a suddenly bashful Maggie toward the bandstand.

"Guy, I'd like you to meet Maggie Chapin. She is my right hand here at Hilltop. We could not do all we do without her."

"Well, Maggie Chapin, I am pleased to meet you. After the break we're going to play *Little Brown Jug*. Be sure you are down front with Gertie. I always dance a few bars with the loveliest and most important ladies in the room." He smiled and she tried not to swoon.

The Mills Band was the first of a parade of celebrity entertainers who found their way to Hilltop. Stories of the wonderful venue spread. Many who came to Washington, DC, to entertain the troops, came to Hilltop. Support for Hilltop USO was at times overwhelming.

"Maggie, the budget and parade of celebrities are more than we can manage. The financial management, programs, and entertainment will have to go totally to the USO. The time has come to change how Hilltop is run. Our job will be managing volunteers, hosting and keeping the food fresh. I've called Colonel Collins to come and meet with us again." Gertie sighed. "He was just waiting to get the word from us."

"I agree."

"Hilltop USO has become more than I could envision." She took Maggie by the shoulders and pulled her into a hug. "Maggie, we did it!"

❧

Gertie came to Hilltop often, but not every day. She still had responsibilities at the bank and at the hospital. Her time at the hospital stayed constant. No one could do that job for her. Daily she went to the wounded and wrote their letters, listened to their stories, and gave them a part of herself. The patients that came to Ft. Meade were mostly doing extensive rehabilitation. She made it her mission to get a patient well enough to come to Hilltop. Often the draining work at the hospital brought her to Hilltop to be regenerated.

Gertie never forgot what her patients had faced. She never forgot what happy men and women enjoying Hilltop would have to face in Europe, North Africa, Italy or the Pacific. She knew families were suffering in the absence of their loved ones as she was for William. She never forgot all that Jesse did to support her in these duties and she never forgot Edward.

If a family member of a fallen warrior came to Hilltop, there were specific orders to all volunteers as part of their initial training—Gertie was to be called and the visitor was to be made comfortable until she arrived. Under no circumstances was Gertie to miss such an important visitor.

"Gertie, can you come to Hilltop?" Maggie called her at the bank. "There are visitors from Oregon. They need to see you."

Gertie arrived at the mansion not knowing if she would meet a grieving parent, spouse, sibling, or sweetheart. *Did they lose a soldier, a sailor, an airman, or a marine? Was he dead, missing in action or severely wounded?*

"Mr. and Mrs. Walker, this is Gertie Morgan.

"I am pleased to meet you," She took Mrs. Walker's hand and then Mr. Walker's, looking each in the eye. Invariably the conversation would begin with the story of Hilltop being shared with the family in a letter from their fallen family hero. Often the letter was on Hilltop USO vellum, written in a quiet corner of Gertie's house.

"Johnny wrote about Hilltop USO. In fact he spent a three day pass here."

That struck a familiar note with Gertie—three day pass—Oregon.

"Johnny will not be coming home." Mrs. Walker spoke; Mr. Walker could not. "We wanted to see the place that Johnny enjoyed so much before he shipped out."

"I'm so sorry for your loss. I remember your son, I remember his broad smile. John was on the lawn, cutting our grass. He wanted to be sure he earned his keep while on leave. It wasn't necessary, but he loved doing it."

"We have a big lawn. He always enjoyed…." The story and connection came. Gertie let them talk without interruption or haste.

Emotion ran its course. "He was happy here. You gave him a home away from home. We cannot thank you and your staff enough."

"No need to thank us. We are delighted to have you here just as we were privileged to have Johnny. Let me show you around." Gertie could not always say she remembered a lost boy, but on this day, she could—because she did. It was apparent the Walkers were visualizing their Johnny sitting on the stairs, walking the grounds, dancing to the music just as men and women were doing at this very moment.

Sometimes Gertie was summoned to greet a warrior coming back, not quite the whole piece he once was. He wanted to be at Hilltop so he could relive better days and see the wonders of Hilltop again.

These visitors, not in uniform, were precious to Gertie. She had all the time in the world for each and every one.

❦

One day she found a note from Maggie top and center on her desk.

I need to talk to you. Come find me. Mag

Gertie found her sorting records by the dance floor. "Hi, Mag. What's up?"

"We have a call from the Washington Post. They want to do a story on Hilltop USO. I have a number to call back. John Silverstone. I told him that he would have to talk to you."

"Thanks a lot, friend. What do you think?"

"I don't know, Gertie. It can't hurt. Maybe other people will be inspired to do the same thing. I guess you have to be careful that he gets the story right."

"What do you mean?"

"Make sure he tells what you want him to."

"Oh. I don't like this but I will return his call. Give me the number."

"Hey, Mag. When are we going to do something for fun?" She wanted to change the subject and try to ignore the paper with the number on it.

"I thought this was fun." She threw her arms in a wide circle to encompass the scene.

"You know what I mean."

"Let's go into Baltimore and eat a crab cake and have a beer. Or we can go to Little Italy and stuff ourselves on spaghetti."

"Sounds good. Tomorrow after work?"

"Meet you at the bank at five."

Gertie stared at the number and then put it down on the desk next to the phone. *I don't want to talk to a reporter.* Could this encourage others to open their homes to the USO? Still, she decided to wait until tomorrow. After gathering her things, she headed down the stairs and paused to read the comments in the guest book. She took time to look at the names and all the different states represented. Her hand was on the door knob when the door pushed open almost knocking her down.

"I'm sorry."

"That's alright. Excuse me; my fault."

"I am John Silverstone; looking for Gretta Morgan."

"You have found me, Mr. Silverstone."

"Can I have a minute of your time?"

"You are from the Washington Post. Do you really mean a minute?"

He laughed and his eyes wrinkled kindly. "Five minutes?"

They went up to her office where Gertie offered him a seat in one of the arm chairs by the window. She took the chair beside him, not wanting to sit at the desk and make his five minutes seem more official.

"What can I do for you Mr. Silverstone?"

"I would like to tell the world about Hilltop USO. Take some pictures, do some history and interview some staff, volunteers, and service people."

"I'm trying to see the advantage of that. We really are not looking for any notoriety. We are just a service club like many others. Why not come out to Ft. Meade and do the story? We have a USO on post."

"This is the first USO in this area that is in a private home. It is a community effort and we would like to tell other communities about it. I beg to differ, Mrs. Morgan. Hilltop is not like all the others. My five minutes is up. Here is my card. I would love to get a call from you saying you'll do it."

"Thank you Mr. Silverstone. I will think about it." She was impressed at his discipline to keep it to five minutes as promised.

As he reached the door, he turned, "One thing more. You can read and edit the piece before it goes to press." He smiled; her returned smile was weak.

"I wish I hadn't stopped to look at the guest book," she said to the back of the door John Silverstone had just closed.

Gertie did not want to be interviewed. She did not want to tell her story to the world. She just wanted uniformed heroes to enjoy the beauty and serenity of Jesse's home. Hilltop was special and she knew it. She often wished other towns would do what the citizens of Laurel were doing here. Would this article be important to the men and women she cared so much about? Was she keeping it under a bushel instead of multiplying her talent like the Bible said? All night long she tossed and turned trying to hold her position, but in the morning she knew what she had to do.

"John Silverstone, this is Gretta Morgan."

"I am glad to hear from you, Mrs. Morgan."

"You can call me Gertie—everybody does."

❦

The piece John Silverstone did was beautiful, accurate, and almost complete. The pictures showed the manor, the volunteers, and the service people making the best of the war situation. Gertie worked with Mr. Silverstone to make sure the volunteers, churches, and businesses in Laurel, were given credit for success at Hilltop. Her name was only mentioned once as owner of Hilltop and founder of USO services at Ft. Meade. He went round and round with her as she demanded that the history of Hilltop USO did not include her. He tried and tried to highlight Gertie, but she was steadfast. She controlled the piece and it went to press—not quite complete.

$

Gertie controlled what went into John Silverstone's article, but she had no control over the letters that poured into the newspaper after it went to press. Space would not permit them all to be published, but, a few were printed in the Letters to the Editor section. Gertie was surprised when Maggie came into the office with the paper a week after the Hilltop USO article was published.

"Look at this smarty pants!"

Three letters were printed and each was about the work that Gertie was doing for service men and women. One was from a young man from Alabama who was now serving in Africa. Another was from the mother of a serviceman who had found a home away from home at Hilltop. The last was from a widow in Ohio who quoted from a letter written to her while her husband was sitting in the library at Hilltop just before he was deployed and killed.

"Emma, it is quiet in this library, music is drifting from across the foyer and I feel a peace I haven't felt since I left you and the children. I am away from training, weapons, and impending dangers. It is lovely and kind here. Hilltop USO, nestled in the hills of Maryland is giving me what I need on my last day stateside…."

They were powerful and touching.

Gertie cried. Maggie gave her a tissue and took one for herself.

"That's what it is really all about. You know," said Maggie

"Yes, I know." was all that Gertie could manage.

$

The next day the Washington Post's Editor did his editorial on Hilltop USO.

We can expect our human interest stories to stir emotions, but the reaction to the story done by John Silverstone on Hilltop USO has been more than amazing. It is a truly wonderful piece on a marvelous group of citizens of *Laurel, Maryland who asked themselves, "What can I do?" and came up with a good answer.*

Since the pictures and story went to press we have received almost a thousand letters from military men, women and their families who have been touched by the efforts of one woman who has been serving our service men and women at Ft. George G Meade for most of her life. Mrs. Gretta Morgan started visiting wounded soldiers at the hospital during World War I, founded one service club at the hospital, then another at the recreation center on post. Her latest effort was to unite the community of Laurel to sponsor a USO in their town at her private residence. She is quick to tell you that it is the work of many and we do not dispute that. We also know it takes an idea, an individual and a beginning step to bring a dream to reality. We have read the letters. Space will not allow us to print them all. Let it suffice to note that Mrs. Morgan is a very important person to some very important people—people who have put their lives on the line for us and people who have given the ultimate sacrifice. She shows us that we cannot thank our service men and women enough, even if we did it every day. We salute you, Gretta Morgan.

Chapter 39

Tenth Street was home, but lonely for Gertie. It was different when William's room was waiting for him during his Naval Academy years. Even different from the years he was away before the war. Always before, his bed was made and his treasures decorated the corners, anticipating his return to them. During all those years of youth and adulthood William was her boy, in her mind. Not anymore. A man, not a boy, would come home to Tenth Street—someday. Gertie longed for William's return, but the days they shared under the wall lamp in the kitchen were gone. The world was different.

Gertie took her cup of coffee to the sunny window and longed to look out on the hills at Hilltop. "I'm not the only woman living without a man." She looked at homes down the street. In many, Neal women were longing for husbands spread across the country or across the globe in harm's way. Sadly, two homes on this block in the west end were no longer waiting; their men would not come home again.

"Yuck," Gertie exclaimed, unable to get used to weak unsweetened coffee mandated by coffee and sugar rationing. *We MacGregors like strong coffee with plenty of sugar.* "That's why we can't get used to this." She continued her conversation with the aromatic brew.

Gertie's gas ration coupons were used to get to the hospital, Hilltop and Bear Creek. She resumed walking to the bank each morning and did her shopping at Slater's on her walk home. Her small deprivations were easily adapted to, but not always easy to live with. Cold houses and bare pantries were common in her modest neighborhood. She took everything extra to Hilltop except coal. Gertie shared that with Edward's cousins with small children.

Sacrifice was not the word she used for her reduced life style. Gertie preferred to feel *patriotic* and it was a pervasive feeling. Hilltop was her sacrifice for the war effort and she embraced it, most of the time, but there were times when it hurt—like this morning. At times in the quiet of Tenth Street she wept for the presence of Jesse at Hilltop. It was not easy to leave his home and set up her bed at Tenth Street. It was a homecoming, but it was also a parting.

❦

General Kellogg sought her one afternoon as she was leaving the hospital.

"Gertie we would like to have a brunch for the USO volunteers. Will that work for you? Two weeks from Saturday at ten? The Officer's Club."

"That would be great, sir. Shall I tell Maggie to get invitations out?"

"No, my office will. Get me a list. Except for the list, you, Maggie, and the volunteers don't have to do a thing. The shuttle will pick up everyone at Hilltop at 9:30."

For this special occasion, Gertie went to the safe deposit box and brought the cameo home. Ever since William graduated from the Naval Academy, it had been secure, but unseen like a treasure buried, yet never forgotten.

The beautiful brooch in its small box lay under insurance papers, marriage and birth certificates, in the metal box in the vault. Today she retrieved it from its dark place. She was again struck by its beauty. Grandmother Amsterdam had impeccable taste. The large pin, almost two inches from top to bottom was oval, the delicate gold filigree frame framed the beautiful face carved in *bas relief*. "Sixteen," she counted. The diamonds were small and brilliant. Soft peach color and pure white artistry brought life to the piece. The delicately carved face was beautiful. Gertie looked closer. *Grandmother? Mom Neal?* For the first time, she saw a resemblance. *My imagination?* She wondered.

"Silly, you are missing those ladies." She exclaimed while still in the vault. The box was slipped carefully into her purse before returning the safe deposit box and turning the key.

Imagination or not, Gertie could hardly wait to get home and look at it again. She laughed at herself as she walked back to her office.

In the lamp light at the table that evening the cameo looked back at her. "It *is* Grandmother." Gertie wondered why she hadn't seen it before. On the back, she found a mark and a signature. With the help of a magnifying glass, she looked again. It was a small hand holding a flame and the signature was *Morellini*. Gertie took a pencil and paper, tried to reproduce the mark, wrote the name, folded the paper and put it in her wallet. She resolved to go to the library and research them, but never found time to sit in the library. What she did do was buy a deep coral dress with a large white square collar—a dress that would show her cameo off to perfection at the volunteer's brunch.

The occasion was gracious and informal. A large thank-you cake centered the table. It was wonderful to have all the volunteers from Hilltop and the post together to socialize.

General Kellogg spoke a few words and invited Gertie to come to the microphone.

"I would like to add my thanks to those of General Kellogg. Our efforts on behalf of the men and women serving our country, is never a chore; it is a privilege and a pleasure. Working with you makes it more so. We will serve as long as we are needed. God Bless the United States of America."

❧

Several days later Father Sheegan visited Hilltop to show a fellow priest the USO and the work done there by his parishioners.

"Is Gertie here, Mag? I would like for her to meet Father Oranzio."

"Yes. She's upstairs. I'll get her." Mag returned and invited the two men to come to Gertie's office. "Go up the stairs. It is the second door on the right. You'll see the open door; she's expecting you. Would you like coffee or tea?"

"Coffee would be nice."

Gertie was delighted to greet her old friend and to meet the priest from Italy. The activities downstairs filtered up with soft sounds of a Benny Goodman record.

"Gertie, this is my friend, Father Oranzio."

"Pleased to meet you, Father."

"How is William? What do you hear?"

"I get letters sporadically and each one is a life line. The Japanese claimed they sank his ship, the North Carolina, four times. But, thankfully, I have an inside line at Ft. Meade and they assure me, each time, its propaganda. I'm keeping the faith along with all the families, Father."

"I will pray for William in all my supplications, my child."

"Thank you." She took a deep breath and brought her thoughts back to Hilltop. "Did you take Father Oranzio around Hilltop so he could see all that is happening downstairs?" she asked.

"It is wonderful," replied Father Oranzio in perfect English with an Italian accent.

It was very easy to talk about Hilltop, Gertie's favorite subject. "In the war effort, we are all looking for something we can do."

"I have been working mostly with saving the artifacts of our poor war torn country. The war has been very hard on Italy. I have been here in America all the time raising money to get the art work to safe places. Fortunately or unfortunately, I was here when the war broke out and the Vatican decided I could do more from here." Father Oranzio's face showed his compassion for his native land. "It has been very rewarding, but at times I feel guilty that I'm not in Italy to bear the cross of fascism." He turned his attention and his countenance to a happier thought. "The generosity of Americans is amazing, and not only Americans of Italian descent are helping with this rescue effort. We are getting support from all quarters."

"So you are a student of the arts; how wonderful to work to save those treasures."

"No, I was an accountant in the Vatican. Now, I collect monies to save art. But, we have to accept our new roles just as the carpenter becomes a warrior. I knew very little about the artifacts, except how beautiful they are. I have spent much time in museums and libraries to become somewhat of an expert.... a lot of time studying art and architecture in the last three years. When you go to a parish to beg for money you need to explain what you are trying to save."

"Father Oranzio was able to identify that lovely vase that was saved from the ashes in the Baltimore fire. Remember seeing it in my reception room?"

"Yes. I remember."

"It is seventeenth century Venetian glass, blown by Federico Pastaulli with twenty-four carat overlay. A real treasure."

"I wonder, Father Oranzio, does the name Morellini mean anything to you? It is on a piece of jewelry I have."

"No, my dear. I am sorry; I do not know that name and do not handle any jewelry. The Vatican has its own expert in that department."

The visit went on for a while and they enjoyed a cup of coffee before the priests departed. Gertie was disappointed that she did not find an easy answer to her question, but enjoyed the visit immensely. "Gertie, Father Oranzio is doing the eleven o'clock mass tomorrow if you would like to join your Catholic friends. We look forward to your visit to St. Mary's."

"I'm sorry Father. I am leaving shortly to spend the weekend with my family at Bear Creek near Baltimore."

At the door Father Sheegan placed his hand over hers. "I saw the article and editorial in the Washington Post. Excellent, excellent." He had waited to the last moment to say this because he knew Gertie this compliment would cause her some embarrassment.

"Thank you, Father. Good-bye. *Arrivederci,* Father Oranzio."

❦

The following Wednesday a note was placed on her desk asking Gertie to return a call to John Petrone. She had no idea who this was and was a bit put out that her secretary did not get her some information about the reason for the call. It had been a hard day—one of those days when the tellers did not prove and the Federal Reserve was changing some policies that would affect cash flow. She called a meeting of the board and didn't have time to guess who John Petrone was. On the other hand, if he was from the Federal Reserve, she needed to return the call. Gertie quickly shuffled though some bank documents on her desk to see if that name appeared on any she had to present to the board. Nothing there.

"Sandra." she called her secretary. "Do you have a clue on this message to call John Petrone? Is it bank business?"

"Sorry, Gertie. He gave his name and number and before I could ask—hung up."

Gertie had ten minutes before the meeting. She dialed the number and found herself talking to a child. She left a message, but had no confidence it would be delivered to John Petrone. At least she knew he was not Federal Reserve. Gertie wadded the note and discarded it from her desk and mind.

The following Friday, Maggie announced to Gertie that John Petrone was down in the foyer, asking to see her. It took a minute to recall the phone message of last week. Gertie's curiosity was tweaked. She rose to greet him.

"Hello, Mrs. Morgan. I'm John Petrone a friend of Father Oranzio."

He was dressed in a suit and tie, but everything about him was unkempt. The tie was cocked, his suit un-pressed and his dark hair had not yielded to the comb. His pockets seemed to be stuffed with unimaginable treasures. He looked Gertie straight in the eye and smiled a most friendly smile. He reminded her of a younger version of Poppa— his pockets were always full of treats for the kids and horses.

"Oh, yes, yes." *Father Oranzio*, she remembered. "Come, have a seat."

John Petrone sat and had trouble finding a place for his hands—not folded across his chest, not in his lap. He grasped the arm rest as if to control them there. It didn't matter, as soon as he started talking, his hands were flying.

"Father asked me to come and see you about a piece of jewelry possibly made in Italy? He thought I might be able to help you and suggested that I come to Hilltop instead of the bank." John Petrone went on to explain his credentials as a jewelry appraiser specializing in Italian pieces. "Do you want to talk to me about your item? I don't want to seem forward in coming here, Mrs. Morgan. I'm not a buyer; you understand?"

She liked him and the way he explained himself. "Please call me Gertie, and may I call you John?" He nodded and his full shock of hair nodded too.

"It was very nice of Father Oranzio to send you to me. I would love to talk to you about my cameo." She paused for emphasis. "I would never sell it. It is much too dear to me. I have had it for a long time. I got it out to wear to an important occasion and became curious about it. Unfortunately the lovely lady who gave it to me has passed away."

"I see."

"It has the name Morellini on it."

John Petrone sat up straight and his tie came straight, too. "I know Morellini's work. Could I possibly see it?"

"I'd like to show it to you but it is not here at Hilltop. Could we make an appointment for you to come back? I will bring it here." Gertie could see he was excited, and she was excited to show it to him.

$

John Petrone arrived back at Hilltop right on time for their appointment. They took coffee on the porch where the morning sun warmed the corners.

"John, thanks for making two trips here. I appreciate it."

There were very few people at Hilltop this morning, but the volunteers were busy getting ready for the Saturday crowd that would begin to assemble at noon. This would be a special night as the Second Army Band from Ft. Meade would be here. John was curious about Hilltop and they took a minute to talk about the goings on and to watch the preparations in the great room. Coffee and sweet rolls were on the table along with fresh flowers and the small box. They looked out across the orchard, heavy with fruit.

"Do I see apples?"

"Yes. Unfortunately, I can't get them harvested. We pick for our use and occasionally a soldier will walk over and pick enough to make pies for our guests but even with occasional pickers, too many go to waste."

"Oh, Gertie. I have seven children and five of them are old enough to pick fruit. It would be so good for them to spend some time picking apples."

"Bring them anytime and you can keep all the fruit you want." If there was one thing Gertie loved, it was finding people who wanted to share fruit from Hilltop's orchard.

John reached into his sport coat pocket, rummaged around and drew out his eyeglass as Gertie passed the box to him. He was subdued by the cameo. He took his time looking at the front and turning it over. He studied the carving, and the gold work. And then, he did it all again.

"The person who gave this to you… how old would she be if she were alive today?"

"Let me see…Grandmother Amsterdam would be about 90 or 92."

"Hmmm…." Gertie poured more coffee as John again turned the cameo and studied with the glass to his eye. Finally, he put the glass down, held the piece, and looked at it with the naked eye. He handed it to Gertie as if he had taken too much of it for himself.

"It's a wonderful cameo. Not often do I get to see such a work of art. I can tell you about the artist and the marks. Morellini is one of the best cameo makers, if not the best of Italian carvers. His work is well known and highly prized. The hand and flame is his mark and it interprets his name. There is also a small mark on the gold filigree. Look here." He gave Gertie the glass and pointed so she could see the sword.

"That's Tiffany. I believe the cameo was carved in Italy, sent to New York and set by Tiffany & Co."

"Morellini died in 1901. This was made prior to the turn of the century—probably mid nineteenth. Do you think it was purchased in New York or is it possible it was bought in Italy and brought to Tiffany by your benefactor?"

"I don't know. John. When I took it from the box recently I was struck by the resemblance of the cameo to Grandmother Amsterdam, She gifted the brooch to me. At first, I thought it was my imagination, but I have studied it and it does resemble her. Is it possible it is her image?"

"Ah. That is such a delicious clue!" John could not believe his good fortune and could not resist taking the cameo again, in his hands. At times, an appraiser came across pieces that were so valuable and other times a piece so rare. Of the two, it was the rare one that made his blood rush. He had become immune to the high sparkle of expensive jewels unless they were set in a unique way. He would never cease to be enthused when a rare piece spoke clearly of art. He was holding one right now. He had many questions for the lovely woman sitting patiently, allowing him to enjoy the cameo.

"Did your Grandmother go to Italy as a young girl? Could she have met Morellini? Did she tell you this was her image?"

"I am sorry, I don't know if she ever went to Italy and she never said it was a likeness. She was my husband's Grandmother and I didn't meet her until we were married. I do know they were a family of means and her father traveled a lot."

"Well, this is exquisitely carved. I would like to do some more studies on Morellini to see if he did other likenesses. As far as appraisals, this piece has several values depending on what your intentions are. You are not interested in the auction value."

"No."

"For insurance purposes it should be insured for $15,000 to $18,000. However, if we had provenance to prove it is a likeness, its value would almost double as Italian museums would be interested."

"I'll take your advice and insure it and if you discover anything else about Morellini and my cameo, I'd love to know it."

"It has been my pleasure, Gertie. I'll surely thank Father Oranzio for bringing us together. You'll get a report from me on the cameo."

"Thank you, John…and don't forget to include a bill for your time."

"You can pay me in apples." he laughed.

As she walked him to the door, she remembered one more thing. "John, I have a picture of Grandmother when she was a girl that is so like the cameo. Wait, I will run get it."

They sat on the bottom step of the beautiful staircase and looked at the picture and the cameo side by side.

"Amazing." was all that John Petrone could say.

The true story of Gertie's cameo lay in the wooden chest labeled *Edward's Things*, and stored with William's things. Deep in the chest Edward's manuscript has a chapter titled *Grandmother Amsterdam*. It had her story of her trip to Italy long, long ago as told to her favored grandson. It did not matter; this cameo would never be sold or loaned to an Italian museum.

Neither William's box nor the manuscript would change what Gertie believed about the wedding gift. Grandmother Amsterdam knew life with her disturbed grandson would not be easy for his bride. Her advice to keep it safe and in reserve was like a safety net or parachute to Gertie. Just knowing she had it made her feel secure enough to take important risks in her life.

Gertie went to the bench in the orchard with the cameo in her hand. Before she started her contemplations, she picked a ripe apple and bit though its sharp red skin to the juicy sweet body. She spoke to the serene face looking back from its soft, velvety, diamond circled setting.

"Grandmother, this gift gave me strength and I hope some of your style. I am truly the only one who can appraise its worth. I look at it with my heart."

Grandmother had thought long and hard about giving the cameo to this girl. She prayed for guidance. God, should I give this gift to Edward's bride?

Her precious brooch was meant for Mary Neal's firstborn and yet she could not trust it to Edward. She wanted to give her grandson something wonderful, but the most she could hope was that this gift given the girl he married, would sustain them in life. The gift that Grandmother gave was not the cameo to Gertie...it was Gertie to the cameo. Gertie had to believe she deserved it and she had to believe she could save it— as well as save herself.

❦

Gertie would not be sitting on this bench, at Hilltop, in the orchard eating an apple, holding the cameo, if she had been less than Grandmother hoped. The divine intervention in her life wasn't the precious jewel, it was Grandmother's faith.

Chapter 40   1945

Hilltop was Jesse. To Gertie, they were one and the same. The beautiful colonial manor house wrapped Gertie in Jesse's love and it allowed her to return to those years with him. But, the old house at 403 Tenth Street gave her a place to weather the war. She restored 403 to its turn of the century beauty both inside and out. The wide front porch had white wicker and ferns and the siding gleamed white. The shutters were dark green almost black. Rooms were arranged to the original floor plan. Gertie needed this house. She returned from the bank, the hospital, or Hilltop USO, tired and spent to smile at visible reminders of times spent here with her son.

When war news was dark and false reports continued on the fate of William's ship, she needed Tenth Street. When air raid exercises required black shades, and when Gabriel Heatter detailed battles in his broadcasts, she needed Tenth Street. When fear that tranquil life with William and Louisa would never come, she needed her home on Tenth Street. She needed to see the Neal house next door; she needed to see the garden grow across the fence in summer and the painted maple trees in fall. And she needed to walk up Fergus Hill and down Montgomery Street to the bank, because that was who she was… and with war-time's drama blasting her senses… it was sometimes hard for Gertie to remember who she was.

❦

On September 3, 1945 Gertie stepped on the porch of 403 Tenth Street and joined her neighbors. The news had just arrived. It was time to celebrate. Japan surrendered yesterday, ending the war in the Pacific. The Neals and their neighbors celebrated four months earlier when Germany surrendered, but until the three west end navy men, including

William, were out of harm's way, the celebration was tempered. Today it was unconditional joy and Gertie wept.

❧

Gertie pulled herself from sleep and lifted the phone receiver. "Yes."

"Gertie Morgan, I have a long distance call from San Diego."

She was full awake now. "Yes, this is Gertie Morgan."

"One moment, please."

"Gertie, Louisa. William just called me from Hawaii."

"Oh, Louisa. Praise God. How is he?"

"He's great." Louisa started to cry tears of relief. "He's safe." Sob. "He's on our—" sob, "—side of the ocean." Sob. "I'm sorry Gertie. I can't stop crying."

Gertie was crying, too. "We've been waiting for this call, Louisa. Don't apologize for your tears, I'm crying, too."

"The war ended, but until he. . ." Louisa broke down completely.

"—until he was safe," Gertie finished her thought. "I know, dear one. Until he was safe, we could not cry these tears of joy. When will you see him?"

"Su... Sunday. He'll be in port *here* in seven days. We'll call."

The operator interrupted, "Two minutes."

"Good night, Gertie."

"Good night, Louisa...and thank you."

Gertie put the phone on its cradle and slid out of bed to her knees.

"Heavenly Father, thank you for bringing William out of harm's way. Please accept my grateful prayer for all returning warriors and their families. We praise your Name and your mercy. Help us to be worthy of the blessing of William's safe return. Amen."

She rose from the floor and crawled back in bed. But, it was useless, she could not sleep. Peaceful sleep on Tenth Street was gone. She picked up the phone again.

"Bertha, I'm sorry to waken you."

"I's not be sleepin' yet. Anythin' wrong, Miss Gertie?"

"Everything is wonderful. Louisa called to tell me William is safely back in Hawaii."

"Dat's sooo good."

"I'm coming to Hilltop. I'll be there in twenty minutes."

"Meetcha at the do'r. Miss Gertie. Come on home."

As soon as she decided to go she felt comforted. Her joy and her relief had to be shared with Jesse and that could only happen in the orchard at Hilltop.

🐌

"Sam! Sam!" Gertie called as she ran over the Hilltop's lawn toward the stables. "Where are you?" She waved a letter.

"This better be important," he called back. "I'm mucking stalls. I *love* this job and hate interruptions." He laughed as he saw the grin on his sister's face. "Must be news from William." he correctly surmised.

"The North Carolina is headed to Norfolk."

"OK, we expected that…"

"Then it is assigned to the Naval Academy for training midshipmen. William is really coming home."

"I'm happy for you, Gertie. Really happy." He pulled his gloves off and rubbed her hair. "William is coming home…" Sam was for a moment, overcome.

"That's not all. He said Louisa is getting ready to come to Maryland… and she's pregnant."

"William used his time in California wisely. That's my boy. Good ole American returning hero. Lots of babies born will be born this year and next."

"1946—August." Gertie got pensive. "A grandchild in August. 'My cup runneth over.' He'll call me when he gets to Norfolk. I can hardly wait."

🐌

The call came. William was finally home. The long wait was over. Life was to be reclaimed.

Gertie, William and Louisa gathered on the porch at 403.

"Louisa and I are ready to start our life on Tenth Street. We want you to stay with us—here, at 403. We have plenty of room and would love to have you. We don't want to take your home away from you."

"It's your home, William. I want to see you and Louisa playing with William, Jr. or Little Elizabeth Mae in this yard. You're not taking anything from me. I've been living in your house, but now it's time for me to move back to Hilltop, and I'm ready." She took William's hand. "I need time with Jesse in his home. I'm actually looking forward to reclaiming Hilltop as my own. And, my mind is made up." William understood his mother and yielded to her MacGregor mind.

"I get that, but it's so big."

"I have Bertha and she needs me now that Jed is gone. I have a plan and if Maggie—you remember Maggie, my right hand at Hilltop USO? If she's agreeable, I won't be there alone. I'm going to ask her to move in with me."

Gertie hatched a plan when it became apparent that the work of Hilltop USO was done. Maggie was delighted at the invitation to live there with Gertie, but had some concerns.

"I'd love to live at Hilltop but, frankly, Gertie, I can't. I can't pay my way."

"I have an idea. Come sit down."

The two ladies went into the library to draw on the natural comfort of the room. Bertha had set a dessert tray and coffee service on the game table.

"Are you trying to ply me with Bertha's apple pie? What's your scheme, Gertie?"

"Alright, I admit, I have a scheme," she replied as she sliced the pie.

Maggie took her pie and coffee and let Gertie continue.

"'Hilltop Orchard Bed, Breakfast, and Apple Pie'. I can see the sign by the drive. It will have the white mansion and a big apple tree loaded with red apples. How inviting is that with *Apple Pie* on the sign? Tell me, who could resist? "

"Mmmm. . . delicious," Maggie replied with a mouth full of sweet apples and flaky crust.

"Are you talking about the pie or the idea?"

"The *idea!*" Maggie gulped to clear her mouth. "Gertie if you decide to do that, I'll work my tail off for you."

"Oh, I've decided…and I can't do it without you."

"When do we start?"

"As soon as we can move in and begin." Gertie opened her notebook. "Here are some things we have to think about."

Maggie saw that Gertie was prepared. Her tenure as bank president had taught her about organization. "I have a list."

"Why am I not surprised?" Maggie replied as she took another small piece of pie.

"I'm going to be right up front with you. A bed and breakfast will not support this place, but it will give me and Bertha, and you, a purpose. I want to keep Hilltop lovely. I hope income from our little enterprise will help me maintain the interior to my husband's standards." Gertie broke her own rule and had a second small slice of pie. Took a bite and began to talk with the taste of pie in her mouth. "And—" she interrupted her own thoughts. "—this pie is so good. Why am I continually surprised at Bertha's cooking?" She cleared her palate with coffee. "Maggie, I have a bigger dream. I would eventually like to have a full restaurant here. I haven't told Bertha yet, but I want her to write down her recipes. I want Bertha to retire at Hilltop and watch master chefs prepare her dishes. Can you imagine? People will come in droves for Bertha's southern comfort food."

"Yes, I can imagine that.

The next morning, Gertie was sitting on the bench in the orchard when the sun broke the horizon and gave the first rays of sunshine to the promised beautiful day. The trees were budded with promise, too. A few had burst and slight pink color dotted the trees that would soon be saturated with pink and white beauty. Her sweater kept her shoulders and arms warm to match the feeling she had inside.

Gertie focused on an open blossom in the lowest branch before her. *I love you little blossom.* And, almost unbidden the next thought came. *I see the apple.*

The sun pushed all the night shadows away and advanced to the bench. "Good morning, Jesse." She was quiet for a moment while she waited for her soul to acknowledge that he was there. "We saw the apple in the blossom, didn't we, Love?"

His answer came on the first warm spring breeze.

Gertie left the bench and orchard with one last thought, which she put in the air over Hilltop. "Bertha and I are going to make apple pies—lots of apple pies!" She laughed and almost danced back across the lawn to the house.

Chapter 41   1946

As the Army limousine drove up to Hilltop, Gertie straightened her light blue gabardine dress for the umpteenth time. The white collar on the matching blue jacket was straight and her cameo was pinned on the left. The mirror in the entry hall reflected her stubborn lock of curly hair. Gertie tucked it into the bun on her neck and started a dialogue with the woman in the mirror. Before she could go to the day ahead, she had to pause for some memories here in Hilltop's foyer.

"Fifty-one birthdays. Where have the years gone? When I was twenty-one I let my hair down and it was shocking. Full circle, Gertie, your hair is back in a bun." She looked twice at the strands of grey she saw among her curls and longed for Jesse's touch. It was a longing that made her young again. She turned from the reflection with a knowing smile directed up the stairs.

Then her eyes traveled down her throat to the cameo.

Funny how this can bring a rush of emotion, she thought as her fingers circled it instinctively. Gertie remembered Grandmother Amsterdam. *I came close to selling. But, I still have it and someday it will go to our namesake, Elizabeth Mae.* She touched William's daughter's picture on the table.

The beautiful cameo and Hilltop Manor were two material things that Gertie loved. And yet, it was who they represented that stirred her emotion.

It is time to go. Gertie took her clutch purse under her arm and went out the door. The general's aide opened the limo door and she slipped comfortably into the plush back seat, and looked around at the interior and out at Hilltop. The car's modern interior and window made a frame for the stately white house. At that irony, Gertie smiled.

Already seated in the car was John H. Grantham, Adjutant General of Ft. George G. Meade, Maryland.

"Good Morning, Gertie. You look lovely."

"Thank you, Sir. I hope my nervousness doesn't show."

"Not at all. You look your usual calm self. No need to be nervous. This is a special day for you. Relax so you can enjoy and take it all in."

"I know. I've been telling myself," she replied, actually relaxing a little with his conversation.

"Let me tell you a little about what to expect. When we arrive, the Protocol Officer will brief us on everything—where to stand, how to greet dignitaries and the program. If you have questions, don't hesitate to ask. Eleanor Roosevelt nominated you for this honor and the United States Army wrote your recommendation. I'll introduce you and recount some of the USO activities at Ft. Meade and Hilltop Manor. I don't know how many honorees there will be today. We will be told when we arrive. We could be first; we could be last Are you prepared to say a few lines to accept the award?"

"Yes, sir. Thanks for giving me a heads-up on that. I've been working on it for weeks. Three weeks—three lines. I should be able to do that," she smiled.

The General smiled with her, enjoying her company and genuine effort to do this as she had tackled every task he had seen her accomplish since his assignment at Ft. Meade. He long ago decided that she was the warmest standoffish woman he had ever met. She gave every man notice, without saying a word—hands off. General Grantham, a widower, had a crush on her early on, but he had long since gotten past that impossible path. "Lieutenant," he spoke to the driver, "see if you can get some good music on that radio. We are going to enjoy this ride into DC." The car moved down Montgomery Street to US 1. Gertie looked at the train station where Edward first worked and where she met Jesse. She shook her head to bring her thoughts back to this day.

The day was overcast but warm. The trees were showing tarnished leaves heralding the end of summer. They crossed the District line and read the sign, "Welcome to The Nation's Capital City – Washington, DC – God Bless America." Rows of brick and stone town houses lined like a parade along their route. People were busy on their daily missions and hardly noticed the limousine in this town of important people and important cars.

Gertie listened to the sounds of Frank Sinatra and his latest #1 hit for 1946, *Come Rain or Come Shine*. She let her mind wander back over the years to William's graduation, thirteen years ago.

"Where is William now?" General Grantham knew Gertie's favorite subject.

"William finished his post war assignment at the Naval Academy. We were so fortunate that he was so close to home this past year. His new assignment is Manila, Philippines. He left three weeks ago. He would have loved to be here, but that was impossible. The Navy isn't too concerned about what's important to his mother back home."

"There will be pictures taken. You can send him one. Does he like his duty?"

"It isn't as exciting as the war years, you know. He loved working with midshipmen at the Academy, but he wanted to be at sea. Now he is decommissioning battleships and bringing them home. But I am happy with his duty and grateful that he passed through the war safely."

"I know; I feel the same about my boys. John is out now and enrolled at Yale. Ron hasn't decided if he wants to make the Marines a career. He's at Lejeune and has plenty of time to make up his mind."

"Here we are at Pennsylvania Avenue, Sir," said the lieutenant. "We pick up the escort now...there they are just like clockwork."

The small motorcades preceded them to the West Gate and onto the White House drive. Gertie was speechless as she looked over the magic world inside the high iron fence. The General did not talk; he did not want to interrupt her experience.

The White House glistened like a pearl under the clearing blue sky and atop the green lawn. Never had the red, white and blue seemed so vibrant and perfect, blowing overhead. Each Marine guard, in perfect dress uniforms, was magnificent. The huge hanging light in the portico and the green topiaries flanking the door were just as they were always pictured. The limo door opened and Gertie stepped into the scene.

Gertie was introduced to the President's chief advisor, General Grantham offered his arm, and she was on her way into the *People's House*.

I've got to remember all of this, she made the mental note. *William*, her mind called to him.

The protocol officer was introduced, but Gertie, in all the emotion, did not get her name. That didn't matter. General Gantham had her arm, and she listened carefully to instructions. She heard the line-up and realized that both the president and former first lady would be standing beside her.

"You are the only honoree in today's ceremony, Mrs. Morgan. Do you have any questions?"

"No."

"I will be standing by if you need me. I'll tell the President—we are ready."

Harry S. Truman was a small figure with a warm smile that could have lived on Tenth Street. He was shorter than Eleanor Roosevelt, who matched General Grantham in stature. Gertie tried to keep from being awestruck by these national heroes as they came to the portico. The President advanced to her, extended his hand, and with great charm, put her at ease.

"I am so pleased to meet you Gretta Morgan. Allow me to introduce Eleanor Roosevelt."

"Mrs. Morgan, I have looked forward to meeting you since I became aware of the work you have done for our uniformed troops. Is Hilltop USO still open"? Eleanor Roosevelt was as gracious and warm as her reputation. They talked as they walked into the house.

"Yes, Mrs. Roosevelt, but, we have scaled back considerably and are preparing to close by the end of the year. I will be making Hilltop my home again, soon."

"I would love to visit."

"I hope you will. It would be our pleasure and honor. Please come soon."

Eleanor Roosevelt turned to her assistant. "Find a time on my calendar and call Mrs. Morgan."

President Truman stepped up beside the two ladies. "Mrs. Morgan, I have been briefed on all you have accomplished on behalf of our service men and women. You are to be commended and I am about to do that."

"Thank you Mr. President. It is not easy to be so honored and singled out when many have done the same. It has been a privilege for me to be in the company of our military. We could never do enough."

"That is precisely why you are here today. You represent many, I know, but you have set precedence for using community resources and volunteers. You have been a pioneer and your leadership brought many communities into like service." He looked up at his aide who signaled from the door. "Let us go forward for the ceremony." He took her arm and turned her toward the Rose Garden where a podium was waiting and an audience was seated. "Relax and enjoy this. This place can be overwhelming, but it is just a house with a yard." He smiled with a twinkle in his eye.

The US Army Band played *Hail to the Chief.* The Commander in Chief saluted, everyone took their seats. Gertie looked out across the gathered people and first noticed they were all in uniform. Then she noticed a familiar face—General Kellogg, Nurse Parker, Nurse Shaw—and another and another. . . .

Gertie began to look at individual familiar faces and in the front row she saw...William.

William, you are here! She wanted to run to him. A broad smile lit her face.

President Truman spoke. "We have gathered men and women who have passed through your care, Gretta Morgan."

William stood when the President spoke his mother's name. He walked to the space that suddenly opened between Gertie and Eleanor Roosevelt. Then everyone rose to their feet, led in applause by President Truman, Eleanor Roosevelt, General Grantham, and William.

It took all of her concentration to stand there but it became easier when William stood beside her, slipped his arm under hers, and gripped tightly. He leaned over and whispered, "Gertie."

Dear William . . . and all these dear people.

General Grantham advanced to the microphone as everyone else took a seat.

"It is my pleasure to introduce Gretta Morgan. She has served you, and many others through World War I and World War II. Mrs. Morgan took a place at the bedside of patients at Ft. Meade Army Hospital for the last twenty seven years, and continues to do so today. It is quite possible that at this important moment in her life, she is thinking about a soldier in a bed at Ft. Meade Army Hospital." He paused to smile at her. "Mrs. Morgan activated service clubs in the hospital and on post. When the USO came into being in 1942, she worked to turn those two clubs into USO's for the thousands of military who processed through Ft. Meade. But she did not stop there. Mrs. Morgan turned her home, Hilltop Manor, into a special USO and enlisted the whole

Laurel, Maryland community to make sure it was a success. Because of her actions, many communities located near military facilities, did likewise. Mrs. Morgan answered the question—*what can I do?*— in a most wonderful way. Join me in a warm welcome for our honoree, Gretta Morgan."

Eleanor Roosevelt advanced to the microphone. "Gretta Morgan, I have been contacted by families of service men and women who have passed under the umbrella of your care. You have cheered and welcomed many, but more importantly, you have comforted and blessed many. Your service at the bedside is valued high above any honor we can bestow today. When a mother, father, wife, husband or child takes the time to write to me about you, I know you have put your mark on their lives and served your country unselfishly. I was most happy and privileged to recommend you for this award."

William escorted Gertie from her seat to stand beside the President who stood next to the podium.

"In recognition of your dedicated service to our veterans and service men and women it is my pleasure to bestow the Medal of Freedom to you, Gretta Morgan on behalf of the American people. This medal honors civilians whose actions aided in the war efforts of the United States. Since 1918, you have given your time and resources so that those serving our country, at home and abroad, would know they were appreciated. The White House has received many letters from families thanking us for the service you have rendered to their loved ones. Mrs. Eleanor Roosevelt nominated you and the distinguished Senator from Maryland introduced the bill to Congress on Dec 7, 1945, the fourth anniversary of Pearl Harbor Day. Your success in developing three USO centers is well documented. Your own home, Hilltop Manor, in Laurel, Maryland became a home away from home for many of those assembled. I am also aware of the countless hours you have spent at veterans hospitals. You came to the bedsides of our wounded taking the place of family who could not be with their loved one. Mrs. Morgan, we are touched by the number of wounded and dying service personnel you have served. In spite of hardship and personal obligations, you have never failed to come to the bedside when needed. The Medal of Freedom is designed to honor civilians who have served over and above expectations in our successful war effort. Gretta Morgan, you have earned this honor. One of the best jobs that come with the Presidency is stepping up to say, thank you on behalf of my fellow Americans. Thank you..." he fixed his gaze on her. "...and congratulations Gretta Morgan." President Truman placed the medal, pinned to red white and blue ribbon, around her neck.

Led by the President, applause filled the air as everyone rose to their feet. Gertie was overwhelmed. She concentrated on William's arm, strong under hers as he led her to the microphone. It would be a challenge to deliver her few lines after such an emotional display. William stepped back and she was alone in the center of the universe, but she had a strange feeling of being at home—at Hilltop when she would descend the staircase and see the same sea of uniforms she was looking upon now. It was that same feeling as walking into the hospital and meeting whatever challenges her sick charges may present. It was that same ability to meet those challenges that brought her voice—loud and clear.

"Mr. President, Mrs. Roosevelt, distinguished guests; I am honored to receive the Medal of Freedom, which I will cherish. It is dedicated to the continuation of work on behalf of our service men and women. Not *one* of them should ever wonder if their sacrifices are appreciated. Their courage begins when they put on that uniform and walk away from the safety and love of their families and goes on across the globe as they meet every test. I am one of many who volunteer in USOs and VA Hospitals around the world and I humbly accept this for them." Her hand traced the medal and she looked into the camera that was recording. "And, I ask my fellow Americans to greet a uniformed hero warmly wherever you might see them. They are your sons and daughters far from home. Tell them, *thank you*." Gertie's face and demeanor changed. She became an advocate of service and continued with unprepared remarks. *"Join* me at the bedside of a veteran. You are needed and you will be rewarded tenfold for being there. Remember their sacrifice is for us and our wonderful United States of America. Thank you."

President Truman stepped back to the microphone. "We have assembled many who would like time to reminisce with you. There is a reception prepared in the Blue Room. The 2nd Army Band is here from Ft. Meade to serenade this occasion. Let the photographers take their pictures and then Commander Neal, please escort your mother into the White House."

The President leaned in closely. "Before I leave, Bess asked me to greet you. I'm to call you *Gertie*, at least once. My wife was always known by her nickname and we love yours. All good wishes from the Trumans... Gertie."

"Thank you, sir. Mrs. Truman and I have something very nice in common. I appreciate your good wishes."

As William walked to the entrance with his Mother on his arm, those assembled in this magnificent room, called out, in unison, "Gertee. Ger-tee. Ger-tee." And it continued until she left William's arm and began to circulate.

William looked down as his mother melted into the sea of blue, white, and khaki uniforms. It was her universe. *One of a kind. They think she's wonderful and they don't know the half of it!* He decided to wade into the sea of men and women who loved his mother and join their conversations.

Gertie was as clear-headed as she had ever been in her life as her beloved service men and women stepped forward to talk to her. Every face did not have a name, but each one was familiar. Each one had shared a difficult or treasured moment with Gertie and each savored this new moment together. Gertie was not in this astonishing beautiful National Monument—she was at the Ft. Meade Army Hospital, or at the post USO Clubs, or at Hilltop USO, and her chatter was easy—as always. The warmth and affection shown her was returned.

"Gertie, I loved Hilltop USO. Will there be apples this summer?"

"Yes, soldier. And apple pies too. Come visit again, when you can."

Gertie reached down to touch his twisted hand on the wheel of his chair. She did not see the scars on his face but she felt the damage to his limbs. The connection was complete. The hero and the brave woman were one.

🍂

William saw Gertie touching the cameo and he wanted to share her thoughts of Grandmother Amsterdam, so he lightly kissed her cheek.

🍂

Edward was looking down—handsome face and winning smile. The question he asked as he was dying had been answered by his one true love. Edward knew he had something to do with her life of service and he claimed its redeeming power.

❧

Jesse moved closer. He stood just behind her shoulder as she talked to a sailor. His hand went around her waist and she was supported again with a warmness that infused her. She heard him above the mingling sounds, "I love you, Gertie." She fingered the wedding band on her finger. She felt the swirl of gold that Jesse designed to remind her of the ocean, and thought of the words he had inscribed inside.

*Love never fails. JRM *GMM*

Gertie recalled the day she read her favorite Bible chapter to Jesse— *I Corinthians 13 7-8.*

> *Love always protects, always trusts, always hopes, always perseveres. Love never fails.*

The memorized words came to mind; her smile was broad and mystical. Jesse's love circled and swirled around her like the gold on her finger.

Our love will never fail, Jesse.... and my love for Edward did not fail, either.

❧

Gertie turned back to the assembled heroes and took an outstretched hand. "Tommy, I'm so happy to see you again. Tell me, did you marry that girl?"

The tall, handsome Marine, in glorious dress uniform, gave Gertie a broad, all encompassing smile that spoke volumes about the future.

THE END

Epilogue

The manuscript journaling Edward Neal's life stayed in William's safe deposit box almost three decades before he finally opened and read his father's efforts to put his troubled life on paper. He discovered that his father had a unique style that brought you into his story.

There were two manuscripts. The first was his early years. Edward put into words the anger, fear, selfishness, and mistrust that made those years a disaster. It began when he was a neighborhood boy, growing up on Tenth Street. The story was intense as he told of leaving home at seventeen and his marriage to Gertie. His words were brutally frank and revealing.

In the second, Edward began trying to unravel himself as his marriage came apart. He explained his metamorphosis while in the Army culminating in war torn Germany. It was full of intense experiences that changed his outlook. Edward finally grew up and became introspective and aware of his place as part of the human race.

It was all there, from Edward's point of view: the scenes on Tenth Street that drove him away; the family on Fergus Hill who gave him his bride; the terrible pressures settling for life on Eleventh Street; the untold trials with anger management; the decision to go into the army; his deep regret when he thought of Gertie and his son; the tough lessons learned in the war. The words and events were compelling and delivered in a message of redemption. Edward faced his actions and the effect they had on the two women he loved, Mary Neal and Gretta MacGregor. He faced the pain he caused and the losses he endured because of his actions. Edward had disappointed William, Grandmother Amsterdam and his father. He suffered much in his late-coming realizations. It was not a tale of events; it was a story of life and growth and feelings.

The whole story was a powerful lesson worthy of sharing.

As he read, William began to understand his father and reconcile his love for him.

William included the story of his father's supplication to Gertie in his final letter before dying in Germany in WW I. He told of her life of service because of the letter. Gertie's devotion to every soldier who lay in a bed at Ft. Meade Army Hospital, from the day of Edward's memorial to her walk into the Rose Garden at the White House was not part of Edward's manuscript, but William included it. Her dedication was a part of Edward's life.

William edited and prepared the manuscript for publication. His first step was getting Gertie's approval. With Gertie's blessing, he worked tirelessly to polish the book for publication. It became his labor of love for the father he never had the opportunity to do anything for. Edward had a literary career posthumously.

Grandmother Amsterdam who always believed in Edward's possibilities would have been delighted with the book. She had prayed that Gertie could save Edward, but it turned out that William was the one to do that. Grandmother would be just as happy—as long as Edward was not lost or unredeemed.

<u>Tenth Street is Universal</u> co-authored by Private Edward William Neal and Captain William Neal, USN, was published in 1950, and in six months, was on the non-fiction bestsellers list. The world cared about a soldier's memoirs and a woman's patriotism.

Edward's story was picked up by a Broadway producer. All three scenes were set in the west end of Laurel, Maryland in homes along Tenth Street, Eleventh Street, and Fergus Hill.

Edward's and Gertie's love story was dramatic. His early death was tragic and could have left his troubled early years as his only legacy, but a young tender, true love gave him redemption after death. The book was poignant and touching as both characters were admired and applauded for the trials they endured.

The play ended with the spirit of Edward Neal as a hero. Gertie was happy with that. She sat in the front row with William and both had tears streaming down their faces as the handsome actor, who played Edward, faded away and the curtain came down.

Edward's story was told.

Perhaps more congratulatory than applause, was the moment of silence, as the audience rose, with tearful shouts of, "bravo, bravo." Then applause rained down on the only two people still seated—William and Gertie.

Bertha's Apple Pie

<u>Prepare Apples</u>
Peal, core and slice 8 to 10 apples—enough to fill the pie plate and pile high. Don't slice too thin or too thick. Place in a big bowl and drizzle with 1 Tbs molasses.

<u>Blend</u>
1 cup sugar
1 tsp cinnamon
Dash nutmeg
2 ½ Tbs flour
½ tsp salt

Toss sugar mixture over apples. Stir several times in the next 30 minutes before starting crust. Set aside and make the crust.

<u>Crust</u>
2/3 cup of chilled lard
2 cups flour
1 tsp salt
2 Tbs sugar
½ cup ice water

Blend dry ingredients in a large bowl. Cut in lard using two knives, working quickly until it is in pea size pieces. Sprinkle water over all. Pull together with a fork until soft ball. Divide in two saving half for the lattice top. Roll the other half on a floured board until it fits a 10 inch glass pie plate. Crimp edges.

<u>Assembly</u>
Fill pie crust with prepared apples. Dot with 2 Tbs butter that has been cut into small pieces. Drizzle with 2 Tbs fresh lemon juice. Return to the ice box while preparing the lattice.

Roll the remaining half of pie crust on a floured board. Cut into ¾ inch strips. Weave the lattice pie crust strips across the pie and pinch edges into the crimped edge of the bottom crust. Brush with small amount of milk and sprinkle with 1 tsp cinnamon sugar.

Bake

Bake in preheated 350 degree oven. 45 – 55 minute. Pie needs to be bubbling up and golden brown. Time varies according to apples.

This recipe was developed from watching Bertha make apple pies without a recipe.
She added this advice: "Yo' be careful, ladies. Dis pie gonna bubbly over de stove. I always puts a tray 'neath it."
fg

Book Club Discussion Questions

1. Titling this book was the subject of discussion with many differing opinions. Do you think it was titled correctly? Can you suggest an alternate title? Discuss Gretta's nickname, what she thought of it, and what effect it had on her life?

2. The MacGregor and Neal families are very different in character. Discuss the families and the resulting differences in their children. Were they both *good* families?

   In the following pairs there are basic similarities and differences. Discuss

Clay	-	Edward
Elizabeth	-	Mary
Gertie	-	Liddy
Edward	-	Jesse

3. The courtship of Mary and Clay was in some ways like the courtship of Gertie and Edward. Discuss the feelings of the women and the attitudes of the men. As the marriages of these couples became less than the women wanted, what were their choices? What drove the path Mary took and the path Gertie took?

4. Mary Neal was a sad character. How did she illicit sympathy? Anger? Did you understand her? If the following characters were asked to describe Mary Neal, how would they? Clay? Elizabeth? Edward? William? Did anyone understand her?

5. Clay had a tough unyielding persona. How did your opinion of Clay evolve? What events gave the reader a different side of the man? Why was he so hard on Mary and Edward?

6. What did you learn about Edward from his grandmother, Elizabeth Amsterdam?

7. How did your feelings toward Edward change as you read the book? Did they change after he died? If so, what factors brought the change?

8. The author refers to Edward as a 'sub-hero' in this book. What do you think she meant and do you agree?

9. Patricia MacGregor said she believed the divorce helped Edward. Do you see that? Can you speculate on Edward's life if Gertie had not divorced him?

10. Who was your favorite supporting character? Why?

11. Do you have any experience with the attitude toward divorce in the early 1900's? Compare Gertie's decision to live single, raise her son and seek a career in 1914 with women who make those choices today.

12. Do you agree with Jesse's comment that Gertie *allowed* the town's attitude against her?

13. In Chapter 27, on William's Gradation Day from the USNA, the author tells a metaphoric story about a rabbit and a fox. What was the author's intent? Was she building fear or confidence?

14. Many times Gertie reassessed her feeling for Edward. Discuss Gertie's feeling for Edward as they surfaced though out the story.

15. Discuss the ease or difficulty in three of Gertie's major decisions: to marry Edward, to divorce Edward, to form a relationship with Jesse?

16. Two homes, Tenth Street and Hilltop Manor, are characters in this book. What were the differences in them? The similarities? Which one meant the most to Gertie?

17. How did Bear Creek serve Gertie? Does everybody need (have) a Bear Creek in their lives? If you could visit 403 Tenth Street, Hilltop Manor or Bear Creek today, which one would you chose, and why?

18. There were two important threads running though this story—the cameo and the apple orchard. Discuss their importance.

19. Today relationships like Jesse and Gertie's are common place. What were the risks they took in 1924? How difficult would it be to have a secret life today? Was keeping it secret easier in early 1900's? In your opinion, did Gertie have good reasons to refuse Jesse's proposals? Why did she finally agree?

20. Gertie's life of service to veterans became all encompassing. Discuss the factors that led to this and the reasons she gave so much to it.

21. During and after World War II social standards and rules changed. William discusses this as does Gertie. Discuss the changes. How would Gertie's story differ if she had divorced after the war?

22. Discuss <u>Gertie's</u> patriotic message. Is it passé or does it resonate today? Why?